CW01433673

On being the patient people of God

Freedom of religion, Christian conscientious objection, and the call to patient holiness in today's world

Martin Davie

GILEAD
B O O K S
PUBLISHING

To Lydia
With the prayer that she and her generation will know the freedom given to them by God and live accordingly.

GileadBooksPublishing.com

First published in Great Britain, February 2025
2 4 6 8 10 9 7 5 3 1

Copyright ©Martin Davie 2025
British Library Cataloguing-in-Publication Data:
A catalogue record for this book is available from the British Library.

ISBN: 978-1-8381828-5-4

All rights reserved.
No part of this publication may be reproduced, stored in a retrieval system or transmitted in any form or by any means, electronic, mechanical, photocopying, recording or otherwise, without the prior permission of the publisher.

Unless otherwise stated scripture quotations are from the Revised Standard Version, copyright © 1946, 1952, and 1971 National Council of the Churches of Christ in the United States of America. Used by permission. All rights reserved.

The publisher makes every effort to ensure that the papers used in our books are made from trees that have been legally sourced from well-managed and credibly certified forests by using a printer awarded FSC & PEFC chain of custody certification.

Indexer: Lyndsay Marshall
Cover design: Nathan Ward

Contents

Introduction

Daniel 6:1-10

'It pleased Darius to set over the kingdom a hundred and twenty satraps, to be throughout the whole kingdom; and over them three presidents, of whom Daniel was one, to whom these satraps should give account, so that the king might suffer no loss. Then this Daniel became distinguished above all the other presidents and satraps, because an excellent spirit was in him; and the king planned to set him over the whole kingdom. Then the presidents and the satraps sought to find a ground for complaint against Daniel with regard to the kingdom; but they could find no ground for complaint or any fault, because he was faithful, and no error or fault was found in him. Then these men said, 'We shall not find any ground for complaint against this Daniel unless we find it in connection with the law of his God.'

Then these presidents and satraps came by agreement to the king and said to him, 'O King Darius, live for ever! All the presidents of the kingdom, the prefects and the satraps, the counsellors and the governors are agreed that the king should establish an ordinance and enforce an interdict, that whoever makes petition to any god or man for thirty days, except to you, O king, shall be cast into the den of lions. Now, O king, establish the interdict and sign the document, so that it cannot be changed, according to the law of the Medes and the Persians, which cannot be revoked.' Therefore King Darius signed the document and interdict. When Daniel knew that the document had been signed, he went to his house where he had windows in his upper chamber open toward Jerusalem; and he got down upon his knees three times a day and prayed and gave thanks before his God, as he had done previously.'

Acts 5:17-32

'But the high priest rose up and all who were with him, that is, the party of the Sad'ducees, and filled with jealousy they arrested the apostles and put them in the common prison. But at night an angel of the Lord opened the prison doors and brought them out and said, 'Go and stand in the temple and speak to the people all the words of this Life.' And when they heard this, they entered the temple at daybreak and taught.

Now the high priest came and those who were with him and called together the council and all the senate of Israel, and sent to the prison to have them brought. But when the officers came, they did not find them in the prison, and they returned and reported, 'We found the prison securely locked and the sentries standing at the doors, but when we opened it we found no one inside.' Now when the captain of the temple and the chief priests heard these words, they were much perplexed about them, wondering what this would come to. And some one came and told them, 'The men whom you put in prison are standing in the temple and teaching the people.' Then the captain with the officers went and brought them, but without violence, for they were afraid of being stoned by the people.

And when they had brought them, they set them before the council. And the high priest questioned them, saying, 'We strictly charged you not to teach in this name, yet here you have filled Jerusalem with your teaching and you intend to bring this man's blood upon us.' But Peter and the apostles answered, 'We must obey God rather than men. The God of our fathers raised Jesus whom you killed by hanging him on a tree. God exalted him at his right hand as Leader and Savior, to give repentance to Israel and forgiveness of sins. And we are witnesses to these things, and so is the Holy Spirit whom God has given to those who obey him.'

Pliny the Younger, Epistle X

'...This is the course that I have adopted in the case of those brought before me as Christians. I ask them if they are Christians. If they admit it I repeat the question a second and a third time, threatening capital punishment; if they persist I sentence them to death. For I do not doubt that, whatever kind of crime it may be to which they have confessed, their pertinacity and inflexible obstinacy should certainly be punished. There were others who displayed a like madness and whom I reserved to be sent to Rome, since they were Roman citizens.'[1]

---

[1] Text in Henry Bettenson (ed), *Documents of the Christian Church* (Oxford: OUP, 1979), p.3.

'French gender equality minister wants priest prosecuted for saying homosexuality is sinful 'weakness,' _The Christian Post_, April 2024

'A French government official has called for the prosecution of a Roman Catholic priest over a video he posted to social media describing homosexual inclinations as 'a weakness' that must be fought like any other sin.

Father Matthieu Raffray, 45, posted the video to his more than 60,000 Instagram followers on March 15, admonishing them to resist their sinful weaknesses, including homosexuality among them.

'We all have weaknesses: those who are greedy, those who are angry, those who have homosexual tendencies!' Raffray said in the incriminating video, according to French Catholic media outlet _Famille Chrétienne._

Raffray's comments drew the ire of Aurore Bergé, a 37-year-old politician who has served as France's minister for gender equality, diversity and equal opportunities since January.

Bergé released a statement on March 20 saying that Raffray's comments about homosexuality were 'unacceptable' and that she was reporting him to the Interministerial Delegation for the Fight against Racism, Anti-semitism, and Anti-LGBT Hatred (DILCRAH) to be prosecuted under Article 40 of the French penal code.

'I will not let anything go in the face of hatred, whatever it may be,' Bergé said in an X post.

DILCRAH—a delegation that works with various government ministries to devise, coordinate and manage French government policy on combating racism, anti-Semitism and anti-LGBT hate crimes—replied to Bergé's tweet about 20 minutes later by noting they had forwarded Raffray's comments to the public prosecutor at her request.

'So-called 'conversion therapy' has been illegal since 2022,' the delegation tweeted. 'Talking about homosexuality as a weakness is shameful…'

In the video, the priest reminded his listeners that everyone has the requisite spiritual weapons to combat such weaknesses, but that Satan tempts them to believe the battle is 'too hard' and to give up.

Raffray, who has a sizable social media following and outreach to young French people, has remained unapologetic regarding his position and has not removed the video despite ruffling the feathers of the French diversity minister.

The priest told *Famille Chrétienne* that his video was about 'temptations in general' and that his intention was not to single out homosexuality but rather 'to make it clear that we are not obliged to give in to all our temptations, to all our desires.'

'I cite homosexuality, among other things,' he said. 'Homosexual acts are a sin, but I think people no longer know what a sin is. Denouncing a sin does not mean denouncing the person who commits the sin! You could have blamed me if I had said something clumsy or hurtful, but that's not the case here.'

'Not only am I not homophobic; in addition, as a priest, I am careful about the vocabulary I use on this issue because I know that the subject is sensitive and that people can easily be hurt,' he said.

Raffrey believes the French government is attacking the Catholic Church and its teachings through him. 'What is at stake is not me, but the freedom to be Christian today,' he was quoted as saying. 'I hope that all the faithful realize that it is Christian morality and the entire Church that are under attack.' [2]

I have begun my book with these four quotations because they illustrate the reality that my book addresses. This reality is the fact that attempts to restrict freedom of religion have been taking place for thousands of years and that they continue today, even in Western democratic countries such as France, even though freedom of religion is specifically protected under the Universal Declaration of Human Rights, the European Convention on Human Rights and other national and international legal documents.

[2] The article can be found at https://www.christianpost.com/news/france-may-prosecute-priest-who-called-homosexuality-a-weakness.html

In this book I shall undertake to answer four questions in the light of this reality.

1. Why is it important that there should be freedom of religion?

2. How has freedom of religion come to have legal protection?

3. Why is Christian freedom of religion still under attack today, even in Western democratic societies?

4. How should Christians understand attacks on their freedom of religion theologically, and how should they respond to them practically?

In order to try to answer these four questions my book is divided into three parts.

In part 1, chapters 1-3, I explain how the Christian belief in freedom of religion and freedom of conscience as part of this is rooted in the belief that the God who is free in himself wishes to be worshipped freely by his human creatures. I also explain how the Christian belief in freedom of religion, firstly explicitly expressed by Tertullian and Lactantius in the early Patristic period, eventually produced the commitment to the principle of freedom of religion, belief and conscience that can be found in national and international law today.

In part 2, chapters 4-6, I give an overview of how freedom of religion is under attack in the world today, how attacks on Christian freedom of religion in the Western world are linked to the fact that Western society has become increasingly less religious and Christian believers have come to be widely viewed as the 'bad guys' as a result, and how in theological terms this development has to be seen as the result of the Devil distorting the positive impact that Christianity has had on the Western world.

In part 3, chapters 7-9, I begin by noting that in spite of the developments noted in chapters 4-6 Christians still have the God given freedom to live in the way he wants them to live. I then go on to argue that living in this way involves a conscientious refusal to act in ways that are contrary to God's will for his human creatures as summarised in the Ten Commandments. Finally, I argue that Christians need to continue to advocate for freedom of religion, need to work with others for the common good, and need to follow the example of the Early Church by living lives of patient Christian holiness that will commend the Christian faith to those who are currently unbelievers.

In my conclusion in chapter 10 I summarise my argument and suggest six specific ways that Christians can seek to patiently obey the great commission in Matthew 28:19-20 whatever specific plans God has for the immediate future of the Church in Western society.

In writing this book I have been dependent on the expertise of scholars in a variety of different fields including biblical studies, law, church history and missiology. I wish to acknowledge my debt to them and to express the hope that my attempt to provide a creative synthesis of the results of their work will help Christians to better understand the challenges they face in today's world and what a proper Christian response to these challenges should look like.

Chapter 1
The theological basis for freedom of religion

The Freedom of God and the freedom of human beings

When thinking about freedom of religion the place we must begin is with the freedom of God. The reason that this is where we need to begin is because the freedom of God is the basis of all human freedom, including freedom of religion.

As John Webster notes in his book *Confessing God*, the Christian faith teaches us that through his activity in the world God has revealed his personal identity as the Triune God who has freely created the human race, who has freely reconciled it to himself when it turned away from him, and who is now freely bringing it to its final fulfilment. 'His freedom is the freedom of the one who does this work, and in so doing manifests that his freedom is to be God for us and with us.' [3]

Expanding on this basic point, Webster explains that God's freedom is first his freedom as God the Father:

> God's freedom is his freedom is God the Father, creator of heaven and earth. God's freedom is not simply arbitrary power or unfocused will. Rather, because God's freedom is made known in the act of creation, it is a freedom which is actual in his purposive bringing into being of another reality to exist alongside himself. God's freedom is not an infinite reserve of potency which could be actualized in ways other than those which he determines for himself as creator; it is rather the undeflected energy with which God follows the direction in which he determines to be himself. His freedom is this freedom for fellowship with the creature. As creator, *God is free* - standing under no necessity, having no external claims upon himself, in no need of the creature; as free Lord, God the Father is and creates *ex nihilo*. But because God is free *as creator*,

[3] John Webster, *Confessing God* (London and New York: T&T Clark, 2005), p.221.

his freedom is not merely an empty or formal idea but a very definite direction and act of relation. And, moreover, as an act of relation, God's freedom is teleological - it involves not simply an initial act of making heaven and earth, but also the preservation and governance of the creaturely realm. As creator, that is, God's freedom is the grace in which he promises himself or commits himself to the creature. The free creator is the free Lord of the covenant, the origin and sustainer of fellowship with himself. [4]

Secondly, God's freedom is his freedom as God the Son:

God's freedom is his freedom as God the Son, the reconciler of all things. God's freedom as Father involves the grace with which he pledges to maintain fellowship. That pledge is enacted in God the Son, who restores the covenant between God and his creatures after it has been broken by the creature's wicked and false attempt to be free from God... In this situation of the absolute jeopardy of the creature, God's freedom demonstrates itself not as freedom to withdraw from fellowship, but precisely as an utter determination to maintain fellowship (whatever else it may mean, this is part of what is set before us in the story of Noah). And God's maintenance of fellowship culminates in the person and work of the Son who, as God in the flesh, is reconciliation embodied and effective. He *is* Emmanuel, the fulfilment of the free divine resolve and promise: I will be your God, you will be my people. The fulfilment of this resolve, is of course, entirely gratuitous - God fulfils his freedom in that 'the word *became* flesh'. But, as in the Father's work of creation, so here in the Son's work of reconciliation: God's freedom is freedom for and with, not freedom apart from or against.[5]

Thirdly, God's freedom is his freedom as God the Holy Spirit:

God's freedom is his freedom as God the Holy Spirit, who brings all things to their perfection. In the work of the Holy Spirit, the

---

[4] Webster, pp.221-222.
[5] Webster, p.222.

reconciliation of the creature which has been willed by the Father and accomplished in the person and work of the Son becomes real as the creature's own history. By the power of the free Spirit, God sanctifies the creature, completing his purpose for it and so finally accomplishing the work begun in creation and maintained in reconciliation. It is the Spirit who thus consummates the purpose of God, not the creature itself. The perfecting of the creature by the Spirit is no less a free work of divine sovereignty than any other of God's works. But the Spirit's freedom is known in the work of making real the relation to God in which the creature has life. The Spirit is Lord, sovereignly free, majestic and unfettered; but as Lord the Spirit is also the life-giver, bestowing upon the creature the life (and therefore the freedom) forfeited in the creature's betrayal of the covenant. As free Spirit, God directs his ways to the final realization of fellowship with those whom he has created and redeemed for life with himself.[6]

The free activity of God which Webster describes is the foundation of freedom of religion for two reasons.

First, it is because of God's free activity in creation (which has his free activity in reconciliation and sanctification as its goal)[7] that human beings exist at all (Genesis 1:26-31, Psalm 100:3, John 1:1-2). If God did not have the capacity to freely create there would be no human beings and therefore of necessity no human freedom and thus no freedom of religion.

---

[6] Webster, pp.222-223.

[7] When God created, he knew and intended that this would lead to the reconciling work of Christ and the sanctifying work of the Holy Spirit. This must be so because God knows 'the end from the beginning' (Isaiah 46:10). In the words of the Christian philosopher Boethius '...since God abides for ever in an eternal present, His knowledge, also transcending all movement of time, dwells in the simplicity of its own changeless present, and embracing the whole infinite sweep of the past and the future contemplates all that falls within its simple cognition as if it were now taking place.' (Boethius, *The Consolation of Philosophy*, Bk V.6 (London: Elliot Stock, 1897) Kindle edition p.141).

Secondly, the nature of God's freedom is the freedom of uncompelled love (I John 4:8 'God is love'). From eternity to eternity, God the Father and God the Son love each other through God the Holy Spirit. 'God loves; God answers with love; and the love wherewith God loves and answers is God: Three Persons, One God.' [8]

We know this because it is what we see in the Gospels in which the life of God is lived out for us on the stage of human history. In the Gospels we see Jesus, God the Son incarnate, experiencing the free love of God the Father through the Spirit and through the Spirit freely responding in love to God the Father.

God's free decision to create and maintain fellowship between his human creatures and himself is his free decision that they should be creatures who are capable of sharing through the Spirit in the free love which God the Son has for God the Father.[9] As Kallistos Ware explains, this also means that God has decided that human beings should be creatures who possess freedom of choice:

> As a Trinity of love, God desired to share his life with created persons made in his image, who would be capable of responding to him freely and willingly in a relationship of love. Where there is no freedom, there can be no love. Compulsion excludes love; as Paul Evdokimov used to say, God can do everything except compel us to love him. God, therefore – desiring to share his love – created, not robots who would obey him mechanically, but angels and human beings endowed with free choice. [10]

---

[8] William Temple, *Christus Veritas* (London: Macmillan, 1949), p.284.
[9] See Romans 5:5 and 8:15.
[10] Kallistos Ware, *The Orthodox Way* (London and Oxford: Mowbrays, 1979), pp.74-75. As Boethius explains, the free choices that human beings made are eternally known by God, but this does not mean that these choices are not genuinely free. In his words: 'all things will come to pass which God foreknows as about to happen, but of these certain proceed of free will; and though these happen, yet by the fact of their existence they do not lose their proper nature, in

Freedom of choice in the Bible

We see the truth that God has endowed his human creatures with the gift of free choice reflected throughout the Bible.

The Old Testament

In the Old Testament the whole point of the story of the Fall at the beginning of the book of Genesis rests on the fact that Adam and Eve, the first parents of the human race, are given the choice of whether or not to obey God's command not to eat of the tree of the knowledge of good and evil (Genesis 2:15-17, 3:1-6).

Later on in Genesis, Abraham is called by God to 'Go from your country and your kindred and your Father's house to the land that I will show you' (Genesis 12:1), but there is no suggestion that God compels him to make the journey. Abraham himself has to make the free decision whether to do what God calls him to do or not. Furthermore, Abraham's decision to have faith in God's promise of innumerable offspring as a result of which is reckoned as righteous (Genesis 15:6) is again a free choice. God does not force him to believe.

Moving on to the book of Exodus, we find that having been delivered from slavery in Egypt the people of Israel have to choose to enter into covenant with God at Sinai. When they declare 'All the words which the Lord has spoken we will do' (Exodus 24:3) no one, not even God, is forcing them to make this declaration. They must make it because they want to do so.

The truth that Israel must make a choice whether to live in an obedient relationship to God is reiterated subsequently by Moses and Joshua. In Deuteronomy 30:19 Moses tells the people of Israel 'I call heaven and earth to witness against you this day, that I have set before you life and death, blessing and curse, therefore choose life, that you and your descendants may live.' Similarly in Joshua 24: 14-15 Joshua tells them:

virtue of which before they happened it was really possible that they might not have come to pass' (Boethius Bk V.6 in James, p.142).

14

Now therefore fear the Lord, and serve him in sincerity and in faithfulness; put away the gods which your fathers served beyond the River, and in Egypt, and serve the Lord. And if you be unwilling to serve the Lord, choose this day whom you will serve, whether the gods your fathers served in the region beyond the River, or the gods of the Amorites in whose land you dwell; but as for me and my house, we will serve the Lord.

We see the same truth highlighted by the prophet Elijah during the period of the monarchy. In I Kings 18:20-21 Elijah lays out the choice that the people of Israel have to make between following God or following Baal:

So Ahab sent to all the people of Israel, and gathered the prophets together at Mount Carmel. And Elijah came near to all the people, and said, 'How long will you go limping with two different opinions? If the Lord is God, follow him; but if Baal, then follow him.'

The reality of freedom of choice is also reflected in God's words to the people of Israel through the prophets Isaiah and Ezekiel.

In Isaiah 55:6-7 God says to the people of Israel:

Seek the Lord while he may be found,

  call upon him while he is near;

let the wicked forsake his way,

  and the unrighteous man his thoughts;

let him return to the Lord, that he may have mercy on him,

  and to our God, for he will abundantly pardon.

This appeal from God presupposes that the people whom God is addressing have the capacity to respond to it. They are free to either stay as they are or to return to God and receive his mercy. It is their choice.

In Ezekiel 33:11 God likewise instructs Ezekiel to say to the people of Israel:

> As I live, says the Lord God, I have no pleasure in the death of the wicked, but that the wicked turn from his way and live; turn back, turn back from your evil ways; for why will you die, O house of Israel?

What God tells Ezekiel to say here once again highlights the need (and therefore the possibility) of the wicked choosing to renounce their wickedness and turn back to God, and also highlights the fact that God will not compel them to do it. They must decide for themselves.

We also see freedom of choice at work in the story of the renewal of the covenant in Nehemiah 7:73-10:39. Following their return from exile in Babylon, 'the children of Israel' hear 'the book of the law of Moses which the Lord had given to Israel' read and expounded by Ezra and they then make the choice to renew the covenant between God and Israel in accordance with what is written in this book. There is no compulsion. It is a choice which the people decide to make.

Finally, if we turn to the Old Testament's vision for the long-term future, we read in Isaiah 2:2-4:

It shall come to pass in the latter days

  that the mountain of the house of the Lord

shall be established as the highest of the mountains,

  and shall be raised above the hills;

and all the nations shall flow to it,

  and many peoples shall come, and say:

"Come, let us go up to the mountain of the Lord,

  to the house of the God of Jacob;

that he may teach us his ways

  and that we may walk in his paths."

For out of Zion shall go forth the law,

  and the word of the Lord from Jerusalem.

He shall judge between the nations,

  and shall decide for many peoples;

and they shall beat their swords into ploughshares,

  and their spears into pruning hooks;

nation shall not lift up sword against nation,

  neither shall they learn war any more.

Here we see the nations coming to Zion to learn to live in obedience to God. What we do not see, however, is anyone forcing them to do so. Rather God's word goes out into the world from Jerusalem and the nations then freely decide to respond to it.

The New Testament
Moving on to the New Testament we find the exercise of free choice in the response of Mary and Joseph to the forthcoming birth of Jesus.

In Luke 1:26-37 we read how Mary is told by the angel Gabriel that she is going to become the mother of the Messiah as a result of the miraculous work of the Holy Spirit even though she is unmarried, and she responds by giving her free consent to what God is going to do in her life. 'Behold, I am the handmaid of the Lord; let it be to me according to your word.'

As George Caird writes in his commentary on Luke, when Gabriel says to her: 'Do not be afraid, Mary, for you have found favour with God' (v.30):

Mary is addressed…as the favoured one, the recipient of a privilege, the beneficiary of God's sovereign and unconditioned choice; and her answer – *'let it be to me according to you word'* – is the only response that anyone can properly make to the free and gracious bestowal of God's favour, the response of humility, faith, and obedience.[11]

However, even though Mary's response is the only one that can properly be made, she still has to make it. As Scott McKnight notes in his book *The Real Mary*, the reason that Mary's words of assent are a model of 'courageous faith' is because she had to choose to utter them and accept the potential consequences in terms the destruction of her relationship with her fiancée and of her standing in her community if he turned his back on her. [12] Her decision only had moral value as an example of 'courageous faith' because she had the choice of whether to make it or not.

In Matthew 1:18-25 we likewise read how Joseph is instructed by an angel to take Mary as his wife, and, in spite of his doubt about the cause of her pregnancy, he chooses to accept the angel's message and acts upon it. In the words of David Dickson, Joseph is a model of 'quiet faith and ready obedience' [13] and once again this faith and obedience involve freedom of choice. No one forces Joseph to make his decision to listen to the angel's message and marry Mary. His faith and obedience are free, not coerced.

We also see the exercise of free choice in the accounts of the response of the shepherds and wise man to the birth of Jesus in Luke 2:8-20 and Matthew 2:1-12. Both sets of people respond to the revelation they receive from God by going to visit the infant Jesus in Bethlehem, but no one makes them do so. They choose to make their respective visits.

[11] George Caird, *Saint Luke* (Harmondsworth: Penguin, 1963). p.53.
[12] Scott McKnight, *The Real Mary* (London: SPCK, 2007), ch.2.
[13] David Dickson, *Matthew* (Edinburgh: Banner of Truth, 1981), p.8.

Turning to the subsequent life of Jesus, we find that as that the second Adam, the model of what it means to live rightly as a human being, Jesus exercises freedom of choice. We can see this, for example, in the narratives about his temptation in the wilderness by the devil in Matthew 4:1-11, Mark 1:12-13 and Luke 4:1-13. These narratives only make sense if the temptation was real and for it to be real Jesus had to be free to decide whether to remain faithful to God the Father or listen to the voice of the tempter.

Similarly, Jesus' agony in the garden recorded in Matthew 26: 36-46, Mark 14:32-42 and Luke 22:31-34 only makes sense if Jesus was faced with a choice of being willing to accept his forthcoming death or rejecting it. Jesus' prayer 'My Father, if it is possible, let this cup pass from me; nevertheless, not as I will, but as thou wilt' (Matthew 26:39) only has moral value because it is the manifestation of a choice by Jesus to obey his heavenly Father's will even though he wished there was an alternative.

In similar fashion, the reality of Jesus' freedom of choice is reflected in the words of the writer of the Epistle to the Hebrews:

> In the days of his flesh, Jesus offered up prayers and supplications, with loud cries and tears, to him who was able to save him from death, and he was heard for his godly fear. Although he was a Son, he learned obedience through what he suffered; and being made perfect he became the source of eternal salvation to all who obey him, being designated by God a high priest after the order of Melchizedek. (Hebrews 5:7-10)

Here again Jesus' 'godly fear' has value because (like Adam) Jesus had a choice about whether to be obedient or not. His fear was godly because he freely chose to obey God to the point of death, and it was this that mean that 'he became the source of eternal salvation to all who obey him.'

What we also find in the New Testament is that in order for people to receive the salvation that God offers through Jesus they have to make a free choice to do so.

We can see this truth laid out, for example, in John 3:16-18:

> For God so loved the world that he gave his only Son, that whoever believes in him should not perish but have eternal life. For God sent the Son into the world, not to condemn the world, but that the world might be saved through him. He who believes in him is not condemned; he who does not believe is condemned already, because he has not believed in the name of the only Son of God.

In these verses receiving eternal life is dependent on belief and belief is not something that can be the result of compulsion. Individuals have to decide for themselves whether they will believe or not. Furthermore, the culpability of unbelief which is also emphasised in these verses only makes sense if the person concerned has a choice in the matter. They can believe, but they choose not to.

This truth can also be found in Paul's words in Romans 3:23-26:

> ...since all have sinned and fall short of the glory of God, they are justified by his grace as a gift, through the redemption which is in Christ Jesus, whom God put forward as an expiation by his blood, to be received by faith. This was to show God's righteousness, because in his divine forbearance he had passed over former sins; it was to prove at the present time that he himself is righteous and that he justifies him who has faith in Jesus.

In these words, Paul makes clear that being in a right relationship with God ('justified') in the face of our sin depends on 'faith.' That is to say, it depends on believing the apostolic message about the saving work of God in Jesus Christ and living in the light of it (which is what Paul means when he writes about the 'obedience of faith' in Romans 1:5). Such belief and obedience cannot be compelled. It has to be something that someone chooses to do for themselves. No one can force faith on anyone else.

It is because salvation depends on free choice, that in the Gospels we see no attempt by Jesus to engage in any form of religious compulsion. He preaches, teaches, performs miracles and calls people to follow him, but he does not make, or seek to make, anyone do anything. To quote the 'Declaration on Religious freedom' issued by Vatican II:

In attracting and inviting His disciples He used patience.(13) He wrought miracles to illuminate His teaching and to establish its truth, but His intention was to rouse faith in His hearers and to confirm them in faith, not to exert coercion upon them.(14) He did indeed denounce the unbelief of some who listened to Him, but He left vengeance to God in expectation of the day of judgment.(15) When He sent His Apostles into the world, He said to them: 'He who believes and is baptized will be saved. He who does not believe will be condemned' (Mark 16:16). But He Himself, noting that the cockle[14] had been sown amid the wheat, gave orders that both should be allowed to grow until the harvest time, which will come at the end of the world.(16) He refused to be a political messiah, ruling by force:(17) He preferred to call Himself the Son of Man, who came 'to serve and to give his life as a ransom for the many' (Mark 10:45). He showed Himself the perfect servant of God, (18) who 'does not break the bruised reed nor extinguish the smoking flax' (Matt. 12:20).

He acknowledged the power of government and its rights, when He commanded that tribute be given to Caesar: but He gave clear warning that the higher rights of God are to be kept inviolate: 'Render to Caesar the things that are Caesar's and to God the things that are God's' (Matt. 22:21). In the end, when He completed on the cross the work of redemption whereby He achieved salvation and true freedom for men, He brought His revelation to completion. For He bore witness to the truth, but He refused to impose the truth by force on those who spoke against it. Not by force of blows does His rule assert its claims. It is established by witnessing to the truth and

---

[14] In the more familiar English translation, 'tares'.

by hearing the truth, and it extends its dominion by the love whereby Christ, lifted up on the cross, draws all men to Himself.[15]

The same is true in Acts. As Jesus continues his ministry through the apostles and those who work with them, there is again preaching, teaching and the working of miracles and people are exhorted to believe and be baptised, but there is, again, not attempt to compel anyone to do anything. People have to choose to become and live as Christians (as we see happening, for example, in Act 2:37-47). To quote the 'Declaration on Religious Freedom' once more:

Like Christ Himself, the Apostles were unceasingly bent upon bearing witness to the truth of God, and they showed the fullest measure of boldness in 'speaking the word with confidence' (Acts 4:31) before the people and their rulers. With a firm faith they held that the Gospel is indeed the power of God unto salvation for all who believe. Therefore they rejected all 'carnal weapons': they followed the example of the gentleness and respectfulness of Christ and they preached the word of God in the full confidence that there was resident in this word itself a divine power able to destroy all the forces arrayed against God and bring men to faith in Christ and to His service.[16]

Likewise, In Revelation we are given an account of the history of the world until the coming of the new creation. John describes how God's people will triumph, and he says that they will do so not by engaging in religious compulsion (which is in fact described as a mark of the work of the beast in Revelation 13), but by means of freely chosen belief in Christ and fidelity to that belief in the face of tribulation and persecution. In the words of Revelation 12:15, the saints conquer 'the dragon,' that is Satan and all the powers of evil working under him 'by the blood of the lamb and the word of their testimony, for they loved not their lives even unto death.' As T F Torrance comments:

[15] Vatican II, 'Declaration on Religious Freedom, ch.2 in Walter Abbott (ed) *The Documents of Vatican II* (London: Geoffrey Chapman, 1967), pp.690-69.
[16] Declaration on Religious Freedom,' ch.2, in Abbott, p.691.

They overcome the devil by the blood of the lamb and by the word of their testimony and they love not their lives under death. That is a real faith. Hold onto the cross in the very teeth of death even if these teeth be dragons' teeth. Hold on to the word of your testimony no matter who accuses you. He that endures to the end, says the Word of God shall be saved. This is what John calls the patience of the Saints.

All that is the work of the man-child born out of Israel. That is the way, and the only way the kingdoms of his earth can become the Kingdom of God – by the might of the Lamb, by the word of the living God and by the blood of the Cross in the heart and in the conscience of men. That is the most potent force in heaven and earth.[17]

Believing this means trusting in God's prescribed method for the fulfilment of his purposes in the world, the proclamation of the Word by God's patiently enduring saints and not falling for the temptation to try to help God along by the coercive use of political force. To quote Torrance again, the message of Revelation is not to:

...drag the Kingdom of God down to the patterns and politics of this strange evil world. Let us rather hold fast to the Word of God, the Word that promises a new heaven and a new earth. As yet the Kingdom of God is invisible, unobservable, except to the eye of faith, but God is working. We may understand but little of God's strange work in history. All that we are able to see may be the beastly shapes of human pride and lust for power rampant in the earth, but one day these weird and crooked patterns will pass away and the promise of God will be revealed as perfectly fulfilled.[18]

Freedom of choice and the biblical commandments
As Augustine observes in his treatise *On Grace and Free Will*, the commands of God which are found throughout both the Old and New

---

[17] Thomas Torrance, *The Apocalypse Today* (London: James Clarke, 1960), p.98.
[18] Torrance, p.109.

Testaments also imply that God has given human beings free will, that is the power to make free choices, and expects them to exercise it. Augustine writes as follows:

> What is the import of the fact that in so many passages God requires all His commandments to be kept and fulfilled? How does He make this requisition, if there is no free will? What means 'the happy man,' of whom the Psalmist says that 'his will has been the law of the Lord'? Does he not clearly enough show that a man by his own will takes his stand in the law of God? Then again, there are so many commandments which in some way are expressly adapted to the human will; for instance, there is, 'Be not overcome of evil,' (Romans 12:1) and others of similar import, such as, 'Be not like a horse or a mule, which have no understanding;' and, 'Reject not the counsels of your mother;' (Proverbs 1:8) and, 'Be not wise in your own conceit;' (Proverbs 3:7) and, 'Despise not the chastening of the Lord;' (Proverbs 3:11) and, 'Forget not my law;' (Proverbs 3:1) and, ('Forbear not to do good to the poor;' (Proverbs 3:27) and, 'Devise not evil against your friend;' (Proverbs 3:29) and, 'Give no heed to a worthless woman;' (Proverbs 5:2) and, 'He is not inclined to understand how to do good;' and, 'They refused to attend to my counsel;' (Proverbs 1:30) with numberless other passages of the inspired Scriptures of the Old Testament. And what do they all show us but the free choice of the human will?

> So, again, in the evangelical and apostolic books of the New Testament what other lesson is taught us? As when it is said, 'Lay not up for yourselves treasures upon earth;' (Matthew 6:19) and, 'Fear not them which kill the body;' (Matthew 10:28) and, 'If any man will come after me, let him deny himself;' (Matthew 16:24) and again, 'Peace on earth to men of good will.' (Luke 2:14) So also that the Apostle Paul says: 'Let him do what he wills; he sins not if he marry. Nevertheless, he that stands steadfast in his heart, having no necessity, but has power over his own will, and has so decreed in his heart that he will keep his virgin, does well.' (1 Corinthians 7:36-37) And so again, 'If I do this willingly, I have a reward;' (1

Corinthians 9:17) while in another passage he says, 'Be sober and righteous, and sin not;' (1 Corinthians 15:34) and again, 'As you have a readiness to will, so also let there be a prompt performance;' (2 Corinthians 8:11) then he remarks to Timothy about the younger widows, 'When they have begun to wax wanton against Christ, they choose to marry.' So in another passage, 'All that will to live godly in Christ Jesus shall suffer persecution;' (2 Timothy 3:12) while to Timothy himself he says, 'Neglect not the gift that is in you.' (1 Timothy 4:14) Then to Philemon he addresses this explanation: 'That your benefit should not be as it were of necessity, but of your own will.' (Philemon 14) Servants also he advises to obey their masters 'with a good will.' (Ephesians 6:7) In strict accordance with this, James says: 'Do not err, my beloved brethren…and have not the faith of our Lord Jesus Christ with respect to persons;' and, 'Do not speak evil one of another.' (James 4:11) So also John in his Epistle writes, 'Do not love the world,' (1 John 2:15) and other things of the same import. Now wherever it is said, 'Do not do this,' and 'Do not do that,' and wherever there is any requirement in the divine admonitions for the work of the will to do anything, or to refrain from doing anything, there is at once a sufficient proof of free will. No man, therefore, when he sins, can in his heart blame God for it, but every man must impute the fault to himself. Nor does it detract at all from a man's own will when he performs any act in accordance with God. Indeed, a work is then to be pronounced a good one when a person does it willingly; then, too, may the reward of a good work be hoped for from Him concerning whom it is written, 'He shall reward every man according to his works.' (Matthew 16:27)[19]

Freedom of choice and damnation

A final point to note is that according to the Bible the seriousness with which God takes the gift of free choice that he has given to his human

---

[19] Augustine, *On Grace and Free Will,* ch.4 in *The Nicene and Post Nicene Fathers,* 1st Series, Vol. V (Edinburgh and Grand Rapids, T&T Clark/Eerdmans, 1997), p.444-445.

creatures is shown by the fact that he allows them to exercise it even if the consequence of their doing so is the eternal damnation referred to in passages such as Matthew 25:46, 2 Thessalonians 1:9-10 and Revelation 21:8.

As J I Packer notes, the content of the various biblical pictures used to describe damnation is that the damned will experience the result of their choices:

> ...what does it mean to lose our souls? To answer this question, Jesus uses His own solemn imagery – 'Gehenna' (hell in Mark 9:47 and then other gospel texts), the valley outside Jerusalem where rubbish was burned; the 'worm' that 'dieth not' (Mark 9:48), an image, it seems for the endless dissolution of the personality by a condemning conscience; 'fire' for the agonising awareness of God's displeasure; 'outer darkness' for knowledge of the loss, not merely of God, but of all good, and everything that made life seem worth living; 'gnashing of teeth' for self-condemnation and self-loathing. These things are, no doubt, unimaginably dreadful, though those who have been convicted of sin know a little of their nature. But they are not arbitrary inflictions; they represent, rather, a conscious growing into the state in which one has chosen to be. The unbeliever has preferred to be by himself, without God, defying God, having God against him, and he shall have his choice.[20]

Freedom of choice and divine grace

When considering the truth that God has given his human creatures freedom of choice, or free will as it is sometimes described, it is important to explore the issue of how the Bible's teaching about freedom of choice relates to its teaching about divine grace.

This issue is raised for example, by Paul's account of salvation in Ephesians 2:8-10:

---

[20] J I Packer, *Knowing God* (London: Hodder and Stoughton 1973), pp.169-170.

For by grace you have been saved through faith; and this is not your own doing, it is the gift of God— not because of works, lest any man should boast. For we are his workmanship, created in Christ Jesus for good works, which God prepared beforehand, that we should walk in them.

At first sight, what Paul says in these verses can seem to emphasise the grace of God to the extent that there is no place left for the exercise of human free choice. God, it seems, does everything, and we do nothing.

In the well-known words of Martin Luther, it can appear that the human will is like a beast of burden that cannot choose its rider:

If God rides it, it wills and goes where God wills, as the Psalm says: 'I am become as a beast (before thee) and I am always with thee' (Psalm 73:22ff). If Satan rides it, it wills and goes where Satan wells; nor can it choose to run to either of the two riders or to seek him out, but the riders themselves contend for the possession and control of it. [21]

To use another image, it can appear that Paul is saying that we are totally passive in the process of salvation, like clay in the hands of the divine potter (Isaiah 29:16, 64:8).

However, this is a too simplistic reading of Paul's words. What Paul is really saying is helpfully expounded by Charles Gore in his study of Ephesians as follows:

It is all pure grace - the free outpouring of unmerited love. The Christians are 'God's workmanship,' his new creation. He, in Christ, had wrought the work all by himself. They, the subjects of it, had contributed nothing. It remained for them only to welcome and to correspond. This is the summing up of man's legitimate attitude towards God. This is faith. It is at first stage simply the acceptance

---

[21] Luther, *On the Bondage of the Will*. Pt I, in Gordon Rupp and Philip Watson (eds), *Luther and Erasmus: Free Will and Salvation* (Philadelphia: Westminster Press, 1969), p.140.

of a divine mercy in all its undeserved and unconditional largeness; but it passes at once, as soon as ever the nature of the divine gift is realised, into a glad cooperation with the divine purpose. [22]

The point that Gore's exposition brings out is that the grace of God does not mean that the free choices of human beings have no role. God's grace makes salvation available through the death and resurrection of Jesus Christ and through the work of the Holy Spirit makes it possible for human beings to accept what Christ has done for them and live in the light of it. However, human beings still have their role to play. Enabled by grace, they have to choose to accept the salvation that God has wrought for them and to choose to walk in good works as a consequence.

What Don Carson says about the teaching of John's Gospel also applies to the teaching of Paul and of the Bible as a whole:

...[it] maximises human responsibility while simultaneously abolishing merit theology. It maximises God's sovereignty in salvation history and in election while simultaneously demanding that men believe.[23]

The truth that salvation involves both grace and the exercise of human free will in choosing to accept and respond to grace is underlined in two key statements on the issue produced by the Anglican Reformers in the sixteenth century.

The first statement is Article X of the *Thirty-Nine Articles of 1571* ('Of Free-Will') which runs as follows:

The condition of Man after the fall of Adam is such, that he cannot turn and prepare himself, by his own natural strength and good works, to faith, and calling upon God: Wherefore we have no power

---

[22] Charles Gore, *The Epistle to the Ephesians* (London: John Murray 1909), pp.100-101.
[23] Don Carson, *Divine Sovereignty and Human Responsibility* (London: Marshall, Morgan and Scott, 1981), p.219.

to do good works pleasant and acceptable to God, without the grace of God by Christ preventing us, that we may have a good will, and working with us, when we have that good will.

As Oliver O'Donovan explains in his commentary on the *Thirty-Nine Articles,* this article does not deny human free will, but insists that the grace of God is needed to provide the right context for its exercise. In his words, according to the article:

Mankind was lacking, not in the capacity to make free decisions as such, but the capacity to make decisions which would affect in any way his moral standing under God's judgement. This, of course, was assumed in the gospel message itself, that God had to take the initiative in sending his Son to earth to redeem mankind. But then the question arose: granted that the deed of salvation, by which mankind was redeemed, was one that only God could effect, what about each individual's *belief* in that deed? Belief is, to a certain extent, a moral act and turns on our moral disposition. Must we not say that it is up to men whether they believe or not? Plainly in one sense we must say this, since belief is a decision of man for which he is responsible, as he is for all his other acts. We would be wrong to suggest that human beings come to believe in Christ only by the *suspension* of a capacity which they otherwise exercise. In that case, as we would now say, belief would be inauthentic.' So much may reasonably be said - but it is possible to be too impressed by this power of human decision and to forget the context within which it must be exercised. For the act of belief, too, can occur only as God evokes it: no one can say 'Jesus is Lord' says Saint Paul, accept through the Holy Spirit (1 Corinthians 12:3).[24]

The references at the end of the article to God's grace 'preventing us' and 'working with us' are references to what Christian theology, following Augustine, has come to call 'prevenient' and co-operating'

[24] Oliver O'Donovan, *On the Thirty Nine Articles* (Exeter: Paternoster Press, 1986), pp.73-74.

grace. Prevenient grace (referred to in biblical texts such as John 6:44, Acts 16:14, Romans 10:20 and Ephesians 2:10) is the grace of God that precedes our human response, inclining our wills to choose the good. Co-operating grace (referred to in biblical passages such as John 15:4-5, 1 Corinthians 15:10, Galatians 2:20 and Philippians 2:13) is the grace of God that assists us to act rightly once our wills have already been inclined towards the good.' To quote O'Donovan again, the grace of God in Christ 'acts on us first, producing a good will; and then it goes on working with us, because there is never a time when we become independent of God for our response to him.' [25]

The second statement is Article X of Thomas Cranmer's *Forty-Two Articles* of 1553 ('Of Grace') which states:

> The grace of Christ, or the Holy Ghost by Him given doth take away the stony heart and give us an heart of flesh. And though, those that have no will to do good things, He maketh them to will, and those that would evil things, He maketh them not to will the same: yet nevertheless he enforceth not the will. And therefore no man when he sinneth can excuse himself, as not worthy to be blamed or condemned, by alleging that he sinned unwillingly or under compulsion.[26]

This article makes four important points:

- Grace is not an impersonal force but the personal action of God the Holy Spirit in someone's life.

- This work of the Holy Spirit fulfils the promise given by God to the prophet Ezekiel:

'A new heart I will give you, and a new spirit I will put within you; and I will take out of your flesh the heart of stone and give you a heart of

---

[25] O'Donovan, p.75.
[26] Text from O'Donovan, p.139.

flesh. And I will put my spirit within you, and cause you to walk in my statutes and be careful to observe my ordinances.' (Ezekiel 36:26-27)

- God's grace does not operate by enforcing the will. The human will remains free. Human beings can still make meaningful choices. They do not become robots or puppets.

- The freedom that human beings have means that they cannot blame God for their sinful desires or actions.

Because it makes these four points, Cranmer's earlier article provides an important supplement to what is said in Article X of the *Thirty-Nine Articles*. As Harold Browne declares it reminds us that:

> God must give the will, must set the will free from its natural slavery, before it can turn to good; but then it moves in the freedom which he has bestowed upon it, and never so truly uses that freedom, as when it follows the motions of the Spirit. Yet clearly there remains some power to resist and do evil. For 'those that have no will to do good things God maketh them to will; Yet, nevertheless He enforces not the will.' And so, although he must work in us yet we, under His influences, must strive and press forward, not resisting him, not neglecting but stirring up his gift in our hearts.[27]

Freedom of religion and human fallenness
A further point that is not generally considered, but is very important to note, is that to understand freedom of religion properly we have to acknowledge both that human beings still possess freedom in spite of the Fall (as we have seen), but that the way that they exercise this freedom has been (and is) shaped by their fallen condition.

The reason that freedom of religion has been and continues to be such a problematic issue is because there is huge disagreement among human beings (including among Christians) about the subject of religion,

---

[27] Harold Browne, *An Exposition of the Thirty Nine Articles* (London: John W Parker, 1847, pp.272-273.

embracing issues such as whether God exists at all, what God is like, and how he wants his human creatures to live.

This disagreement is a result of our fallen condition. God knows the truth about all things. This is what is meant when Job 28:24 tells us that God 'looks to the ends of the earth and sees everything under heaven' and Hebrews 4:13 declares 'before him no creature is hidden, but all are open and laid bare to the eyes of him with whom we have to do.' As creatures made in God's image human beings are also created to know the truth. We can see this in the account of creation in Genesis in which we are told that 'the LORD God formed every beast of the field and every bird of the air, and brought them to the man to see what he would call them; and whatever the man called every living creature, that was its name' (Genesis 2:19). What is described here is an act of truthful discernment. Adam is not just arbitrarily assigning names to the birds and the animals, he is discerning truthfully what they are. Like God he knows the true nature, 'the name,' of things.

If all human beings engaged in this kind of truthful discernment all of the time. then there would never be any disagreement between them. We would all know the truth and we would all freely agree about the truth. Tragically, however, the result of the big lie told by the devil and accepted by the first human beings (Genesis 3) is that we have lost the ability to always see things as they really are and to always be honest about what we do see. It is for that reason that human beings disagree.

Fortunately, God has provided a remedy for this situation. Jesus is truth incarnate (John 14:6 'I am the truth') and he has come to restore our ability to know the truth. In John 8:31-32 Jesus declares 'if you continue in my word, you are truly my disciples, and you will know the truth, and the truth will make you free.' This comes about through the work of the Holy Spirit who is sent by Jesus to 'guide you into all the truth' (John 16:13). Like the whole of our re-creation through Jesus, our ability to discern the truth is a work in progress. At the moment 'our knowledge is imperfect' (1 Corinthians 13:9), but in heaven we shall understand fully in the same way that we ourselves are fully understood by God (1 Corinthians 13:12). As C S Lewis puts it in his book *The Great Divorce*, human beings are created with an innate desire for truth and this desire will one day be satisfied. God will bring us to a place where we can taste truth 'like honey and be embraced by it like a bridegroom. Your thirst shall be quenched.' [28]

What all this means is that the term 'good disagreement' is an oxymoron like 'virtuous sin'. Disagreement can never in itself be good. We disagree because in our fallen condition we either don't know the truth, or are unwilling to accept it when it is presented to us.

In this situation the vocation of the Church is to be a community where as far as possible disagreement ceases to exist because truth is universally known, accepted and celebrated, and to make an ever-increasing number of people part of this community. However, until Christ comes in glory and ushers in the new creation where truth can be tasted like honey, this vocation will always be a work in progress. This means that there will continue to be disagreement about religion both inside the Church, and between those inside the Church and those as yet outside it.

The reason why there needs to be freedom of religion, in the sense of freedom to disagree about matters of religious belief and practice, is because this is the case. In this world disagreement about religion will always exist, we have to find the best way to handle it, and allowing freedom of religion is the best way to do so.

The reason why people have historically found freedom of religion difficult to accept is because they have not wanted a world in which there is disagreement about religion. They have wanted a world where everyone agrees. However, the reason for allowing the existence of freedom of religion, even when this means the acceptance of continuing disagreement about religious matters, is because trying to bring such disagreement to an end through coercive activity aimed at forcing agreement in belief and practice fails to respect the freedom of choice

---

[28] C S Lewis, *The Great Divorce* (Glasgow: Fontana, 1972), p.41.

which God has given to his human creatures and the non-coercive character of the commission that God has given his Church.

God in his wisdom has decided to allow a situation in which disagreement about religion resulting from the Fall will continue until Christ returns in glory. Respecting God's decision means not trying to second guess God by trying to bring disagreement to an end prematurely by means of our own coercive activity.

God's freedom, our freedom and freedom of religion
In this chapter we have seen that:

1. God is free in himself as Father, Son and Holy Spirit

2. God the Father freely loves the Son through the God Holy Spirit and God the Son loves the God Father through God the Holy Spirit

3. In his freedom God has made his human creatures to freely share in the love between the Father and the Son through the Holy Spirit

4. Because love by its nature cannot be compelled, God has created human being with the gift of free choice.

5. In the life of Jesus we see the perfect example of a human being rightly exercising this God given gift of freedom to choose.

6. Throughout the Bible we also see numerous other examples of human beings either exercising, or being called to exercise, the freedom of choice that God has given them.

7. The saving faith In Christ through which human beings enter into a right relationship with God involves the exercise of free choice.

8. God respects the freedom that he has given his human creatures to the extent that he allows them to damn themselves through the wrong exercise of it.

9. In the Gospels and Acts we see that the saving activity of Jesus takes the form of preaching, teaching, the working of miracles and people being called to become disciples. However, there is no attempt to compel people to believe in and follow Jesus.

10. Human beings are saved by grace, but this grace does not take away human freedom, but rather allows them the ability to exercise their freedom rightly.

These ten points provide the theological foundation for a Christian belief in freedom of religion. The basic point is that human beings must not think they know better than God.

Firstly, God has created people to exercise freedom of choice in their relationship with him and we must not go against God's decision by trying to force people to relate rightly to him. We have to respect their God given right to choose, even if the result of their choice is that they are eventually damned.

Secondly, it is pointless and arguably blasphemous to try to force people into a right relationship with God, because this means that we are trying to substitute our own activity for God's supernatural work of grace. We would be seeking to do in our own strength what only God working through the Holy Spirit can do.

Thirdly, being obedient to God means accepting the pattern given to us in the New Testament for the spreading of the Gospel. The job God has given to Christians is preach, teach and baptise. That is how the Gospel is to be spread, not through compulsion. In terms of Isaiah 2:1-4, God's will is that the nations should come to Zion because of their free acceptance of the good news about God going forth from Jerusalem to the ends of the earth and not because earthly authorities have made them do so.

Fourthly, God has decided to allow disagreement about religion resulting from the effects of the Fall to endure until Christ returns in glory. We need to respect this fact and not seek to bring disagreement to an end before then by means of coercion. This does not mean that we should not try to bring disagreement to an end as much as possible. We should, but we have to do it in God's way and not attempt to do it by means of force.

In his chapter we have set out the theological foundation for freedom of religion. In the next chapter we shall look at how subsequent Christian theology has built upon this foundation, beginning with the work of Tertullian and Lactantius in the Patristic period.

Additional note 1: Restriction of freedom of religion in ancient Israel, a model for the world today?

In this chapter we have seen that in the Old Testament people are given freedom to decide whether or not to obey God and to be in covenant relationship with him. What is also true, however, is that in the Old Testament ancient Israel is a theocracy in which only one form of religion is meant to exist, and in which departure from this form of religion is subject to strict punishment (including the death penalty), and kings such as Hezekiah and Josiah are praised for insisting on religious conformity and stamping out ungodly forms of religious activity. Thus, we read in 2 Kings 23: 24-25:

> ...Josi'ah put away the mediums and the wizards and the teraphim and the idols and all the abominations that were seen in the land of Judah and in Jerusalem, that he might establish the words of the law which were written in the book that Hilki'ah the priest found in the house of the Lord. Before him there was no king like him, who turned to the Lord with all his heart and with all his soul and with all his might, according to all the law of Moses; nor did any like him arise after him.

The question this latter truth raises is whether the theocratic polity of ancient Israel is meant to provide a model for a Christian theocratic form of society in the world today in which only Christianity would be tolerated and in which the world would be governed by biblical law. [29]

[29] For an exploration of such thinking see Bruce Barron, *Heaven on earth? the social & political agendas of dominion theology* (Grand Rapids: Zondervan, 1992).

The answer to this question is 'No' and the reason it is 'No' is because the idea that ancient Isael is meant to be a model for Christian theocracy today fails to do justice to the way in which according to the Bible the story of ancient Israel is meant to serve as both a warning and a promise to subsequent generations of God's people.

It serves as a warning because it tells us that the attempt to undo the effects of the Fall through the creation of a godly human political society are bound to fail. As a number of commentators on the Old Testament have pointed out, Israel's exodus from Egypt and entry into the promised land represents a new start for the human race. In the words of Peter Leithart, by bringing Israel through the wilderness and into the land of Canaan: 'God is making the world new and putting Israel in it so that they can be a nation of new Adams and Eves.' [30]

Unfortunately, the people of Israel fail to do any better than the first Adam and Eve. Just as the Mosaic law was unable to make individuals godly (Romans 7:1-25), so Israel's theocratic polity was unable to produce a godly nation. As the Old Testament makes clear, the people of Israel constantly rebel against God and the laws he has given Israel to observe, and the reformations introduced by kings such as Hezekiah and Josiah are unable to change this situation. As a result, just as Adam and Eve were exiled from Eden so Israel is eventually exiled from the land that God has given them.

By telling us that Israel's theocratic polity failed in this way the Bible is warning future generations of God's people that they should not think of going down the same road again. It is saying that a this-worldly political system along Israelite lines is not the way that God's purposes in the world will be achieved and that, like all other human projects in a fallen world, any attempt to create one will inevitably end in failure.

See also, for the Roman Catholic version of the same basic approach known as 'integralism,' see the Catholic Website *The Josias* at. https://thejosias.com/
[30] Peter Leithart, *A House for My Name – A Survey of the Old Testament* (Moscow: Canon Press, 2000), Kindle Edition, p.97.

However, the Bible also sees the form of government that existed in ancient Israel as a promise because it points forward in a typological fashion to the way in which God's purposes in the world are being and will be fulfilled.

Typology means the way in which the Old Testament provides us with types or symbols which point forward to the greater realities which came into being when the new covenant was instituted through Christ. For example, the Exodus from Egypt is a type of the deliverance from sin and death brought about by Jesus' death and resurrection, and the Old Testament sacrificial system is a type of the once for all sacrifice made by Jesus through the offering of himself on the cross.

Viewed typologically ancient Israel points forward to the life of the people of God in two ways.

First, it points to the present existence of the people of God as a voluntary remnant among the nations (the Catholic Church), with a distinction existing between the Church and the world outside, in which many different forms of religion will continue to exist, and with disobedience to God being addressed not by means of coercive political power, but by the spiritual discipline exercised on behalf of Christ by the ministers of the Church (the 'power of the keys' referred to in Matthew 16:18-19, 18:15-20, John 20:22-23).

In the words of the seventeenth century Puritan writer Roger Williams:

> ...the state of Israel as a national state made-up of spiritual and civil power so far as it attended upon the spiritual, was merely figurative and typing out of the Christian Churches consisting of both Jews and Gentiles, enjoying the true power of the Lord Jesus establishing, reforming, correcting, defending in all cases concerning his Kingdom and Government. [31]

---

[31] Roger Williams, *The Bloody Tenent of Persecution* (London: J Haddon, 1848), p.316.

Secondly, it points forward to the new creation in which Jesus, the promised descendant of king David, will rule as the undisputed king, and in which there will be total and absolute obedience to the will of God and from which the ungodly will have been excluded forever (Revelation 21:1-22:15).

When understood typologically in these two ways, Old Testament Israel does not point to the need to try to replace religious freedom with some form of Christian theocracy in the world today. To do so would be confuse the civil authority of the rulers of the nations of the world with the spiritual authority of Jesus Christ exercised in the Church in the ways laid down in the New Testament, ways which do not include seeking to establish a theocratic polity in which civil rulers play the part of the kings of Israel.

Additional note 2: Could Jesus have sinned?

The fact that Jesus possessed freedom of choice in the course of his life on earth has led to theologians asking the question about whether it was possible for Jesus to exercise that free choice by choosing to sin. We know that in fact he did not do so, but could he have done? To use traditional theological language, was Jesus *peccable* (capable of sinning) or was he *impeccable* (incapable of sinning).

Theologians have differed on this point, but as R Carlton Wynne argues in his article 'Could Jesus have sinned?' the view that Jesus was impeccable fits in best with an orthodox understanding of the person of Christ. As he explains, Jesus' impeccability follows from the 'solidarity or harmony' between his divine and human wills:

As with Christ's two natures, his two wills are not equally ultimate, but his human will was necessarily submissive to and reflective of his pre-existent divine will as the Son obeyed his Father on earth. As a man, the incarnate Son necessarily expressed his inexhaustible purity as the second person of the Trinity, including his infallible divine desire to pursue only what is holy and righteous and good (cf. Romans 7:12), as he delighted in his Father's good will regarding his messianic mission (see John 4:34; Hebrews 3:1–2).

39

While additional qualifications may be offered for Christ's human obedience, the ultimate reason for his impeccability throughout his earthly life was the deity of his person as the incarnate Mediator. As Geerhardus Vos explains, 'Will or intellect or emotion in the human nature could not have sinned unless the underlying person had fallen from a state of moral rectitude.' In other words, the very act of the Son's incarnation ensured his lifelong impeccability from its inception. In assuming a human nature and all of its essential attributes, the divine Son lived, obeyed, and suffered as one whose human will was a creaturely organ of the eternal Son, assumed 'inconfusedly, unchangeably, indivisibly,' and 'inseparably' to himself as a member of the Godhead.[32]

To put the matter simply, Jesus could only sin if God can sin. God cannot sin. Therefore, Jesus cannot sin. Hence Jesus is impeccable.

However, this does not mean that Jesus' choices and his resistance to temptation were not real and voluntary. God freely wills to do only what is good and this is true also of Jesus as God incarnate. He freely wills to do only what his heavenly Father wants him to do, even when faced with the temptation to want the opposite.

In line with what was said earlier in this chapter, Wynne notes that what the gospels tell us about Jesus' agony in the Garden of Gethsemane proves this point. He writes:

One biblical example will suffice to prove the thoroughly voluntary quality of Christ's human obedience, highlight the misery of his temptations, and illustrate how his human will flawlessly reflected his divine will as the Son in obedience to his Father. Fully aware of the inexpressible pain and suffering that would attend his final acts of earthly obedience, Jesus faced his most intense trial of temptation in the garden of Gethsemane, which Luke describes as

[32] R Carlton Wynne, 'Could Jesus Have Sinned? - The Temptations and Triumph of Christ,' *Desiring God*, 2 September 2019 at https://www.desiringgod.org/articles/could-jesus-have-sinned

such 'agony' that 'his sweat became like great drops of blood falling down to the ground' (Luke 22:44). The weight of impending judgment that would be undeservedly his was so horrendous that Jesus the man even pleaded for another way to fulfil his messianic mission. Mark recounts, 'He fell on the ground and prayed that, if it were possible, the hour might pass from him. And he said, 'Abba, Father, all things are possible for you. Remove this cup from me'' (Mark 14:35–36)

This was not a moment of Trinitarian schizophrenia, with the divine Son wavering in his commitment to save, but was instead a sorrowful cry issuing from the human heart of Christ. Facing the excruciating final demand of his holy mission, Christ displayed the capacity to think and will as a man in distinction from his divine mind. As an innocent and holy man, Jesus wanted the cup removed. He did not want to face the wrath of God for sin. And yet, the impeccable character of his human will impelled him to offer himself as a human sacrifice to the Father ('Nevertheless, not my will, but yours, be done,' Luke 22:42). Despite the disrupting thoughts of his imminent pain, the uncoerced human will of Christ, united to the eternal Son, cherished obedience to the Father above all else.[33]

[33] Wynne, 'Could Jesus have sinned?'

Chapter 2
Freedom of religion in the history of the Christian Church

In chapter 1 we looked at the theological basis for freedom of religion. In this chapter we shall go on to look at how the teaching of the Christian Church on this issue has developed from the Patristic period to the present day.

It is often assumed that belief in freedom of religion only emerged at the time of the European Enlightenment in the eighteenth century.[34] What we shall see in this chapter is that this assumption is mistaken. What we shall see is that the Christian Church has a tragically mixed record in upholding religious freedom in practice, and there have been Christian writers who have rejected freedom of religion in principle. Nevertheless, there has been an unbroken tradition of Christian thought, rooted in the theological principles set out in the last chapter, that holds that religious faith and practice may not rightly be coerced and that therefore people must be free to worship God, both individually and in religious communities, in the way that they conscientiously believe to be right.

This tradition of Christian thoughts has its roots in the writings of Tertullian and Lactantius in the third and fourth centuries, continued to be upheld in the later Patristic and medieval periods and was then extensively developed during the sixteenth and seventeenth centuries. The growing acceptance of freedom of religion across the Christian Church from the eighteenth to the twenty-first centuries is a further development of this inherited pattern of thought. It is not saying something new but rather reiterating a very ancient part of Christian belief.

---

[34] See, for example, Perez Zagorin, *How the idea of religious toleration came to the West* (Princeton: Princeton: University Press, 2003).

Tertullian

The foundations for later Christian teaching about freedom of religion were laid by the North African Christian writer Tertullian in his two works *Apology* and *To Scapula* in which he attacks the attempts by the imperial authorities to force Christians to worship the gods of Rome.

In chapters 24 and 28 of his *Apology,* which was produced in 197, Tertullian writes as follows:

> Let one man worship God, another Jupiter; let one lift suppliant hands to the heavens, another to the altar of Fides; let one—if you choose to take this view of it—count in prayer the clouds, and another the ceiling panels; let one consecrate his own life to his God, and another that of a goat. For see that you do not give a further ground for the charge of irreligion, by taking away religious liberty, and forbidding free choice of deity, so that I may no longer worship according to my inclination, but am compelled to worship against it. Not even a human being would care to have unwilling homage rendered him; and so the very Egyptians have been permitted the legal use of their ridiculous superstition, liberty to make gods of birds and beasts, nay, to condemn to death anyone who kills a god of their sort.[35]

> But as it was easily seen to be unjust to compel freemen against their will to offer sacrifice (for even in other acts of religious service a willing mind is required), it should be counted quite absurd for one man to compel another to do honour to the gods, when he ought ever voluntarily, and in the sense of his own need, to seek their favour. [36]

In chapter 2 of *To Scapula,* which was produced in 212, he further writes:

---

[35] Tertullian, *Apology* 24 in *The Ante-Nicene Fathers*, Vol. III (Edinburgh and Grand Rapids: T&T Clark/Eerdmans, 1997), p.39.
[36] Tertullian, *Apology* 28, p.41.

We are worshippers of one God, of whose existence and character Nature teaches all men; at whose lightnings and thunders you tremble, whose benefits minister to your happiness. You think that others, too, are gods, whom we know to be devils. However, it is a fundamental human right, a privilege of nature, that every man should worship according to his own convictions: one man's religion neither harms nor helps another man. It is assuredly no part of religion to compel religion—to which free-will and not force should lead us—the sacrificial victims even being required of a willing mind. You will render no real service to your gods by compelling us to sacrifice. For they can have no desire of offerings from the unwilling, unless they are animated by a spirit of contention, which is a thing altogether undivine.

As Robert Wilken notes, what we see in these three passages is that according to Tertullian there has to be liberty for everyone (Christians included) to worship as they see fit because:

Religion consists of more than dutiful gestures and solemn rituals; it arises from inner conviction. Intention gives authority to religious devotion; feigned observance makes a mockery of piety. Persecution fosters not genuine devotion but irreligion.[37]

Although Tertullian does not specifically refer to the Bible in these passages, his claim in *To Scapula* that it is a 'human right' and a 'privilege of nature' that everyone should be able to worship in accordance with their convictions is based on the teaching of Genesis 1:26-27 that God has created human beings in his image and likeness. For Tertullian the creation of human beings in God's image and likeness is shown precisely in their ability to exercise free will (including in matters concerning religion). In the words of Tertullian in his work *Against Marcion*:

---

[37] Robert Wilken, *Liberty in the Things of God* (New Haven and London: Yale University Press, 2019), Kindle edition p.11.

I find, then, that man was by God constituted free, master of his own will and power; indicating the presence of God's image and likeness in him by nothing so well as by this constitution of his nature. For it was not by his face, and by the lineaments of his body, though they were so varied in his human nature, that he expressed his likeness to the form of God; but he showed his stamp in that essence which he derived from God Himself (that is, the spiritual, which answered to the form of God), and in the freedom and power of his will. This his state was confirmed even by the very law which God then imposed upon him. For a law would not be imposed upon one who had it not in his power to render that obedience which is due to law; nor again, would the penalty of death be threatened against sin, if a contempt of the law were impossible to man in the liberty of his will. So in the Creator's subsequent laws also you will find, when He sets before man good and evil, life and death, that the entire course of discipline is arranged in precepts by God's calling men from sin, and threatening and exhorting them; and this on no other ground than that man is free, with a will either for obedience or resistance.[38]

To put it simply, God has created human beings with the possibility of offering him free-obedience and religion only has value if it is an exercise of this free obedience. Hence there must be freedom of religion.

Lactantius
The other early Christian writer who helped shape subsequent Christian thinking about freedom of religion was Lactantius, who worked in the court of the Emperor Constantine as tutor to his son Crispus.

Lactantius' work *The Divine Institutes,* which was written sometime between 303 and 310, was a systematic defence and exposition of

---

[38] Tertullian, *Against Marcion*, Book II, Chapter V in in *The Ante-Nicene Fathers*, Vol. III (Edinburgh and Grand Rapids: T&T Clark/Eerdmans, 1997), p.301.

Christian teaching in response to its pagan critics. In Book V of this work Lactantius attacks religious persecution (such as the persecution instituted by the Emperor Diocletian from 303 onwards) on the grounds that the exercise of free-will is fundamental to religion and therefore to seek to force religious observance is to attack religion itself. In his words:

But, they say, the public rites of religion must be defended. Oh with what an honourable inclination the wretched men go astray! For they are aware that there is nothing among men more excellent than religion, and that this ought to be defended with the whole of our power; but as they are deceived in the matter of religion itself, so also are they in the manner of its defence. For religion is to be defended, not by putting to death, but by dying; not by cruelty, but by patient endurance; not by guilt, but by good faith: for the former belong to evils, but the latter to goods; and it is necessary for that which is good to have place in religion, and not that which is evil. For if you wish to defend religion by bloodshed, and by tortures, and by guilt, it will no longer be defended, but will be polluted and profaned. For nothing is so much a matter of free-will as religion; in which, if the mind of the worshipper is disinclined to it, religion is at once taken away, and ceases to exist. The right method therefore is, that you defend religion by patient endurance or by death; in which the preservation of the faith is both pleasing to God Himself and adds authority to religion. For if he who in this earthly warfare preserves his faith to his king in some illustrious action, if he shall continue to live, because more beloved and acceptable, and if he shall fall, obtains the highest glory, because he has undergone death for his leader; how much more is faith to be kept towards God, the Ruler of all, who is able to pay the reward of virtue, not only to the living, but also to the dead! Therefore, the worship of God, since it belongs to heavenly warfare, requires the greatest devotedness and fidelity. For how will God either love the worshipper, if He Himself is not loved by him, or grant to the petitioner whatever he shall ask, when he draws near to offer his prayer without sincerity or reverence? But these men, when they come to offer sacrifice, present to their gods nothing from within, nothing of their own—no uprightness of mind, no reverence or fear.[39]

The Edict of Milan

In their original contexts the works of Tertullian and Lactantius that we have just looked at are intended to show that it is wrong for the upholders of traditional Roman religion to persecute Christians for their religious nonconformity. However, in subsequent Christian thought the basic point they are making, that it is wrong in principle to force people engage in any particular kind of religious observance, came to be seen as applying not only to non-Christians, but to Christians as well. If religious coercion is wrong in principle, then it would be just as wrong for Christians in positions of power to seek to coerce pagans or Jews as it was for pagans to seek to coerce Christians.

This later point is first reflected in what is commonly known as the Edict of Milan. This name is misleading because it was a letter to provincial governors rather than an edict and it was posted from cities in in the Eastern Roman Empire rather than Milan. However, it is a very significant document because it sets out the policy on religious matters agreed by the two co-emperors Constantine and Licinius when they met in Milan in the winter of 313.

The first part of the letter runs as follows:

> When we, Constantine and Licinius, emperors, had an interview at Milan, and conferred together with respect to the good and security of the commonweal, it seemed to us that, among those things that are profitable to mankind in general, the reverence paid to the Divinity merited our first and chief attention, and that it was proper that the Christians and all others should have liberty to follow that mode of religion which to each of them appeared best; so that that God, who is seated in heaven, might be benign and propitious to us, and to every one under our government. And therefore we judged it

---

[39] Lactantius, *The Divine Institutes,* Book V.20 in the Ante-Nicene Fathers Vol.VII (Edinburgh and Grand Rapids: T&T Clark/Eerdmans, 1994), p.157.

a salutary measure, and one highly consonant to right reason, that no man should be denied leave of attaching himself to the rites of the Christians, or to whatever other religion his mind directed him, that thus the supreme Divinity, to whose worship we freely devote ourselves, might continue to vouchsafe His favour and beneficence to us. And accordingly we give you to know that, without regard to any provisos in our former orders to you concerning the Christians, all who choose that religion are to be permitted, freely and absolutely, to remain in it, and not to be disturbed any ways, or molested. And we thought fit to be thus special in the things committed to your charge, that you might understand that the indulgence which we have granted in matters of religion to the Christians is ample and unconditional; and perceive at the same time that the open and free exercise of their respective religions is granted to all others, as well as to the Christians. For it befits the well-ordered state and the tranquillity of our times that each individual be allowed, according to his own choice, to worship the Divinity; and we mean not to derogate anything from the honour due to any religion or its votaries. [40]

This section of the letter declares that rather than there being any form of religious coercion there should be unconditional freedom for both Christians and non-Christians alike to follow whatever form of religion seems best to them.[41] As Elizabeth DePalma Digeser argues, what is said

---

[40] Lactantius, *Of the manner in which the persecutors died*, XLVIII, in in the Ante-Nicene Fathers Vol. VII (Edinburgh and Grand Rapids: T&T Clark/Eerdmans, 1994), p.320.

[41] It is interesting to contrast the unconditional freedom of religion permitted by the Edict of Milan and the more restricted tolerance granted to the Christians in the Sasanian [Persian] Empire by King Yazdegerd I in 409. in the words of William Wigram: 'Permission was formally given to the Christians to worship openly, and to rebuild their churches. Confessors who were still in prison were set at liberty, and bishops were given free leave to travel in their dioceses. This decree was practically the Edict of Milan for the Assyrian Church. It was the formal recognition of the Christians as being in law what they had hitherto been in fact, viz. a *melet* [community] with the right to exist. and worship in the Persian Empire. Of course this toleration was something very far removed from liberty or equality, as we

in this 'paradigmatic statement of religious liberty' carries the 'fingerprints' of Lactantius. [42] The similarity between what is said here and what is said in the *Divine Institutes* indicates that what we have in the Edict of Milan is the developing thought of Lactantius reflected through Constantine. Constantine as the senior co-emperor determined the policy set out in the letter, and he in turn was influenced by Lactantius.

As Digeser further observes, what the first part of the Edict of Milan reflects is Lactantius' vision for the religious policy of a Christian Rome:

> When considering how Romans should treat Christians...Lactantius appealed for a policy of tolerance. But a Christian Rome would also exercise forbearance. It would certainly disapprove of and disagree with the practise of traditional cult, but such an objection would not license the use of force to achieve conformity - although again, rational arguments about what he saw as the truth of Christianity would be allowable. The same principles that argue for a tolerant Roman state would also justify Christian forbearance: Christians must allow God to punish impiety and must allow people free choice to convert to Christianity. Finally, because Lactantius thinks that the only way people can become genuine Christians is to have free choice, and because he thinks that with enough time and sufficiently skilled teachers the traditional religions will disappear...the result for a Christian state would be a policy seeking concord, not tolerance. Such a state would forbear polytheism, for

understand the words. First, the decree was valid only *durante beneplacito*—till it was the pleasure of the Shah-in-Shah to withdraw it; and next, while in existence, the toleration that it gave was limited. A Christian might exist, but not proselytize. Apostasy from Magianism was as much a capital offence as ever; and the leave to rebuild old churches did not (and does not) imply the right to build new ones.' (W A Wigram, *An Introduction to the History of the Assyrian Church*, London: SPCK 1910, pp.89-90).

[42] Elizabeth De Palma Digeser, 'Lactantius on Religious Liberty and His Influence on Constantine' in Timothy Shah and Allen Hertzke (eds), *Christianity and Freedom – Volume I: Historical Perspectives* (New York: CUP, 2016), p.96.

example, not because it despaired over converting such people (toleration) but because forbearance was precisely what would achieve conversion (concord). [43]

A Christian Rome would seek to convert non-Christians to Christianity, but it would do so in a non-coercive manner that continued to give people free choice in matters of religion.

Wilken notes that the second part of the letter, which is about the return to Christians of church buildings that they have lost during the preceding period of persecution is also significant because it suggests that there is a distinction between the Christian Church and the state:

> After the general statement about freedom to practise one's religion, the emperors made clear that with respect to the Christians they also have in mind not simply individuals but the freedom of the church, the body (*corpus*) of Christians. The Christians are known, they write, to have places 'in which they have the habit of assembling' and where they own property. For that reason Licinius and Constantine state that the places where they gather 'belong by right to their body [*ius corporis*],' that is to the churches not to individuals.' This statement is no less novel than the general policy on freedom in religious matters, for it suggests that the emperors sensed, if only dimly, that a new form of religion existed in their midst, having its own corporate life independent of the state. It is a truth Christians would always honour, even when the line between the spiritual and the temporal was so fine as to seem non-existent.[44]

The importance of the principle that the Church is a body independent of the state is that it means that the Church has the right to run its own affairs under its own leaders and cannot simply be subject to state policy.

[43] Digeser, p.94.
[44] Wilken, p.23.

From the Edict of Milan to the end of the Middle Ages

If we move on from the Edict of Milan through the later Roman Empire and the Middle Ages we find that the ideas of religious freedom which we find in the works of Tertullian and Lactantius were not always upheld by later generations of Christians.

Tragically, once they had obtained political and social power, Christians frequently abandoned a policy of forbearance with regard to non-Christians and to Christian groups such as the Donatists and the Cathars who they judged to be schismatic or heretical and instead frequently subjected them to discrimination, persecution and attempts at forced conversion. In addition, the distinction between church and society and church and state often got blurred and those who were viewed as being heretical or schismatic were subject to coercion and punishment by the church and the state acting together.[45]

However, this having been said, what we also find is that there has also been a continuous tradition of Christian thinking that has continued to uphold freedom of religion in a number of different ways.

First, we find a succession of statements maintaining the two key principles that non-Christians should not be subject to forced conversion and that they should be free to practice their own religion.

At the turn of the fifth and sixth centuries we see these two principles reflected in two letters from Pope Gregory the Great.

In a letter on the forced baptism of Jews in Marseilles who had been 'brought to the font more by coercion than by preaching' Gregory writes:

---

[45] It is worth noting that when the Spanish Bishop Priscillian was executed for heresy in 385, this was condemned by Pope Siricius, Bishop Ambrose of Milan and Bishop Martin of Tours and those responsible including the Emperor Maximus were excommunicated with Ambrose declaring that he did not wish to have anything to do with bishops who sent heretics to their deaths.

I consider the intention worthy of praise and grant that it comes from love of our Lord. But I fear that such intention, unless supported by the evidence to the holy scriptures, will not lead to a good outcome, and may (God forbid) result in the loss of souls we would want to save. For when anyone is brought to the font of baptism, not by the sweetness of preaching, but by compulsion, he will return to his former superstition and die in a worse state because he had been reborn. So, my brother, may you stir up such men by frequent preaching so that they may desire to change their life more by the sweetness of their teacher.[46]

In another letter, written to Bishop Paschasius of Naples, Gregory insists that while it is right to seek their conversion, the Jews in Naples must be allowed to freely celebrate their festivals:

Those who with pure intent desire to bring to the true faith aliens from the Christian religion should study kindness, and not asperity; lest such as reason rendered with smoothness might have appealed to should be driven far off by opposition. For whosoever act otherwise, and under cover of such intention would suspend people from their accustomed observance of their own rites, are proved to be intent on their own cause rather than on God's. To wit, the Jews dwelling in Naples have complained to us, asserting that certain persons are endeavouring unreasonably to drive them from certain solemnities of their holidays, so that it may not be lawful for them to observe the solemnities of their festivals, as up to this time since long ago it has been lawful for them and their forefathers to keep and observe them. Now, if this is true, these people appear to be taking trouble to no purpose. For what is the use, when even such long unaccustomed prohibition is of no avail for their faith and conversion? Or why should we lay down rules for the Jews as to how they should observe their ceremonies, if we cannot thereby win them? We should therefore so act that, being rather appealed to

---

[46] Gregory 1, Epistle 1.45 cited in Robert Wilken, 'The Christian Roots of Religious Freedom,' in Shah and Hetzke, pp.67-68.

by reason and kindness they may wish to follow us, and not to fly from us; and that proving to them from their own Scriptures what we tell them, we may be able, with God's help, to convert them to the bosom of Mother Church.

Wherefore let your Fraternity, so far as may be possible, with the help of God, kindle them to conversion, and not allow them any more to be disquieted with respect to their solemnities; but let them have free licence to observe and celebrate all their festivals and holidays, even as hitherto both they and their forefathers for a long time back have kept and held them.[47]

At the end of the eighth century Alcuin of York warned Charlemagne against trying to forcibly convert the pagan Saxons:

Faith arises from the will, not from compulsion. You can persuade a man to believe, but you cannot force him. You may be able to force him to be baptized, but this will not instil the faith within him.[48]

In 1120, in response to attacks on Jews across Europe, Pope Callistus II issued a Papal Bull entitled *Sicut Iudaeis* ('As for the Jews') which came to be seen as the authoritative statement on how Christians should relate to the Jewish community. This forbad under pain of excommunication forced baptism of Jewish people, or any attacks on their persons, their property or their customs:

[The Jews] ought to suffer no prejudice. We, out of the meekness of Christian piety, and in keeping in the footprints of Our predecessors of happy memory, the Roman Pontiffs Calixtus, Eugene, Alexander, Clement, admit their petition, and We grant them the buckler of Our protection.

---

[47] Gregory the Great, *Epistles*, Book XIII.XII, in *The Nicene and Post Nicene Fathers*, Vol. XIII (Edinburgh and Grand Rapids: T&T Clark/Eerdmans, 1997), pp.96-97.
[48] Alcuin, Letter 113 cited in Wilken, 'The Christian roots of religious freedom,' p.68.

For we make the law that no Christian compel them, unwilling or refusing, by violence to come to baptism. But, if any one of them should spontaneously, and for the sake of the faith, fly to the Christians, once his choice has become evident, let him be made a Christian without any calumny. Indeed, he is not considered to possess the true faith of Christianity who is not recognized to have come to Christian baptism, not spontaneously, but unwillingly.

Too, no Christian ought to presume...to injure their persons, or with violence to take their property, or to change the good customs which they have had until now in whatever region they inhabit.

Besides, in the celebration of their own festivities, no one ought disturb them in any way, with clubs or stones, nor ought any one try to require from them or to extort from them services they do not owe, except for those they have been accustomed from times past to perform.

...We decree...that no one ought to dare mutilate or diminish a Jewish cemetery, nor, in order to get money, to exhume bodies once they have been buried.

If anyone, however, shall attempt, the tenor of this decree once known, to go against it...let him be punished by the vengeance of excommunication, unless he correct his presumption by making equivalent satisfaction."[49]

In the thirteenth century Pope Innocent IV addressed the question of whether Christians could lawfully wage war on Muslims. His response was that they could do so under just war theory if Muslims were in serious breach of the natural law to which all human beings are

---

[49] Pope Callistus II, *Sicut Iudaeis*, in Edward Synan, *The Popes and the Jews in the Middle Ages* (Lightning Source Inc.2008) pp.231–232.

subject,[50] but that they could not do so for the purpose of seeking to forcibly convert Muslims to Christianity[51]

Also in the thirteen century, Thomas Aquinas taught in the *Summa Theologiae* that while it was legitimate for Christians to defend their faith against the actions of unbelievers it was not legitimate for Christians to try to compel unbelievers to accept the Christian faith:

> Among believers there are some who have never received the faith, such as the heathens and the Jews: and these are by no means to be compelled to the faith, in order that they may believe, because to believe depends on the will: nevertheless they should be compelled by the faithful, if it be possible to do so, so that they do not hinder the faith, By their blasphemies, or by their evil persuasions, or even by the open persecutions. It is for this reason that Christ's faithful often waged war with unbelievers, not for the purpose of forcing them to believe because even if they were to conquer them, and take them prisoners, they should still leave them free to believe if they will, but in order to prevent them from hindering the faith of Christ.[52]

Finally, right at the end of the Middle Ages we find the Spanish Dominican theologian Bartholome De Las Casas drawing on the work of his Patristic and Medieval predecessors in his defence of the rights of the native inhabitants of the New World.

In his work *Entre los remedios* (Among the remedies) published in 1552 he argued that it would be wrong to force the Amerindians to accept the Christian faith:

> In order to receive our holy faith the freedom of the will is required among those who accept it. God left in the hand of each person the

---

[50] For instance, by invading someone else's country.
[51] Ian Levy, 'Liberty of Conscience and Freedom of Religion in the Medieval Canonists,' in Shah and Hertzke, p.157.
[52] Thomas Aquinas, *Summa Theologiae* II-II, Q.10, Art 8.

free choice to accept it or not. And since this is the end that God has assigned to the entire affair of the Indies, it remains established in the voluntary will of these peoples, and not in any force or violence done to them. Undoubtedly, most esteemed Lord, in everything else done nothing should be against their will, But in agreement with it, respecting their approval and consent.[53]

In his *Apologia* he also argued that the existing religious practices of the Amerindians should be respected:

Nature itself teaches that the whole human race must worship God. Since divine worship consists in ceremonies, it follows that, just as man cannot live without the true God, or a false god considered true, they cannot live without the exercise of some ceremonies, especially seeing that the strong belief among the gentiles has been the entire welfare of a commonwealth is preserved in happiness by means of ceremonies and sacrifices. Therefore, if against their wills we were to destroy their ceremonies, they would have, besides the many other offences that would follow, only a thin adherence to the Catholic faith and Christian religion, and we would appear deranged in compelling them to receive that faith, which is prohibited.[54]

In addition to the belief that non-Christians should not be subject to forced conversion and should be able to practice their own religion, we also find the consistent belief that there was a distinction between civil and ecclesiastical jurisdiction. Emperors and Kings ruled over the temporal sphere, but the bishops of the Church had authority in spiritual matters.

[53] Casas, Bartholome De Las, *Entre los remedios* in David Latingua, 'Faith, Liberty and the Defense of the Poor' in Shah and Hertzke, p.193.
[54] Casas, Bartholome De Las, *Apologia* 7.43, in Lantigua, p.196. The same approach to the rights of the Amerindians had previously been taken by another Spanish theologian, Francisco Vitoria, in his work 'On the evangelization of unbelievers' published in 1534-35.

The classic statement of this belief, which shaped Christian thinking into the sixteenth century, was a letter written by Pope Gelasius I to the Emperor Anastasius in 494. The letter runs as follows:

There are two powers, august Emperor, by which this world is chiefly ruled, namely, the sacred authority of the priests and the royal power. Of these that of the priests is the more weighty, since they have to render an account for even the kings of men in the divine judgment. You are also aware, dear son, that while you are permitted honourably to rule over humankind, yet in things divine you bow your head humbly before the leaders of the clergy and await from their hands the means of your salvation. In the reception and proper disposition of the heavenly mysteries you recognize that you should be subordinate rather than superior to the religious order, and that in these matters you depend on their judgment rather than wish to force them to follow your will.

If the ministers of religion, recognizing the supremacy granted you from heaven in matters affecting the public order, obey your laws, lest otherwise they might obstruct the course of secular affairs by irrelevant considerations, with what readiness should you not yield them obedience to whom is assigned the dispensing of the sacred mysteries of religion. Accordingly, just as there is no slight danger in the case of the priests if they refrain from speaking when the service of the divinity requires, so there is no little risk for those who disdain - which God forbid -when they should obey. And if it is fitting that the hearts of the faithful should submit to all priests in general who properly administer divine affairs, how much the more is obedience due to the bishop of that see which the Most High ordained to be above all others, and which is consequently dutifully honoured by the devotion of the whole Church.[55]

---

[55] Fordham University, 'Gelasius I on Spiritual and Temporal Power, 494' at https://sourcebooks.fordham.edu/source/gelasius1.asp.

The importance for freedom of religion of the distinction between civil and ecclesiastical jurisdiction set out in this letter is that it established the principle that there is an authority in spiritual matters which is separate from the authority in temporal matters enjoyed by those with civil power. This in turn meant that the members of the Church were not bound to do what those with civil power told them to do in matters of religion. This distinction between civil and religious authority later came to be described, on the basis of Luke 22:35-38 as the 'doctrine of the two swords.'

The principle that the Church had an authority in spiritual matters separate from that enjoyed by civil rulers in temporal matters, also meant that the Church had the right to call Christian rulers to account when they acted in ways in ways contrary to the law of God. The classic example of this principle in action was the excommunication of the Emperor Theodosius by Bishop Ambrose of Milan on account of his having unjustly ordered the killing of the inhabitants of the city of Thessalonica in 390. In the words of the church historian Sozomen:

> The occasion of the sin was as follows. When Buthericus was general of the troops in Illyria, a charioteer saw him shamefully exposed at a tavern, and attempted an outrage; he was apprehended and put in custody. Some time after, some magnificent races were to be held at the hippodrome, and the populace of Thessalonica demanded the release of the prisoner, considering him necessary to the celebration of the contest. As their request was not attended to, they rose up in sedition and finally slew Buthericus. On hearing of this deed, the wrath of the emperor was excited immediately, and he commanded that a certain number of the citizens should be put to death. The city was filled with the blood of many unjustly shed; for strangers, who had but just arrived there on their journey to other lands, were sacrificed with the others. There were many cases of suffering well worthy of commiseration, of which the following is an instance. A merchant offered himself to be slain as a substitute for his two sons who had both been selected as victims, and promised the soldiers to give

them all the gold he possessed, on condition of their effecting the exchange. They could not but compassionate his misfortune, and consented to take him as a substitute for one of his sons, but declared that they did not dare to let off both the young men, as that would render the appointed number of the slain incomplete. The father gazed on his sons, groaning and weeping; he could not save either from death, but he continued hesitating until they had been put to death, being overcome by an equal love for each. I have also been informed, that a faithful slave voluntarily offered to die instead of his master, who was being led to the place of execution. It appears that it was for these and other acts of cruelty that Ambrose rebuked the emperor, forbade him to enter the church, and excommunicated him. Theodosius publicly confessed his sin in the church, and during the time set apart for penance, refrained from wearing his imperial ornaments, according to the usage of mourners. He also enacted a law prohibiting the officers entrusted with the execution of the imperial mandates, from inflicting the punishment of death till thirty days after the mandate had been issued, in order that the wrath of the emperor might have time to be appeased, and that room might be made for the exercise of mercy and repentance.[56]

A final belief that was important in the Middle Ages was that conviction that one should act according to conscience. If conscience and authority are in conflict then one must obey one's conscience, one's interior conviction that obedience to God required doing one thing rather than another. This is because it would be a sin to disobey what you believed obedience to God required.

Two examples illustrate this point.

The first is the discussion by the thirteenth century Parisian theologian Godfrey of Fontaines about 'Whether a master of theology ought to

---

[56] Sozemen, *Church History,* Book VII:25 in *The Nicene and Post Nicene Fathers*, 2nd series (Edinburgh and Grand Rapids: T&T Clark, 1997), p.394.

speak out against a statement of a bishop if he believes the opposite to be true.' His conclusion was that while generally one should submit to a bishop as one's ecclesiastical superior, if a matter concerned salvation, then the bishop's error must be opposed. As Ian Levy explains, for Godfrey:

> In those cases when the truth is clear from Scripture and reason, the bishop's sentence has no force. Admittedly, it is possible that the master could sincerely believe that the Bishop is wrong when the Bishop is actually correct. In that case, the master should still speak out what he believes to be true. Godfrey insisted that one is to follow conscience even if in error, since one actually sins more gravely in violating the dictates of erroneous conscience then acting in accord with that same erroneous conscience.[57]

The second example is provided by the case of a woman in the diocese of Bourges in France who became convinced that she was too closely related to her husband for her marriage to be lawful before God. This raised the theoretical question of whether a wife in this situation should obey her conscience and refuse to have sexual intercourse with her husband even if this meant becoming subject to excommunication for breaking church law by refusing intercourse within a legitimate marriage. The ruling of Pope Innocent III on the matter was that she obey her conscience even if it meant excommunication because 'to proceed against one's conscience is the path to hell.' The commentary on the Pope's decision in what is known as the *Ordinary Gloss* adds:

> It is better to sustain excommunication then to commit mortal sin. For no one should act against conscience; it is better to follow one's conscience than the determination of the church when one is certain in this case. One should rather suffer all manner of evil rather than commit a mortal sin against one's conscience.[58]

---

[57] Levy, p.166.
[58] Levy, p.163.

The emphasis on the importance of conscience reflected in these two examples is important because it establishes the principle that freedom of religion is not just a matter of the freedom of a religious community to believe and act in a particular way, but also involves taking seriously the obligation of individuals to believe and act according to their conscience even when this means saying 'no' to the authorities of a religious community (or to the civil authorities)

Writings from the sixteenth and seventeenth centuries

The medieval emphasis on the importance of conscience just mentioned can be seen to have been at the heart of the Reformation in the sixteenth century. Why did the Reformers break with Rome? They did so because their consciences, informed by Scripture and reason, told them that they had to oppose the teaching of the late Medieval Church. Thus, when called upon at the Diet of Worms in 1521 to repudiate his teaching Martin Luther famously replied:

> Unless I am convicted by Scripture and plain reason – I do not accept the authority of popes and councils, for they have contradicted each other – my conscience is captive to the Word of God. I cannot and I will not recant anything, for to go against conscience is neither right nor safe. God help me. Amen.[59]

Sadly, however, the exercise of freedom by the Protestant Reformers led to problems of conscience for those unable to accept their challenge to traditional Catholic theology and practice. For example, when Nuremburg became a Lutheran city, the civic authorities tried to make the sisters of the Franciscan convent of St Clare abandon their monastic way of life. In her diary, which has survived, the Abbess of the convent, Caritas Pirckheimer, protested that she and the other sisters were being pressured to act against their consciences. To quote Wilken:

> Again and again she says that the sisters are being deprived of their spiritual freedom. We hope, she writes, that the 'honourable City Council will not apply pressure in matters which concern our

---

[59] Martin Luther quoted in Roland Bainton, *Here I Stand* (Tring: Lion, 1978), p.185.

conscience' and force us to act against our wills to confess what the authorities want us to say.' To which she adds: 'We cannot find in our conscience that we should believe and hold fast to what everyone wants us to' and abandon the 'faith and order of the Holy Church.' The 'entire convent,' she writes 'stood up and indicated to me that they concurred with what I had said.' Do not ask us to accept a faith we do not believe in. Even the Turks do not 'coerce' anyone.[60]

As Wilken further notes, Pirckheimer also told the city council that: 'They knew very well that we had always obeyed them in all *temporal* things. But in what concerned our soul, we could follow nothing but our own conscience.'[61]

To quote Wilken, Pirckheimer was not:

> ...simply complaining to the magistrate that they had disrupted the life of her religious community; Pirckheimer was making, however succinctly, a principled argument based on the medieval distinction of powers. It was not the task of civic rulers to determine spiritual matters; the magistrates had transgressed a boundary Christians held sacred.[62]

To put the point a different way, the argument between Pirckheimer and the city council in Nuremburg was whether the civil ruler has the right to wield the spiritual as well as the temporal sword. To put it more simply, has the magistrate the right to take action in matters concerning religion?

The city council in Nuremburg thought that the answer to this question was 'yes' and they were not alone in this conviction. On both the Roman Catholic and the Protestant sides of the Reformation it was seen to be

---

[60] Wilken, p.50 quoting Caritas Pirckheimer, *A Journal of the Reformation Years, 1524-1528* (Cambridge: Boydell and Brewer, 2006), pp.36 and 56.
[61] Wilken, p.50 quoting Pirckheimer, p.39.
[62] Wilken, p.50.

not only the right, but the responsibility, of civic authorities to enforce true religion and suppress irreligion and heresy.

On the Catholic side, for instance, the Emperor Charles V told the German rulers gathered at the Diet of Worms:

> I am descended from a long line of Christian emperors of this noble German nation, and of the Catholic kings of Spain, the archdukes of Austria, and the dukes of burgundy. They were all faithful to the death to the Church of Rome, and they defended the Catholic faith and the honour of God. I have resolved to follow in their steps. A single friar who goes counter to all Christianity for a thousand years must be wrong. Therefore I am resolved to stake my lands, my friends, my body, my blood, my life, and my soul. Not only I, but you of this noble German nation, would be forever disgraced If by our negligence not only heresy but the very suspicion of heresy would survive. After having heard yesterday the obstinate defence of Luther, I regret that I have so long delayed in proceeding against him and his false teaching. I will have no more to do with him. He may return under his safe conduct without preaching or making any tumult. I will proceed against him as a notorious heretic, and ask you to declare yourself as you promised me.[63]

On the Protestant side John Calvin, for example, wrote in the *Institutes of the Christian Religion*:

> The duty of magistrates, its nature, as described by the word of God, and the things in which it consists, I will here indicate in passing. That it extends to both tables of the law, did Scripture not teach, we might learn from profane writers; for no man has discoursed of the duty of magistrates, the enacting of laws, and the common weal, without beginning with religion and divine worship. Thus, all have confessed that no polity can be successfully established unless piety be its first care, and that those laws are absurd which disregard the rights of God and consult only for men. Seeing then that among

---

[63] The Emperor Charles V quoted in Bainton, p.186.

philosophers religion holds the first place, and that the same thing has always been observed with the universal consent of nations, Christian princes and magistrates may be ashamed of their heartlessness if they make it not their care. We have already shown that this office is especially assigned them by God, and indeed it is right that they exert themselves in asserting and defending the honour of him whose vice regents they are, and by whose favour they rule. Hence in Scripture holy kings are especially praised for restoring the worship of God when corrupted or overthrown, or for taking care that religion flourished under them in purity and safety. On the other hand, the sacred history sets down anarchy among the vices, when it states that there was no king in Israel, and, therefore, everyone did as he pleased (Judges 21:25). This rebukes the folly of those who would neglect the care of divine things, and devote themselves merely to the administration of justice among men; as if God had appointed rulers in his own name to decide earthly controversies and omitted what was of far greater moment, his own pure worship as prescribed by his law. [64]

Because of the religious divide at the Reformation, which was not simply between Roman Catholics and Protestants but between Roman Catholics and different kinds of Protestants, was replicated in a religious divide between the civic rulers, the result was a religious patchwork across Europe with different forms of Christianity being supported in different political jurisdictions. As the famous Latin tag put it, *cuius regio, eius religio* (whoever rules, his will be the religion).

During the course of the sixteenth and seventeenth centuries, however, a growing number of Christian voices joined Pirckheimer in protesting against the idea that the temporal ruler had the right to wield the spiritual sword. Drawing on Scripture and Christian writers as far back as Tertullian and Lactantius, they argued that religion was a matter for each individual, or group of individuals, rather than for the civic

---

[64] John Calvin, *Institutes of the Christian Religion*, Book IV, Ch.9 (Grand Rapids; Eerdmans, 1975), Vol.II, pp.657-658.

authorities, and that consequently there should be freedom of religion not only for various different kinds of Christians, but also for Jews and Muslims.

The following selection of writings from the sixteenth and seventeenth century writers illustrates this point.

Georg Froelich

Georg Froelich was a clerk in the city chancellery in Nuremburg. In 1530 he wrote an anonymous memorandum entitled *Whether Secular Government has the right to wield the sword in matters of faith*. Addressing 'Evangelical' (i.e. Protestant) rulers he declares:

> I would very much like to hear where they get the right to control faith either by executing those who do not wish to be of their faith or else by tearing them from property and goods, wife and children, and banishing them from the territory.[65]

As he sees it, by contrast with the Old Testament:

> ...the New Testament speaks of two kingdoms on earth, namely the spiritual and the secular. The spiritual kingdom is the kingdom of Christ in which Christ is king. Similarly, the secular realm also has its king, namely the emperor and other authorities. Just as each kingdom has its own distinct king, so each has its own distinct sceptre, goal, and end. The sceptre of the spiritual realm is the word of God; the goal and end to which this sceptre should attract and move us is that men turn to God and after this life be saved. The sceptre of the secular realm, on the other hand, is the sword; the goal and end toward which it should drive and force men is that external peace be maintained.

---

[65] Georg Froelich, *Whether Secular Government has the right to wield the sword in matters of faith*, text in German History in Documents and images, 'Radicals vs. Protestants – An Attack on Religious Claims to Temporal Authority (1530),' p.1, at https://germanhistorydocs.ghidc.org/sub_document.cfm?document_id=4316

That this is the proper division and distinction between the two kingdoms is powerfully demonstrated in the New Testament, where Christ and his agents, the apostles, observe the order of his kingdom most precisely, ruling in no other wise than with their sceptre, the word of God. With this word they teach, admonish, and censure men, and proclaim that he who accepts and believes it will be saved, while he who does not will be damned. [Mark 16:16] This is their method of government; they leave it at that and thereby their office is fulfilled. Nowhere does one find that if someone did not adhere to their doctrine and preaching but rather believed or taught some other faith, that they appealed to the secular government either to force such a person to accept their faith or else not to tolerate him. Nor does one find anywhere in the New Testament that any government that did this of its own accord was praised for it. On the contrary, Christ forbids it, as can be especially well observed in his explanation of his parable of the good seed and the tares, Matthew 13[:24-30, 37-43], where he says that the good seed are the children of the kingdom, sown by the Son of Man; the tares are the children of evil, sown by the devil; the harvest is the end of the world, the reapers the angels. He concludes that the tares should not be rooted up but rather allowed to remain, lest the wheat also be rooted up with them. For just as the tares are gathered and burned in the fire, so it will be at the end of the world: the Son of Man will send his angels, who will gather out of his kingdom all those that offend and cast into the furnace all those that work iniquity.[66]

This makes it, clear, he argues:

...that Christ does not wish the sword of the secular government to be used to root anything out of his kingdom, but wishes rather to do combat there solely by his word until the end of the world. As the prophet Isaiah proclaims and says, Christ will do battle 'with the breath of his mouth and with the rod of his lips,' [Isaiah 11: 4] not

[66] Froelich. pp.1-2.

with the sword of secular government. Here it is clearly stated that Christ himself will fight, not the secular government for him, with the rod of his mouth and with the breath of his lips, not with the sword of secular government. The prophet Daniel agrees with this and says that Antichrist (that is, all that sets itself against Christian faith and doctrine) shall be destroyed "without hand." [Daniel. 8:25] Whoever, then, seeks by secular power to defend true faith and doctrine or to drive out false faith and doctrine does nothing else than despise and mock the entire New Testament and the prophets as well. And, contrary to what Isaiah and Daniel say—that Christ will do battle in his kingdom by the breath of his mouth and that Antichrist will be destroyed without [human] hand—he also falsely maintains that the breath of Christ's mouth does not do it and that one must accomplish it with one's hand.[67]

For Froelich, 'the sum and substance of the whole matter' is that:

...a government that wishes to discharge its office and not claim more than has been entrusted to it should and must leave it entirely to Christ the king to determine and judge, by means of the sceptre of his divine word, whether any teaching about faith, how man may come to God and be saved, be true or false. Just as one clearly sees that in his kingdom Christ does both things, namely, teaches the true faith and condemns the false, pours the holy spirit into the heart and drives the devil out, doing both through his sceptre, the word, and calls on no secular authority to assist. Hence it is not proper for secular authority to do this. Rather it should use its sceptre or sword in the secular realm against external misdeeds, so that no one may be harmed in his body or goods. In such matters the secular sword is effective and God has established it for that reason. But the sword is of no use in forcing people to adhere to this or that faith. In the final analysis, whether you hang or drown them,

---

[67] Froelich, p.2.

the choice must still be left to those who do not want to go to heaven to go down to hell to the devil or his mother instead.[68]

Menno Simons

Menno Simons (after whom the Mennonite Christian tradition is named) was a Dutch Roman Catholic Priest who joined the radical Protestant group known as the Anabaptists in 1536. He became a recognised leader of the Anabaptists and wrote a number of works explaining and defending their theological convictions.

In these works he argues that the secular magistrates should not meddle in matters of religion. Thus, in a response to an attack on the Anabaptists published by a Reformed minister called Gellius Faber, Simons declares:

> Christ Jesus and his powerful word and Holy Spirit is the protector and defender of his church; and not the emperor, king, or any worldly potentate. The kingdom of the Spirit must be protected and defended by the sword of the Spirit, and not by the sword of the world. This is too clear to be controverted, according to the doctrine and example of Christ and his apostles.

> I would further say, If the magistracy rightly understood Christ and his kingdom, they would, in my opinion, rather choose death, than to meddle with their worldly power and sword in spiritual matters, which are not subject to the judgment of man, but to the judgment of the great and Almighty God alone. But they are taught by their pastors that they should proscribe, imprison, torture and slay those who are not obedient to their doctrine, as may, alas, be seen in many different cities and countries.[69]

In similar fashion, in his *Brief complaint or apology of the despised Christians and exiled strangers to all the theologians and preachers of the*

---

[68] Froelich, p.2.
[69] Menno Simons, *The Complete Works of Menno Simons* (Elkhart: John F Funk, 1871), p.104.

German Nations he argues that it is wrong for Christians to seek to rule over the consciences of others by means of the sword of the magistrate and that the proper was to deal with heretics was by shunning them rather than killing or imprisoning them:

> Say, beloved, where do the Holy Scriptures teach that we shall rule the consciences and faith of others, in the kingdom and church of Christ, by force of the sword, violence, and tyranny of the magistracy—something which is left entirely to the judgement of God? In what instance has Christ and the apostles ever done, recommended or commanded this?
>
> Christ says, 'Beware of false prophets;' and Paul commands that we shall shun an heretic after one or two admonitions; John teaches that we shall not greet nor receive the transgressor into our houses, who does not bring the doctrine of Christ, Matt. 7: 15; Tit. 3: 10; 2 John 1: 9; they say not: Down with the heretics, accuse them before the magistrates, imprison, exile, and cast them into the fire or water, as the Romans have done for many years, and as many of you would do, you who pretend to preach the word of God.[70]

In his response to Faber, Simons also appeals to Jesus' parable of the wheat and tares (Matthew 13:24-30) arguing that the parable shows that it is wrong to try to seek to destroy those who are judged to be the tares lest those who are wheat get uprooted in the process:

> This first parable is explained by Christ himself, saying, 'He that soweth the good seed is the Son of man; The field is the world' (understand it rightly, Christ says, It is the world, and not the church, as Gellius claims); 'the good seed are the children of the kingdom; but the tares are the children of the wicked one; the enemy that sowed them is the devil; the harvest is the end of the world; and the reapers are the angels,' Matt. 13:37-39.

---

[70] Simons, p.118.

Reader, understand it rightly. Christ, the Son of man, sows his seed (God's word), through his Spirit, in the world; all who hear, believe and obey it, are called the children of the kingdom. In the same manner the opponent sows his tares (false doctrine), in the world, and all that hear and follow him are called the children of evil. Now, both wheat and tares grow together in the same field, namely, in the world. The husbandman does not want the tares to be plucked out before their time, that is, he will not have them destroyed by rooting them up, but wants them left until the harvest, lest the wheat be destroyed with the tares, Matt. 13:29, 30.

O, reader, if the preachers rightly understood this parable and feared God, they would not cry so loudly against us, who, alas, are everywhere called tares, heretics and conspirators, 'Down with the heretics;' even if we were heretics, from which God save us. Oh! what noble wheat they destroy! But what does it avail? Satan must rebel and murder; for it is his nature and work, as the Scriptures teach, Gen. 3:4; John 8.[71]

Sebastian Castellio

Sebastian Castellio was a French Reformed theologian who served as the principal of the College of Geneva before moving on to teach Greek at the University of Basel after a disagreement with John Calvin. In 1553, following the execution of Michael Servetus in Geneva for Trinitarian Heresy, he published under the pseudonym Martin Bellius a work entitled *Concerning heretics – whether they should be persecuted*.[72] This was a collection of Christian texts dating from the Patristic period to his own day, which was designed to show that the persecution of heretics, and particularly their execution, was un-Christian.

In the dedication to the original edition of this work to Duke Christoph of Wurtemburg, Castellio declares that there are two great dangers. The first is that 'he be held for a heretic, who is not a heretic.' The second is

---

[71] Simmons, p.88.
[72] It is thought that it was co-authored with two other scholas, Laelius Socinus and Celio Secondo Curione.

that 'he who is really a heretic be punished mores severely or in a manner other than that required by Christian discipline.'[73] In his book, he writes, he has collected 'the opinions of many who have written on this matter, in order that a consideration of their arguments may lead to less offense.'[74]

In the dedication of the French edition to Prince William of Hesse, he distinguishes between the disciplinary roles of the magistrate and the church. He allows the magistrate to punish an obstinate heretic who continues to disturb the peace even after excommunication, but rules out the imposition of the death penalty.

Sins of the heart, such as infidelity, heresy, envy, hate, etc are to be punished by the sword of the Spirit which is the Word of God. If anyone disturbs the Commonwealth by an assault under colour of religion, the magistrate may punish such a one not on the score of religion, but because he has done damage to bodies and goods, like any other criminal. If anyone conduct himself amiss in the church, both in his life and in his doctrine, the Church should use the spiritual sword which is excommunication, if he will not be admonished.

Then, if after excommunication, he perseveres in his evil doings to the point of disturbing the peace, the Christian magistrate may see to it that he no longer troubles the church with his heresies and blasphemies plainly contrary to the Word of God. Of such a character is the teaching of those who deny the creation of the world, the immortality of souls and the resurrection, as well as of those who repudiate the office of the magistrate in order they may better disturb the state to their hearts content without reproof. These men thrive on disturbance, to which the Spirit of God is utterly alien. If they continue to disobey princes and

---

[73] Sebastian Castellio, *Concerning heretics, whether they are to be persecuted and how they are to be treated – A collection of the opinions of learned men both ancient and modern,* (New York: Columbia University Press, 1935), p.126.
[74] Castellio, p.126.

magistrates, they may be punished, but not with the death penalty as St. Augustine teaches.[75]

Examples of the extracts from earlier writers he cites are as follows:

Martin Luther, 'On Civil Government':

> First of all we must observe the children of Adam fall into two groups, the one in the Kingdom of God under Christ, the other in the Kingdom of the world under the magistrate as we have said above. These two groups have two sets of laws for every Kingdom must have laws for without law no Kingdom can stand as daily experience reveals. Civil government has law which extends only to bodies and goods on earth. God, who alone has jurisdiction and all authority over the soul will not suffer it to be subject to mundane laws. When civil government undertakes to legislate for souls then it encroaches upon the province of God and merely perverts and corrupts souls. I wish to make this as clear as day that bishops and princes may see what fools, not to say scoundrels, they are when they seek to coerce men by laws and commandments to believe this or that.

> If a man imposes laws according to his fancy upon the souls of men this certainly is not in accordance with the Word of God and must of necessity displease God, who desires that our faith be built solely upon his Word, as he says in the sixteenth chapter of Matthew 'On this rock I will build my church' [Matthew 16:18] and John, the tenth chapter, 'My sheep hear my voice and know me. A stranger they will not know, but will flee from him. [John 10:4-5].[76]

John Brenz, 'Whether the magistrate has the authority to put to death anabaptists and other heretics':

---

[75] Castellio, p.137.
[76] Castellio, pp.142-143.

Before the world heretics may perfectly well appear as upright if not orthodox. So long, then, as they do not commit murder, adultery, and theft, do violence to no man and keep the civil peace; so long as they render to all their dues: tribute to whom tribute is due; custom to whom custom; fear to whom fear; honour to whom honour, as Saint Paul writes to the Romans, civil punishment has no jurisdiction over them. Paul says that the magistrate is a 'minister of God...A revenger to execute wrath upon him that doeth evil.' This text is by all means to be referred to civil offence and not to spiritual unbelief. Murderers, criminals, and public enemies are subject to civil punishment. Unbelievers and heretics, who live uprightly before the world, are subject to the gospel and God in the next world. This was the command of Christ to his disciples in the 13th chapter of Matthew that they should not root out the tares, but let them grow together until the harvest etc. Christ means that Christians should not root out unbelievers and heretics - these are the tares -with the bodily sword but fight only with spiritual weapons until the harvest, then the heretics will receive their punishment if they have not changed. If unbelievers and heretics are put to death they are deprived not only of their bodies here, but also of their souls hereafter, because they might have turned from unbelief to the true faith from which they have been prevented by the tyranny of the magistrate.[77]

Lactantius, 'Divine Institutes Book 5, Chapter twenty':

For they know that there is nothing more excellent in life than religion and that this ought to be defended with the greatest energy, but as they are deceived with regard to religion so also as to the manner of its defence. Religion is to be defended not by killing, but by dying; not by cruelty, but by patience; not by guilt, but by faith. The first are the characteristics of the evil, the second of the good, and in religion the good is to be employed and not the bad. If you wish to defend religion with blood, with torments, with evil, then

[77] Castellio, pp.156-157.

she is not defended but defiled. Nothing is so free as religion. If the heart is averse to sacrifice, then religion is taken away, is not. The proper method is to defend religion by patience or death in which faith is conserved and is pleasing to God and enhances religion. [78]

Urbanus Rhegius, 'The theological topics on the end of the chapter on heretics':

The spirit of Christians is clement and burns only with the fire of love 'ye know what manner of spirit you are of.' It seeks not vengeance, but the repentance of sinners. The godly dispute not obstinately, but with a mind humble and desirous of the truth after the manner of Acts seventeen 'They searched the Scriptures daily, whether these things were so,' and sought not their own victory but that of the truth.

God does not teach us to burn erring sheep but, as in Ezekiel 34 to heal the sick and feed the lean, etc.[79]

John Chrysostom, 'In Homily Forty Seven on Matthew Thirteen':

'Wilt thou then that we go and gather them up?' But the Lord forbade them lest in gathering up the tares they root up the wheat. This he said that he might prohibit wars and effusion of blood. For if heretics were put to death a truceless war would be let loose upon the world. By two reasons he restrained the servants, first lest the wheat be hurt, and second, that the tares will be punished eventually if incurable. If then, you wish to punish them without hurt to the wheat, wait until the proper time. And what is the meaning of this 'lest you root out the wheat with them?' Either he means that if you resort to arms and slay the heretics many of the saints will necessarily be slain with them, or else he means that in all probability many of the tears may change and become wheat if

---

[78] Castellio, p.198.
[79] Castellio, p.205.

then you root them up prematurely the wheat will perish which would have been produced by a change in the tares.[80]

Texts from the Netherlands Revolt

From 1568-1648 there were eighty years of conflict in the territories which are now Belgium and the Netherlands between the Spanish ruling authorities and various groups opposed to Spanish rule. Part of this conflict was a religious conflict between Catholics and Protestants and as in Germany and Switzerland this aspect of the conflict resulted in the production of writings making the case for freedom of religion. Two key documents from these writings are the anonymous *Good Admonition to the Good Citizens of Brussels* published in 1579 and *Discourse of a nobleman, a patriot partial to public peace, upon peace and war in these Low Countries*, which was published in 1584 and which has been attributed to the Burgomaster of Antwerp, Manix of St Aldegonde.

The importance of these documents lies in their insistence on the right to freedom of conscience and its exercise in outward religious activity. Building on the idea of natural rights developed by late medieval thinkers such as the French theologian Jean Gerson, the *Good Admonition* defends freedom of conscience in matters of religion as a natural (i.e. God given) right:

It is well known that human freedom is located particularly in the soul, which is the chief part of us and in view of which we are called human. Freedom of the soul means freedom of conscience. This freedom means that the person may accept and hold such a religion as his conscience witnesses to him and that no one has the right or the power to hinder him in it or to forbid it violently. This freedom does not have its origin in the Pacification of Ghent,[81] but properly belongs to an individual by nature and by natural right because religion is a bond that the person has with God. It is for this reason that he owes an account to no one besides God alone. This whole

---

[80] Castellio, p.209.
[81] The Pacification of Ghent was a treaty between the provinces of Spanish Netherlands signed in 1576.

thing is well known and requires no proof. If people did not have the freedom to accept and hold such religion as they deemed good according to conscience, then the Christian religion could never have gotten its start. On the contrary, our parents would have had to stay in the heathen religion which they had once accepted without ever being able to change it. [82]

In the words of Wilken, this statement insists that freedom of conscience in matter of religion 'is not a privilege granted by government, not an accommodation or an act of clemency. It is a right given at birth and it cannot be taken away by laws or decrees' [83]

In the *Discourse* it is then argued that the promise to respect Protestant freedom of conscience made by the Spanish authorities was meaningless because it carried the proviso that 'There is no public worship and no offence is given.' This is because:

...this is only to trap and ensnare us. For it is well known that conscience, which resides in peoples minds, is always free and cannot be examined by other men and still less be put under their control or command. And in fact, no one has ever been executed or harassed merely on grounds of conscience, but always for having committed some public act or demonstration, either in words, which are said to be an offence, or in acts which are described as exercise of religion. There is no difference between so-called freedom of conscience without public worship and the old rigour of the edicts and inquisition of Spain...How is it possible to grant freedom of conscience without exercise of religion? For what are the consequences for people who want to enjoy the benefits of this freedom? If they have no ceremonies at all and do not invoke God to testify to the piety and reverence they bear him, they are in fact left without any religion and without fear of God. But if they do have ceremonies and want to show openly that they honour God, their

---

[82] *Een goede vermaninghe aen de goede borgers von Brussele* (Ghent, 1597) translation in Wilken, pp.108-109.
[83] Wilken, p.110.

religious services must be conformable to their conscience as this is allowed to be free. [84]

Leonard Busher

In England, as in Germany and Switzerland, there was a church supported by the state, in this case the Church of England, and those who refused to be part of it were subject to persecution. During the sixteenth century those who remained Roman Catholics protested against this, and from the beginning of the seventeenth century those who had joined separatist Protestant congregations outside the Church of England started to protest as well.

One of the earliest of these Protestant protests was made by Leonard Busher in his 1614 tract *Religion's Peace: A plea for liberty of conscience* which was addressed to King James I and his parliament. In the introduction to this tract Busher sets out his basic case as follows, arguing that persecution is against the mind of Christ and that no bishop or king can command faith:

> Therefore may it please your majesty and parliament to understand that by fire and sword, to constrain princes and peoples to receive that one true religion of the gospel, is wholly against the mind and merciful law of Christ, dangerous both to king and state, a means to decrease the kingdom of Christ, and a means to increase the kingdom of antichrist; as these reasons following do manifest. The which, I humbly beseech your majesty and parliament carefully to consider and that according to the word of God which shall *judge every man according to his deeds* [Matthew 16:27]. And persecution is a work well pleasing to all false prophets and bishops, but is contrary to the mind of Christ *who came not to judge and destroy men's lives but save them* [Luke 9:55-56]. And though some men and women believe not at the first hour, yet may they at the eleventh hour, if they be not persecuted to death before.

---

[84] E H Kossman and A F Mellink (eds), *Texts concerning the Revolt of the Netherlands* (Cambridge: CUP, 1974), pp.265-266.

And no king nor bishop can, or is able to command faith; *that is the gift of God, who worketh in us both the will and the deed of his own good pleasure* [Ephesians 2:8]. Set him not a day therefore, in which, if his creature hear not and believe not, you will imprison and burn him. Paul was a blasphemer and also a persecuter, and could not be converted by the apostles and ministers of Christ; yet at last was received to mercy, and converted extraordinarily by Christ himself who is *very pitiful and merciful, and would have no man to perish, but would that all men come to repentance* [1 Timothy 1:13]. But not by persecution but by the word of reconciliation which he hath committed to his ministers. And as kings and bishops cannot command the wind, so they cannot command faith: and *as the wind bloweth where it listeth, so is every man but is born of the Spirit* [John 3:8]. You may force men to church against their consciences but they will believe as they did afore when they come there; for God gives a blessing only to his own ordinance and abhorreth antichrist's.[85]

Roger Williams

Roger Williams, who I have already mentioned in chapter 1, was another separatist writer. Having been banished from the Massachusetts Bay Colony for his religious views, he founded Providence Plantation (what is now Rhode Island) in 1635 as a haven for religious liberty. In 1644 he published a book called *The Bloudy Tenent of Persecution*[86] setting out the case for toleration in matters of religion for Christians and non-Christians alike.

The book is very long and very detailed, but at the beginning William provides a preface in which he lists the twelve principle arguments contained in the book.

[85] Leonard Busher, *Religion's peace: A plea for liberty of conscience* in Edward Underhill (ed), *Tracts on Liberty of Conscience and Persecution, 1614-1661* (London: J Haddon, 1846), pp.17-18.
[86] 'Bloudy' and 'tenent' are the archaic forms of 'bloody' and 'tenet.'

First. That the blood of so many hundred thousand souls of protestants and papists, spilt in the wars of present and former ages, for their respective consciences, is not required nor accepted by Jesus Christ the Prince of Peace.

Secondly. Pregnant scriptures and arguments are throughout the work proposed against the doctrine of persecution for cause of conscience.

Thirdly. Satisfactory answers are given to scriptures and objections produced by Mr. Calvin, Beza,[87] Mr. Cotton,[88] and the ministers of the New English churches, and others former and later, tending to prove the doctrine of persecution for cause of conscience.

Fourthly. The doctrine of persecution for cause of conscience, is proved guilty of all the blood of the souls crying for vengeance under the altar.

Fifthly. All civil states, with their officers of justice, in their respective constitutions and administrations, are proved essentially civil, and therefore not judges, governors, or defenders of the spiritual, or Christian, state and worship.

Sixthly. It is the will and command of God that, since the coming of his Son the Lord Jesus, a permission of the most Paganish, Jewish, Turkish[89], or anti-Christian consciences and worships be granted to all men in all nations and countries: and they are only to be fought against with that sword which is only, in soul matters, able to conquer: to wit, the sword of God's Spirit, the word of God.

Seventhly. The state of the land of Israel, the kings and people thereof, in peace and war, is proved figurative and ceremonial, and no pattern nor precedent for any kingdom or civil state in the world to follow.

---

[87] Theodore Beza was Calvin's successor as head of the church in Geneva and wrote a work justifying the persecution of heretics in response to Castellio.
[88] John Cotton was the leading minister in the Massachusetts Bay Colony and opposed Williams view on religious toleration.
[89] 'Turkish' here means 'Muslim.'

Eighthly. God requireth not an uniformity of religion to be enacted and enforced in any civil state; which enforced uniformity, sooner or later, is the greatest occasion of civil war, ravishing of conscience, persecution of Christ Jesus in his servants, and of the hypocrisy and destruction of millions of souls.

Ninthly. In holding an enforced uniformity of religion in a civil state, we must necessarily disclaim our desires and hopes of the Jews' conversion to Christ.

Tenthly. An enforced uniformity of religion throughout a nation or civil state, confounds the civil and religious, denies the principles of Christianity and civility, and that Jesus Christ is come in the flesh.

Eleventhly. The permission of other consciences and worships than a state professeth, only can, according to God, procure a firm and lasting peace; good assurance being taken, according to the wisdom of the civil state, for uniformity of civil obedience from all sorts.

Twelfthly. Lastly, true civility and Christianity may both flourish in a state or kingdom, notwithstanding the permission of divers and contrary consciences, either of Jew or Gentile.[90]

As Wilken notes, Williams:

> ...asserts that liberty of conscience applies equally to Jews, Muslims, and Catholics - indeed to all men, not only to dissenting Christians. Recent studies have shown that Williams had personal contact with Muslims. His brother was a 'Turkey-Merchant,'[91] and on one of his trips to the eastern Mediterranean, perhaps Izmir, Istanbul, or Aleppo, he had obtained a Bible purchased from a merchant in the Ottoman Empire, Williams also had done some study of Islam. In one writing he mentioned that Muhammad is considered the seal of the prophets, superseding Moses and Jesus. At the same time he

---

[90] Williams, *The Bloody Tenent of Persecution*, Preface.
[91] I.e. someone who traded with the Ottoman Empire (not a purveyor of Turkeys!).

was critical of Muslim beliefs and considered Muhammad an impostor who would be condemned to hell for misleading his followers. Yet he does not budge from his central argument that all men must be granted liberty of conscience. In his *The Bloudy Tenent Yet More Bloudy* he says that he has 'impartially pleaded for the freedom of the consciences of the Papists themselves, the greatest enemies and persecutors...of the Saints and Truths of Jesus. It is their due and right, as it is of all others. 'Soul-freedom' - one of Williams' terms for freedom of conscience - belongs to all men, for no one can believe and consent to what is imposed on him.[92]

Jeremy Taylor

It can easily be assumed that it was only separatists such as Busher and Williams who were arguing for freedom of religion in England and its colonies in the seventeenth century. However, this was not the case. There were those who conformed to the Church of England who also argued for religious liberty. The prime example is Jeremy Taylor.

Taylor was a clergyman and academic who was a protégé of the Archbishop of Canterbury, William Laud, and as result of Laud's influence he became a chaplain to King Charles I. Following the defeat of the Royalist side in the English Civil War in 1645, he became the principal of a school in West Wales and served as private chaplain to the Earl of Carbery. During his time in Wales he produced a plea for toleration in religious matters entitled *Discourse of the Liberty of Prophesying shewing the unreasonableness of prescribing to other men's faith; and the iniquity of persecuting different opinions.*[93]

In the introduction to this work deplores the religious divisions in the British Isles in his day, declaring that:

These are all become instruments of hatred; thence come schisms and parting of communions, and then persecutions, and then wars

---

[92] Wilken, p.148.
[93] Jeremy Taylor, *Discourse of the Liberty of Prophesying* (London: Joseph Rickerby, 1836).

and rebellion, and then the dissolutions of all friendships and societies.[94]

'All these mischiefs,' he writes, are not the result of the fact that there is a lack of unanimity on religious matters, 'for that is neither necessary nor possible,' but because:

...every opinion is made an article of faith, every article is a ground of a quarrel, every quarrel makes a faction, every faction is zealous, and all zeal pretends for God, and whatsoever is for God cannot be too much. We by this time are come to that pass, we think we love not God except we hate our brother; and we have not the virtue of religion, unless we persecute all religions but our own: for lukewarmness is so odious to God and man, that we, proceeding furiously upon these mistakes, by supposing we preserve the body, we destroy the soul of religion; or by being zealous for faith, or which is all one, for that which we mistake for faith, we are cold in charity, and so lose the reward of both.[95]

As E Cattermole explains in his introductory essay to the 1836 edition of Taylor's work, Taylor's major argument is for mutual tolerance between Christians based on their joint acceptance of the teaching contained in the Apostles Creed:

The general principle advanced in the Liberty of Prophesying, is this: that as truth on all minor dogmas of religion is uncertain, and of small moment in its bearings upon the conduct of men, while peace and charity are things of undoubted certainty and importance, our desire to obtain the former ought to yield to the necessity of securing the latter; and every one, for the good of the community at large, ought to tolerate the differences of all others, while in turn he receives toleration for his own. But as it is indispensable somewhere to draw the line—as some standard of truth must be acknowledged, unless men were to rush into

[94] Taylor, p.6.
[95] Taylor, p.6.

boundless anarchy, or sink into mere indifference, of opinion, he proposes the confession of the apostles' creed, as the test of orthodoxy, and condition of union and communion among Christians.[96]

Despite this generally liberal approach to differences between Christians, Taylor argues that heresy is a serious matter which requires a response from both the Church and the civil authorities:

...heresy being a work of the flesh, and all heretics criminal persons, whose acts and doctrine have influence upon communities of men, whether ecclesiastical or civil, the governors of the republic, or church, respectively, are to do their duties in restraining those michiefs which may happen to their several charges, for whose indemnity they are answerable. [97]

If the issue involved is false doctrine, then this is a spiritual matter which needs to be dealt with by the authorities of the Church by means of ecclesiastical discipline. As he puts it:

If it be false doctrine in any capacity, and doth mischief in any sense, or teaches ill life in any instance, or encourages evil in any particular....these men must be silenced; they must be convinced by sound doctrine, and put to silence by spiritual evidence, and restrained by authority ecclesiastical; that is, by spiritual censures, according' as it seems necessary to him who is most concerned in the regimen of the church. For all this we have precept, and precedent apostolical, and much reason. For by thus doing the governor of the church uses all that authority that is competent, and all the means that is reasonable, and that proceeding which is regular, that he may discharge his cure and secure his flock.[98]

---

[96] Taylor, pp.XIX-XX.
[97] Taylor, p.300.
[98] Taylor, pp.300-301.

However, Taylor says, the Church's discipline needs to be 'restrained and prudent,' and this rules out the application of the death penalty for heresy:

> ...as the church may proceed thus far, yet no Christian man, or community of men, may proceed farther. For if they be deceived in their judgment and censure, and yet have passed only spiritual censures, they are totally ineffectual, and come to nothing; there is no effect remaining upon the soul, and such censures are not to meddle with the body so much as indirectly. But, if any other judgment pass upon persons erring, such judgments whose effects remain, if the person be unjustly censured, nothing will answer and make compensation for such injuries. If a person be excommunicate unjustly, it will do him no hurt; but if he be killed, or dismembered unjustly, that censure and infliction is not made ineffectual by his innocence, he is certainly killed and dismembered. [99]

In Taylor's view, the prince, by which he means the ruling authority in a given state, may take action against religious activity if this should 'disturb the public peace.'[100] However, with this exception, it is not only allowable, but necessary that the prince should tolerate the existence of different forms of religious belief because to do otherwise would be to usurp the role of God:

> ...it is not only lawful to tolerate disagreeing persuasions, but the authority of God only is competent to take notice of it, and infallible to determine it, and fit to judge; and therefore no human authority is sufficient to do all those things which can justify the inflicting temporal punishments upon such as do not conform in their persuasions to a rule or authority which is not only fallible, but supposed by the disagreeing person to be actually deceived.[101]

---

[99] Taylor, p.302.
[100] Taylor p.307.
[101] Taylor, p.307.

John Owen

Like Jeremy Taylor, the great seventeenth century English Puritan theologian, John Owen was ordained into the Church of England, only departing from it after being unable to accept the re-imposition of episcopacy and the Book of Common Prayer in 1662.

Owen, addressed the issue of religious toleration in a number of his works, but his two key texts on this is issue were his *Discourse of Toleration*, which was published in 1649 and *Truth and Innocence Vindicated*, which was published in 1670.

In his *Discourse of Toleration* he takes an equivocal attitude to the role of those with civil authority in relation to religious matters. On the one hand, he declares that there is no biblical basis for those with civil authority to punish those who will not agree with them about matters of religion:

> Non-toleration—in the latitude which is for persons in authority enjoying the truth (or supposing they do enjoy it) to punish in an arbitrary way, according to what they shall conceive to be condign, men who will not forsake their own convictions about any head or heads of Christian religion whatsoever, to join with what they hold out, either for belief or worship, after the using of such ways of persuasion as they shall think fit—is no way warranted in the gospel; nor can any sound proof for such a course be taken from the Old Testament.[102]

On the other hand, he also goes on to declare that it is not only the right, but the positive duty, of the magistrate to repress certain forms of religious practice. He writes:

> That the magistrate ought not to make provision of any public places for the practice of any such worship as he is convinced to be an abomination unto the Lord. When I say he ought not to make provision, I understand not only a not actual caring that such be,

---

[102] John Owen, 'A Discourse of Toleration,' in *The Sermons of John Owen*, pp.172-173 at https://ccel.org/ccel/owen/sermons/sermons.ii.iii.vi.html

but also a caring that such may not be. He should not have a negation of acting as to anything of public concernment. His not opposing here is providing. For instance, he must not allow—that is, it is his duty to oppose—the setting apart of public places under his protection for the service of the mass (as of late in Somerset House), or for any kind of worship in itself disallowed, because not required, and so not accepted. This were to be bound to help forward sin, and that such sin whereof he is convinced;—which is repugnant to the whole revealed will of God. A magistrate, I told you before, is not to act according to what he may do, but what he must do. Now, it cannot be his duty to further sin.[103]

This means, he writes, that the magistrate should not permit:

Outward monuments—ways of declaring and holding out false and idolatrous worship—he is to remove; as the Papists' images, altars, pictures, and the like; Turks' mosques; prelates' service-book.

...Such things as, in their whole use and nature, serve only for the carrying on of worship in itself wholly false, and merely invented; as altars, images, crosses.

...Such as are used for the carrying on of worship true in itself, though vilely corrupted; as praying and preaching;—such are those places commonly called churches. [104]

However, in his 1670 book *Truth and Innocence Vindicated* he defends religious toleration in a more unequivocal fashion in response to a book by the Church of England writer Samuel Parker called *A Discourse of Ecclesiastical Polity* which attacked the idea that any 'indulgence and toleration' should be offered to those like Owen who refused to conform to the episcopally led Church of England which had been restored in 1662.

---

[103] Owen, 'A Discourse of Toleration,' pp.193-194.
[104] Owen, 'A Discourse of Toleration,' p.194.

In his book Owen argues that everyone ought to be allowed to act according to their conscience in relation to their form of worship. As he puts it:

> This, therefore, is the sum of what is asserted in this matter: Conscience, according to that apprehension which it hath of the will of God about his worship (whereunto we confine our discourse), obligeth men to act or forebear accordingly. If their apprehensions are right and true, just and equal, what the Scripture, the great rule of conscience, doth declare and require, I hope none, upon second thoughts, will deny but that such things are attended with a right onto a liberty to be practised, while the Lord Jesus Christ is esteemed the lord of lords and the king of kings, and is thought to have power to command the observance of his own institutions. Suppose their apprehensions to be such as may in those things, be they more or less, be judged not to correspond exactly with the great rule of conscience, yet supposing them also to contain nothing inconsistent with, or of a disturbing nature to, civil society and public tranquillity, nothing that gives countenance to any vice or evil, or is opposite to the principle truths and main duties of religion, wherein the minds of men in a nation do coalesce, nor to carry any politic entanglements along with them; and add thereunto the peaceableness of the persons possessed with those apprehensions, and the impossibility they are under to divest themselves of them; -and I say natural right, justice, equity, religion, conscience, God himself in all, and his voice in the hearts of all unprejudiced persons, do require that neither the persons themselves, on the account of their consciences, have violence offered under them, nor their practises in pursuit of their apprehensions be restrained by severe prohibitions and penalties. [105]

---

[105] John Owen, *Truth and Innocence Vindicated* (Louisville: GLH Publishing, 2020), Kindle edition, Loc.2320.

As Wilken notes, when Owen refers to 'natural right' and 'equity' there is an unacknowledged reference to Tertullian's *To Scapula*. As we have seen, Tertullian declared that it is a 'fundamental human right, a privilege of nature, that every man should worship according to his own convictions' and for Owen this translates into the innate right of everyone to act in accordance with their conscience in relation to the worship of God.

Owen further argues that it is proper for action to be taken against forms of religion that are subversive of civil government, but adds that this is not a charge that can rightly laid against Owen and his fellow dissenters from the Church of England. In his words:

Let it be granted, as it must and ought to be, that all principles of the minds of men, pretended to be from apprehensions of religion, that are in themselves inconsistent with any lawful government, in any place whatever, ought to be coerced and restrained; for our Lord Jesus Christ, sending his gospel to be preached and published in all the nations and kingdoms of the world, then and at all times under various sorts of governments, all for the same end of public tranquillity and prosperity, did propose nothing in it but what a submission and obedience unto might be consistent with the government itself, of what sort soever it were. He came, as they used to sing of old,' to give men a heavenly Kingdom, and not deprive them or take from them their earthly temporal dominions.' There is, therefore, nothing more certain than that there is no principle of the religion taught by Jesus Christ which either in itself, or in the practice of it, is inconsistent with any righteous government on the earth. And if any opinions can truly and really be manifested so to be, I will be no advocate for them nor their abettors. But such as these our author shall never be able to justly to affix on them whom he opposeth, nor the least umbrage of them, if he do but allow the gospel and the power of Christ to institute those spiritual ordinances, and require their administration, which do not, which cannot, and extend undo anything wherein a magistrate, as such, hath the least concernment in point of prejudice...[106]

Finally, Owen suggests that what is being proposed is that princes or magistrates should try to usurp the place of God by the 'assuming of a dominion over the souls and consciences of men in the worship of God'[107] and asks the rhetorical question as to whether the persecution of godly people advocated by Parker is in accordance with the spirit of the gospel and the mind of Christ. To quote Owen:

Let the merit of the case be a stated and considered, which is truly as above proposed, and no other; set aside prejudices, animosities, advantages from things past and bygone in political disorders and tumults wherein it hath no concern, - and it will quickly appear how little it is, how much, if possible, less than nothing, that is or can be pleaded for the countenancing of external severity in this case. Does it suit the spirit of the gospel [of Christ] or his commands, to destroy *good wheat*, for standing, as his supposed, *a little out of order*, who would not have men pluck up the tares, but let them stand quietly in the field until harvest? [Matthew 13:24-30]. Doth it answer his mind to destroy *his disciples*, who profess to love and obey him, from the earth, who blamed his disciples of old for desiring to destroy the Samaritans, his enemies, with fire from heaven? [Luke 9:54-55] We are told that 'he who was born after the flesh persecuted him who was born after the promise;' [Galatians 4:29] and a work becoming him it was. And if men are sincere disciples of Christ, though they may fall into some mistakes and errors, the outward persecuting of them on that account will be found to be of the works of the flesh. [108]

William Penn

William Penn, the founder of Pennsylvania, originally belonged to the Church of England. Having studied under John Owen and the French

---

[106] Owen, *Truth and Innocence Vindicated,* Loc. 2580-2591.
[107] Own, *Truth and Innocence Vindicated,* Loc 3446.
[108] Owen, *Truth and Innocence Vindicated,* Loc, 3594.

Reformed theologian Moise Amyraut, he eventually became a member of the Society of Friends (the Quakers) in 1666. In 1670 he wrote a defence of freedom of religion entitled *The Great Case of Liberty of Conscience* while in the Newgate prison in London on account of his beliefs.

Penn defines 'liberty of conscience' as involving not only freedom of belief, but also freedom of worship:

> ...not only a mere Liberty of the Mind, in believing or disbelieving this or that Principle or Doctrine, but the Exercise of ourselves in a visible Way of Worship, upon our believing it to be indispensably required at our Hands, that if we neglect it for Fear or Favour of any Mortal Man, we Sin, and incur Divine Wrath: Yet we would be so understood to extend and justify the Lawfulness of our so meeting to worship God, as not to contrive, or abet any Contrivance destructive of the Government and Laws of the Land, tending to Matters of an external Nature, directly, or indirectly; but so far only, as it may refer to religious Matters, and a Life to come, and consequently wholly independent of the secular Affairs of this, wherein we are supposed to Trangress.[109]

He then argues that there are five reasons why 'Imposition, Restraint, and Persecution' in matters relating to liberty of conscience 'directly invade the Divine Prerogative, and Divest the Almighty of a Due, proper to none besides himself.' These five reasons are:

> First, If we do allow the Honour of our Creation, due to God only, and that no other besides himself has endowed us with those excellent Gifts of Understanding, Reason, Judgment, and Faith, and consequently that he only is the Object as well as Author, both of our Faith, Worship, and Service, then whosoever shall interpose their Authority to enact Faith and Worship, in a Way that seems not to us congruous with what he has discovered to us to be Faith and

---

[109] William Penn, *A Collection of the Works of William Penn* (London: J. Sowle, 1726), p.447, spelling updated in this and subsequent extracts from Penn.

Worship (whose alone Property it is to do it) or to restrain us from what we are persuaded is our indispensable Duty, they evidently usurp this Authority and invade his incommunicable Right of Government over Conscience: For the Inspiration of the Almighty gives Understanding: And Faith is the Gift of God, says the Divine Writ. [Job 32:8]

Secondly. Such magisterial Determinations carry an evident Claim to that Infallibility, which Protestants have been hitherto so jealous of owning, that to avoid the Papists, they have denied it to all, but God himself. Either they have forsook their old Plea, or if not, we desire to know when, and where, they were invested with that divine Excellency, and whether Imposition, Restraint, and Persecution, were deemed by God ever the Fruits of his Spirit: However, that itself was not sufficient; for unless it appear as well to us, that they have it, as to them who have it, we cannot believe it upon any convincing Evidence, but by Tradition only; an Anti-Protestant Way of Believing.

Thirdly, It enthrones Man as King over Conscience, the alone just Claim and Privilege of his Creator, whose Thoughts are not as Men's Thoughts but has reserved to himself, that Empire from all the Caesars on Earth; for if Men in Reference to Souls, and Bodies, things appertaining to this and the other World, shall be subject to their Fellow-Creatures, what follows? but that Caesar (however he got it) has all, God's Share, and his own too; and being Lord of both, Both are Caesar's and not God's.

Fourthly, It defeats God's Work of Grace, and the invisible Operation of his Eternal Spirit, which can alone beget Faith, and is only to be obeyed, in and about Religion and Worship, and attributes Men's Conformity to outward Force and Corporal Punishments. A Faith subject to as many Revolutions as the Powers that enact it.

Fifthly and Lastly, Such Persons assume the Judgment of the great Tribunal unto themselves; for to whomsoever Men are imposedly or restrictively subject and accountable in Matters of Faith, Worship and Conscience; in them alone must the Power of Judgment reside; but it is equally true that God shall judge all by Jesus Christ, and that no Man is so accountable to his fellow Creatures, as to be imposed upon, restrained, or persecuted for any Matter of Conscience whatever.[110]

Penn also lists twelve 'testimonies of Divine Writ' which show that 'Imposition, Restraint and Persecution are repugnant to the plain Testimonies and Precepts of the Scriptures.' These testimonies are:

1. The Inspiration of the Almighty gives Understanding, Job 32. 8. If no Man can believe before he understands, and no Man can understand before he is inspired of God, then are the Impositions of Men excluded as unreasonable, and their Persecutions for non-Obedience as inhuman.

2. Wo unto them that take Counsel, but not of me, Isa. 30. 1.

3. Woe unto them that make a Man an Offender for a Word, and lay a Snare for him that reproves in the Gate, and turn aside the Just for a Thing of Nought, Isa. 29. 15. 21.

4. Let the Wheat and the Tares grow together, until the Time of the Harvest, or End of the World. Matt. 13. 27, 28, 29.

5. And Jesus called them unto him, and said ye know that the Princes of the Gentiles, exercise Dominion over them, and they that are great exercise Authority upon them, but it shall not be so amongst you. Matt. 20. 25, 26.

6. And Jesus said unto them, Render unto Caesar the Things that are Caesar's, and unto God the Things that are God's. Luke 20. 25.

7. When his Disciples saw this (that there were Non-conformists then as well as now) they said, wilt thou that we command Fire to come down from Heaven and consume them, as Elias did; but he

---

[110] Penn, p.448.

turned, and rebuked them, and said, Ye know not what Spirit ye are of; for the Son of Man is not come to destroy Men's Lives but to save them, Luke 9. 54, 55, 56.

8. Howbeit, when the Spirit of Truth is come, he shall lead you into all Truth, John 16. 8. 13.

9. But now the Anointing which ye have received of him, abides in you, and you need not that any Man teach you, (much less impose upon any, or restrain them from what any are persuaded it leads to) but as the same Anointing teaches you of all Things, and is Truth and is no Lye, 1 John 2. 27.

10. Dearly Beloved, avenge not yourselves, but rather give Place unto Wrath (much less should any be Wrathful that are called Christians, where no Occasion is given) therefore if thine Enemy Hunger feed him, and if he Thirst, give him Drink; Recompense no Man Evil for Evil, Rom. 12. 19, 20, 21.

11. For though we walk in the Flesh (that is in the Body or visible World) we do not war after the Flesh, for the Weapons of our Warfare are not Carnal. 2 Cor. 10. 3. (but Fines and Imprisonments are, and such use not the Apostle's Weapons that employ those) for a Bishop, 1 Tim. 3. 3. (saith Paul) must be of good Behaviour, apt to teach, no Striker, but be gentle unto all Men, Patient, in Meekness instructing (not Persecuting) those that oppose themselves, if God peradventure will give them Repentance to the Acknowledging of the Truth, 2 Tim. 2. 24, 25.

12. Lastly, We shall subjoin one Passage more, and then no more of this particular; Whatsoever ye would that Men should do you, do ye even so to them. Mat. 7. 12. Luke 6. 31. Now upon the whole we seriously ask, Whether any should be imposed upon, or restrain'd, in Matters of Faith and Worship? Whether such Practices become the Gospel, or are suitable to Christ's meek Precepts and suffering

Doctrine? And lastly, Whether those, who are herein guilty, do to us, as they would be done unto by others.[111]

Penn also gives an eclectic list of citations of quotations in favour of religious freedom taken from writers from classical times onwards. Among those cited are Tertullian ('that Learned and Judicious Apologist'), *To Scapula* chapter 2, Lactantius, *Divine Institutes* 5.20 and Jeremy Taylor, *Discourse of Liberty of Prophesying*. [112]

John Locke

The final Christian voice from the seventeenth century we shall note is the English philosopher John Locke who wrote his work *A Letter Concerning Toleration* while he was living as a fugitive in Holland.[113] This work, which is actually an essay rather than a letter, became very influential in the eighteenth century. To quote Andrew Murphy, its significance is 'not because it advances new or previously unheard-of arguments for toleration, but because it so concisely synthesizes nearly a century of ongoing debate on this vexing problem.'[114]

In his essay Locke argues that the kind of religious violence which had been seen in the British Isles and in Europe as a whole during the sixteenth and seventeenth centuries is bound to occur when church

---

[111] Penn, pp.449-450.
[112] Penn, pp.460-462.
[113] John Locke has frequently been portrayed as an Enlightenment philosopher rather than a Christian writer, but this argument does not do justice to the Christian basis of Locke's thought. For this point see C Ryan Fields, 'A Generous Reading of John Locke: Reevaluating His Philosophical Legacy in Light of His Christian Confession' *Themelios*, Vol 45. 3 at https://www.thegospelcoalition.org/themelios/article/a-generous-reading-of-john-locke-reevaluating-his-philosophical-legacy-in-light-of-his-christian-confession/ and Jeremy Waldron, *God, Locke and Equality: Christian Foundations of Locke's Political Thought* (Cambridge University Press, 2002).
[114] Andrew Murphy, Conscience and Community: Revisiting Toleration and Religious Dissent in Early Modern England and America (University Park: Pennsylvania State University Press, 2001), p.126.

leaders combine with the 'magistrates' (i.e. those with civil authority) to take action against religious dissent:

The heads of the church, driven by greed and an insatiable hunger for control, have exploited the magistrates' ambition (often out of control) and the (always stupid) superstition of the multitude, arousing the populace against those who dissent from themselves, by preaching to them, contrary to the laws of the Gospel and to the precepts of charity, that schismatics and heretics should be deprived of their possessions and wiped out. In this they have mixed together two things that are really utterly different, the church and the commonwealth. When men are stripped of the goods they have acquired by honest work, industry, and, contrary to all the laws of equity, human and divine, are exposed to other men's violence and robbery, it is very difficult for them to put up with this patiently. Especially when they are otherwise entirely blameless, and the 'reason' for this treatment lies right outside the magistrate's jurisdiction and is a matter for the individual's conscience and the salvation of his soul, for which he is accountable only to God. When these men, growing weary of the evils under which they labour, eventually come to think it lawful for them to resist force with force, and to defend their natural rights (which are not forfeitable on account of religion) with arms as well as they can, what else could we expect?[115]

As well as arguing that attempts to suppress religious dissent inevitably lead to conflict Locke also puts forward an argument that such attempts are wrong in principle.

In this argument Locke contends that a church is a body within society which people join voluntarily and as such its laws ought to be determined solely by its members or by those authorised by them to do so (and therefore not by the magistrate).

---

[115] Jonathan Bennet (ed.), John Locke, *Toleration,* pp.24-25. Text at http://www.earlymoderntexts.com/assets/pdfs/locke1689b.pd

A church seems to me to be a free society of men who voluntarily come together to worship God in a way that they think is acceptable to Him and effective in saving their souls. I repeat: a 'free' society that men join 'voluntarily'. No-one is born a member of a church; otherwise the religion of parents and grandparents would be inherited by the children in the same way that they inherit wealth and land—and you can't imagine anything more absurd than that. So there it is: No-one is by nature bound to any particular church or sect; everyone voluntarily joins the society in which he thinks he has found the creed and mode of worship that is truly acceptable to God. He joined that communion in the hope of salvation, and that hope is the only reason he can have for staying there. If later on he discovers something erroneous in the doctrine or unsuitable in the worship, he should be just as free to leave that society as he was to join it in the first place. He can't be held by any bonds except what come from the certain expectation of eternal life. A church, then, is a society of members voluntarily uniting for that purpose. What we have to consider now is what power this church has and what laws it is subject to. No society, however free it is, and however slight the basis is for its existing—whether it is a society of scholars for doing philosophy, of merchants for transacting business, or of men of leisure for conversation and the exchange of ideas, —can survive and not fall to pieces unless it is regulated by some laws; and the same holds for any church. Place and time of meeting must be agreed on; conditions for membership and for exclusion must be established; and so on...But since the members of this society ·or church· joined it freely and without coercion, as I have shown, it follows that the right of making its laws must belong to the society itself—or anyway to those whom the society has by common consent authorised to do this.[116]

He further contends that the job of magistrate is the preservation and promotion of the public good:

[116] Ibid, p.5.

The commonwealth seems to me to be a society of men constituted only for the purpose of preserving and promoting the public good. By 'the public good' I mean: life, liberty, freedom from bodily illness and pain, and the possession of things such as money, land, ·houses·, furniture, and so on. The civil magistrate's job is to secure, for the people in general and for each one in particular, the just possession of these worldly things. If anyone tries to violate the laws governing this, he should be deterred by the fear of punishment, consisting of the lessening or outright loss of the goods that he otherwise might and ought to enjoy. Because no-one willingly allows himself to be punished by the loss of any of his goods, let alone his liberty or his life, the magistrate in punishing those who violate any other man's rights is armed with the force and strength of all his subjects.[117]

Having defined the role of the magistrate in this way he then puts forward three arguments which he says 'show conclusively that the magistrate's jurisdiction doesn't extend beyond these civic concerns' to encompass religious matters to do with 'the salvation of souls.' [118]

First, Locke follows the teaching of New Testament passages John 3:16-18, Galatians 3:6-8 and Hebrews 11:6 in arguing that personal faith lies at the heart of true religion. This means, he argues, that the care of souls is not given to the magistrate by God and cannot be given to the magistrate by the people:

> The care of souls is not committed to the civil magistrate any more than it is to other men. It isn't committed to him by God, because it seems that God hasn't ever given any man the authority to compel someone else to join his religion. And such a power can't be given to the magistrate by the people, because no-one can be so unconcerned about his own salvation that he blindly leaves it to someone else—whether monarch or subject—to tell him what faith

---

[117] Ibid. p.3.
[118] Ibid. p.3.

or worship to embrace. And anyway the life and power of true religion consists in faith, faith involves believing·, and no-one can just believe what someone else tells him to believe, even if he wants to. Whatever we ·audibly· say, whatever outward worship we conform to, if we aren't fully convinced that what we say is true and how we worship is pleasing to God, we'll merely have set up obstacles to our salvation by adding hypocrisy and contempt of God's majesty to our catalogue of sins.[119]

Secondly, the magistrate's power consists in the use of outward force whereas religion has to do with faith, which cannot be compelled by such force:

It can't be up to the magistrate to take care of souls, because his power consists only in outward force, whereas true and saving religion consists in the inward faith of the soul, without which nothing can be acceptable to God, and which the nature of the human mind won't allow to be compelled by any outward force. Confiscation of goods, imprisonment, torture—nothing like that can make men change their inward judgments about things. But you say: 'The magistrate can use arguments that will draw the heterodox to the truth, and effect their salvation.' So he can, but so can anyone else. In teaching, instructing, and correcting error by reason, he can certainly do what any good man can fittingly do; being a magistrate doesn't stop him from still being human and Christian. But it is one thing to persuade, another to command; one thing to press with arguments, another with judicial rulings. The civil power should not try to establish any articles of faith or doctrine, or any forms of worship, by the force of its laws. Laws without penalties have no force, and in our present context penalties are just silly, because they have no power to change anyone's mind. The only way to change men's opinions is through light, and you can't produce light in someone's mind· by torturing him.[120]

[119] Ibid, pp.3-4.
[120] Ibid. p.4.

Thirdly, even if the imposition of legal penalties by the magistrate could change people's beliefs about religious matters this would not contribute to the salvation of their souls:

> It can't be the civil magistrate's job to care for the salvation of men's souls, because even if laws and penalties could change men's minds, that would do nothing for the salvation of their souls. Even if there were only one truth, one road to the heavenly home, what hope is there that more men would be led into it if they had to walk out on the light of their own reason, oppose the dictates of their own consciences, and blindly submit to the will of their governors and worship God in the way that was established by law in the countries where they were born? In the variety of opinions in religion, the narrow way into heaven would be narrow indeed! It would be open only to those from one geographical region; whether a man received eternal happiness or eternal misery would depend on where he was born—which is utterly absurd and not worthy of God.[121]

According to Locke, however, although these considerations mean that religious matters should normally be determined by religious bodies themselves and the magistrates should give them the freedom to do so, this does not mean that there should be unlimited tolerance.

First, while religious bodies can do whatever is lawful in wider society for the purposes of religion, they cannot do what is unlawful in wider society:

> ...if people who had gathered for religious purposes wanted to sacrifice a calf, I deny that that should be prohibited by a law. The calf's owner can lawfully kill his calf at home and burn any part of it he likes; for this does no harm to anyone; and for the same reason he may kill his calf also in a religious meeting. Whether doing this is pleasing to God is for the calf-killers to think about. The magistrate's only role is to ensure that the commonwealth isn't

---

[121] Ibid. p.4.

harmed and that no individual suffers personal or financial harm. If the interests of the commonwealth required all slaughter of beasts to be suspended for a while, so as to rebuild stocks that had been destroyed by some extraordinary epidemic, it's obvious that in that case the magistrate can forbid all his subjects to kill any calves for any purpose. But that law would be made about a political matter, not a religious one; what it prohibits is not sacrificing calves but killing them. This shows us how a church differs from the commonwealth. Something that is lawful in the commonwealth can't be prohibited by the magistrate in the church. If any man can lawfully take bread or wine in his own house, the law oughtn't to deprive him of that same liberty in his religious worship; though in the church the use of bread and wine is very different because there it is applied to the mysteries of faith and rites of Divine worship. But things that are forbidden by law because in their ordinary use they are harmful to the public ought not to be permitted to churches in their sacred rites. But the magistrate should be very careful not to misuse his authority by oppressing some church, on the pretext of securing the public good.[122]

Secondly, a church cannot be tolerated if it means people accepting the authority of a foreign ruler:

A church can't have any right to be tolerated by the magistrate if it is constituted on a basis such that anyone who joins it is thereby giving himself over to the protection and service of a different monarch. For this would establish a foreign jurisdiction in his own country; the magistrate would be allowing enemy soldiers to be enlisted from among his own people.

The frivolous and fallacious distinction between the Court and the church is no help here, especially when both Court and church are equally subject to the absolute authority of the same person, who not only has power to persuade the members of his church to do

---

[122] Ibid, p.15.

whatever he likes—either as purely religious, or as contributing to the good of religion—but can also order them to do it on pain of eternal fire. It would be absurd for anyone to claim to be a Moslem only in his religion and in everything else a faithful subject of a Christian magistrate, if he admits that he is bound to give blind obedience to the Mufti of Constantinople, who himself is entirely obedient to the Ottoman Emperor and invents the 'oracles' of that religion to suit himself. And this Moslem living among Christians would renounce their government even more openly if he acknowledged the supreme magistrate in the state to be also the head of his church.[123]

Thirdly, there should no tolerance for those who are atheists:

No-one should be tolerated who denies the existence of God. Promises, covenants, and oaths, which are the bonds of human society, can have no hold on an atheist: this all dissolves in the presence of the thought that there is no God. And atheists can't claim on religious grounds that they should be tolerated! As for other practical opinions, including ones that have some error in them, there's no reason why they shouldn't be tolerated as long as they don't tend to establish domination over others or claim civil impunity for the church in which they are taught. [124]

The eighteenth to twenty-first centuries

From the eighteenth century onwards there has been an ever widening acceptance across the Christian churches of the principles that both individuals and religious communities should be allowed freedom of belief and practice, and that while civil authorities may legitimately support religious activity they may neither enforce it, dictate the form it should take, or limit it, unless it would harm the temporal well-being of those for whom the civil authorities are responsible.

---

[123] Ibid, p.21.
[124] Ibid. p.21.

The following five examples illustrate the widening acceptance of these principles.

James Madison's Memorial and Remonstrance, 1785

In 1784 there was a proposal by members of the Protestant Episcopal Church that there should be a tax in the state of Virginia to support 'teachers of the Christian religion,' with taxpayers being given the choice as to which 'society of Christians' their money should support.

This proposal was opposed by the Virginian politician James Madison (later the fourth president of the United States) because he believed that any regulation of religious matters by the state was an infringement of religious liberty and therefore wrong in principle. To build support against the proposal he published anonymously in 1785 a 'Memorial and Remonstrance, the first two articles of which oppose the proposal for the following reasons:

1. Because we hold it for a fundamental and undeniable truth, 'that Religion or the duty which we owe to our Creator and the manner of discharging it, can be directed only by reason and conviction, not by force or violence.' The Religion then of every man must be left to the conviction and conscience of every man; and it is the right of every man to exercise it as these may dictate. This right is in its nature an unalienable right. It is unalienable, because the opinions of men, depending only on the evidence contemplated by their own minds cannot follow the dictates of other men: It is unalienable also, because what is here a right towards men, is a duty towards the Creator. It is the duty of every man to render to the Creator such homage and such only as he believes to be acceptable to him. This duty is precedent, both in order of time and in degree of obligation, to the claims of Civil Society. Before any man can be considered as a member of Civil Society, he must be considered as a subject of the Governour of the Universe: And if a member of Civil Society, who enters into any subordinate Association, must always do it with a reservation of his duty to the General Authority; much more must every man who becomes a member of any particular Civil Society, do it with a saving of his allegiance to the Universal Sovereign. We

maintain therefore that in matters of Religion, no mans right is abridged by the institution of Civil Society and that Religion is wholly exempt from its cognizance. True it is, that no other rule exists, by which any question which may divide a Society, can be ultimately determined, but the will of the majority; but it is also true that the majority may trespass on the rights of the minority.

2. Because if Religion be exempt from the authority of the Society at large, still less can it be subject to that of the Legislative Body. The latter are but the creatures and vicegerents of the former. Their jurisdiction is both derivative and limited: it is limited with regard to the co-ordinate departments, more necessarily is it limited with regard to the constituents. The preservation of a free Government requires not merely, that the metes and bounds which separate each department of power be invariably maintained; but more especially that neither of them be suffered to overleap the great Barrier which defends the rights of the people. The Rulers who are guilty of such an encroachment, exceed the commission from which they derive their authority, and are Tyrants. The People who submit to it are governed by laws made neither by themselves nor by an authority derived from them, and are slaves.[125]

The belief of Madison and others that the religion should be free of state interference and control was subsequently reflected in 1791 in the first amendment to the United States constitution which states:

'Congress shall make no law respecting an establishment of religion, or prohibiting the free exercise thereof; or abridging the freedom of speech, or of the press; or the right of the people peaceably to assemble, and to petition the Government for a redress of grievances.'

It should be noted, however, that this amendment was a compromise. It was designed to prevent the creation by Congress of an established

[125] James Madison, *Memorial and Remonstrance*, 1785, text at https://founders.archives.gov/documents/Madison/01-08-02-0163

church at the national level, along the lines of the Church of England, but it did not rule out the individual states having established churches (Massachusetts, for example maintained a Congregational established church until the 1830s) or the federal government supporting the Christian religion (something for which again there is plentiful evidence in the early years of the American republic). To put it another way, what the Fathers of the American resolution wanted was a religious, and indeed Christian, republic, but not one with a single national established church.[126]

This American development was significant, because the American revolution initiated a political tradition hospitable to, and supportive of, freedom of religion, as opposed to the anti-clerical and anti-religious political tradition stemming from the French and Russian revolutions.

The Barmen Declaration, 1934

The Barmen Declaration was the result of a joint meeting of Lutheran and Reformed theologians (the most prominent of whom was the Swiss theologian Karl Barth) in Barmen in Germany in 1934. These theologians were concerned by the threat posed by the Nazi inspired 'German-Christian' movement which supported the subordination of the German Protestant churches to the German state and to Nazi ideology.

Section 5 of the Declaration rejects any confusion between the respective roles of the state and the Church. The state must not act in a totalitarian fashion, seek to control everything including the Church, and conversely the Church must eschew the temptation to try to take on the role of the state. The Church must remain free of the control of the state and the state must be free of the control of the Church.

'Fear God, honour the king (1 Peter 2:17)

---

[126] For this point see Michael Novak, *On Two Wings – Humble Faith and Common Sense at the American Founding* (New York and London, Encounter Books, 2002).

The Bible tells us that according to divine arrangement the state has the responsibility to provide for justice and peace in the yet unredeemed world, in which the church also stands, according to the measure of human insight and human possibility, by the threat and use of force.

The church recognises with thanks and reverence toward God the benevolence of this, his provision. She reminds men of God's Kingdom, God's commandment and righteousness, and thereby the responsibility of rulers and ruled will stop she trusts and bays the power of the word, through which God maintains all things.

We repudiate the false teaching that the state can and should expand beyond its special responsibility to become the single and total order of human life, and also thereby fulfilled the commission of the church.

We repudiate the false teaching that the church can and should expand beyond special responsibility to take on the characteristics, functions and dignities of the state, and thereby become itself an organ of the state.[127]

The World Council of Churches and the International Missionary Council, *Declaration on Religious Liberty*, 1948

In the aftermath of the Second World War, and in their light of their experiences of Fascism, Nazism and Soviet Communism, the churches represented in the newly established World Council of Churches were deeply concerned that the new world order that was being put in place should protect freedom of religion, not just for Christians, but for people of all religions. They expressed this belief in a declaration produced by the World Council of Churches and the International Missionary Council in September 1948 and unanimously adopted by the WCC's first assembly. As we shall see in the next chapter, this declaration forms part of the background to the article on freedom of

[127] *The Barmen Declaration,* section 5, text in John Leith (ed), Creeds of the Churches, rev. ed. (Oxford: Basil Blackwell, 1973), pp.521-522.

religion contained in the Universal Declaration of Human Rights which was agreed by the United Nations in November of the same year.

The declaration runs as follows:

An essential element in a good international order is freedom of religion. This is an implication of the Christian faith and of the world-wide nature of Christianity. Christians, therefore, view the question of religious freedom as an international problem. They are concerned that religious freedom be everywhere secured. In pleading for this freedom, they do not ask for any privilege to be granted to Christians that is denied to others. While the liberty with which Christ has set men free can neither be given nor destroyed by any Government, Christians, because of that inner freedom, are both jealous of its outward expression and solicitous that all men should have freedom in religious life. The nature and destiny of man by virtue of his creation, redemption and calling, and man's activities in family, state and culture establish limits beyond which the government cannot with impunity go. The rights which Christian discipleship demands are such as are good for all men, and no nation has ever suffered by reason of granting such liberties. Accordingly:

The rights of religious freedom herein declared shall be recognized and observed for all persons without distinctions as to race, colour, sex, language, or religion, and without imposition of disabilities by virtue of legal provision of administrative acts.

1. Every person has the right to determine his own faith and creed.

The right to determine faith and creed involves both the process whereby a person adheres to a belief and the process whereby he changes his belief. It includes the right to receive instruction and education.

This right becomes meaningful when man has the opportunity of access to information. Religious, social and political institutions have the obligation to permit the mature individual to relate himself to sources of information in such a way as to allow personal religious decision and belief.

The right to determine one's belief is limited by the right of parents to decide sources of information to which their children shall have access. In the process of reaching decisions, everyone ought to take into account his higher self-interests and the implications of his beliefs for the well-being of his fellowmen.

2. Every person has the right to express his religious beliefs in worship, teaching and practice, and to proclaim the implications of his beliefs for relationships in a social or political community.

The right of religious expression includes freedom of worship both public and private; freedom to place information at the disposal of others by processes of teaching, preaching and persuasion; and freedom to pursue such activities as are dictated by conscience. It also includes freedom to express implications of belief for society and its government.

This right requires freedom from arbitrary limitation of religious expression in all means of communication, including speech, press, radio, motion pictures and art. Social and political institutions should grant immunity from discrimination and from legal disability on grounds of expressed religious conviction, at least to the point where recognized community interests are adversely affected.

Freedom of religious expression is limited by the rights of parents to determine the religious point of view to which their children shall be exposed. It is further subject to such limitations, prescribed by law as are necessary to protect order and welfare, morals and the rights and freedoms of others. Each person must recognize the rights of others to express their beliefs and must have respect for authority at all times, even when conscience forces him to take issue with the people who are in authority or with the position they advocate.

3. Every person has a right to associate with others and to organize with them for religious purposes.

This right includes freedom to form religious organizations, to seek membership in religious organizations, and to sever relationships with religious organizations.

It requires that the rights of association and organization guaranteed by a community to its members include the right of forming associations for religious purposes.

It is subject to the same limits imposed on all associations by non-discriminatory laws.

4. Every religious organization, formed or maintained by action in accordance with the rights of individual persons, has the right to determine its policies and practices for the accomplishment of its chosen purposes.

The rights which are claimed for the individual in his exercise of religious liberty become the rights of the religious organization, including the right to determine its faith and creed; to engage in religious worship, both public and private; to teach, educate, preach and persuade; to express implications of belief for society and government. To these will be added certain corporate rights which derive from the rights of individual persons, such as the right: to determine the form of organization, its government and conditions of membership; to select and train its own officers, leaders and workers; to publish and circulate religious literature; to carry on service and missionary activities at home and abroad; to hold property and to collect funds; to co-operate and to unite with other religious bodies at home and in other lands, including freedom to invite or to send personnel beyond national frontiers and to give or to receive financial assistance; to use such facilities, open to all citizens or associations, as will make possible the accomplishment of religious ends.

In order that these rights may be realized in social experience, the state must grant to religious organizations and their members the same rights which it grants to other organizations, including the right of self-government, of public meeting, of speech, of press and publications, of holding property, of collecting funds, of travel, of ingress and egress, and generally of administering their own affairs.

The community has the right to require obedience to non-discriminatory laws passed in the interest of the public order and well-being. In the exercise of its rights, a religious organization must respect the rights of other religious organizations and must safeguard the corporate and individual rights of the entire community.[128]

Vatican II, Declaration on Religious Freedom, 1965

During the nineteenth century a number of Papal statements, such as the encyclical *Mirari Vos* issued by Pope Gregory XVI in 1832 and the encyclical *Quanta Cura* issued by Pope Pius IX in 1864, rejected the recognition of freedom of conscience and freedom of religion along with other liberal political developments of their time. As Daniel Philpott writes:

The Popes of this period were unwilling to separate civil liberties such as freedom of speech, freedom of the press, and freedom of religion, all of which they condemned explicitly from the relativism they saw in the French Revolution. They thought that political, theological, and philosophical liberalism were bundled inextricably.[129]

Although subsequent Popes were more open to the development of political democracy, until the Second Vatican Council none 'departed from the political theology that called for the establishment of the

---

[128] World Council of Churches, *Declaration on Religious Liberty*, 1948 at: https://original.religlaw.org/content/religlaw/documents/wccdecreliglib1948.htm
[129] Daniel Philpott, 'Christianity: A Straggler on the Road to Liberty?' in Shah and Hertzke, pp.358.

church and denied religious freedom as a universal right' [130] However, the 1965 *Declaration on Religious Freedom* to which I referred in chapter 1 departed radically from this theology. Influenced by Roman Catholic theologians such as John Henry Newman, John Murray and Jacques Maritain, the declaration reached back behind more recent Papal teaching to the biblical, Patristic and medieval teaching about the God given dignity of all human beings (hence its Latin title *Dignitas Humanae – Of the Dignity of the Human Person*) and on that basis gave unequivocal support to the legal recognition of freedom of conscience and freedom of religion.

Thus, chapter 2 of the Declaration states:

> This Vatican Council declares that the human person has a right to religious freedom. This freedom means that all men are to be immune from coercion on the part of individuals or of social groups and of any human power, in such wise that no one is to be forced to act in a manner contrary to his own beliefs, whether privately or publicly, whether alone or in association with others, within due limits.

> The council further declares that the right to religious freedom has its foundation in the very dignity of the human person as this dignity is known through the revealed word of God and by reason itself. This right of the human person to religious freedom is to be recognized in the constitutional law whereby society is governed and thus it is to become a civil right.

> It is in accordance with their dignity as persons-that is, beings endowed with reason and free will and therefore privileged to bear personal responsibility-that all men should be at once impelled by nature and also bound by a moral obligation to seek the truth, especially religious truth. They are also bound to adhere to the truth, once it is known, and to order their whole lives in accord with the demands of truth. However, men cannot discharge these

[130] Philpott, p.357.

obligations in a manner in keeping with their own nature unless they enjoy immunity from external coercion as well as psychological freedom. Therefore, the right to religious freedom has its foundation not in the subjective disposition of the person, but in his very nature. In consequence, the right to this immunity continues to exist even in those who do not live up to their obligation of seeking the truth and adhering to it and the exercise of this right is not to be impeded, provided that just public order be observed.[131]

Chapter 4 then goes on to further state that religious freedom has to do with the freedom not just of individuals, but also of religious communities:

The freedom or immunity from coercion in matters religious which is the endowment of persons as individuals is also to be recognized as their right when they act in community. Religious communities are a requirement of the social nature both of man and of religion itself.

Provided the just demands of public order are observed, religious communities rightfully claim freedom in order that they may govern themselves according to their own norms, honor the Supreme Being in public worship, assist their members in the practice of the religious life, strengthen them by instruction, and promote institutions in which they may join together for the purpose of ordering their own lives in accordance with their religious principles.

Religious communities also have the right not to be hindered, either by legal measures or by administrative action on the part of government, in the selection, training, appointment, and transferral of their own ministers, in communicating with religious authorities and communities abroad, in erecting buildings for religious

---

[131] Vatican II, 'Declaration on Religious Freedom,' ch.2 in Abbott, pp.678-680.

purposes, and in the acquisition and use of suitable funds or properties.

Religious communities also have the right not to be hindered in their public teaching and witness to their faith, whether by the spoken or by the written word. However, in spreading religious faith and in introducing religious practices everyone ought at all times to refrain from any manner of action which might seem to carry a hint of coercion or of a kind of persuasion that would be dishonorable or unworthy, especially when dealing with poor or uneducated people. Such a manner of action would have to be considered an abuse of one's right and a violation of the right of others.

In addition, it comes within the meaning of religious freedom that religious communities should not be prohibited from freely undertaking to show the special value of their doctrine in what concerns the organization of society and the inspiration of the whole of human activity. Finally, the social nature of man and the very nature of religion afford the foundation of the right of men freely to hold meetings and to establish educational, cultural, charitable and social organizations, under the impulse of their own religious sense.[132]

The Cape Town Commitment 2010

The Lausanne Movement is an international movement of Evangelical Christians which exists to support and encourage Christian evangelism around the world. Its 'Third Lausanne Congress on World Evangelization,' which was held in Cape Town in 2010 issued the 'Cape Town Commitment' which stressed that 'Living the love of Christ among people of other faiths' involves working for universal religious freedom and being willing to put that freedom into practice by rejecting the commands of the state when it is necessary to do so in order to be obedient to God. The Commitment declares:

---

[132] 'Declaration on Religious Freedom,' ch.4, in Abbott, pp.681-683.

LOVE WORKS FOR RELIGIOUS FREEDOM FOR ALL PEOPLE. Upholding human rights by defending religious freedom is not incompatible with following the way of the cross when confronted with persecution. There is no contradiction between being willing personally to suffer the abuse or loss of our own rights for the sake of Christ, and being committed to advocate and speak up for those who are voiceless under the violation of their human rights. We must also distinguish between advocating the rights of people of other faiths and endorsing the truth of their beliefs. We can defend the freedom of others to believe and practise their religion without accepting that religion as true.

A. Let us strive for the goal of religious freedom for all people. This requires advocacy before governments on behalf of Christians and people of other faiths who are persecuted.

B. Let us conscientiously obey biblical teaching to be good citizens, to seek the welfare of the nation where we live, to honour and pray for those in authority, to pay taxes, to do good, and to seek to live peaceful and quiet lives. The Christian is called to submit to the state, unless the state commands what God forbids, or prohibits what God commands. If the state thus forces us to choose between loyalty to itself and our higher loyalty to God, we must say No to the state because we have said Yes to Jesus Christ as Lord.

In the midst of all our legitimate efforts for religious freedom for all people, the deepest longing of our hearts remains that all people should come to know the Lord Jesus Christ, freely put their faith in him and be saved, and enter the kingdom of God.[133]

---

[133] The Lausanne Movement, *The Cape Town Commitment*, 2010, Part 2 C6, pp.82-83 at https://lausanne.org/wp-content/uploads/2021/10/The-Cape-Town-Commitment-%E2%80%93-Pages-20-09-2021.pdf

The key ideas noted in this chapter

The writings we have looked at in this chapter do not all say the same thing, or say the same thing in the same way. Nevertheless, an agreed set of key ideas can be seen to be present in these writings.

1. Religion is ultimately a matter between an individual and God.

2. To have value, religion must be freely chosen and freely exercised.

3. In matters of religion people should always act in accordance with their conscience even if this means breaking civil or religious laws.

4. It is not right for either the civil authorities or the Church to try to coerce people into accepting or practicing a particular form of religion.

5. Civil authorities should allow freedom of religious belief and practice by individuals and religious communities except when this would lead to its citizens suffering temporal harm.

6. Christians may rightly practice forms of spiritual discipline within the Church, but such spiritual discipline may not rightly include the death penalty.

What we do not see in these writings, but what has also come to be accepted across the churches, is that freedom of religion has to go hand in hand with the freedom not to be religious. If religious belief and practice has to be freely chosen and may not rightly be imposed, it follows, contrary to what Locke argues, that people have to be free to be atheists or agnostics.

In the next chapter we shall go on to see how these key ideas, first developed in the Christian Church, have come to be reflected in national and international law since the 1940s.

Additional note 1: Augustine 'Compel them to come in.'

In a letter to Donatus, a priest of the Donatist church, written in 416 Augustine interprets Jesus' parable of the great banquet in Luke 14:15-24, and particularly the instruction in v. 23 'compel them to come in,' as providing justification for the Catholic Church, having achieved a position of power, to use coercive force to bring people into the Church and thus to salvation.

I hear that you have remarked and often quote the fact recorded in the gospels, that the seventy disciples went back from the Lord, and that they had been left to their own choice in this wicked and impious desertion, and that to the twelve who alone remained the Lord said, 'Will ye also go away?' John 6:67 But you have neglected to remark, that at that time the Church was only beginning to burst into life from the recently planted seed, and that there was not yet fulfilled in her the prophecy: 'All kings shall fall down before Him; yea, all nations shall serve Him;' and it is in proportion to the more enlarged accomplishment of this prophecy that the Church wields greater power, so that she may not only invite, but even compel men to embrace what is good. This our Lord intended then to illustrate, for although He had great power, He chose rather to manifest His humility. This also He taught, with sufficient plainness, in the parable of the Feast, in which the master of the house, after He had sent a message to the invited guests, and they had refused to come, said to his servants: 'Go out quickly into the streets and lanes of the city, and bring in hither the poor, and the maimed, and the halt, and the blind. And the servant said, Lord, it is done as you have commanded, and yet there is room. And the Lord said to the servant, 'Go out into the highways and hedges, and compel them to come in, that my house may be filled.' Luke 14:21-23 Mark, now, how it was said in regard to those who came first, 'bring them in;' it was not said, 'compel them to come in,'— by which was signified the incipient condition of the Church, when it was only growing towards the position in which it would have strength to compel men to come in. Accordingly, because it was right that when the Church had been strengthened, both in power and in extent, men should be compelled to come into the feast of everlasting salvation, it was afterwards added in the parable, 'The servant said, Lord, it is done as you have commanded, and yet there is room. And the Lord said to the servants, Go out into the highways and hedges, and compel them to come in.' [134]

As William Barclay notes, Augustine's great reputation as a theologian has meant that his interpretation of the parable has had a long and very damaging influence on the subsequent history of the Church:

> It was used as a command to coerce people into the Christian faith. It was used as a defence of the inquisition, the thumbscrew, the rack, the threat of death and imprisonment, all those things which are the shame of Christianity. [135]

However, in spite of its influence, what Augustine writes in Letter 173 is not a good interpretation of Jesus' parable. This is for two reasons.

First, the parable is about the immediate future of the Church rather than a prediction of its long-term history in the way that Augustine's argument requires.

Secondly, in its original context 'compel' in verse 23 means convincing people that they really are welcome rather than coercing them into attending.

Both of these points are helpfully brough out by Kenneth Bailey in his commentary on the parable in his book *Jesus Through Middle Eastern Eyes*. Bailey writes as follows, citing the renowned eleventh century Syriac biblical scholar Ibn al-Tayyib:

> The point the master is making is that he knows how the strangers on the highway will respond.

[134] Augustine, 'Letter 173,' in *The Nicene and Post Nicene Fathers*, Vol.1 (Edinburgh and Grand Rapids: T&T Clark/Eerdmans, 1994), p.544.
[135] Willam Barclay, *The Gospel of Luke* (Edinburgh: St Andrew Press, 1981, p.183.

When an outsider, with no social status, is invited to a banquet in the home of a nobleman, the outsider has a very hard time Believing that he is really wanted. On first exposure, grace is unbelievable. The recipient of the invitation will at once feel, *They don't really want me. Impossible! Look at who I am. The intent of the invitation is to impress me with the nobility of the master, but the invitation itself is not serious.*

The messenger who delivers such an extraordinary invitation will need some special way to convince the outsiders that they are indeed invited and wanted. Understanding this, the master suggests, 'When they are reluctant, grab them by the hand and drag them in if you have to. I want you, by all means, to convince them that the invitation is indeed serious and that they are genuinely welcome and wanted at my banquet.

Ibn al-Tayyib writes:

'Oblige them to come in.' This does not mean compulsion or force or persecution, but refers to the strength of the need for urgent solicitation, because those living outside the town see themselves as unworthy to enter into the places of the rich and eat banquets. Such outsiders need someone to confirm that there is indeed a welcoming wedding there.'

It has long been affirmed that the third round of guests symbolises the Gentiles, who during Jesus' lifetime had not been approached. In the parable this last command is given, but the story stops before it is carried out. The parable fits historically into the life and ministry of Jesus.

When Paul and his friends go to the Gentile world with the message of the gospel, they are fulfilling a vision verbalised by Isaiah (IS 49:6) and reaffirmed by Jesus in this parable and elsewhere.[136]

Additional note 2: Thomas Aquinas on the legitimacy of executing heretics

As we have seen in this chapter Christian theologians have also argued that heretics should be subject to the death penalty. Even those who have held that that unbelievers should not be coerced into conversion have held that those inside the Church who depart from the orthodox faith and refuse to repent should be punished in this way.

The classic example of someone who held this position was Thomas Aquinas. As we have seen, he argued that non-believers 'are by no means to be compelled to the faith, in order that they may believe, because to believe depends on the will.' However, in the *Summa Theologiae* he nevertheless argued for the execution of heretics:

> With regard to heretics two points must be observed: one, on their own side; the other, on the side of the Church. On their own side there is the sin, whereby they deserve not only to be separated from the Church by excommunication, but also to be severed from the world by death. For it is a much graver matter to corrupt the faith which quickens the soul, than to forge money, which supports temporal life. Wherefore if forgers of money and other evil-doers are forthwith condemned to death by the secular authority, much more reason is there for heretics, as soon as they are convicted of heresy, to be not only excommunicated but even put to death.

> On the part of the Church, however, there is mercy which looks to the conversion of the wanderer, wherefore she condemns not at once, but 'after the first and second admonition,' as the Apostle directs: after that, if he is yet stubborn, the Church no longer hoping for his conversion, looks to the salvation of others, by

---

[136] Kenneth Bailey, *Jesus Through Middle Eastern Eyes* (London: SPCK, 2008), pp.317-318. Italics in the original.

excommunicating him and separating him from the Church, and furthermore delivers him to the secular tribunal to be exterminated thereby from the world by death. For Jerome commenting on Galatians 5:9, 'A little leaven,' says: 'Cut off the decayed flesh, expel the mangy sheep from the fold, lest the whole house, the whole paste, the whole body, the whole flock, burn, perish, rot, die. Arius was but one spark in Alexandria, but as that spark was not at once put out, the whole earth was laid waste by its flame.'[137]

Aquinas is right to take heresy seriously. If, as the Athanasian Creed tells us 'Whoever will be saved: before all things all things it is necessary that he hold the Catholic Faith' and if heresy leads people away from the Catholic faith, then it is indeed a truly dreadful thing that needs to be opposed by all legitimate means. However, using temporal power to execute heretics is not legitimate. We have already seen the reason for this in the words of Menno Simons quoted earlier in this chapter.

Say, beloved, where do the Holy Scriptures teach that we shall rule the consciences and faith of others, in the kingdom and church of Christ, by force of the sword, violence, and tyranny of the magistracy—something which is left entirely to the judgement of God? In what instance has Christ and the apostles ever done, recommended or commanded this?

Christ says, 'Beware of false prophets;' and Paul commands that we shall shun an heretic after one or two admonitions; John teaches that we shall not greet nor receive the transgressor into our houses, who does not bring the doctrine of Christ, Matt. 7: 15; Tit. 3: 10; 2 John 1: 9; they say not: Down with the heretics, accuse them before the magistrates, imprison, exile, and cast them into the fire or water, as the Romans have done for many years, and as many of you would do, you who pretend to preach the word of God.

Aquinas says nothing that answers these points made by Simons.

---

[137] Thomas Aquinas, *Summa Theologiae* II-II, Q.11. Art.3.

Chapter 3
Freedom of religion, belief and conscience in international and national law

In chapter 2 we noted that the American revolution initiated a political tradition hospitable to, and supportive of, freedom of religion.

The idea that the first amendment to the American constitution shows that the founders of the United States were attempting to create a secular (in the sense of non-religious) state is completely mistaken. On the contrary, they believed that religion was vital to the prosperity of their new republic. This point was made with great clarity, for example, by George Washington in his farewell address as the first president of the United States in 1796, in which he declared:

> Of all the dispositions and habits which lead to political prosperity, religion and morality are indispensable supports. In vain would that man claim the tribute of patriotism who should labour to subvert these great pillars of human happiness, these firmest props of the duties of men and citizens. The mere politician, equally with the pious man, ought to respect and to cherish them. A volume could not trace all their connections with private and public felicity. Let it simply be asked where is the security for property, for reputation, for life, if the sense of religious obligation desert the oaths, which are the instruments of investigation in courts of justice? And let us with caution indulge the supposition that morality can be maintained without religion. Whatever may be conceded to the influence of refined education on minds of peculiar structure, reason and experience both forbid us to expect that national morality can prevail in exclusion of religious principle.[138]

---

[138] *Washington's Final Address to the People of the United States*, p.16 at: https://www.senate.gov/artandhistory/history/resources/pdf/Washingtons_Farewell_Address.pdf

What the founders of the United States did believe, however, as a result of the influence of that ancient Christian tradition of support for religious freedom that we looked at in the last chapter,[139] was that the United States should be a religious country, but also one in which individuals and communities should be free to choose which particular type of religion they wished to follow.

Not only was this intention of the American founders, but it was something that they managed to achieve. As the French writer Alexis de Tocqueville commented in the 1830s, in order to understand American society correctly it was necessary to see it as:

...the product (and this point of departure ought constantly to be present in one's thinking) of two perfectly distinct elements that elsewhere have often made war with each other, but which, in America, they have succeeded in incorporating somehow into one another and combining marvellously. I mean to speak of the *spirit of religion* and the *spirit of freedom*. [140]

To put it another way, the influence of Christian thinking about religious freedom resulted in the United States being a country in which freedom of religion was understood to be both a part of and as Washington said, an indispensable support for, a free society. In the twentieth century this American understanding of the importance of religious freedom then resulted in freedom of religion being legally recognised around the world.

---

[139] As Wilken writes, the provenance of the thinking of Madison and others about freedom of religion is the Christian tradition. 'It was early Christian teachers who first set forth ideas of the freedom of the human person in matters of religion; it was Christian thinkers who contended that conscience must be obedient only to God; and it was the dualism of political and spiritual authority in Christian history that led to the idea that religious beliefs and civil government must be kept separate' (Wilken, p.180).

[140] Alexis de Tocqueville, *Democracy in America* (Chicago: Chicago University Press, 2000), p.43. Italics in the original.

The four freedoms

The starting point for this development was the annual State of the Union address given to the United States' Congress by President F D Roosevelt on 6 January 1941.

The background to his address that year was the war that was taking place between the Allied forces led by Britain and its Empire and the Nazi and Fascist dictatorships in Germany and Italy. In the light of this, the bulk of the speech was a promise that America, while still remaining officially neutral, would aid the cause of freedom by giving material support to the Allied war effort:

> We Americans are vitally concerned in your defense of freedom. We are putting forth our energies, our resources and our organizing powers to give you the strength to regain and maintain a free world. We shall send you, in ever-increasing numbers, ships, planes, tanks, guns. This is our purpose and our pledge.[141]

However, the address is best remembered for its peroration in which Roosevelt outlined the four freedoms for which the Allied forces were fighting and for which the United States also stood.

In the future days, which we seek to make secure, we look forward to a world founded upon four essential human freedoms.

The first is freedom of speech and expression—everywhere in the world.

The second is freedom of every person to worship God in his own way—everywhere in the world.

The third is freedom from want—which, translated into world terms, means economic understandings which will secure to every nation a healthy peacetime life for its inhabitants-everywhere in the world.

---

[141] F D Roosevelt, State of the Union address, 6 January 1941 at:
https://www.presidency.ucsb.edu/documents/annual-message-congress-the-state-the-union

The fourth is freedom from fear—which, translated into world terms, means a world-wide reduction of armaments to such a point and in such a thorough fashion that no nation will be in a position to commit an act of physical aggression against any neighbor—anywhere in the world.

That is no vision of a distant millennium. It is a definite basis for a kind of world attainable in our own time and generation. That kind of world is the very antithesis of the so-called new order of tyranny which the dictators seek to create with the crash of a bomb.[142]

This peroration was the personal vision of Roosevelt himself, rather than something that was put together by his speech writers [143] and the inclusion of freedom of worship as the second freedom reflected both his own sense of the importance of religion[144] and the way in which freedom of worship had come to be seen as a fundamental American principle since the time of the passing of the first amendment to the Constitution.

This sense that freedom of worship was something that was essential to American life, and which Americans should seek to ensure around the world is clearly expressed, for example, in an essay written by the American historian and philosopher William Durant and published in the American newspaper the Saturday Evening Post on 27 February 1943.

[142] Roosevelt, State of the Union.
[143] For this point see Jean Edward Smith, *FDR* (New York: Random House, 2008), pp.487-488.
[144] As a Frances Perkins wrote 'he had no doubts. He just believed with a certainty and simplicity that gave him no pangs or struggles. The problems of the higher criticism, of the application of scientific discoveries to the traditional teachings of the Christian faith and the Biblical record, bothered him not in the least. He knew what religion was and he followed it. It was more than a code of ethics for him. It was a real relationship of man to God, and he felt as certain of it as of the reality of his life.' Frances Perkins *The Roosevelt I Knew*, quoted in Smith, p.302.

By 1943 the United States was at war and the four freedoms set out by Roosevelt in 1941 had come to be seen as summarising the moral imperatives for which the country was fighting. The prominent American artist Norman Rockwell had produced a series of four paintings on the four freedoms[145] and the Saturday Evening Post reproduced these with an essay accompanying each one. Durant's essay on Freedom of Worship runs as follows:

Down in the valley below the hill where I spend my summers is a little white church whose steeple has been my guiding goal in many a pleasant walk

Often, as I passed the door on weekdays when all was silent there, I wished that I might enter, sit quietly in one of the empty pews, and feel more deeply the wonder and the longing that had built such chapels—temples and mosques and great cathedrals—everywhere on the earth.

Man differs from the animal in two things: He laughs, and he prays. Perhaps the animal laughs when he plays, and prays when he begs or mourns; we shall never know any soul but our own, and never that. But the mark of man is that he beats his head against the riddle of life, knows his infinite weakness of body and mind, lifts up his heart to a hidden presence and power, and finds in his faith a beacon of heartening hope, a pillar of strength for his fragile decency.

These men of the fields, coming from afar in the uncomfortable finery of a Sabbath morn, greeting one another with bluff cordiality, entering to worship their God in their own fashion—I think, sometimes, that they know more than I shall ever find in all my books. They have no words to tell me what they know, but that is because religion, like music, lives in a world beyond words, or thoughts, or things. They have felt the mystery of consciousness

---

[145] See Rockwell's Four Freedoms at https://rockwellfourfreedoms.org/about-the-exhibit/rockwells-four-freedoms/

within themselves, and will not say that they are machines. They have seen the growth of the soil and the child, they have stood in awe amid the swelling fields, in the humming and teeming woods, and they have sensed in every cell and atom the same creative power that wells up in their own striving and fulfilment. Their unmoved faces conceal a silent thankfulness for the rich increase of summer, the mortal loveliness of autumn and the gay resurrection of the spring. They have watched patiently the movement of the stars, and found in them a majestic order so harmoniously regular that our ears would hear its music were it not eternal. Their tired eyes have known the ineffable splendor of earth and sky, even in tempest, terror, and destruction; and they have never doubted that in this beauty some sense and meaning dwell. They have seen death, and reached beyond it with their hope.

And so they worship. The poetry of their ritual redeems the prose of their daily toil; the prayers they pray are secret summonses to their better selves; the songs they sing are shouts of joy in their refreshened strength. The commandments they receive, through which they can live with one another in order and peace, come to them as the imperatives of an inescapable deity, not as the edicts of questionable men. Through these commands they are made part of a divine drama, and their harassed lives take on a scope and dignity that cannot be cancelled out by death.

This little church is the first and final symbol of America. For men came across the sea not merely to find new soil for their plows but to win freedom for their souls, to think and speak and worship as they would. This is the freedom men value most of all; for this they have borne countless persecutions and fought more bravely than for food or gold. These men coming out of their chapel—what is the finest thing about them, next to their undiscourageable life? It is that they do not demand that others should worship as they do, or even that others should worship at all. In that waving valley are some who have not come to this service. It is not held against them; mutely these worshipers understand that faith takes many forms, and that men name with diverse words the hope that in their hearts is one.

It is astonishing and inspiring that after all the bloodshed of history, this land should house in fellowship a hundred religions and a hundred doubts. This is with us an already ancient heritage; and because we knew such freedom of worship from our birth, we took it for granted and expected it of all mature men. Until yesterday, the whole civilized world seemed secure in that liberty.

But now suddenly, through some paranoiac mania of racial superiority, or some obscene sadism of political strategy, persecution is renewed, and men are commanded to render unto Caesar the things that are Caesar's, and unto Caesar the things that are God's. The Japanese, who once made all things beautiful, begin to exclude from their realm every faith but the childish belief in the divinity of their emperor. The Italians, who twice littered their peninsula with genius, are compelled to oppress a handful of hunted men. The French, once honored in every land for civilization and courtesy, hand over desolate refugees to the coldest murderers that history has ever known. The Germans, who once made the world their debtors in science, scholarship, philosophy, and music, are prodded into one of the bitterest persecutions in all the annals of savagery by men who seem to delight in human misery, who openly pledge themselves to destroy Christianity, who seem resolved to leave their people no religion but war, and no God but the state.

It is incredible that such reactionary madness can express the mind and heart of an adult nation. A man's dealings with his God should be a sacred thing, inviolable by any potentate. No ruler has yet existed who was wise enough to instruct a saint; and a good man who is not great is a hundred times more precious than a great man who is not good. Therefore, when we denounce the imprisonment of the heroic Niemoller, the silencing of the brave Faulhaber, we are defending the freedom of the German people as well as of the human spirit everywhere. When we yield our sons to war, it is in the trust that their sacrifice will bring to us and our allies no inch of alien soil, no selfish monopoly of the world's resources or trade, but only the privilege of winning for all peoples the most precious gifts in the orbit of life—freedom of body and soul, of movement and enterprise, of thought and utterance, of faith and worship, of hope and charity, of a humane fellowship with all men.

If our sons and brothers accomplish this, if by their toil and suffering they can carry to all mankind the boon and stimulus of an ordered liberty, it will be an achievement beside which all the triumphs of Alexander, Caesar, and Napoleon will be a little thing. To that purpose they are offering their youth and their blood. To that purpose and to them we others, regretting that we cannot stand beside them, dedicate the remainder of our lives.[146]

In this essay it is made clear that freedom of worship is at the heart of what America is fighting for. It is, Durant says, 'the freedom men value most of all.' Why are American young men offering their 'youth and blood'? So that all people everywhere can have the same liberty of worship as those gathered in the 'little white church' Durant describes in his essay.

The Universal Declaration of Human Rights

Following the end of World War II, Roosevelt's emphasis on the importance of freedom of worship became the basis for the declaration of freedom of religion as a basic human right by the newly created United Nations.

The United Nations was established in October 1945 with the aim of preventing future World Wars. At the preparatory conference held in San Francisco the three major Allied powers, Great Britain, the United States and the Soviet Union, saw the chief purpose of the United Nations as being to provide mechanisms to settle disputes between nations in

---

[146] Will Durant, 'Freedom of Worship' at https://www.saturdayeveningpost.com/2017/12/will-durants-freedom-worship/Will Durant Freedom of Worship

peaceful manner and to prevent nations engaging in future in the sort of armed aggression that had been undertaken by Germany, Italy and Japan. However, the delegates from Latin America, who were the largest group at the conference, wanted a transnational declaration on human rights to be included in the United Nations Charter. Accordingly, a reference to human rights was included in the Charter, with Chapter 1, Article 1, section 3 of the Charter stating that among the purposes of the United Nations was to promote and encourage 'respect for human rights and for fundamental freedoms for all without distinction as to race, sex, language, or religion.'[147]

This reference to freedom of religion in the United Nations charter, in line with the inclusion of 'freedom of worship' in Roosevelt's four freedoms, was then developed through the work of the newly created United Nations Commission on Human Rights, which was chaired by President Roosevelt's widow, Eleanor Roosevelt. The first task given to this Commission by the United Nations was the preparation of an 'international bill of rights,' what eventually became the Universal Declaration of Human Rights, and Eleanor Roosevelt, working with the Lebanese Orthodox Christian Charles Malik and the American Lutheran O Frederick Nolde (who was the director of the Commission on International Affairs of the World Council of Churches), saw to it that the Universal Declaration included a robust article on freedom of religion that would be in line with the WCC's statement on this topic that we looked at in chapter 2. [148]

The Universal Declaration of Human Rights was agreed at a meeting of the United Nations in Paris on 10 December 1948 with forty-two votes in favour, eight abstentions and no votes against. The Preamble to the Declaration references Roosevelt's four freedoms when it states that:

---

[147] United Nations Charter, Chapter 1: Purposes and Principles at https://www.un.org/en/about-us/un-charter/chapter-1
[148] See Mary Ann Glendon, *The Forum and the Tower* (New York: OUP, 2011) chapter 12 and John Nurser, *For All Peoples and All Nations – Christian Churches and Human Rights* (Geneva: WCC Publications, 2005).

...the advent of a world in which human beings shall enjoy freedom of speech and belief and freedom from fear and want has been proclaimed as the highest aspiration of the common people. [149]

Article 18 then goes on to say that:

Everyone has the right to freedom of thought, conscience and religion; this right includes freedom to change his religion or belief, and freedom, either alone or in community with others and in public or private, to manifest his religion or belief in teaching, practice, worship and observance.[150]

This article has subsequently been the basis for subsequent international and national statements on freedom of religion. In line with the Christian tradition that we explored in chapter 2, it states that freedom of religion is a universal right and one that covers all aspects of religious activity, and not just freedom of belief:

It belongs to every person. It includes the interior or 'private' right to believe in accordance with one's own conscience as well as the exterior or 'public' right to manifest one's religion in 'teaching, practice, worship and observance.' It is a right that all persons must have the freedom to express as individuals ('alone') and with others ('in community'). [151]

The International Covenant on Civil and Political Rights

The Universal Declaration of Human Rights was a statement of principles. It had moral but not legal authority. Therefore, in order to try to ensure that the principles in the Declaration were put into practice it was decided to produce and legally binding multilateral treaty to complement it. The United Nation's Commission on Human

[149] *The Universal Declaration of Human Rights*, Preamble, at https://www.un.org/en/about-us/universal-declaration-of-human-rights
[150] *The Universal Declaration of Human Rights*, Article 18.
[151] Timothy Shah, Matthew Franck and Thomas Farr (eds), *Religious Freedom: Why Now? Defending an Embattled Human Right (*Princeton: Witherspoon Institute, 2012), Kindle edition, Loc 1090-1101.

Rights was given the job of drawing up this treaty, but eventually political disagreement about including all kinds of rights in one treaty led the General Assembly of the United Nations to draft two separate covenants on different aspects of human rights. These were produced in 1966 and came into force in 1976. Together with the Universal Declaration of Human Rights they form what is known as the International Bill of Human Rights, which is the basic legal foundation for human rights around the world today.

The first of the two covenants was the International Covenant on Economic, Social and Cultural Rights. As Andrew Chapman explains, this Covenant of thirty-one articles 'covers human rights in areas including education, food, housing, and health care, as well as the right to work and to just and favourable conditions of work. A state that becomes a party to the Covenant agrees to takes steps for the progressive realization of these rights to the full extent of that state's available resources.'[152]

The second was the International Covenant on Civil and Political Rights. As Chapman further explains, this covenant of fifty-three articles 'safeguards rights such as rights to life, liberty, fair trial, freedom of movement, thought conscience, peaceful assembly, family, and privacy. It also prohibits slavery, torture, cruel, inhuman, and degrading treatment and punishment, discrimination, arbitrary arrest, and imprisonment for debt.'[153]

Article 18 of the Covenant on Civil and Political Rights covers freedom of thought, conscience, and religion. It states:

1. Everyone shall have the right to freedom of thought, conscience and religion. This right shall include freedom to have or to adopt a religion or belief of his choice, and freedom, either individually or in

[152] Andrew Chapman, *Human Rights, A Very Short Introduction* (Oxford: OUP, 2007). Kindle edition, ch.2.
[153] Ibid. Ch.2.

community with others and in public or private, to manifest his religion or belief in worship, observance, practice and teaching.

2. No one shall be subject to coercion which would impair his freedom to have or to adopt a religion or belief of his choice.

3. Freedom to manifest one's religion or beliefs may be subject only to such limitations as are prescribed by law and are necessary to protect public safety, order, health, or morals or the fundamental rights and freedoms of others.

4. The States Parties to the present Covenant undertake to have respect for the liberty of parents and, when applicable, legal guardians to ensure the religious and moral education of their children in conformity with their own convictions.[154]

The first section reiterates what was said in Article 18 of the Universal Declaration of Human Rights and sections 2-4 then forbid the infringement of freedom of religion through coercion, specifies the limitations which may be imposed on the manifestation of religion or belief and safeguard the right of children or legal guardians to ensure that children are educated in line with their beliefs.

Declaration on the Elimination of All Forms of Intolerance and Discrimination Based on Religion or Belief

In 1981 the United Nations General Assembly built on what was said about freedom of religion in the Universal Declaration of Human Rights and the International Covenant on Civil and Political Rights by issuing a Declaration on the Elimination of All Forms of Intolerance and Discrimination Based on Religion or Belief.

The 1981 Declaration, which consists of a declaration and eight articles, runs as follows:

---

[154] International Covenant on Civil and Political Rights, Article 18 at https://www.ohchr.org/en/instruments-mechanisms/instruments/international-covenant-civil-and-political-rights

The General Assembly

Considering that one of the basic principles of the Charter of the United Nations is that of the dignity and equality inherent in all human beings, and that all Member States have pledged themselves to take joint and separate action in co-operation with the United Nations to promote and encourage universal respect for and observance of human rights and fundamental freedoms for all, without distinction as to race, sex, language or religion,

Considering that the Universal Declaration of Human Rights and the International Covenants on Human Rights proclaim the principles of non-discrimination and equality before the law and the right to freedom of thought, conscience, religion, or belief,

Considering that the disregard and infringement of human rights and fundamental freedoms, in particular of the right to freedom of thought, conscience, religion or whatever belief, have brought, directly or indirectly, wars and great suffering to mankind, especially where they serve as a means of foreign interference in the internal affairs of other States and amount to kindling hatred between peoples and nations,

Considering that religion or belief, for anyone who professes either, is one of the fundamental elements in his conception of life and that freedom of religion or belief should be fully respected and guaranteed,

Considering that it is essential to promote understanding, tolerance and respect in matters relating to freedom of religion or belief and to ensure that the use of religion or belief for ends inconsistent with the Charter, other relevant instruments of the United Nations and the purposes and principles of the present Declaration is inadmissible,

Convinced that freedom of religion or belief should also contribute to the attainment of the goals of world peace, social justice, and friendship among peoples and to the elimination of ideologies or practices of colonialism and racial discrimination,

Noting with satisfaction the adoption of several, and the coming into force of some, conventions, under the aegis of the United Nations and of the specialized agencies, for the elimination of various forms of discrimination,

Concerned by manifestations of intolerance and by the existence of discrimination in matters of religion or belief still in evidence in some areas of the world,

Resolved to adopt all necessary measures for the speedy elimination of such intolerance in all its forms and manifestations and to prevent and combat discrimination on the ground of religion or belief,

Proclaims this Declaration on the Elimination of All Forms of Intolerance and of Discrimination Based on Religion or Belief:

Article 1
1. Everyone shall have the right to freedom of thought, conscience, and religion. This right shall include freedom to have a religion or whatever belief of his choice, and freedom, either individually or in community with others and in public or private, to manifest his religion or belief in worship, observance, practice, and teaching.

2. No one shall be subject to coercion which would impair his freedom to have a religion or belief of his choice.

3. Freedom to manifest one's religion or belief may be subject only to such limitations as are prescribed by law and are necessary to protect public safety, order, health or morals or the fundamental rights and freedoms of others.

Article 2
1. No one shall be subject to discrimination by any State, institution, group of persons, or person on the grounds of religion or belief.

2. For the purposes of the present Declaration, the expression "intolerance and discrimination based on religion or belief" means any distinction, exclusion, restriction or preference based on religion or belief and having as its purpose or as its effect nullification or impairment of the recognition, enjoyment or exercise of human rights and fundamental freedoms on an equal basis.

Article 3

Discrimination between human beings on the grounds of religion or belief constitutes an affront to human dignity and a disavowal of the principles of the Charter of the United Nations, and shall be condemned as a violation of the human rights and fundamental freedoms proclaimed in the Universal Declaration of Human Rights and enunciated in detail in the International Covenants on Human Rights, and as an obstacle to friendly and peaceful relations between nations.

Article 4

1. All States shall take effective measures to prevent and eliminate discrimination on the grounds of religion or belief in the recognition, exercise and enjoyment of human rights and fundamental freedoms in all fields of civil, economic, political, social, and cultural life.

2. All States shall make all efforts to enact or rescind legislation where necessary to prohibit any such discrimination, and to take all appropriate measures to combat intolerance on the grounds of religion or belief in this matter.

Article 5

1. The parents or, as the case may be, the legal guardians of the child have the right to organize the life within the family in accordance with their religion or belief and bearing in mind the moral education in which they believe the child should be brought up.

2. Every child shall enjoy the right to have access to education in the matter of religion or belief in accordance with the wishes of his parents or, as the case may be, legal guardians, and shall not be compelled to receive teaching on religion or belief against the wishes of his parents or legal guardians, the best interests of the child being the guiding principle.

3. The child shall be protected from any form of discrimination on the ground of religion or belief. He shall be brought up in a spirit of understanding, tolerance, friendship among peoples, peace and universal brotherhood, respect for freedom of religion or belief of others, and in full consciousness that his energy and talents should be devoted to the service of his fellow men.

4. In the case of a child who is not under the care either of his parents or of legal guardians, due account shall be taken of their expressed wishes or of any other proof of their wishes in the matter of religion or belief, the best interests of the child being the guiding principle.

5. Practices of a religion or belief in which a child is brought up must not be injurious to his physical or mental health or to his full development, taking into account article 1, paragraph 3, of the present Declaration.

Article 6
In accordance with article 1 of the present Declaration, and subject to the provisions of article 1, paragraph 3, the right to freedom of thought, conscience, religion, or belief shall include, inter alia, the following freedoms:

(a) To worship or assemble in connection with a religion or belief, and to establish and maintain places for these purposes;

(b) To establish and maintain appropriate charitable or humanitarian institutions;

(c)　To make, acquire and use to an adequate extent the necessary articles and materials related to the rites or customs of a religion or belief;

(d)　To write, issue and disseminate relevant publications in these areas;

(e)　To teach a religion or belief in places suitable for these purposes;

(f)　To solicit and receive voluntary financial and other contributions from individuals and institutions;

(g)　To train, appoint, elect, or designate by succession appropriate leaders called for by the requirements and standards of any religion or belief;

(h)　To observe days of rest and to celebrate holidays and ceremonies in accordance with the precepts of one's religion or belief.

Article 7
The rights and freedoms set forth in the present Declaration shall be accorded in national legislation in such a manner that everyone shall be able to avail himself of such rights and freedoms in practice.

Article 8
Nothing in the present Declaration shall be construed as restricting or derogating from any right defined in the Universal Declaration of Human Rights and the International Covenants on Human Rights.[155]

The 1981 Declaration builds on what has already been said about freedom of religion in Article 18 of the Universal Declaration of

---

[155] Declaration on the Elimination of All Forms of Intolerance and Discrimination Based on Religion or Belief at: https://www.ohchr.org/en/instruments-mechanisms/instruments/declaration-elimination-all-forms-intolerance-and-discrimination

Human Rights in 1948 and in Article 18 of the International Covenant on Civil and Political Rights in 1966. However, it goes beyond these two previous statements in recognizing that the right to freedom of religion and belief:

...generates a host of specific rights, including the rights of parents or legal guardians 'to organise the life within the family in accordance with their religion or belief;' the right to establish humanitarian institutions, the right disseminate relevant publications; the right to teach a religion or belief; the right to train, appoint, elect or designate appropriate leaders 'Called for by the requirements and standards of any religion or belief,' and the right to establish and maintain communications with individuals and communities in matters of religion and belief at the national and international levels.[156]

As Derek Davis notes, the 1981 Declaration can rightly be seen as the most important international document concerning the right to freedom of religion and belief. In his words:

If the importance of a document were measured in terms of its pathbreaking qualities, the 1948 Universal Declaration would undoubtedly be most important. If importance were measured in terms of an instrument's enforceability in courts, the 1966 Covenant would be the most important. But if by importance we refer to the comprehensiveness of rights addressed and the degree to which a document is looked to by the international community to define the religious rights that should be respected, then it is clearly the 1981 Declaration that deserves the 'most important' label.[157]

---

[156] Shah, Franck and Farr, Loc.1113.
[157] Derek Davis, 'The Evolution of Religious Freedom as a Universal Human Right: Examining the Role of the 1981 United Nations Declaration on the Elimination of All Forms of Intolerance and of Discrimination Based on Religion or Belief,' *BYU Law Review*, Volume 2002, Issue 2, Article 2, p.228 at:

As Davis also notes, the reference to 'whatever belief' in the preamble and in Article 1(1) was included in order to make clear that the rights covered in the Declaration extend not only to different forms of religious belief, but to different forms of non-religious belief as well.

In the document's preparation, communists argued that use of the word 'religion' did not extend the principle of intolerance to atheism. They felt that non-belief should be protected on the same level as belief and that the use of the word 'religion' favored belief over non-belief. Several Westerners countered with the view that the document was intended to protect *religious* rights, that atheism was not religious in nature, but that atheism would likely find adequate protection in the text in any event. A compromise was worked out: the insertion of the word 'whatever' before the word "belief" in the preamble and in Article 1(1) In retrospect, this has turned out to be a successful compromise since everyone now understands that the Declaration protects all world views, including agnosticism, atheism, and rationalism.[158]

The insertion can be seen to follow the logic generally accepted across the Christian churches and noted at the end of chapter 2 of this book, namely that freedom of religion has to go hand in hand with the freedom not to be religious. If religious belief and practice has to be freely chosen and may not rightly be imposed, it follows that people have to have the right to be atheists or agnostics and this right needs to be respected. Just as atheists or agnostics must not seek to force people to abandon religious belief and practice, so also those who are religious should not seek to force atheists or agnostics to adopt them.

In addition, the inclusion of Article 8 in the Declaration reflects controversy during the drafting of the Declaration about whether a right to conversion should be recognized within it in the way it had been in the 1948 and 1966 texts which guaranteed to an individual the

https://digitalcommons.law.byu.edu/cgi/viewcontent.cgi?article=2109&context=lawreview
[158] Davis, pp.228-229.

'freedom to change his religion or belief' and the freedom 'to adopt a religion or belief of his choice.'

To quote Davis again:

Since Muslim law generally considers conversion from Islam to any other religion an act of blasphemy, Muslims objected to language in these instruments that would have made converting from one religion to another an unqualified right. Based on this belief, most Muslim regimes have little tolerance for non-Muslim missionaries and view their proselytizing efforts as encouraging Muslims to commit blasphemy. In drafting the 1981 Declaration, references to the right to change one's religion were deleted from the text in both the preamble and Article 1, departing, therefore, from the language used in the Universal Declaration and the 1966 Covenant. Consequently, the text of the 1981 Declaration was weakened, but to satisfy those who objected to the deletion, a new Article 8 was added, which provides that '[n]othing in the present Declaration shall be construed as restricting or derogating from any right defined in the Universal Declaration of Human Rights and the International Covenants on Human Rights.' Thus, nations that do not ratify the Covenants can claim that the right to change one's religion, although included among the rights enumerated in the Universal Declaration and the 1966 Covenant, cannot be afforded the status of international law. Advocates of the right to convert to a new religion were not particularly happy about this development but were pleased that at least the right to change one's religion was not derogated, specifically in the text. In fact, there are some who suggest that the inclusion of Article 8 preserves the integrity of the right to change one's religion as fundamental. When examining the combined effect of the Universal Declaration, the 1966 Covenant, and the 1981 Declaration, one expert concludes:

'Although they are varied slightly in wording, all meant precisely the same thing: that everyone has the right to leave one religion or belief and to adopt another or to remain without any at all. This meaning...is implicit in the concept of the right to freedom of thought, conscience, religion, or belief, regardless of how that concept is presented.' [159]

The United Nations Special Rapporteur on Freedom of Religion and Belief

In order to further the goals of the 1981 Declaration and to support the development of the right to freedom of religion more generally, the United Nations Commission on Human Rights established the role of 'Special Rapporteur on Religion Intolerance' in 1986. In 2000 the title of the role was changed to 'Special Rapporteur on Freedom of Religion or Belief' in order make clear that Rapporteur's role also included protecting the right of individuals to change religion or to hold some other non-religious belief system.

The Rapporteur, is an independent expert (at the time of writing the Iranian Nazila Ghanea) appointed by the United Nations Human Rights Council and their mandate is: 'to identify existing and emerging obstacles to the enjoyment of the right to freedom of religion or belief and present recommendations on ways and means to overcome such obstacles.' [160]

Regional conventions on freedom of religion and belief

In addition to the three United Nations statements that we have just looked at, there have also been a number of regional conventions about human rights which have been produced by specific groups of countries. If we look at the following list of these conventions, which is taken from the 2023 report by Nazila Ghanea entitled *Landscape of freedom of religion and belief*,[161] we can see that they all reflect what is

---

[159] Davis, p.229 quoting Elizabeth Odio Benito, 'Study of the Current Dimensions of the Problems of Intolerance and of Discrimination on Grounds of Religion or Belief,' ¶ 190, U.N. Doc. E/CN.4/Sub.2/1987/26 (1987).

[160] For more details see 'Special Rapporteur on Freedom of Religion or Belief' at: https://www.ohchr.org/en/special-procedures/sr-religion-or-belief.

[161] Nazila Ghanea, *Landscape of freedom of religion and belief* (New York: United Nations Human Rights Council, 2023), pp.5-7 at: https://documents-dds ny.un.org/doc/UNDOC/GEN/G23/006/31/PDF/G2300631.pdf?OpenElement

said in the United Nations' statements. To put it simply, the United Nations material has provided the blueprint for the subsequent regional material.

- Article 9 of the European Convention on Human Rights guarantees that: (a) everyone has the right to freedom of thought, conscience and religion; this right includes freedom to change his religion or belief and freedom, either alone or in community with others and in public or private, to manifest his religion or belief, in worship, teaching practice and observance; and (b) freedom to manifest one's religion or beliefs is subject only to such limitations as are prescribed by law and are necessary in a democratic society in the interests of public safety, for the protection of public order, health or morals or for the protection of the rights and freedoms of others.

- The Final Act of the Conference on Security and Cooperation in Europe included the provision that the participating States would respect human rights and fundamental freedoms, including the freedom of thought, conscience, religion, or belief, for all without distinction as to race, sex, language, or religion. Within that framework, the participating States would recognize and respect the freedom of the individual to profess and practice, alone or in community with others, religion or belief acting in accordance with the dictates of his or her own conscience.

- Article 10 of the Charter of Fundamental Rights of the European Union, as adjudicated through the Court of Justice of the

---

In addition, seven countries have appointed special envoys to advance freedom of religion or belief: Canada, Denmark, the EU, Germany, Norway, the Netherlands, the UK, and United States (though not all these remain in place). There is also a European Union Envoy. For more details see: MD Toft and M Christian Green, 'Progress on FoRB? An analysis of European and North American government and parliamentary initiatives, *The Review of Faith and International Affairs*, vol 16, 2018, pp4–18.

European Union, states that: (a) everyone has the right to freedom of thought, conscience and religion; this right includes freedom to change religion or belief and freedom, either alone or in community with others and in public or in private, to manifest religion or belief, in worship, teaching, practice and observance; and (b) the right to conscientious objection is recognized, in accordance with the national laws governing the exercise of that right.

- Article 12 of the American Convention on Human Rights upholds that: (a) everyone has the right to freedom of conscience and of religion; this right includes freedom to maintain or to change one's religion or beliefs, and freedom to profess or disseminate one's religion or beliefs, either individually or together with others, in public or in private; (b) no one is to be subject to restrictions that might impair his freedom to maintain or to change his religion or beliefs; (c) freedom to manifest one's religion and beliefs may be subject only to the limitations prescribed by law that are necessary to protect public safety, order, health, or morals, or the rights or freedoms of others; and (d) parents or guardians, as the case may be, have the right to provide for the religious and moral education of their children or wards that is in accord with their own convictions.

- Article 8 of the African Charter on Human and Peoples' Rights provides that freedom of conscience, the profession and free practice of religion is guaranteed. No one may, subject to law and order, be submitted to measures restricting the exercise of those freedoms.

- Article 30 of the Arab Charter on Human Rights states that: (a) everyone has the right to freedom of thought, conscience and religion and no restrictions may be imposed on the exercise of such freedoms except as provided for by law; (b) the freedom to manifest one's religion or beliefs or to perform religious observances, either alone or in community with others, is to be subject only to such limitations as are prescribed by law and are necessary in a tolerant society that respects human rights and freedoms for the protection of public safety, public order, public health or morals or the fundamental rights and freedoms of others; and (c) parents or guardians have the freedom to provide for the religious and moral education of their children. Article 25 of the Charter states that persons belonging to minorities are not to be denied the right to enjoy their own culture, to use their own language and to practise their own religion and that the exercise of those rights is to be governed by law.

- Article 22 of the Human Rights Declaration of the Association of Southeast Asian Nations (ASEAN), adopted by 11 States, upholds that, every person has the right to freedom of thought, conscience and religion and that all forms of intolerance, discrimination and incitement of hatred based on religion or beliefs is to be eliminated. Non-discrimination on the basis of religion and other status is upheld in article 2 of the Declaration.

- Article 20 of the revised Cairo Declaration of the Organization of Islamic Cooperation states that: (a) everyone is to have the right to freedom of thought, conscience and religion; freedom to manifest one's religion or belief may be subject only to such limitations as are prescribed by law and are necessary to protect public safety, order, health, or morals or the rights and fundamental freedoms of others; (b) no one is to be subject to coercion, which would impair his or her freedom to have or to adopt a religion or belief of his or her choice.

National material on freedom of religion and belief

In addition to the international material on freedom of religion and belief that we have just looked at, countries across the world have their own material which protects freedom of religion and belief. There is too much material to survey in a comprehensive fashion, but the following twelve examples from different regions of the world given an indication of the nature of this national legal material.

From North and South America

Canada

Part 1 (2) of the Canadian Charter of Rights and Freedoms states:

Everyone has the following fundamental freedoms:

a. freedom of conscience and religion;

b. freedom of thought, belief, opinion and expression, including freedom of the press and other media of communication;

c. freedom of peaceful assembly;

d. freedom of association.[162]

Ecuador

Article 66:8 of the constitution of Ecuador states:

The following rights of persons are recognized and guaranteed...

The right to practice, keep, change, profess in public or private one's religion or beliefs and to disseminate them individually or collectively, with the constraints imposed by respect for the rights of others.

The State shall protect voluntary religious practice, as well the expression of those who profess no religion whatsoever, and shall favour an environment of plurality and tolerance.[163]

---

[162] *Canadian Charter of Rights and Freedoms,* Part 1(2) at https://laws-lois.justice.gc.ca/eng/const/page-12.html
[163] *Constitution of the Republic of Ecuador,* 66:8 at:
https://pdba.georgetown.edu/Constitutions/Ecuador/english08.html

From Europe
Finland

Section 11 of the Finnish constitution on 'Freedom of religion and conscience' states:

Everyone has the freedom of religion and conscience.

Freedom of religion and conscience entails the right to profess and practice a religion, the right to express one's convictions and the right to be a member of or decline to be a member of a religious community. No one is under the obligation, against his or her conscience, to participate in the practice of a religion.[164]

Germany

Article 4 of The Basic Law for the Federal Republic of Germany on 'Freedom of faith and conscience' states:

1. Freedom of faith and of conscience and freedom to profess a religious or philosophical creed shall be inviolable.

2. The undisturbed practice of religion shall be guaranteed.

3. No person shall be compelled against his conscience to render military service involving the use of arms. Details shall be regulated by a federal law.[165]

From the Middle East
Israel

Israel does not have a written constitution, but the 1947 *Declaration of the Establishment of the State of Israel* declares that the state:

...will be based on freedom, justice and peace as envisaged by the prophets of Israel; it will ensure complete equality of social and

---

[164] *The Constitution of Finland*, Section 11 at
https://finlex.fi/en/laki/kaannokset/1999/en19990731.pdf
[165] *The Basic Law for the Federal Public of Germany*, Article 4 at
https://www.gesetze-im-internet.de/englisch_gg/englisch_gg.html#p0030

political rights to all its inhabitants irrespective of religion, race or sex; it will guarantee freedom of religion, conscience, language, education and culture; it will safeguard the Holy Places of all religions; and it will be faithful to the principles of the Charter of the United Nations. [166]

Jordan

Article 2 of the Jordanian constitution declares 'Islam is the religion of the State.' However, Article 14 then goes on to state:

The State shall safeguard the free exercise of all forms of worship and religious rites in accordance with the customs observed in the Kingdom, unless such is inconsistent with public order or morality.[167]

From Africa

Kenya

Article 8, section 32, of the Kenyan constitution states:

There shall be no State religion.

1. Every person has the right to freedom of conscience, religion, thought, belief and opinion.

2. Every person has the right, either individually or in community with others, in public or in private, to manifest any religion or belief through worship, practice, teaching or observance, including observance of a day of worship.

3. A person may not be denied access to any institution, employment or facility, or the enjoyment of any right, because of the person's belief or religion.

4. A person shall not be compelled to act, or engage in any act, that is contrary to the person's belief or religion. [168]

---

[166] *Declaration of the Establishment of the State of Israel* at https://www.jewishvirtuallibrary.org/the-declaration-of-the-establishment-of-the-state-of-israel.
[167] *The Constitution of the Hashemite Kingdom of Jordan,* Articles 2 and 14 at: https://www.refworld.org/pdfid/3ae6b53310.pdf

Rwanda

Chapter IV, Article 37 of the Rwandan constitution states:

Freedom of thought, conscience, religion, worship and public manifestation thereof is guaranteed by the State in accordance with the law.

Propagation of ethnic, regional, racial discrimination or any other form of division is punished by law.[169]

From Asia
Pakistan

Article 2 of the *Constitution of the Islamic Republic of Pakistan*, declares that 'Islam shall be the State religion of Pakistan.' However, Article 20 on 'Freedom to profess religion and to manage religious institutions' states:

Subject to law, public order and morality,

a) every citizen shall have the right to profess, practice and propagate his religion; and

b) every religious denomination and every sect thereof shall have the right to establish, maintain and manage its religious institutions.[170]

Singapore

Part 4, Article 15 of the constitution of Singapore states:

1. Every person has the right to profess and practise his religion and to propagate it.

---

[168] *Constitution of Kenya*, Article 8.32 at
https://kmpdc.go.ke/resources/Constitution_of_Kenya_2010.pdf
[169] *Constitution of Rwanda*, Chapter IV, Article 37 at
https://www.constituteproject.org/constitution/Rwanda_2015?lang=en
[170] *Constitution of the Islamic Republic of Pakistan*, Articles 2 and 20 at
1333523681_951.pdf(na.gov.pk)

2. No person shall be compelled to pay any tax the proceeds of which are specially allocated in whole or in part for the purposes of a religion other than his own.

3. Every religious group has the right,

   a. to manage its own religious affairs;

   b. to establish and maintain institutions for religious or charitable purposes;

   c. to acquire and own property and hold and administer it in accordance with law.

4. This Article does not authorise any act contrary to any general law relating to public order, public health or morality.[171]

From Australasia and the Pacific
Australia

Section 116 of the Australian Constitution Act states that the Commonwealth of Australia:

…shall not make any law for establishing any religion, or for imposing any religious observance, or for prohibiting the free exercise of any religion, and no religious test shall be required as a qualification for any office or public trust under the Commonwealth.[172]

Fiji

Section 22 of the Fijian Bill of Rights, covering 'Freedom of religion, conscience and belief,' states:

1. Every person has the right to freedom of religion, conscience and belief.

---

[171] *Constitution of the Republic of Singapore*, Part 4, Article 15 at https://sso.agc.gov.sg/Act/CONS1963?ProvIds=P14-#pr15-.
[172] *The Commonwealth of Australia, Constitution Act,* Section 116 at https://www.aph.gov.au/About_Parliament/Senate/Powers_practice_n_procedures/Constitution/chapter5

2. Every person has the right, either individually or in community with others,

3. in private or in public, to manifest and practise their religion or belief in worship,

4. observance, practice or teaching.

5. Every person has the right not to be compelled to—

    a. act in any manner that is contrary to the person's religion or belief; or

    b. take an oath, or take an oath in a manner, that--

    c. is contrary to the person's religion or belief; or

    d. requires the person to express a belief that the person does not hold.

6. Every religious community or denomination, and every cultural or social

7. community, has the right to establish, maintain and manage places of education whether or

8. not it receives financial assistance from the State, provided that the educational institution

9. maintains any standard prescribed by law.

10. In exercising its rights under subsection (4), a religious community or

11. denomination has the right to provide religious instruction as part of any education that

12. it provides, whether or not it receives financial assistance from the State for the provision

13. of that education.

14. Except with his or her consent or, in the case of a child, the consent of a parent

15. or lawful guardian, a person attending a place of education is not required to receive

16. religious instruction or to take part in or attend a religious ceremony or observance if the

17. instruction, ceremony or observance relates to a religion that is not his or her own or if

18. he or she does not hold any religious belief.

19. To the extent that it is necessary, the rights and freedoms set out in this section

20. may be made subject to such limitations prescribed by law—

    a.   to protect—

    b.   the rights and freedoms of other persons; or

    c.   public safety, public order, public morality or public health; or

    d.   to prevent public nuisance.[173]

The United Kingdom

Although the United Kingdom does not have a written constitution it is obligated to uphold freedom of religion and belief as a signature of the International Covenant on Civil and Political Rights and the European Convention on Human Rights. Because the ICCPR is an unincorporated treaty it does not create a private or public law cause of action under British law. By contrast the European Convention of Human Rights was

---

[173] *Constitution of the Republic of Fiji,* section 22 at
https://www.laws.gov.fj/ResourceFile/Get/?fileName=2013%20Constitution%20of
%20Fiji%20(English).pdf

transposed into UK law vis-à-vis the Human Rights Act 1998, and therefore creates rights which can be defended in court.

In addition, specific protection against discrimination on the grounds of religion and belief is provided by the Equality Act of 2010.[174]

Freedom of Conscience

We saw in chapter 2 that the Christian tradition has seen freedom of conscience as an essential part of freedom of religion, and international and national statements on freedom of religion and belief which have been produced since 1945 have likewise often included a commitment to freedom of conscience. For example, all the United Nations documents on freedom of religion and belief that we have looked at in this chapter have included references to freedom of conscience as have all the regional documents. In addition, seven of the twelve national statements we have looked at (those from Canada, Finland, Germany, Israel, Kenya, Rwanda and Fiji) also contain a guarantee of freedom of conscience.

A helpful explanation of what freedom of conscience means in these modern statements, and why it has been seen as worthy of legal protection, is provided by Adina Portaru and Robert Clarke in their 2020 paper *Freedom of Conscience: Protecting our Moral Compass.*

They begin by quoting with approval the statement by Javier Martinez-Torrron that 'conscience' does not refer to:

> ...any and every intellectual opinion inspired by personal views but the ensemble of supreme personal rules of conduct, rooted in religious or non-religious beliefs, which leave for the individual a compelling force higher than any other normative reference.[175]

---

[174] *Equality Act 2010* at https://www.legislation.gov.uk/ukpga/2010/15/contents.
[175] Adina Portaru and Robert Clarke, *Freedom of Conscience: Protecting our Moral Compass* (Vienna: ADF International, 2020), p.1 quoting Javier Martínez-Torrón, 'Protecting Freedom of Conscience Beyond Prejudice' in Silvio Ferrari (ed), *Routledge Handbook of Law and Religion* (London: Routledge 2015), p.192

They then go on to write that these kinds of belief about how to behave:

> ...either religious or non-religious, have a central place in the individual's moral identity and, for this very reason, must be distinguished from other personal preferences or options. They are 'core or meaning-giving convictions and commitments' that 'allow people to structure their moral identity and to exercise their faculty of judgment.' Consequently, the more a belief is linked to the moral identity of the person, the stronger the legal protection afforded to it must be. [176]

This is because:

> If the law requires behaviour that would contradict the values underpinning the moral identity of a person, then the person finds himself or herself in a conflicting situation that challenges his or her moral integrity.[177]

As an example of how conscience differs from someone's 'preferences, tastes, options and desires' Portaru and Clarke give the example of two people who do not wish to take part in abortion, 'a person who refuses to participate an abortion procedures because he or she has an aversion to blood' and 'a person who refuses to participate in abortion procedures because he or she deeply believes that abortion is the taking of innocent life.' Having to participate in an abortion will be much more serious for the second individual than for the first:

> If someone has to participate in an abortion despite his or her opposition to blood, such participation may cause feelings of uneasiness or discomfort. By contrast, if a person is forced to participate in an abortion despite his conscience-based objection, that would create a sense of moral betrayal and harm the values

---

[176] Portaru and Clarke, p.1 quoting Jocelyn Maclure and Charles Taylor, *Secularism and Freedom of Conscience* (Cambridge Mass: Harvard University Press 2011), p.76.
[177] Portaru and Clarke, p.1.

and beliefs which fundamentally define that person. This is precisely why such core beliefs (whether religious or non-religious) 'play the role of a compass and criteria of judgment in an individual's life.' If they are transgressed, then the person violates his or her deepest moral structure. [178]

Portaru and Clarke next go on to explain that conscientious objection, such as a conscientious objection to taking part in abortion, is a necessary part of the exercise of conscience. In their words:

Conscience is more than just a moral code or a set of beliefs—it is a belief bound up in action. Thomas Aquinas drew the line between conscience and a mere belief by stating that conscience is 'the application of knowledge to what we do.' Therefore, the concept of conscientious objection refers to the refusal, grounded in deeply held religious, moral, ethical, or philosophical beliefs, to fulfil certain legal obligations. The refusal is hence based on the fact that performing the legal obligation in question would lead to a serious conflict with genuinely held beliefs, so as to force the person to act against the dictates of conscience.[179]

In response to the objection that allowing conscientious objection opens the door to general disobedience to the law they further note that:

A proper approach to conscience claims cannot be criticized as providing *carte blanche* for generally disobeying the law or for an absolutist view of individual autonomy. Conscientious objection is distinct from an alleged unreasonable behaviour which goes against the law (*contra legem*), since it is grounded in ethical reasons that are of utmost importance for the individual. They do not usually extend to a wide number of legal obligations, but rather to precise, well-defined moral values that play a structural role in the moral

---

[178] Portaru and Clarke, pp.1-2 quoting Maclure and Taylor, p.90.
[179] Portaru and Clark, pp.2-3 quoting Thomas Aquinas, *Summa Theologica* (1265-1274) Article 13.

identity of the individual. The inextricable link between conscience and action is an important and foundational point and the very reason why any robust protection of conscience must embrace a right to conscientious objection.[180]

In summary, the reasons why freedom of conscience deserves robust legal protection is because:

State limitations on the exercise of freedom of conscience amount to an attempt by the State to abnegate citizens' freedom to object to and refrain from certain actions that they believe are fundamentally wrong and are incompatible with their deeply held beliefs. Such violations of freedom of conscience on matters of fundamental belief assert the paternalistic premise that individuals may be subjected to penalties and other significant consequences, either personal or professional, for not performing acts which directly violate his or her deeply held beliefs. Expressions of conscientious belief are of fundamental importance and represent one of the cornerstones of a democratic, broad-minded, and pluralistic society, which safeguards respect for diversity of opinion:

'Freedom of thought and conscience is one of the most vital elements that go to make up the identity of believers and their conception of life, but it is also a precious asset for atheists, agnostics, skeptics and the unconcerned. The pluralism indissociable from a democratic society, which has been dearly won over the centuries, depends on it.'

Inherent in the concept of a pluralistic, inclusive, and democratic society is the idea that the public square must be populated by people holding diverse viewpoints, beliefs, and moral convictions regarding what conduct ought to be permitted or proscribed.[181]

---

[180] Portaru and Clarke, p.3.
[181] Portaru and Clarke, pp.3-4 quoting *Kokkinakis v. Greece* App No 14307/88 (25 May 1993) p.31/.

Further helpful clarification about conscientious objection is provided by Gregor Puppinck in his 2016 *Brief Presentation on Conscientious Objection*.[182]

Puppinck notes that: 'In Human Rights law, the right to conscientious objection is implicitly guaranteed as a component of freedom of conscience and religion in its negative dimension.' What he means by this is that: 'Like every freedom, freedom of conscience and religion has two sides–positive and negative–which guarantee the freedom to act and not to act.'[183] The right to conscientious objection is the right not to act in particular circumstances.

He further explains that conscientious objection has come to be recognised as both a duty and a right.

Conscientious objection, he says, was recognised as a duty at the Nuremberg trials after World War II and then subsequently by the European Court of Human Rights after the fall of Communism in Eastern Europe at the end of the twentieth century:

> ...in cases where Nazi and Communist agents were condemned for not having objected to legal orders. Faced with a seriously unjust order, the subordinate must refuse to obey: conscientious objection is for him a duty, assuredly a heroic one, but a duty towards humankind (to which he belongs), and the non-respect of which justifies his condemnation. The International Law Commission expressed this principle in the following terms: 'The fact that a person acted pursuant to [an] order of his Government and of a superior does not relieve him from responsibility under international law, provided a moral choice was in fact possible to

---

[182] Gregor Puppinck, *Brief presentation on Conscientious Objection*, European Centre for Law and Justice, 2016 at http://media.aclj.org/pdf/Brief-presentation-on-conscientious-objection---ECHR-Seminar.pdf. A fuller version of Puppinck's argument can be found at Gregor Puppinck, *Conscientious Objection and Human Rights: A Systematic Analysis* (Leiden: Brill, 2015).
[183] Puppinck, *Brief Presentation*, p.4.

him.' This possibility of 'moral choice' is precisely the faculty exercised by conscience. Nazi and Soviet agents were condemned for obeying to orders rather than to their conscience. These are authentic situations where conscientious objection is a moral and legal duty, beyond and despite the absence, in the national legal order, of an explicit right to objection.[184]

Conscientious objection has also come to be recognised as a right granted by states to their citizens. According to Puppinck, this second type of recognition involves a contradiction in that: 'a single legal order imposes an obligation and simultaneously allows the refusal to comply to it.' The existence of such a contradiction is a recent phenomenon and it resulted from the development of modern liberal societies:

> ...for it accepts the coexistence of two levels of morality: a social level and a private one. Indeed, liberal societies are characterized by tolerance, that is to say by the affirmation of illegitimacy of all moral judgement ad extra: the morality of an individual action may only be judged by the concerned party, and not by society nor other individuals. This results in a differentiation between a public morality and a private morality which leads people to publicly tolerate practices which they disapprove of in private.

> Yet, if this tolerance is trouble-free for the majority of citizens, it is not so for the minority directly concerned by the carrying out of the practice in question; because, to use a concrete example, it is one thing to tolerate euthanasia, but it is another to have to practice it oneself. If it is possible to make two moralities coexist within a society, it is not possible within a single person. In this way, the 'freedom' that liberal society offers to individuals with regard to practices which are morally debatable and have often long been prohibited can only be fair if the society guarantees those who morally disapprove the practice at stake the right to not be forced

---

[184] Puppinck, *Brief Presentation,* p.5, quoting the *International Law Commission Yearbook*, 1950, vol. II, pp.374-378.

to take part in it. The 'conscience clause' guarantees precisely this right, it avoids the 'dictatorship of the majority' and facilitates the smooth functioning of the pluralist and liberal society.[185]

Examples of recognised types of conscientious objection

A range of legitimate forms of conscientious objection have come to be recognised. To quote Puppinck again:

> Freedom of conscience and religion applies to refusals to take part, between others, to military service, to abortion, to euthanasia, to hunting, to celebrating homosexual unions, to religious teachings and practises, as well as to refuse to take on oath on the Bible, to be vaccinated, to shave one's beard, or to reveal one's religious convictions.[186]

Three specific examples which illustrate this range of recognised conscientious objection are the German acceptance of conscientious objection to military service, the British acceptance of conscientious objection to abortion, and the Australian acceptance of conscientious objection to euthanasia.

---

[185] Puppinck, *Brief Presentation*, p.5. The Grand Chamber of the European Court of Human Rights has explicitly affirmed rights of conscientious objection for sincerely held religious and moral beliefs as falling within the ambit of Article 9 of the Convention. ECHR, Bayatan v. Armenia [GC], (2012) 54 E.H.R.R. 15., paras. 124-126. The Grand Chamber based its reasoning on several premises:
• That where conscientious objection was not for a personal benefit, but was based on a sincerely held religious or philosophical belief, a system should have been put in place whereby violence would not be done to that belief;
•A refusal to allow conscientious objection fails to strike a proper balance between the interests of society as a whole and the fundamental rights of the individual;
•Democracy does not simply mean that the views of the minority must be subordinated to those of the majority;
•And that far from creating inequalities or discrimination in a democratic society, provision of rights of conscience ensure a cohesive and stable pluralism and promote religious harmony and tolerance in society.
[186] Puppinck, *Brief Presentation*, p.6.

As we saw earlier in this chapter, Article 4(3) of Germany's Basic Law lays down that: 'No person shall be compelled against his conscience to render military service involving the use of arms.'

In the United Kingdom, section 4 of the 1967 *Abortion Act* covers conscientious objection by medical practitioners to taking part in abortion. The section states:

1. Subject to subsection (2) of this section, no person shall be under any duty, whether by contract or by any statutory or other legal requirement, to participate in any treatment authorised by this Act to which he has a conscientious objection:

Provided that in any legal proceedings the burden of proof of conscientious objection shall rest on the person claiming to rely on it.

2. Nothing in subsection (1) of this section shall affect any duty to participate in treatment which is necessary to save the life or to prevent grave permanent injury to the physical or mental health of a pregnant woman.

3. In any proceedings before a court in Scotland, a statement on oath by any person to the effect that he has a conscientious objection to participating in any treatment authorised by this Act shall be sufficient evidence for the purpose of discharging the burden of proof imposed upon him by subsection (1) of this section.[187]

In Australia the state of Queensland makes provision for conscientious objection by health practitioners, speech pathologists and other health care workers to taking part in voluntary assisted dying. The provision runs as follows:

---

[187] *Abortion Act 1967*, Section 4 at https://www.legislation.gov.uk/ukpga/1967/87

Conscientious objection

A conscientious objection is when a person declines to participate in a lawful process or procedure due to their personal beliefs, values, or moral concerns.

A healthcare worker has the right to refuse to participate in the process if they conscientiously object to voluntary assisted dying. However, registered health practitioners and speech pathologists have obligations under the Act that apply if they hold a conscientious objection.

Registered health practitioner obligations

Registered health practitioners who conscientiously object to participating have obligations under the Voluntary Assisted Dying Act 2021 (the Act).

A registered health practitioner who conscientiously objects to voluntary assisted dying has the right to refuse to:

- participate in the request and assessment process

- participate in an administration decision

- prescribe, supply or administer a voluntary assisted dying substance

- be present at the time of the administration of a voluntary assisted dying substance

- provide information to another person about the voluntary assisted dying process.

If a registered health practitioner refuses to participate in any of the above steps due to conscientious objection, they must give the person:

- information about a health practitioner, provider, or service they believe is likely to be able to assist; or

159

- the Queensland Voluntary Assisted Dying Support Service (QVAD-Support) contact details.

Speech pathologist obligations

While speech pathologists are not registered health practitioners, the Act protects their right to conscientiously object to participating in voluntary assisted dying.

A speech pathologist who conscientiously objects to voluntary assisted dying has the right to refuse to:

- participate in the request and assessment process

- participate in an administration decision

- be present at the time of the administration of a voluntary assisted dying substance

- provide information to another person about voluntary assisted dying.

If a speech pathologist refuses to provide speech pathologist services for any of the above steps due to conscientious objection, they must:

- inform their employer or the other person that they conscientiously object

- inform their employer or the other person of another provider who they believe is likely to be able to assist with providing speech pathology services to the person requesting access to voluntary assisted dying, and

- not intentionally impede the person's access to voluntary assisted dying.

If a speech pathologist is employed or engaged by a health service provider that is likely to provide voluntary assisted dying, they must also:

- inform the health service provider of their conscientious objection

- discuss with the health service provider how they can practise in accordance with their beliefs without placing a burden on their colleagues or compromising a person's access to voluntary assisted dying.

Healthcare workers

Healthcare workers who are not registered health practitioners or speech pathologists can conscientiously object to participating in any stage of the voluntary assisted dying process.

Only registered health practitioners and speech pathologists are required to provide information to the patient. However, it is good clinical practice for healthcare workers to:

- provide the person with:

  o information about a health practitioner, provider, or service they believe is likely to be able to assist; or

  o the Queensland Voluntary Assisted Dying Support Service (QVAD-Support) contact details.

- inform their employer and the person seeking access to voluntary assisted dying of their objection

- ensure the person's treatment or care is not impacted if they choose to request information or services elsewhere.[188]

Summary and Conclusion

What we have seen in this chapter is that the Christian teaching about the importance of freedom of religion that we looked at in chapter 2

---

[188] Queensland Government, Queensland Health, Conscientious Objection at https://www.health.qld.gov.au/clinical-practice/guidelines-procedures/voluntary-assisted-dying/information-for-healthcare-workers/conscientious-objection.

resulted from the end of the eighteenth century in the establishment of a strong tradition of freedom of religion in the United States. This tradition formed the background to the declaration of the need for freedom of worship in President Roosevelt's 'Four Freedoms' speech in 1941 and the eventual result of that speech was that from 1945 onwards freedom of religion has become legally protected around the world.

The precise form that this protection takes varies from jurisdiction to jurisdiction, but it very widely takes the form of freedom of religion, belief (i.e. non-religious belief) and conscience. What is protected is not just the freedom to privately believe certain things, but also the freedom to publicly practice one's religion or belief both as an individual and together with others. It also includes the freedom to change one's religion or belief.

Similarly, freedom of conscience involves freedom to act in accordance with one's conscience and this involves the freedom both to do certain things and the right to conscientiously object to doing others and being permitted not to do them.

What we have also seen, however, is that freedom of religion, belief, or conscience is not seen as absolute. To quote the United Nations' *Covenant on Civil and Political Rights*, the view that has been taken is that freedom of religion, belief and conscience may rightly be subject: 'to such limitations as are prescribed by law and are necessary to protect public safety, order, health or morals or the fundamental rights and freedoms of others.' For example, there is no jurisdiction that would allow murder or theft on the basis of freedom of religion and belief.

As writers such as Tom Holland, Rodney Stark and Glen Scrivener have pointed out,[189] the modern world has been shaped by influence of the

---

[189] Tom Holland, *Dominion–The Making of the Western Mind* (London: Little, Brown, 2019), Rodney Stark, *The Victory of Reason* (New York: Random House,

Christian faith. It is as it is because of the impact of Christianity. This is true not only in places where the majority of the population adheres to Christianity, but also in places where the majority adhere to some other religion or have become secular.

The current worldwide acceptance of freedom of religion and belief that we have looked at in this chapter is a case in point. If we ask where its origin lies, the answer is that it is the outworking of the Christian belief in freedom of religion that we looked at in chapters 1 and 2. It was this tradition that led Roosevelt to proclaim freedom of religion as one of the Four Freedoms in 1941 and it was this tradition, mediated through the work of Eleanor Roosevelt, Charles Malik and the World Council of Churches that led to Article 18 of the Universal Declaration of Human Rights in 1948, and the other global, regional and national commitments to freedom of religion and belief that have followed from it.

The same is also true with regard to freedom of conscience and the recognition of the right to conscientious objection. As we have seen, belief in freedom of conscience emerged in the Christian tradition and the practice of conscientious objection flowed from it. The woman from Bourges mentioned in chapter 2 who refused to have sex with a man to whom she believed she was not legitimately married was practicing conscientious objection, as was Luther when he refused to submit to calls to recant at the Diet of Worms, as have been members of 'peace churches' such as the Quakers and the Mennonites who have conscientiously refused to take part in military service. The modern legal recognition of conscientious objection is simply the contemporary recognition of this ancient tradition.

From a Christian perspective therefore the modern recognition of the right to freedom of religion, belief and conscience is a reflection of the impact of the work of Jesus Christ through his Church around the world,

2006), Glen Scrivener, *The Air We Breathe* (Epsom, The Good Book Company, 2022).

even among those who are not themselves Chistian believers. Jesus has changed the world for the better and the recognition of freedom of religion, belief and conscience is one aspect of this fact.

It is true, of course, that the existence of freedom of religion, belief and conscience is not an absolute good. As we saw in chapter 1, the result of the Fall is that freedom results in disagreement and that disagreement is not in itself a good thing. However, what we also saw is that it is not legitimate to use coercion to try to bring such disagreement to an end prior to the return of Christ. God has decided to allow his human creatures to disagree until Christ comes again and it is not legitimate for us to second guess his decision. We have to manage disagreements about matters of religion and belief as best we can in a non-coercive fashion, and allowing freedom of religion, belief and conscience is the best way to do this. It is the best provisional good we can achieve in the world as it is.

What is also good, however, is the recognition in the various international and national documents about freedom of religion, belief, and conscience that governments can put restrictions on the exercise of this freedom. As we saw in chapter 2, the Christian view is that civil authorities have a God given responsibility for ensuring the temporal wellbeing of those in their charge. Protecting 'public safety, order, health or morals or the fundamental rights and freedoms of others' from the misuse of freedom of religion belief or conscience to bring temporal harm to others is a good because it is part of the proper discharge of this responsibility.

In summary, the post 1945 international consensus that there should in principle be freedom of religion, belief and conscience is something that Christians should welcome. The problem is that this consensus is not being reflected in what is actually happening in the world today. As we shall go on to see in the next chapter, the religious freedom of Christians in particular is under attack around the world, even in those countries in the Western world where the freedom of Christian to freely practice their faith has until recently been taken for granted.

Chapter 4
Attacks on freedom of religion in the contemporary world

Russian attacks on freedom of religion in Ukraine

It is generally accepted that Russian forces have committed numerous human rights violations since their full-scale invasion of Ukraine in February 2022. Among these violations have been attacks on freedom of religion. As the report on 'Russia's religious freedom violations in Ukraine' from the United States Commission on International Religious Freedom explains these recent violations of freedom of religion are part of a pattern of attacks on freedom of religion by the Russian Federation dating back to Russia's annexation of parts of Ukraine in 2014.

In the words of the report:

> For nearly ten years, the Russian Federation—through its military and proxy forces—has committed gross religious freedom violations in Ukraine. In February 2014, Russian forces seized the Crimean Peninsula, and a month later illegally annexed it. In April 2014, fighting between Russian-backed separatists and the Ukrainian army began in Ukraine's eastern Donbas region. That same month, pro-Russian activists unlawfully declared their independence from Ukraine and proclaimed the unrecognized "Luhansk People's Republic" (LPR) and "Donetsk People's Republic" (DPR), which together comprised a third of the Donbas region.

> In the years following, Russian-installed authorities in Crimea and Donbas imposed repressive Russian laws that severely curtailed religious freedom and targeted religious minorities. Officials banned religious literature and prohibited certain forms of religious activities and speech. They also outlawed entire religious groups either by depriving them of legal registration or declaring them 'extremist' or 'terrorist,' despite the fact they had peacefully and legally practiced their religion in Ukraine for years.

Since Russia launched its full-scale invasion of Ukraine on February 24, 2022, its military has dismantled religious life and stifled religious diversity throughout other parts of Ukraine. On the frontlines of the war, Russian artillery and military forces frequently damaged and destroyed religious buildings and other sites and killed or injured those sheltering or worshiping in these places. In areas under Russian control, de-facto authorities have abducted and tortured religious leaders and enforced the same repressive Russian legal mechanisms that were instituted in Crimea and Donbas.[190]

What these Russian attacks on freedom of religion highlight is the point raised at the end of the last chapter, namely, that in spite of the international consensus in favour of freedom of religion, freedom of religion is nonetheless under attack.

Article 28 of the Russian constitution declares:

Everyone shall be guaranteed the freedom of conscience, the freedom of religion, including the right to profess individually or together with other any religion or to profess no religion at all, to freely choose, possess and disseminate religious and other views and act according to them. [191]

As this article shows, the Russian Federation, formally at least, accepts the international consensus in favour of freedom of religion. The problem is that this fact does not stop Russia from attacking freedom of religion in practice.[192] In similar fashion, in numerous other places

---

[190] United States Commission on International Religious Freedom, 'Russia's religious freedom violations in Ukraine,' July 2023 at:
https://www.uscirf.gov/sites/default/files/20207/2023%20Russias%20Religious%20Freedom%20Violations%20in%20Ukraine%20Issue%20Update_07.05.2023.pdf
[191] *The Constitution of the Russian Federation*, Article 28 at http://www.constitution.ru/en/10003000-03.htm
[192] What is not clear is why Russian attacks on freedom of religion have occurred. One suggestion is that they are due to the continuing influence of the philosophical idea known as *sobornost* which sees Russia as a community united

around the world freedom of religion is under attack even though it is a recognised human right and should therefore be upheld.

A useful overview of the current situation with regard to attacks on freedom of religion around the world is provided by the *Religious Freedom Report* for 2023 published by the Roman Catholic charity Aid to the Church in Need (ACN). The key findings of the report are as follows:

> During the period under review, intense persecution became more acute and concentrated, and impunity grew. This persecution included extreme violations of Article 18 of the UN Universal Declaration of Human Rights, the right to freedom of thought, conscience, and religion.
>
> 1. Globally, the retention and consolidation of power in the hands of autocrats and fundamentalist group leaders led to increased violations of all human rights, including religious freedom. A combination of terrorist attacks, destruction of religious heritage and symbols (Turkey, Syria), electoral system manipulation (Nigeria, Iraq), mass surveillance (China), proliferation of anti-conversion laws and financial restrictions (Southeast Asia and Middle East) increased the oppression of all religious communities.
>
> 2. 'Hybrid' cases of 'polite' and bloody persecution became more frequent. Occurring mostly without protest, governments applied controversial laws restricting freedom of religion or discriminated against certain religious communities (cf anti-conversion laws). At the same time, violent attacks against those of the 'wrong' religion were 'normalized' and mostly not prosecuted (Latin America).

by its commitment to Russian Orthodoxy and another is that is that the Russian authorities see non-Russian orthodox religious bodies as likely to be centres of resistance to Russian rule. What is not in doubt, however, is that serious attacks on freedom of religion have taken place.

This was also observed in Western nations but there was better recourse to justice.

3. An increase in the number of majoritarian religious communities suffering persecution. To date, most faith groups suffering persecution were from minority religious communities. Increasingly majoritarian religious communities were also experiencing persecution (Nigeria, Nicaragua).

4. An increasingly muted response from the international community towards atrocities by 'strategically important' autocratic regimes (China, India), demonstrated a growing culture of impunity. Key countries (Nigeria, Pakistan) escaped international sanctions and other punishment following revelations of religious freedom violations against their own citizens.

5. The rise of 'opportunistic caliphates' During the review period, transnational jihadist networks in Africa increasingly changed tactics. By degrees, they shifted from conquering and defending fixed territories towards hit and run attacks aimed at creating isolated communities (cfr Mozambique) in poorly defended rural areas, (preferably ones) with mineral resources (cfr D.R. Congo). Traditional kill and loot strategies gave way to a tendency to impose illegal tax and trade, resulting in a state within a state. The insecurity and lack of government control led to revolts and military coups (two in Mali and one in Burkina Faso).

6. Divergent trends within Muslim communities became more visible. On the one hand, disenfranchised, impoverished, and frustrated youth were increasingly attracted by Islamist terrorist and criminal networks (Africa). On the other hand, recent surveys, notably in Iran, showed growing numbers of Muslims were self-identifying as non-religious.

7. Increased persecution of Muslims, including by other Muslims. Brutal persecution continued in China against the Uyghurs, with Muslims in India and Myanmar also suffering discrimination and persecution. Increasing incidents of intra-Muslim persecution were also reported between Sunni and Shi'a (Hazara in Afghanistan), between national and 'foreign' Muslim interpretations as well as between dominant and so-called 'deviant' forms of Islam (Ahmadi in Pakistan).

8. Reported aggression against the Jewish community in the West increased after the Covid-19 lockdowns. Anti-Semitic hate crimes reported in OSCE countries increased from 582 in 2019 to 1,367 in 2021.

9. Abductions, sexual violence, including sexual enslavement and forced religious conversion continued unabated and remained largely unpunished (West Africa, Pakistan). Abductions and human trafficking were fuelled by worsening poverty and increased armed conflicts. In dozens of countries religious minority women and girls suffered especially from this form of violence.

10. Inflating numbers of faithful as a means of maintaining political power. In some cases, faith communities, seeking to preserve their political, religious, and social status, exaggerated numbers of faithful by giving misleading religious data when officially registering children, or by postponing population census indefinitely (Lebanon, India, Malaysia).

11. Increased scrutiny, including mass surveillance, impacted faith groups. In the West, social media was used to marginalise and target religious groups. These developments undermined fundamental liberties, including freedom of conscience, thought, religion, freedom of expression, movement, and assembly.

12. In the West, 'cancel culture', including 'compelled speech', evolved from (verbal) harassment of individuals, who for religious reasons take different views, to include legal threats and loss of job opportunities. Individuals who, because of their faith, failed to articulate positions specifically endorsing views in line with prevailing ideological demands ('cancel culture') were threatened with legal sanctions. Social media was an important factor driving this trend.

13. Derogatory content about minority faiths was inserted into school textbooks (India, Pakistan) with potentially significant consequences for the future of inter-faith relations.

14. Proliferation of anti-conversion legislation, as well as reconversion initiatives offering economic benefits to those who join the majority religion or return to it (Asia, North Africa). Evidence revealed new legislation and harsher implementation of existing anti-conversion laws where the religious majority sought to entrench political power. Renewed reconversion efforts offered economic privileges to members who revert. Conversely, these benefits were withdrawn from converts compromising the welfare of the entire family in poverty-stricken areas.

15. Increased attacks on religious leaders and other Church personnel by organised criminal groups (Latin America). Religious representatives, champions of migrants and other disadvantaged communities, were targeted – abducted and even murdered – for speaking out against criminal gangs and taking action to stop them.[193]

[193] Aid to the Church in Need, *Religious Freedom Report 2023* at https://acninternational.org/religiousfreedomreport/reports/global/2023

As the mention of the Muslim and Jewish communities in the *Religious Freedom Report* indicates, Christians are not the only religious community under attack in the world today. However, there is no doubt that Christians are under attack and the available evidence suggests that they are in fact the world's most persecuted religious community.[194]

According to the 2023 *World Watch List* from the Christian charity Open Doors more than 360 million Christians worldwide 'suffer high levels of persecution and discrimination for their faith.' The report notes that 1 in 7 Christians are persecuted worldwide, with 1 in 5 suffering persecution in Africa and 2 in 5 suffering persecution in Asia.

The report further explains that the main trends with regard to the persecution of Christians across the world are that:

Violence against Christians in Sub-Saharan Africa has reached new heights

Jihadists are destabilizing countries in West and Central Africa. Entire countries are at risk of collapse into extremist violence. 26 countries in Sub-Saharan Africa face high levels of persecution; half of these have violence scores in the 'extremely high' range.

The jihadist movement, which seeks to expand Sharia across the continent, has forced Christians into constant motion, from their homes

---

[194] 'Today, Christians constitute by far the most widely persecuted religion. The International Society for Human Rights, a secular NGO based in Frankfurt, estimated in 2009 that Christians are the victims of 80 percent of all acts of religious discrimination in the world, a finding that is corroborated by separate human rights observatories. John Allen reports in his recent book, The Global War on Christians, that Christians were the only religious group that was persecuted in all sixteen countries highlighted as egregious offenders by the United States Commission on International Religious Freedom in 2012. The Pew Research Center's 2014 report found that between June 2006 and December 2012, Christians faced harassment and intimidation in 151 countries, the largest number of any religious group.' Daniel Philpott, 'Why Christians Deserve Attention' Georgetown University, Berkley Centre, 2 September 2014 at https://berkleycenter.georgetown.edu/essays/why-christians-deserve-attention.

to displacement camps, or to other countries. The insecurity stemming from this experience of forced displacement makes Christians even more vulnerable to further violence. Christian women, in particular, can be easily targeted for sexual attack, while men are more likely to lose their lives.

China's model of oppression is spreading throughout authoritarian states

The apparent success of China, especially in economic terms, is appealing to many leaders around the world. The promise of growth and prosperity, while being able to control all groups and individuals perceived as deviant, has triggered the interest of leaders from all over the world, no matter their ideological background.

Countries as diverse as Sri Lanka, Myanmar and Malaysia have headed down this same authoritarian path, joining Central Asian states like Azerbaijan, Kazakhstan, Kyrgyzstan, Tajikistan, Turkmenistan, Uzbekistan and Russia.

The mere existence of Christian communities is a thorn in the flesh of the regimes in many of these countries. Even more so if Christian activists raise their voice frustrating the regime's attempts to control its citizens. Using the language of 'stability' and 'security', autocrats put immense pressure on church leaders in response to their persistent call for the respect of human rights, free participation of civil society, the rule of law, and election transparency. Those who refuse to support the ruling party can be branded as 'troublemakers', 'disturbers of the peace' or even 'terrorists.' They face arrest, demolition of church buildings, and the loss of church registration.

The Church in the Middle East is reduced and still under pressure

The church has not been able to recover after the upsurge of Islamic State and the attempts of extremists to wipe out Christianity entirely.

Discrimination and oppression coupled with crippling economic decline means the church is losing hope, particularly for young people.

In the Levant region of the Middle East (Lebanon, Syria, Iraq, Israel/Palestinian Territories and Jordan), the Christian community is shrinking due to deprivation, discrimination and persecution. Ever since the Islamic State group (IS) arrived on the scene, Christians in those areas of Iraq and Syria have been struggling to earn a living; young Christians in particular face high unemployment and continual hostility, thus encouraging their desire to emigrate. When Christian emigration increases, church communities are weakened as a consequence, deprived of the next generation of leaders and families, and so become easier targets for further marginalization.

Elsewhere in the region there has been less violence, fewer killings, but not a better outlook. Converts to Christianity from Islam continue to face high levels of pressure from family and community.

Conditions for the Church have worsened in Latin America
On the 2022 list, three Latin American countries were ranked in the top 50. On the 2023 list, there are now four: Nicaragua is ranked No. 50 in 2023, the first time the country has appeared within the top 50. It joins Colombia (22), Cuba (27) and Mexico (38).

Corrupt and ineffective government has created space for criminal groups and ethnic leaders to emerge, strengthen and become drivers of persecution—especially in rural areas and among indigenous populations.

Government repression in Nicaragua, Cuba and Venezuela has intensified against those who are seen as opposition voices. In Nicaragua especially, communist repression of church leaders became increasingly visible during the year.

Although attacks on Christian religious freedom are less severe in the Western world than in other places, nevertheless, as the ACN report indicates, they exist, they are growing, and they take various forms such as physical attacks on Christians and church buildings, social hostility leading to Christian self-censorship and the use of the law to restrict the exercise of Christian belief.

The next section of this chapter will give examples of attacks on Christian religious freedom across the Western world.

Attacks on Christian freedom in Europe
The trials of Päivi Räsänen and Juhana Pohjola

In January 2022 the Finnish MP, and former Minister of the Interior, Dr Päivi Räsänen went on trial in Helsinki together with the Finnish Lutheran Bishop Juhana Pohjola went on trial in Helsinki accused of breaking Finnish law by inciting hatred against an ethnic group, the group in question being those who are homosexual.

The case against Dr Räsänen and Bishop Pohjola was summarised by the Finnish State Prosecutor as follows:

> The Prosecutor General has filed charges against MP Päivi Räsänen for three incitements against a group of people, and against Juhana Pohjola, an agent and board member of the Finnish Luther Foundation, for incitement against a group of people.
>
> The charges are based on three different sets of issues.
>
> Räsänen has written, 'God created them as men and women. Gay relationships challenge the Christian conception of man.' In her writing, Räsänen has presented opinions and information that denigrate homosexuals. Among other things, Räsänen has claimed that homosexuality is a scientifically proven disorder of psychosexual development. Pohjola has published the article on the websites of the Finnish Luther Foundation and the Finnish Evangelical Lutheran Mission.
>
> In addition, Räsänen has published on her Twitter and Instagram account and Facebook page an opinion that denigrates homosexuals, according to which homosexuality is a shame and a sin.
>
> Räsänen, on the program of the Yle Puhe radio channel, in its episode 'What did Jesus think about gays?' made derogatory statements about homosexuals. In it, Räsänen has said that if

homosexuality is genetic, then it is a genetic degeneration and a genetic disease that causes the disease. In Räsänen's view, homosexuals are also not created by God like heterosexuals.

According to the indictment, the statements further specified in Räsänen's indictments are derogatory and discriminatory against homosexuals. The statements violate the equality and dignity of homosexuals, so they transcend the boundaries of freedom of speech and religion.

The Attorney General believes that Räsänen's statements are likely to cause intolerance, contempt and hatred towards homosexuals.[195]

Following the decision to prosecute her and Bishop Pohjola, Räsänen issued a public statement setting out her view of the matter. In it she wrote:

Yesterday morning, I received by phone the information that the Prosecutor General has decided to prosecute me in three cases. The application for summons has been delivered to the District Court of Helsinki. I am accused of criminal agitation against a minority group, which carries the sentence of a fine or imprisonment for a maximum of two years. The three charges filed against me are about the following cases. Firstly, a pamphlet I wrote in 2004 'Male and female He created them—Homosexual relationships challenge the Christian concept of humanity.' A charge has also been filed against Rev. Dr. Juhana Pohjola, the Dean of Evangelical Lutheran Mission Diocese of Finland. The Evangelical Lutheran Mission Diocese of Finland was in charge of publishing the pamphlet.

The second charge is about a tweet I published 17 June 2019 in my social media accounts. In addition to Twitter, I published my tweet

---

[195] Press release from the Finnish State Prosecutor, 29 April 2021, quoted in Rod Dreher, 'Finland Persecutes Christian Lawmaker,' *The American Conservative*, 29 April 2021, at: https://www.theamericanconservative.com/finland-persecutes-christian-lawmaker-paivi-rasanen/

in Facebook and Instagram. In the tweet, I questioned the Evangelical Lutheran Church's official affiliation with Helsinki LGBT Pride 2019 and accompanied my publication with a photo of the Bible, from the Letter to the Romans 1:24-27. The third charge is about my views presented in one program of the Finnish Broadcasting Corporation, when I visited a talk show series hosted by Ruben Stiller and discussed the topic 'What would Jesus think about homosexuals?'

The decision of the Prosecutor General is surprising, even shocking. I do not think I have committed threatening, defaming or insulting a minority group. In all these three cases, the question is about the Bible's teaching about marriage and sexuality. Ultimately, the three charges brought against me have to do with whether it is allowed in Finland to express your conviction that is based on the traditional teaching of the Bible and Christian churches. I do not see I would have in any way defamed homosexuals whose human dignity and human rights I have constantly said to respect and defend. The Bible's teaching is, however, very clear in the teaching that marriage is a union between man and wife and that practicing homosexuality is against God's will.

The Apostle Paul's teaching is not only about defending marriage between man and woman, but about how a human being is saved into eternal life. If the teachings of God's word about sin are rejected, also the whole core of Christian faith is made empty: the precious sacrifice of Jesus on the cross for the sake of everyone's sins and the way He opened into eternity.

There is a difficulty here far greater than a sentence of a fine or an imprisonment: a demand for censorship: an order to remove my social media postings or a ban on the publication of the pamphlet. If one defies the court's verdict, it leads to demands of penalty payments. This sort of judgement would open up an avenue leading to further publication bans for similar texts and modern book burnings.

It is noteworthy that with regard to the pamphlet case and the TV episode with Stiller, the police stated that there was no reason to suspect a crime. The pre-trial investigation should not have even been commenced according to their decision. The police stated in their decision: 'if some of the views in the Bible were to be regarded as per se fulfilling the criteria of an agitation offense, the dissemination of or making the Bible available would in principle be punishable as an offense of agitation.' This has deeply to do with free speech and freedom of religion.

I will go to the court with a peaceful and brave mind, trusting that Finland is a constitutional state where the freedoms of speech and religion, which both are guaranteed in international agreements and in our constitution, are respected. A conviction based on the Christian faith is more than [a superficial] opinion. The early Christians did not renounce their faith in lions' caves, why should I then renounce my faith in a court room. I will not step back from my conviction nor from my writings. I do not apologize for the writings of the Apostle Paul either. I am ready to defend freedom speech and religion as far as is necessary.[196]

The result of the trial was the unanimous acquittal of Räsänen and Pohjola on all the charges against them. However, that was not the end of the matter.

In April 2022 the Finnish state prosecutor announced that she was going to appeal against this acquittal. In the words of the report from the Christian legal advocacy organisation ADF International, which had supported Räsänen's case:

The Finnish state prosecutor has filed her appeal against the unanimous court decision which exonerated are a Finnish MP and bishop of 'hate speech' allegations for sharing their faith-based beliefs. The prosecution is demanding tens of thousands of Euros in fines and insisting that Räsänen's and Pohjola's publications be

---

[196] Press Statement from Päivi Räsänen quoted in Dreher.

censored. On 30th of March 2022 the Helsinki District Court had dismissed all charges against Räsänen and Pohjola, stating that 'it is not for the district court to interpret biblical concepts.' After announcing their intention to appeal almost a month ago, the prosecution appealed the District Court's not guilty verdict on 30th of April.

'After my full exoneration in court, I am dismayed that the prosecutor will not let this campaign against me drop. And yet, the prosecutor's decision to appeal may lead to the case going all the way to the Supreme Court, offering the possibility of securing a positive precedent for freedom of speech and religion for all Finnish people. Also, I am happy that this decision will lead to the discussion of the Bible's teachings in society. I am ready to defend freedom of speech and religion in all necessary courts. As far as the European Court of Human Rights, if necessary,' said Päivi Räsänen MP.[197]

In a unanimous ruling on 14 November 2023 the Helsinki Appeal court dismissed the appeal by the state prosecutor and upheld the District Court's verdict. It found that there was:

...no reason, on the basis of the evidence received at the main hearing, to assess the case in any respect differently from the District Court. There is therefore no reason to alter the final result of the District Court's judgment.[198]

This was a second major victory for Räsänen and Pohjola, but it came after four years of police investigations, criminal indictments, prosecutions, and court hearings, and the matter is not necessarily over

[197] ADF International, 'Prosecutor files appeal against Finnish MP's major free speech victory' at: https://adfinternational.org/prosecutor-files-appeal-against-finnish-mps-major-free-speech-victory/
[198] ADF International, 'BREAKING: Finnish parliamentarian found NOT GUILTY of "hate speech" for Bible Tweet and other expressions' at: https://adfinternational.org/breaking-finnish-parliamentarian-found-not-guilty-of-hate-speech-for-bible-tweet-and-other-expressions/

since the state prosecutor has said she will appeal against the second acquittal at the Finnish Supreme Court.[199]

As Räsänen makes clear in the previous paragraphs, the issue raised by her case is whether Christians in Finland are free to give expression to their Christian convictions about homosexuality 'based on the traditional teaching of the Bible and Christian churches' without facing the prospect of a criminal prosecution and the possibility of a fine or imprisonment as a result. If they are not free to do so, then freedom of religion guaranteed has become restricted in spite of this freedom being protected (as we have seen) both in the Finnish constitution and in international agreements to which Finland is a signatory.

The cases of Felix Ngole and Bernard Randall
The British cases of Felix Ngole and Bernard Randall raise the issue of Christian religious freedom in a similar way.

Felix Ngole
Felix Ngole is a Christian social worker who was refused employment because of his Christian convictions about same-sex relationships. As the British online magazine *Spiked* explains:

> It seems like social work is no place for Christians in the UK. Felix Ngole, a social worker and pastor, had a job offer withdrawn last year because of his Christian views on same-sex relationships.

> In 2022, Ngole was offered a job at Touchstone, an NHS provider that offers mental-health and wellbeing services to people across Yorkshire. But when the charity learned that Ngole was a Christian who believed that homosexuality was a sin, he was called back in for another interview (Ngole says it felt more like an interrogation). His job offer was then promptly rescinded.

---

[199] 'Finnish state prosecutor to appeal Christian politician's 'not guilty' verdict' *Christian Today*, 13 January 2024, at:
https://www.christiantoday.com/article/finnish.state.prosecutor.to.appeal.christian.politicians.not.guilty.verdict/141260.html

Ngole has taken his case to an employment tribunal in Leeds, where the case is currently ongoing, to argue that his sacking amounts to discrimination under the Equality Act. Certainly, Touchstone's treatment of him looks to be horribly unjust. In defence of its decision to reject Ngole, the charity has made the absurd claim that employing him would have literally led to deaths. Should Ngole be allowed to work at Touchstone, the charity told the tribunal, there would be a serious risk of LGBT service-users killing themselves.

This is a grotesque suggestion. Ngole says that over his 20-year career as a youth worker, pastor and teacher, he has helped people from all kinds of backgrounds and communities, without discriminating against any of them. 'Not long ago I worked with a trans person', he told the tribunal, 'and I treated them as a human being'.

His record would seem to back this up. Indeed, as Ngole's lawyers have pointed out, Touchstone decided he was the best candidate for the role before it found out about his religious beliefs. He scored exceptionally well on every assessment given to him (including in equality and diversity) and was 'enthusiastically' offered the job.

This is not the first time that Ngole has been treated unfairly for his beliefs. In 2015, he was unceremoniously thrown off his university course. While studying for a social-work degree at Sheffield University, Ngole made comments on Facebook calling homosexuality a 'sin'. A fellow student reported him to the university.

After Ngole refused to renounce his opinions, he was removed from the course. Apparently, he was unable to practise within the rules of the Health and Care Professions Council. After various court and appeal hearings, Ngole finally managed to have the decision overturned in 2019 at the Court of Appeal. It was only after Googling Ngole's name and reading about this case that Touchstone learnt about his views on homosexuality.

It is deeply ironic that Ngole has been hounded out of his profession under the guise of 'tolerance'. He hasn't been intolerant towards anyone. He hasn't discriminated against people or even acted unprofessionally. 'I do not believe I have to agree with a person in order to meet their needs', he told the tribunal. He says he had no intention of imposing his views on anyone else.

That, in a nutshell, is what tolerance actually looks like: being free to hold your own opinions, being free to criticise the opinions of others, but ultimately resolving to live and let live. But tolerance has come to mean its precise opposite today. Anyone who doesn't agree with mainstream views on sexuality, say, is deemed beyond the pale, harmful to minorities and perhaps even unworthy of employment.[200]

Bernard Randall

The Revd Dr Bernard Randall was a Christian school chaplain who was reported to the government's terrorist watchdog and lost his job for delivering a sermon in a school chapel that encouraged respect and debate on 'identity ideologies.'

In June 2018, Trent College where Dr Randall worked, invited the leader of a group called Educate and Celebrate, Dr Elly Barnes, into the school to train staff.

Dr Randall, whose job description stated that his role was to 'be the particular voice and embodiment of ... Christian values which are at the heart of Trent's ethos,' was alarmed when, during the training session, Dr Barnes instructed staff to chant 'smash heteronormativity,' 'heteronormativity' being the traditional Christian belief that a heterosexual relationship between a man and a woman is what is normal for human beings.

[200] Lauren Smith, 'The Persecution of Felix Ngole,' *Spiked,* 6 April 2024 at: https://www.spiked-online.com/2024/04/06/the-persecution-of-felix-ngole/

He was also concerned that Dr Barnes wrongly informed staff that 'gender identity,' the sexual identity assumed by an individual regardless of their biological sex, is a protected characteristic under the Equality Act of 2010 and therefore must be legally recognised as a statutory requirement at the school.

Dr Randall raised these concerns with the school authorities and was assured by the headteacher that he would be involved in any decision-making process on whether the school would implement Educate and Celebrate's programme in the light of potential clashes with the school's Christian beliefs and values.

In January 2019, at the next staff training day, Dr Randall was stunned to find out that the school had decided to adopt Educate and Celebrates year-long 'gold standard' programme. This would see an identity politics 'LGBT inclusive curriculum' implemented, even for the nursery provision at the school. When he asked why he had not been included in discussions about this decision he was told that it was because he 'might disagree'.

After asking students what subjects they would like to hear in his sermons during the summer term Christian chapel services, Dr Randall was approached by a student who asked him whether he would address the following: 'how come we are told we have to accept all this LGBT stuff in a Christian school?' He was approached by pupils who had said that they were confused and upset by the issues involved in the new LGBT teaching.

In response to these student requests Dr Randall gave a sermon in the school chapel entitled 'Competing ideologies' in which he looked at a Christian approach to questions of personal and sexual identity. In the sermon he encouraged debate and stressed that no protected characteristic is more protected than another. He also explained that for Christians it is vital to love your neighbour in the face of disagreement, ad that this left no room for personal attacks or abusive language towards anyone.

Presenting the Church of England's Biblical position on marriage and human nature, he emphasised that children at the school were not compelled to 'accept an ideology they disagree with.' Rather, he encouraged the students, aged from 11 to 17, to debate matters of identity and make up their own minds on the issue.

The sermon was part of a service which also included hymns, prayers and a Bible reading.

The following week, he was called into a meeting with the Deputy Head and the school's Designated Safeguarding Lead (DSL). In a hostile interrogation, Dr Randall was told that his beliefs were not relevant and did not matter, and that the sermon had hurt some people's feelings and undermined the School's LGBT agenda. He was also told it was 'offensive' to describe Elly Barnes as an 'LGBT activist', despite her describing herself as such on her Twitter profile at the time.

During this interrogation, Dr Randall was asked what his sources were. for the Church of England's teachings regarding marriage, sexuality and gender. In response he pointed to the Church of England's public liturgy, especially the Book of Common Prayer, and the Church's Canon law.

Dr Randall was immediately suspended, pending an investigation and after this meeting, the DSL began the process of reporting Dr Randall, without his knowledge, to the government's counter-terrorism watchdog, Prevent, as a potentially violent religious extremist. The DSL also reported him to the Local Authority Designated Officer (LADO) as a danger to children, which is the same point of contact for reporting concerns over paedophilia.

On 1 July 2019, a Derbyshire police officer, Richard Barker, responded to the report to Prevent saying that the sermon posed no counter-terrorism risk. However, according to the DSL, he gave his personal opinion that the sermon 'was wholly inappropriate for a school, and society in general. 'Dr Randall only discovered by accident that he had been reported to Prevent and was only casually told that this investigation would not be taken any further.

Following an investigation and disciplinary hearing, Dr Randall received a letter on the 30 August 2019 stating that the Headmaster had concluded that his actions had amounted to gross misconduct and that he would be dismissed. On appeal, his dismissal was overturned by the school's governors, but he was given a final warning instead.

Dr Randall was also provided with twenty conditions that he had to comply with regarding any future sermons. Open censorship of his sermons followed. He was told that every theme and piece of sermon content had to be approved by school leadership in advance and that a staff member would observe to ensure each stipulation was met.

When the United Kingdom went into lockdown due to COVID in March 2020, Dr Randall was immediately furloughed. As restrictions eased, the school refused to reinstate his timetable and planned to reduce his full-time hours to seven hours per week. He was eventually made redundant by the school on 31 December 2020.

Supported by the Christian Legal Centre, Dr Randall took Trent College to court for discrimination, harassment, victimisation and unfair dismissal.

He was eventually cleared of any wrongdoing by the Disclosure and Barring Service (the public body that seeks to prevent unsuitable people working with children or vulnerable adults), Prevent, and the Teaching Regulation Authority (TRA). Despite this, he is still treated as a safeguarding risk by the Church of England which means he cannot engage in public ministry as a minister of the Church.

His dismissal by Trent College was upheld by an employment tribunal in 2023 and his appeal against this decision is expired to be heard sometime in 2024.

Commenting on his reaction when he found out he had been reported to Prevent without his knowledge, Dr Randall said:

'I was terrified. I did not sleep. What was I supposed to tell my family? Being reported as a potential terrorist, extremist and a danger to children are arguably the worst crimes you could be accused of.

"When I found out that they had reported me without telling me, my mind was blown trying to comprehend it. I had gone to such lengths in the sermon to stress that we must respect one another no matter what, even people we disagree with. I am not ashamed to say that I cried with relief when I was told that the report to Prevent was not going to be taken further.

Yet I ended up being told that I had to support everybody else's beliefs, no matter what, while my Christian beliefs, the Church of England's beliefs, were blatantly censored.

During the disciplinary hearing, I was never asked what I thought, they just assumed that I had extreme religious views. I don't think the Church of England is an extremist organisation.

I was doing the job I was employed to do. I wasn't saying anything that I should not have been able to say in any liberal secular institution. Everyone should be free to accept or reject an ideology. Isn't that what liberal democracy means?

My story sends a message to other Christians that you are not free to talk about your faith. It seems it is no longer enough to just 'tolerate' LGBT ideology. You must accept it without question and no debate is allowed without serious consequences. Someone else will decide what is and what isn't acceptable, and suddenly you can become an outcast, possibly for the rest of your life.

I 100% see what has happened to me in Orwellian terms. Truth matters, but increasingly powerful groups in our society do not care about the truth.

My career and life are in tatters. I believe that if this is the Cross that I have to carry to help prevent others from experiencing the same as me, I have no choice but to pursue justice' [201]

Intolerance and discrimination against Christian in Europe—the OIDAC report

The three cases just mentioned, and the similar case of Father Matthieu Raffray mentioned in the Introduction, should not be viewed in isolation. They are a part of growing pattern of intolerance and discrimination against Christians in Europe over the past few years.

For example, the report for 2021 by the Vienna based Observatory on Intolerance and Discrimination against Christians (OIDAC) notes the growth of various forms of both intolerance and discrimination against Christians in Europe in 2021. The report uses 'intolerance' to refer to 'an invisible sentiment towards a certain group, which can manifest in public acts such as vandalism, violence, insults, and other forms of targeted aggression.' It uses 'discrimination' to refer to acts which involve a 'legal dimension' and includes 'discriminatory treatment of individuals and groups by entities such as the authorities, employers, and governmental organisations.'[202]

The OIDAC report contained 13 key findings:

1. In 2021, OIDAC documented over 500 anti-Christian hate crimes. There is a reasonable probability for higher dark numbers, due to limited reporting on Anti-Christian Hate Crimes, the 'chilling effect' among victims and lack of media coverage.

---

[201] Details about Dr Randall's case can be found on the *Christian Concern* website at https://christianconcern.com/cccases/rev-dr-bernard-randall/.
[202] Observatory on Intolerance and Discrimination Against Christians, *OIDAC Europe Annual Report 2021,* p.6 at
https://www.intoleranceagainstchristians.eu/fileadmin/user_upload/publications/files/Annual_Report_2022_-_ONLINE_Web_View_Final.pdf.

2. In 2021, OIDAC documented anti-Christian hate crimes in 19 European countries. There were 14 crimes of physical assault and 4 Christians were murdered.

3. Recent preliminary research and example cases confirm the increasing phenomenon of self- censorship by Christians, in response to perceived intolerance towards their beliefs, resulting in what is termed a 'chilling effect.'

4. Self-censorship by Christians has been identified in five areas of life: education, the workplace, the public sphere, private social interactions, and media platforms.

5. In 2021, Christians from various denominations were subject to negative stereotyping and insensitivity by the media and political groups. This trend emerged particularly in relation to Catholics in Spain.

6. Christian-led organisations were banned from social media platforms for expressing dissenting beliefs, while insult and violent speech against Christians were permitted on the same platforms.

7. Ambiguously worded 'hate speech' laws and public order legislation have undermined the right to Freedom of Speech, leading to several unjustified arrests of street preachers, mainly in the UK.

8. Freedom of Assembly of Christians was contested in courts after some cities in Germany, Spain and the UK implemented 'safe-access buffer zones' around abortion clinics. This criminalizes activities including prayer vigils, conversations with the public, and other forms of peaceful activism.

9. Doctors, bioethics commissions, and medical personnel have voiced concerns about limitations to Freedom of Conscience. Laws have recently been drafted that would

withdraw the right to 'conscientious objection' for controversial medical procedures, endangering the ability of medical staff to practise in accordance with their beliefs.

10. New laws outlawing 'conversion therapy' or introducing sexual education guidelines are infringing on the Rights of Parents to have a say in the education and psychological well-being of their children. These laws are often based on gender theory and employ imprecise language that could result in the criminalisation of dissenting discussions in both public and private context, including private prayer.

11. New trans-laws and abortion laws give minors autonomy to decide to undergo an abortion or gender transition without parental consent, violating Parental Rights.

12. Following the relaxation of COVID-19 lockdown measures for non-essential services and shops, legal scholars, national court rulings and human rights groups stated that some churches were subject to unjustifiable and discriminatory treatment as religious services and in some cases even private worship remained prohibited.

13. In Spain, France and some German cities, misleading statements made by the media and politicians led to a stigmatisation of Evangelical churches and groups, which were labelled 'COVID-19 spreaders' during the pandemic.[203]

The report notes the objection that 'Intolerance and discrimination in Europe are minor issues compared to the violent persecution of Christians in other countries.' Its response is to explain that,

'The most persecuted religion worldwide is Christianity, and many of them face imprisonment and death in other countries.' However, it says 'This does not mean that more subtle forms of intolerance,

[203] *OIDAC Europe Annual Report 2021*, pp.4-5.

such as social exclusion, censorship, discrimination in education or employment are less important or should be ignored.' [204]

The OIDAC report for 2022-2023 notes that the same trends identified in the 2021 continued in 2022 with the number of documented anti-Christian hate crimes rising to 749, and once again the probability that the actual number of 'dark crimes' was higher.[205]

Attacks on Christian freedom in Australia
It is not only in Europe that there are attacks on Christian religious freedom. This is also happening in Australia. Two examples are the introduction of bill banning conversion therapy in the state of Victoria and the proposal that the government should take over the running of a Roman Catholic hospital in the Australian Capital Territory.

Victoria's 'Change or Suppression (Conversion) Practices Prohibition Act 2021' defines such practices as:

...a practice or conduct directed towards a person, whether with or without the person's consent—(a) on the basis of the person's sexual orientation or gender identity; and (b) for the purpose of—(i) changing or suppressing the sexual orientation or gender identity of the person; or (ii) inducing the person to change or suppress their sexual orientation or gender identity.

The objects of the Act are then defined as being to:

(a) to eliminate so far as possible the occurrence of change or suppression practices in Victoria; and

(b) to further promote and protect the rights set out in the Charter of Human Rights and Responsibilities; and

---

204 *OIDAC Europe Annual Report 2021*, pp.3.
205 *OIDAC Europe 2022/2023 Annual Report*, p.7 at https://www.intoleranceagainstchristians.eu/fileadmin/user_upload/publications/files/Annual_Report_2023_-_ONLINE_Version.pdf

(c) to ensure that all people, regardless of sexual orientation or gender identity, feel welcomed and valued in Victoria and are able to live authentically and with pride.

The Act further adds that:

...In enacting this Act, it is the intention of the [Victorian State] Parliament

a. to denounce and give statutory recognition to the serious harm caused by change or suppression practices; and

b. to affirm that a person's sexual orientation or gender identity is not broken and in need of fixing; and

c. to affirm that no sexual orientation or gender identity constitutes a disorder, disease, illness, deficiency or shortcoming; and

d. to affirm that change or suppression practices are deceptive and harmful both to the person subject to the change or suppression practices and to the community as a whole.[206]

As a Baptist pastor from Victoria explained in an interview, this Act constitutes a major restriction on the freedom of Christians in the state:

Speaking to The Christian Institute, Murray Campbell, Lead Pastor at Mentone Baptist Church in Melbourne, said that under the ban, prayers and conversations on issues of gender and sexuality will be prohibited if they are perceived as an attempt to change or suppress someone's sexuality or gender identity, even if they are consensual.

---

[206] Change or Suppression (Conversion) Practices Prohibition Act 2021, Part 1 (5) and Part I Preliminary, at https://content.legislation.vic.gov.au/sites/default/files/2021-02/21-003aa%20authorised.pdf

He added that, while sermons and preaching will not initially be included, the previous Attorney General threatened that they could be included in a wider ban at a later date.

Explaining the impact on gospel freedom, Pastor Campbell said: 'Someone might approach me and say 'Murray, can you pray for me, I'm struggling at the moment with my sexual godliness', and if I do so, I will be breaking the law.

'If someone comes to me for advice and says, for example, 'I'm same-sex attracted, I love Jesus, I want to follow Jesus, I want to be godly with my life, can you walk alongside me and help me and disciple me', and if I do so, I will be breaking the law.

'And even in a Bible-study setting, so you're opening the Bible with say eight other people and maybe you're working through Romans chapter one, and someone puts up their hand and says 'actually, I now identify as gay'. If we were to continue with the Bible study on Romans chapter one, we will be breaking the law because an individual has highlighted the fact that they identify as gay.'

Murray also explained that these scenarios could result in either civil complaints or criminal charges, with prison sentences ranging between five and ten years.

Accusations of wrongdoing can be made by either the alleged victim, or by a third party, 'and so you may well just have the police rocking up at your home door one day and saying 'a complaint's been made against you – you need to come down and explain yourself'.'

The pastor said that for most 'Christian offences', the offender will have to appear before a civil tribunal, where they will have to show documentation, including email history and sermons, and they will then be sent to 'a class where you will be re-educated as to what you need to think about sexual orientation and gender identity'.

He added: 'At the very least, a civil complaint, a civil tribunal. That in itself can be a very long process and a very difficult and expensive process. Worst case scenario, it's ten years imprisonment.'

Murray attended an 'information session' for Christian leaders in the state, where officials from the Victorian Government explained the law and what they can and cannot do.

They said one 'grey area' is a situation involving an individual or a group praying for someone who is not present but is known to be struggling with their sexuality. The officials said this could be a breach of the law, whether the person being prayed for is aware of the prayer or not.

He added that during the session it was made very clear that no person's sexual orientation or gender identity is sinful 'or needs to change in any way and churches are to affirm a person's sexual orientation or gender identity'.

The law is not limited to church leaders, and Murray said one of the most dangerous areas is for parents: 'It's becoming more common for children to be questioning their gender identity and saying 'I don't know if I'm a boy any more, maybe I'm a girl, maybe I'm something else'.

'If parents say to their children 'Slow down, let's wait a couple of years and see how we go', or if they try to dissuade their child of this questioning, they too are falling foul of the law and could be pulled up on charges.

'The ramifications are broad and encompassing, but obviously there are going to be significant challenges for churches, because I think largely the laws are trying to target religious organisations.'

The Melbourne pastor said that the other church leaders he knows are in favour of 'appalling' conversion therapy practices being stopped, but said such instances are almost unheard of.

'It was only I think about four or five years ago that I first heard of these gay conversion practices. I had a journalist call me and say 'Hey Murray, what do you think about it?' And I'm thinking 'What?! This is awful. We don't do this. I don't know anyone who does this'.

'So on the one hand, we're very supportive of the Government saying some things are dangerous and we don't want to see them happening, but on the other hand, there are basic, integral Christian practices that are now, according to the state, against the law – such as speaking to someone, counselling someone, praying with somebody.'[207]

The second example concerns the passing of a bill by the government of the Australian Capital Territory to acquire Calvary Hospital, a hospital currently run by the Roman Catholic Church, in order to change its stance on issues such as abortion, contraception and euthanasia.

According to the report on the issue on the Catholic website *Lifesite,* this move is unprecedented and is an indication of a wider threat to Christianity in Australia.

In a move that points to increasing political hostility in Australia towards Catholic and other Christian institutions, the Australian Capital Territory (ACT) government has moved to mandatorily acquire Canberra's Catholic-run Calvary Hospital.

The takeover required the introduction of a bill, a change in the law – an unprecedented move in Australia's history. The bill stipulates that the ACT government will move into the premises on July 3 and take over the operation of the hospital. This will occur before any compensation is agreed to or paid.

The extreme move and hasty implementation—designed to keep public debate to a minimum—is taking place because the Catholic-owned

[207] Christian Institute, 3 February 2022, 'EXCLUSIVE: Australian pastor explains draconian Victorian conversion therapy ban' at https://www.christian.org.uk/news/exclusive-australian-pastor-explains-draconian-victorian-conversion-therapy-ban/

hospital has a history of being pro-life and of not supporting euthanasia.

A recent ACT government inquiry into abortion and reproductive choice described Calvary Hospital as 'problematic... due to an overriding religious ethos.' The inquiry issued warnings about an 'ethically fraught dependence' on the Sisters of the Little Company of Mary for provision of health services.

The bureaucrats and politicians rely on muted words like 'problematic' and neutral phrases (in the press release) like 'the evolving needs of the ACT community' to create the impression that this is merely an administrative decision.

This is belied by the fact that it was necessary to resort to hasty and unusual moves in the legislature to make the acquisition possible. Such political and bureaucratic deceptions are as routine as they are tedious and insulting.

A more accurate picture was provided by the leader of the federal opposition, Peter Dutton, who said that he was 'just not aware of an action like it elsewhere in the country or, frankly, around the world, where a government has taken a decision based on their opposition to a religion to compulsorily acquire a hospital in these circumstances a facility that's working well and in the greater public interest and good in a local community and just for ideological reasons.'

Father Tony Percy from ACT's Catholic diocese described the move as 'basically religious bigotry writ large,' saying it sets a dangerous precedent that could 'see other Christian-owned properties 'acquired' in Soviet-style takeovers.' He said the takeover could create a precedent for other governments to seize Christian facilities like schools and aged care facilities.

The Archbishop of Canberra, Christopher Prowse, protested against the 'shocking news' in a letter.

'This extraordinary and completely unnecessary government intervention could set the scene for future acquisitions of any faith-based health facility, or, indeed, any faith-based enterprise including education or social welfare. I am also concerned that this action, based on obsessive government control, would deprive future Catholic generations in Canberra of the choice of hospital care based on the ethos of our cherished Catholic faith.'

Rob Norman, the Australian Christian Lobby's ACT director, described the move as an 'authoritarian decision... reminiscent of a Soviet style takeover of non-Government assets.' He said the ACT government has 'no tolerance for religious convictions that oppose the will of the State.'

There are two reasons why the move poses a threat to the fabric of Australian society.

One is the lack of respect for Australia's history. Many of the hospitals and institutions of care in Australia, including Calvary, were established by the Catholic Church without government assistance. This exemplary record of helping the sick and the disadvantaged is widely ignored: not so much religious bigotry as convenient omission. Thus the ACT government can treat Calvary as if it is government property.

The second, more telling issue, is that there is a widely held view in Australia that the nation has a legally enforced separation of Church and state. It is not true, or at least only partly true. Under section 116 of the Constitution there is a guarantee of the Freedom of Religion but these prohibitions only apply to the Commonwealth government, not to the States, which are free to discriminate on the basis of religion.

The ACT is not a state, but a territory, so theoretically it falls under the control of the federal government. But the left-wing Federal Labour government is unlikely to do anything.

The message to Australian Christians is that if they hold to their moral positions, they can expect to be considered hostile to the state.

Kevin Andrews, a former federal defence minister, writes that Australia's domestic law contains very little protection for freedom of religion. 'This is compounded by the incorporation through a series of Commonwealth, state and territory statutes of one universally recognized freedom – against discrimination – into domestic law, but the exclusion of others, including freedom of religion.'

The implication is that in Australia, discrimination against some groups, especially those deemed 'minorities,' is aggressively outlawed, but prejudice against religious groups, particularly Christians, is not considered much of a problem. The move against Calvary Hospital is a clear indication of the consequences of that inequality.[208]

Attacks on Christian Freedom in Canada and the United States

There has also been a rise in attacks on the religious freedom of Christians in the United States and Canada.

For example, a report published by the Family Research Council in December 2022 documents the growth in attacks on church premises across the United States and, as the report's introduction explains, these attacks constitute an assault on the religious freedom of Christians in America:

In June 2021, after surveillance cameras caught footage of two men approaching St. Veronica's Catholic Church in Philadelphia, setting fires at the entrance, and then walking away, Father Joseph Lo Jacono told

---

[208] David James, 'The Australian gov't is forcefully taking over a Catholic hospital because it is pro-life,' *Lifesite* 27 May 2023, https://www.lifesitenews.com/opinion/the-australian-govt-is-forcefully-taking-over-a-catholic-hospital-because-it-is-pro-life/. Another example of the way in which the religious freedom of Roman Catholic Christians in Australia has been infringed is the 2020 Queensland law compelling priests to break the seal of confession in suspected child abuse cases. For details of this see 'Queensland passes law requiring priests to break confessional seal,' Catholic News Agency, 8 September 2024 at https://www.catholicnewsagency.com/news/45756/queensland-passes-law-requiring-priests-to-break-confessional-seal.

local reporters, 'I think it's a sign of a lessening of the faith and a certain anger and hatred to the Catholic faith.'

Father Lo Jacono is not the only person thinking that such incidents indicate a growing animosity toward Catholicism, and Christianity in general. There is ample reason to be concerned about rising hostility to Christianity by a Western culture that increasingly rejects Judeo-Christian values.

In a report published in July 2022, Family Research Council documented 99 incidents of government violations of religious freedom against individual Christians or Christian institutions across 14 Western countries since 2020. But religious hostility can be felt from other sources besides the government.

Tracking physical incidents against churches is an important data point for larger discussions about increasing intolerance toward Christianity in American society. So, Family Research Council set out to analyze publicly available data to determine whether there has been a statistically significant increase in acts of vandalism and destruction of church property over the past five years. Our findings, detailed in this report, indicate that there has been a noticeable increase.

Criminal acts of vandalism and destruction of church property are likely symptomatic of a collapse in societal reverence and respect for houses of worship and religion—in this case, churches and Christianity. Americans appear increasingly comfortable lashing out against church buildings, pointing to a larger societal problem of marginalizing core Christian beliefs, including those that touch on hot—button political issues related to human dignity and sexuality.

The Federal Bureau of Investigation keeps records of hate crimes in the United States, including those motivated by an anti-religious bias. In 2021, the most recent year with available data, the FBI reported 240 anti-Christian 'hate crimes' (the FBI uses the following categories for Christianity: Catholics, Protestants, Eastern Orthodox, and 'other Christians'). This was up from 213 anti-Christian incidents in 2020.

There seems to be a general upward trend over the past few years: the FBI reported 217 anti - Christian incidents in 2019 and 172 in 2018.

In a Western country like the United States, there can be a tendency to brush aside the significance of vandalism or other acts of hostility against churches. This should not be the case. For staff members and congregants, such acts of hostility against their churches can be intimidating. For example, when a statue of Mary outside of a Catholic church is beheaded, it is natural for congregants to feel disturbed and upset, and that may be the vandal's aim. Acts of hostility against churches send the message that churches are not wanted in the community or respected in general. This may cause congregants or church leaders to feel unsafe. In some instances, the goal of the hostility is to interrupt the normal work of the church.

Make no mistake, acts of hostility against churches are a matter of religious freedom. Religious freedom is not maintained by good laws and policies alone; it also relies on cultural support. When church attendees feel targeted by members of their communities or church buildings bear the brunt of outrage over political events, a more grievous assault is occurring on the ability to choose and live out one's faith safely, both at church and in the public square. Violent or destructive incidents that interfere with an individual's lawful free exercise of religion at their house of worship present a significant nationwide challenge. [209]

In a supplementary report the Family Research Council noted a continuing rise in attacks on churches in the first three months of 2023. The report notes:

In the first quarter of 2023, 69 incidents have already occurred. If this rate continues, 2023 will have the highest number of incidents of the six years FRC has tracked, continuing the upward trend. Most of the 2023

[209] Arielle Del Turco, 'Hostility Against Churches Is on the Rise in the United States - Analyzing Incidents from 2018-2022,' Family Research Council, December 2022, No, 1522 LO, p.2-3 at: https://downloads.frc.org/EF/EF22L24.pdf

incidents occurred in January (43); 14 occurred in February, and 12 occurred in March.

Compared to the same time frame in previous years, January through March of 2023 represents a significant increase in acts of hostility. In those same months, 2018 saw 15 acts of hostility against churches; 2019 saw 12; 2020 saw none; 2021 saw 14; and 2022 saw 24.

Criminal acts of vandalism and destruction of church property are symptomatic of a collapse in societal reverence and respect for houses of worship and religion—in this case, churches and Christianity. Some people appear increasingly comfortable lashing out against church buildings, pointing to a larger societal problem of marginalizing core Christian beliefs, including those that touch on hot-button political issues related to human dignity and sexuality.

The anger and division that increasingly characterize American society are endangering churches and eroding religious freedom. When congregants feel targeted by members of their communities or church buildings bear the brunt of outrage over political events, the very ability to live out one's faith safely is under attack. Violent or destructive incidents that interfere with an individual's lawful free exercise of religion at their house of worship present a significant nationwide challenge.[210]

In an updated report published in February 2024 the Family Research Council identified 436 attacks on churches in the United States in 2023 as a whole. It noted that these figures were 'more than double the number identified in 2022 and more than eight times the number

[210] Arielle Del Turco, 'Hostility Against Churches Supplemental Report – First Quarter 2023', Family Research Council, April 2023 | No. IF23D01, pp.2-3, at https://downloads.frc.org/EF/EF23D04.pdf.

identified in 2018' and that they 'suggest that hostility against U.S. churches is not only on the rise but also accelerating.' [211]

In Canada some sixty-eight churches were burned down in 2021 in response to what were claimed to be the discovery of mass graves of indigenous children at former church run residential schools,[212] and in general Canadian society has begun to be a more hostile environment for Christians in recent years with the law increasingly being used to restrict Christian religious freedom. This is a point that is made by Joe Boot in his 2020 article 'On the brink: the criminalisation of Christianity in Canada.' In this article he writes:

> For over two decades in Canada, an alert minority has observed and sought to oppose (thus far fruitlessly) the gradual construction of a human rights and legal apparatus with the potential to severely restrict the freedoms and liberties of Christians. Especially since July 2005 and the scandalous legal fiction redefining marriage in the Canadian state, a steady stream of criminal and administrative law has found its way onto the statute books that can and has been gradually wielded against Christians and their faith by the police, professional bodies, Human Rights Tribunals and the Courts.
>
> In 2017, the Liberal government amended sections of Canada's Criminal Code that deal with 'hatred' toward an 'identifiable group'. Hatred itself is not defined in the Code, but writing, statements or signs deemed to incite or promote hatred could be regarded as criminal (A 2013 Supreme Court of Canada decision states that 'hate speech' is expression that is 'likely to expose a person or persons to detestation and vilification on the basis of a prohibited ground of discrimination'). In the 2017 revision to the Criminal Code sections listing identifiable groups (which already included

---

[211] Arielle Del Turco, 'Hostility Against Churches Is on the Rise in the United States - Analyzing Incidents from 2018-2023,' Family Research Council Issue Analysis February 2024 | No. IS24B01at: https://downloads.frc.org/EF/EF24B78.pdf.
[212] See the Wikipedia article '2021 Canadian church burnings,' at https://en.wikipedia.org/wiki/2021_Canadian_church_burnings.

sexual orientation), the highly controversial ideological concepts generated by radical critical theory – gender identity and expression – were added to the identifiable groups listed in section 318(4) (this list also applies for section 319 – see 319(7)) and in section 718.2(a) (aggravating factors for sentencing) of the Criminal Code. The promoting and inciting of 'hatred' towards these newly created groups now includes making statements in a public place or making statements in any other setting than that of a private conversation. Although religious arguments are ostensibly considered a possible defence if they are made in 'good faith,' the subjectivity of both 'hatred' and 'good faith' give courts incredible latitude in finding someone guilty. In the event of a conviction, the offense carries up to two years in prison.

Whilst the Supreme Court of Canada has acknowledged that these provisions restrict freedom of expression, they have argued that the restrictions are justifiable under Section (1) of the Canadian Charter of Rights and Freedoms—a document that has been used to batter and marginalise Christianity in Canada for over thirty years. As such, the Court has rejected constitutional challenges to both the hate propaganda offences in the Criminal Code, and challenges to the hate publication provisions in human rights legislation.

In addition, the various Human Rights Commissions and Tribunals, enforcing the regularly amended Human Rights Codes, have consistently targeted Christian and conservative individuals and institutions for alleged discrimination. The decisions of the courts have steadily generated a 'hierarchy' of rights – a fact they vigorously deny – in which liberties for Christians are consistently found at the bottom.[213]

As an example of this trend, he points to the case of Trinity Western University:

[213] Joe Boot, 'On the brink: the criminalisation of Christianity in Canada,' Christian Concern, 10 October 2020 at https://christianconcern.com/resource/on-the-brink-the-criminalisation-of-christianity-in-canada/.

...in a landmark case in 2018, Trinity Western University, an evangelical university in British Columbia, lost its battle in Canada's Supreme Court to move ahead with its law school after some Canadian law societies objected that the university was discriminatory. While the court recognised that its final ruling violated religious freedom, it argued that it was 'proportionate and reasonable' to do this in order to ensure access to the University for self-identifying LGBTQ students who might feel unable to sign Trinity Western's Community Covenant that obliged students studying at this Christian institution to respect the Biblical view of human sexuality and abstain from sexual relations other than heterosexual marriage during their studies at the school.[214]

He also points to the significance of the proposed bill by the Canadian Federal Government to ban conversion therapy, a bill which has since become law. He comments:

It seems that many of these steps, steadily eroding Christian freedom, may now be coming to a head at the federal level with an ideologically motivated effort to actually criminalise services and practices that the government believes are rooted in 'myths' about the human person.

Proposed legislation originally called 'Bill C-8', An Act to amend the Criminal Code, had proposed to brandish criminal law against so-called 'conversion therapy' and is now expected to reappear this Fall unchanged but under a different number. Bill C-8 states clearly in its preamble: 'conversion therapy...is based on and propagates myths and stereotypes about sexual orientation and gender identity, including the myth that a person's sexual orientation and gender identity can and ought to be changed.'

Clearly here, Biblical truth (cf. 1 Cor. 6: 9-11) and the historic teaching of the church concerning human sexuality are condemned as myth and Christ's call to repentance from sexual sin is overtly rejected. Justice

[214] Boot.

Minister David Lametti explained his rationale for the ban, saying: 'Conversion therapy is premised on a lie, that being homosexual, lesbian, bisexual or trans is wrong and in need of fixing. Not only is that false, it sends a demeaning and a degrading message that undermines the dignity of individuals.' So, on the authority of Mr. Lametti, God's Word, the authority of Christ, the teaching of the universal Church and centuries of normative understandings of the human person are dismissed as lies to be overthrown, with resisters cast into prison.

With the seriousness of this threat in mind, it would be important to know how 'conversion therapy' is actually being defined. The bill's definition is as follows:

> Conversion therapy means a practice, treatment or service designed to change a person's sexual orientation to heterosexual or gender identity to cisgender, or to repress or reduce non-heterosexual attraction or sexual behaviour.

The language of the bill already presupposes the validity of fictive ideological concepts in queer theory by using terms like 'cisgender' for the biological binary norm of male and female. It seems incredible that such a bill could be coming before the House of Commons from the government, but this is the reality facing Christians in Canada.

The Justice Centre for Constitutional Freedoms, in a paper entitled 'Unconscionable and Unconstitutional (May 12, 2020)', has warned Canadians that:

> 'Bill C-8 directly confronts the teaching of cultural and religious beliefs about sexuality and gender with the threat of imprisonment. It also severely restricts the ability of consenting adults to voluntarily receive the supports of their choice in relation to sexuality and gender by making it criminal to advertise or receive material benefit from 'conversion therapy' as overbroadly defined ...Bill C-8 imposes broad criminal prohibitions that violate Canadian human rights and constitutional freedoms, including Charter rights

to liberty and security of the person, freedom of expression, freedom of conscience and religion and equality.'

What the bill in fact does is remove meaningful personal choice by imposing the affirmation and promotion of homosexuality and/or gender transition as the only acceptable form of counsel, guidance or treatment – especially for children experiencing gender identity distress. Under the cover of outlawing barbaric and harmful 'treatments' that no-one actually practices, a radical and ideologically pagan view of sexuality and gender is enforced by making the definition of 'conversion therapy' so wide (including spiritual, medical and psychological supports) that youth with unwanted feelings or addictions would have no choice but to have 'treatments' that either reinforce these unwanted feelings and addictions, or permanently alter their bodies. It does this by banning alternative supports with the threat of imprisonment, violating the Charter rights and freedoms of children, their parents, church communities and health care professionals.

André Schutten, Fellow of the Ezra Institute and Director of Law and Policy and General Legal Counsel for ARPA Canada, has recently warned pastors in Canada that:

'This bill, if passed as written, would make it a criminal offence to help a person struggling with their sexual orientation (e.g. a same-sex attracted Christian) or sexual thoughts or behaviour (e.g. watching gay porn) or gender identity (e.g. believe they are a man trapped inside a female body) to bring their thoughts, words, and deeds into conformity with the Word of God. But the pastor or counsellor would be free to encourage a man to explore same-sex desires or experiment with same-sex behaviour. Similarly, encouraging a teen girl to love and appreciate and care for the female body God designed and paired with her soul would be a criminal act. But the opposite (encouraging or experimenting with change from cisgender to genderqueer, nonbinary, transgender, etc.) is permitted.'

It is especially important therefore, that Christians become aware that this legislation is not directed merely at health care professionals – though that itself would be serious enough. It directly threatens the sanctity and sphere of authority of the family by invading the child-parent relationship and threatening jail time for parents seeking health and spiritual care alternatives to social, hormonal and physical gender transition of their children who may be experiencing some form of gender dysphoria or other psychological condition.

It likewise threatens the sphere of authority and sanctity of the church. Christians must become alert to the fact that right now, basic pastoral care, prayer counselling and the fundamental teachings of the scriptures and the church, if applied, are literally teetering on the edge of being criminalised in the Dominion of Canada. Schutten likewise warns Canadian pastors that the implications of this bill passing would likely go well beyond banning faithful pastoral care and biblical counselling—it would soon thereafter destroy the charitable legal status of non-compliant churches and Christian organisations:

'If this bill passes unamended, aspects of your ministry (to youth in particular) in an age of sexual confusion would be criminalized. Not only do you face fines and prison time should you continue with biblically faithful counselling, it would be a very simple and logical next step to remove your church's charitable status: why would the CRA give tax receipts to a criminal organization? Through all this, the gospel witness would be marginalized, preventing more from hearing and experiencing the joy and freedom found in Christ Jesus.'[215]

Why are attacks on Christian religious freedom increasing?
The various forms of attack on Christian religious freedom that we have looked at in these chapter all have their own explanations, and these explanations are different in different cases. Thus, the specific reason for the prosecution of Päivi Räsänen and Juhana Pohjola in Finland was

---

[215] Boot.

different from the reason why churches were burned down in Canada. However, what we can also say is that the overarching reason why the religious freedom of Christians has come under increasing attack across the Western world in recent years in Western society is because of changed understanding of the meaning of a 'secular society' and because. Christians are now widely regarded as the 'bad guys.'

A changed understanding of what it means to be secular

As Paul Marshall argues in a survey of 'Patterns of Anti-Christian persecution,' the current 'erosion of religious freedom in the West' is tied 'to the growth of newer interpretations of what it means to be 'secular.'[216]

As he explains:

The term 'secular' along with its cognates, has a range of meanings and is often carried a positive religious meaning - emerging as it did from within Christian thought. The words 'secularism' and 'secularization' were derived from the Latin *saeculum*: the vocation of the priests who withdrew from the world was religious, and the vocation of the priest who took an active role in society was secular. In such usage, 'secular' did not mean the absence of religion but the lack of direct control by the church. One could be religious in the secular realm - the area where most Christians and others live out most of their lives. Hence, religion and its influences could be pervasive in secular society and often were.[217]

However, he continues:

The related idea of a plural, secular society of free religious and secular influences, with opposition to religious discrimination, has been changing into what Charles Taylor describes as a public arena

---

[216] Paul Marshall. 'Patterns of Anti-Christian Persecution' in Allen Hertzke and Timothy Shah (eds), *Christianity and Freedom – Volume II Contemporary Perspectives* (New York: CUP, 2016), p.74.
[217] Marshall, pp.74-75.

that has 'been allegedly emptied of God, or of any reference to ultimate reality,' resulting in an extreme *laicite* and virtual Kemalism. In much current western jargon, the secular arena is no longer treated as a companion to the religious sphere but as its opposite. Parallel to this, as Bishop Tartaglia has pointed out, much of modern liberalism now tends 'to imply that institutions like the family, the church, and other associations exist only with the permission of the state, and to exist lawfully they must abide by the dictates and norms of the state…which is intolerant of anyone who questions it.'[218]

The result of this development, he writes, is that:

…politicians and policy makers, among others, often reduce freedom of religion to freedom of worship, which limits the freedom to practise, express, teach, criticise, or leave a religion publicly, or to introduce religion into the societal and public arena. The freedom to worship is defended only as an essentially private activity, with few civic or public policy implications. There is also a widespread, uncritical assumption that secular societies are tolerant and free, when in fact many of the world's most repressive regimes, including the worst, North Korea, are highly secular. This truncation of religion is combined with a growing hostility to religion. The Pew Research Center's 2012 'Rising Tide of Restrictions on Religion' reports that such restrictions have now risen in many countries that had previously had low or moderate restrictions or hostilities, such as Switzerland and the United States. Simultaneously, countries such as the United Kingdom, Germany, and France experienced a substantial rise in social hostilities involving religion; in fact, those countries scored higher on the Pew Forum's social hostilities index than Iran, Sudan, and Lebanon. [219]

---

[218] Marshall, p.75. The references to '*laicite*' and 'Kemalism' are to the strict separation between the state and religion introduced by the French Government in 1905 and by Kemmal Attaturk in Turkey from 1923.
[219] Marshall, p.75.

Christians as the 'bad guys'

If we ask why such restrictions and hostility have affected Christians in particular, the answer is given by the Christian writer Stephen McAlpine who notes in his book *Being the Bad Guys*:

>...in the eyes of much of Western society, Christianity is the bad guy (or at least is fast becoming so). Christianity is the problem. And it happened so quickly but it's taken us by surprise.

>Only a few generations ago, Christianity was the good guy, the solution to what was bad. Rather than being on the wrong side of the law, we were the law. Christian morality was assumed and passed mainly unchallenged. The cultural, legal and political power structures affirmed Christians. Then something changed. Over the course of the twentieth century, we became just one of the guys: one option among many-a voice to be considered but not to be followed unquestioningly. If Christianity worked for you, fine; if it didn't work for me, also fine.

>Most of us think we still live in that world. Most Christian books, sermons and podcasts assume that we do. In many ways, we've only just worked out how to live well as one of the guys.

>But the problem is that that's not where we are now. The tide has shifted further. Increasingly Christianity is viewed as the bad guy. Christianity is no longer an option; it's a problem. The cultural, political and legal guns that Christianity once held are now trained on us - and it's happened quickly. The number of those professing faith has fallen dramatically. The number of those who reject the faith they held until their late teens has risen dramatically. The seat at the cultural table that we assumed was ours for keeps is increasingly being given to others. We're on the wrong side of history, the wrong side of so many issues and conversations. If this were a Western, we would be the guys wearing the black hats whose appearance is accompanied by the foreboding soundtrack. It's come as a surprise, we're not sure how it happened, we don't

like it, and we don't feel we deserve it - but we are the bad guys now. [220]

A good example of what McAlpine is talking about is provided by the 2022 report from Canada on how to deal with 'systemic racism and discrimination' in the Canadian armed forces.

Recommendation 6 of this report concerns forces chaplains. It declares:

> It is necessary as well to recognize that, for some Canadians, religion can be a source of suffering and generational trauma. This is especially true for many lesbian, gay, bisexual, transgender, queer and two-spirited members of Canadian society. And Indigenous Peoples have suffered unimaginable generational trauma and genocide at the hands of Christian religious leaders through initiatives such as Residential School and Indian Day School programs.

> Another important point is that, at present, some chaplains represent or are affiliated with organized religions whose beliefs are not synonymous with those of a diverse and inclusive workplace. Some of the affiliated religions of these chaplains do not subscribe to an open attitude and the promotion of diversity.

> For example, some churches' exclusion of women from their priesthoods violates principles of equality and social justice, as do sexist notions embedded in their religious dogmas. In addition, certain faiths have strict tenets requiring conversion of those they deem to be 'pagan,' or who belong to polytheistic religions. These faiths' dogmas and practices conflict with the commitment of the Defence Team to value equality and inclusivity at every level of the workplace.

[220] Stephen McAlpine, *Being the Bad Guys* (Epsom: Good Book Company, 2021), Kindle edition, p.11.

If the Defence Team rejects gender discrimination, anti-Indigenous discrimination, and racialized discrimination in every other area and is working hard to remove systemic barriers to the employment of marginalized people, it cannot justify hiring representatives of organizations who marginalize certain people or categorically refuse them a position of leadership.[221]

What the authors of the report are proposing is discrimination against Christians (and also Muslims and Jews). Christians, the recommendation suggests, should not be hired as chaplains because the faith they represent makes them 'bad guys' whose values contradict those of the Canadian military. [222]

Until very recently a recommendation so hostile to Christianity would have been inconceivable. In the next chapter we shall go on to explore why it is now not only conceivable but has actually been made.

We shall look at why it is that the Western world has become secular in the sense described by Marshall, why the Christian world view has been widely superseded by an alternative view of the nature of the world and of human existence within it, and why this new existence of this alternative world view has led to Christian being regarded as the 'bad guys' whose freedoms may be rightly restricted.

---

[221] *Minister of National Defence Advisory Panel on Systemic Racism and Discrimination – Final Report – January 2022,* Part III section 6, Redefining Chaplaincy at https://www.canada.ca/en/department-national-defence/corporate/reports-publications/mnd-advisory-panel-systemic-racism-discrimination-final-report-jan-2022.html

[222] As the Canadian CARDUS think tank points out: 'This commentary demonstrates thinly veiled hostility to a number of Abrahamic religions including adherents of Islam, Judaism, Catholicism, Eastern Orthodoxy, and Protestantism. It shows gross ignorance of the teachings of these faiths and presents caricatures of their adherents as violators of equality and social justice. This defamatory language goes so far as to equate adherents of monotheistic religions with racism.' CARDUS, 'Memo: Redefining Chaplaincy,' 29 April 2022 at https://www.cardus.ca/research/faith-communities/policy-memo/memo-redefining-chaplaincy/.

Chapter 5
Why Christians are the bad guys in a world without God

1.   The development of a world without God

Anyone who watches mainstream Western media might very easily conclude that we live in a world from which God is absent. The content will assume as an unspoken but generally accepted truth that what happens in the world is the result of either the activity of blind natural forces or the activity of human beings. It is acknowledged, of course, that religious believers of various kinds do exist, but a Christian view of the world in which God himself is present and active is certainly not what is reflected in the vast bulk of the content. What is reflected instead is the assumption of God's absence.

The Covid 19 pandemic

Media coverage of the Covid 19 pandemic reveals this point very clearly. In the Church of England's *Book of Common Prayer* there is a section entitled 'Prayers and Thanksgivings upon several occasions.' This section includes the following prayer of intercession for use 'In the time of any common Plague or Sickness':

> O Almighty God, who in thy wrath didst send a plague upon thine own people in the wilderness, for their obstinate rebellion against Moses and Aaron; and also, in the time of king David, didst slay with the plague of pestilence threescore and ten thousand, and yet remembering thy mercy didst save the rest: Have pity upon us miserable sinners, who now are visited with great sickness and mortality; that like as thou didst then accept of an atonement, and didst command the destroying Angel to cease from punishing, so it

may now please thee to withdraw from us this plague and grievous sickness; through Jesus Christ our Lord. Amen.[223]

It also includes a matching prayer of thanksgiving 'For Deliverance from the Plague, or other common Sickness.' This prayer runs:

O Lord God, who hast wounded us for our sins, and consumed us for our transgressions, by thy late heavy and dreadful visitation; and now, in the midst of judgement remembering mercy, hast redeemed our souls from the jaws of death: We offer unto thy fatherly goodness ourselves, our souls and bodies which thou hast delivered, to be a living sacrifice unto thee, always praising and magnifying thy mercies in the midst of thy Church; through Jesus Christ our Lord. Amen.[224]

These prayers refer to the Old Testament accounts of the plagues sent by God upon the people of Israel during their journey through the wilderness and during the time of king David (Numbers 16:41-50, Numbers 21:4-9, 2 Samuel 24:1-15 and 1 Chronicles 21:1-30). They set outbreaks of plague in a clear theological framework, seeing the cause of plague as God's judgement upon sin and its removal as an act of God's undeserved mercy in Christ for which thanksgiving is rightly due.

In the vast amount of Western media coverage of the Covid 19 pandemic this theological dimension was totally missing. The outbreak of the pandemic was attributed to this worldly causes (the two favourite explanations being transfer from the natural world due to poor hygiene at a Chinese food market, or accidental release from a Chinese laboratory) and its containment was seen to be due to the lockdown measures imposed by governments and the development and roll out of vaccines. God didn't feature in the picture.

---

[223] *The Book of Common Prayer*, (Cambridge: Cambridge University Press, N.D.), p.40.
[224] *The Book of Common Prayer,* p.45.

The Covid 19 pandemic was the most world-changing event of recent times and yet, in the view of the Western world as reflected in its media, God (assuming he even exists) had nothing to do with either its outbreak or its containment.

It can also be argued that the unimportance attached to God was shown by the fact that many governments around the world, including the governments of the United States and the United Kingdom, legally enforced the closure of churches during the Covid pandemic on the grounds that holding services of public worships did not constitute an essential public service.

In the words of Roger Kiska, commenting on the situation in the United Kingdom:

> ...these restrictions on freedom of worship are... an indicator of the level of value the government esteems church attendance and participation in a church community. While someone in the United Kingdom is free to purchase alcohol (both off-license and licensed), go to a bicycle shop, secure a loan, go to the chiropractor or dry cleaner, or any other number of activities, church attendance is punishable by fine or forced physical removal to their home. Furthermore, while the government allows churches to continue to function in their public outreach providing services for the vulnerable, they clearly miss the point as to the primary spiritual role of churches. Sadly, it is just another sign of how we have lost the Christian heart of the nation.[225]

The war in Ukraine

A further example of this assumed absence of God can be found in the media coverage of the war in Ukraine. It is acknowledged that there is a religious dimension to the war, but this dimension has to do with the attitudes and actions of the religious believers involved with it in some

---

[225] Roger Kiska, 'Assessing the Coronavirus Act 2020: what you need to know,' *Christian Concern*, 17 April2020 at: https://christianconcern.com/resource/ assessing-the-coronavirus-act-2020-what-you-need-to-know/.

way (as in the case of the support for the Russian war effort provided by the leadership of the Russian Orthodox Church) rather than with any action by God himself.

In the Bible and the subsequent Christian tradition it is held that God either allows wars to happen as a result of his providential government of the world, or actively causes them to happen for the furtherance of his good purposes, and that it is therefore right to pray to God to bring a war to an end, with the outcome of the war being the one he has intended.

This traditional Christian viewpoint is once again reflected in the *Book of Common Prayer* in which the prayer 'In the time of War and Tumults' runs:

O Almighty God, King of all kings, and Governor of all things, whose power no creature is able to resist, to whom it belongeth justly to punish sinners, and to be merciful to them that truly repent: Save and deliver us, we humbly beseech thee, from the hands of our enemies; abate their pride, asswage their malice, and confound their devices; that we, being armed with thy defence, may be preserved evermore from all perils, to glorify thee, who art the only giver of all victory; through the merits of thy only Son, Jesus Christ our Lord. Amen.[226]

The corresponding thanksgiving 'For Peace and Deliverance from our Enemies' then goes:

O Almighty God, who art a strong tower of defence unto thy servants against the face of their enemies: We yield thee praise and thanksgiving for our deliverance from those great and apparent dangers wherewith we were compassed: We acknowledge it thy goodness that we were not delivered over as a prey unto them; beseeching thee still to continue such thy mercies towards us, that

---

[226] *The Book of Common Prayer*, pp.39-40.

all the world may know that thou art our Saviour and mighty Deliverer; through Jesus Christ our Lord. Amen.

In the Western media, and Western society as whole, the understanding of God's relationship to war reflected in these prayers has once again been totally absent in relation to the war in Ukraine. God is seen as playing no part at all in what is going on. What is happening is seen as solely the result of human choices and activity.

The question that these two examples raise is how the Western world reached this 'secular' state of affairs where God's absence is thus assumed.

The rise of incredulity

In the first part of this chapter, I shall explore the answer to this question. Numerous studies have been made of this topic,[227] but I shall be drawing on the overview of the reasons for this development provided by Duncan MacLaren in the section 'The Rise of Incredulity' his 2004 book *Mission Implausible – Restoring Credibility to the Church.* [228] I have chosen to draw on MacLaren's work because it provides a useful synthesis of the work of a variety of other scholars working in this field.

MacLaren notes that there have been three 'broad types of explanation for secularization.' The first attributes it to the development of ideas.

---

[227] See for example Callum Brown, *The Death of Christian Britain* (London, Routledge, 2000), Steve Bruce, *God is Dead: Secularization in the West* (Oxford: Blackwell, 2002), Owen Chadwick, *The Secularization of the European Mind in the Nineteenth Century* (Cambridge: CUP, 1974), Os Guinness, *The Gravedigger File* (London: Hodder & Stoughton, 1987) and Charles Taylor, *A Secular Age* (Cambridge Mass and London: The Belknap Press of Harvard University Press, 2007).
[228] Duncan MacLaren, *Mission Implausible – Restoring Credibility to the Church* (Milton Keynes: Paternoster Press, 2004).

The second links it to a set of social processes. The third sees it as spread by a set of institutional carriers. [229]

a. The development of ideas

In terms of the development of ideas, Maclaren argues that 'three streams of thinking can be identified which give reasons for the decline in Christian thinking and its social significance: the Enlightenment, the growth of science, and the rise of ideology.'[230]

The Enlightenment

Looking first at the Enlightenment, Maclaren writes that this is a term which refers to 'a relatively short period of intellectual endeavour,' which was 'concentrated in the latter half of the eighteenth century' but which is 'often seen as a pivotal moment in the birth of the modern world.' [231] Building on the work of the American missiologist David Bosch,[232] he suggests that seven elements of Enlightenment thought can be seen as paving the way to modern secularism.

- **An emphasis on unaided human reason**

First, the Enlightenment privileged unaided human reason:

> ....as the sole arbiter of knowledge at the expense of traditional sources of theology, such as church tradition, religious experience, and God's revelation in scripture and the natural world.[233]

The result of this way of thinking has been to lead people to the view that religion does not provide us with real knowledge. 'In the modern

---

[229] MacLaren, p.15.

[230] MacLaren, p.16.

[231] Maclaren, p.16. For an introduction to the Enlightenment see Norman Hampson, *The Enlightenment* (London: Penguin, 1990).

[232] The work by Bosch to which MacLaren refers is David Bosch, *Believing in the Future: Towards a Missiology of Western Culture* (Harrisburg: Trinity Press International, 1995).

[233] MacLaren, p.18.

world, the bus timetable counts as real knowledge: the Beatitudes do not.' [234]

It is worth noting on this point that the issue here is not whether it is right for human beings to employ reason. It has been universally accepted within the Christian tradition that the capacity for exercising reason is an intrinsic part of what it means to be a human person (hence the Christian philosopher Boethius' famous definition of a person as being 'an individual substance of a rational nature'[235]). The issue is rather the view of certain influential thinkers that the use of reason precluded making use of traditional Christian sources of knowledge.

- **The critical investigation of the world (and God)**

Secondly, the Enlightenment's division of the world:

> ...into thinking subjects, and objects suitable for analysis and exploitation, led 'man' (and they were men, not women) to become the inquisitor and critic of all reality. Where once nature had been our teacher, now it became our laboratory. Under pressure from this critical principle, the biblical view of the cosmos could no longer be taken on trust, but everything became potential fodder for critical evaluation...just as nature and humanity were placed under the microscope so too was the Bible subjected to critical historical scholarship, casting doubt on its claim to be inspired. Finally, too, even God himself was treated to the same epistemological critique. [236]

According to MacLaren, the result of the development of this critical approach to the investigation of reality has been that:

---

[234] MacLaren, p.19.
[235] Boethius, 'A Treatise Against Eutyches and Nestorius', in H F Stewart *The Theological Tractates* (London: Heinemann, 1918), p.85.
[236] McLaren, p.20.

We have lost our sense of awe and humility before the mysteries of nature and her creator. We have become like the first-year undergraduate who, in a single, disdainful sentence dismisses the life-time's work of an eminent professor. When all is dubious, faith is hard to come by; if our minds are open at both ends, no belief can be held for long. Contemporary people how become compulsive doubters left with no criteria according to which they could believe and no evidence that would ever provide sufficient criteria upon which they could base their trust.[237]

To put it another way, if the Middle Ages can be criticised as an age of excessive credulity, the modern era can be seen as having swung to the opposite extreme with belief in God becoming subject to the same degree of scepticism as everything else.

- **The exclusion of purpose**

Thirdly, the Enlightenment:

...excluded the category of purpose from rational explanation, in favour of causal explanations. A rainbow in the sky was no longer explained in terms of the covenant of God, but as a consequence of the refraction of light. This implied that the universe is a closed system unfolding along predetermined and mechanistic lines. Causal explanations were then treated as fact, whereas explanations in terms of purpose could only be held as private beliefs. [238]

The result of this exclusion of purpose was to make both Christian ethics and the biblical account of God's free action in the world seem increasingly implausible:

...if we no longer know the purpose for which human beings have been created, we have no means of knowing whether or not they are living a right - a mechanistic universe is of necessity an amoral

---

[237] MacLaren, p.20.
[238] MacLaren, p.21.

universe. Without a Christian anthropology, Christian ethics appears as an implausible, arbitrary imposition upon human freedom. Furthermore, the loss of explanations in terms of purpose meant that events in history ceased to be viewed within the framework of the coming kingdom of God. Today, to ask how God is at work in some situation (say, in a general election) would most likely be met with incomprehension or ridicule. Yet the story throughout scripture is the story of a God at work in history -on the battlefield, the storm-tossed sea and the marriage bed. If we can no longer talk of the purposes of God in society and history, it is little wonder that contemporary people struggle to believe the biblical narrative. A world rich with sacred significance has given way to a prosaic, mechanistic view of ourselves and our world. [239]

- **The pursuit of progress**

Fourthly, the Enlightenment was preoccupied with the pursuit of progress. In MacLaren's words:

History may have come to be viewed as without purpose, but this did not stop people inventing one. It has been suggested that Christian eschatology (the doctrine of the 'last things') was simply replaced by secular doctrines of historical progress. [240]

Furthermore, comments MacLaren, belief in human progress continues to dominate people's thinking today:

Despite the twentieth century being the bloodiest the world has ever seen, the belief in progress is still with us. The story of the emancipation of women, the black civil -rights struggle in America, and the emergence of the welfare state in Europe, all testify to the reality of progress in the sphere of politics. Even more striking is the progress of science and technology. We have come to expect that 'new' will mean 'new-improved,' and 'old' will mean 'obsolete'...Science and technology even more than politics, embody

[239] MacLaren, p.21.
[240] MacLaren, p.21.

the ideal of progress in a forceful and convincing way. The sheer instrumental utility of technology is hard to argue with; it confers upon technology a high degree of prestige; technology, like a celebrity at a party, creates an excited buzz, a *frisson*.[241]

'Against the gleaming backdrop of cutting-edge technology,' writes MacLaren:

Christian faith looks a little tired. Its homely doctrine of providence - God is working his purpose out as year succeeds year - cannot compete with the adrenaline-rush injected by scientific and technological progress. Nor can its story compete with technology's underlying evolutionary narrative. More than that, whereas progress exalts the idea of the 'new,' Christianity trades on the value of the 'old,' the traditional, and the authoritative. In a world bewitched by progress, Christianity suffers cognitive dissonance; it tries to tell the old, old story, but people think they have heard it before. Who wants to hear the obsolete, obsolete story? In the modern world, then, while science, 'is a constantly successful - or rather, perhaps better, confident – form of practice, in the West the church is not.' [242]

- **The separation between facts, beliefs and values**

Fifthly, the Enlightenment created a separation between facts on the one hand and beliefs and values on the other:

Facts belong in the public sphere, the sphere of common concern, whereas beliefs, since they cannot be proven with certainty, were gradually consigned to the private dimension of people's lives, along with values, preferences and opinions. Beliefs that were once taken for granted as immutable truths about the world -the reality of creation, sin, judgement and redemption -were relegated to the private sphere of personal interest and whim. Today, to talk

[241] MacLaren, p.22.
[242] MacLaren, pp.22-23 quoting Colin Gunton, *A Brief Theology of Revelation* (Edinburgh: T&T Clark, 1995), p.92, n.11.

theology in public is to commit a social *faux pas*. There is a widely held taboo towards conversation on the religious themes. Try talking about God as a public reality and you will quickly find yourself surrounded by wry, embarrassed, pitying smiles.[243]

Furthermore, if the objects of Christian belief:

...are continually treated as not being real in any objective sense, it becomes difficult even for Christians to maintain the sense that their beliefs refer to something – or someone - real, out there. The privatisation of belief is therefore more than simply a cognitive curfew; it involves the forced adoption of a split personality; it is a tacit invitation to self-deception – to maintain in private a set of beliefs as if they were objectively true, while at the same time living a public life that requires the denial or suppression of these beliefs. No wonder faith is hard to sustain when it is stripped of its sense of reality and denied a public voice.[244]

- **The responsibility of human beings to make things better**

Sixthly, the Enlightenment emphasised the responsibility of human beings to sort out their own problems. To quote MacLaren:

The human condition was no longer to be accepted as inevitable, nor the world to be regarded as a veil of tears to be endured with resignation while we await salvation. Instead, the feeling arose that it was incumbent upon humanity to make full use of human ingenuity to change adverse circumstances, and that all problems were common in principle, solvable.[245]

MacLaren dubs this approach the 'melioristic attitude,' and he writes that:

[243] MacLaren, p.23.
[244] MacLaren, p.23.
[245] MacLaren, pp.23-24.

Meleorism means that humans sought to ameliorate the suffering of the human condition through technical and political means - improved agriculture, industrial technology, medical research, welfare provision - rather than practising prayer, incantation, or spell. This attitude has not made prayer entirely obsolete: there are still crises beyond the reach of modern medicine for which prayer is the only resort. Yet, typically, in the face of practical problems prayer is a last resort, or at best a mere accompaniment to proven technical procedures. The overwhelming practical success of modern technology and the modern welfare state has thrown Christian faith into a crisis of relevance.[246]

- **Autonomy versus religious authority**

Finally, the Enlightenment's emphasis on unaided human reason led Enlightenment thinkers to challenge the tradition of submission to religious authority in favour of an emphasis on individual human intellectual autonomy. In MacLaren's words:

...the Enlightenment rejected the idea of truth as the preserve of an authoritative elite. If reason is the short route to knowledge, it follows that, in principle, every person has equal access to the truth, and need not depend upon the pronouncements of a prophet or priest.[247]

As MacLaren goes on to write:

In reality, the key thinkers of the Enlightenment were themselves authorities: indeed, it may be truer to describe this shift not from authority to autonomy, but from the authority the church to the authority of the academy. Nevertheless, the legacy of this contrast can still be encountered today in the widespread assumption that to be religiously committed involves a 'leap of faith' - an irrational step into the arms of some or other authority which claims privileged

---

[246] MacLaren, p.24 drawing on A D Gilbert, *The Making of Post-Christian-Britain: A History of the Secularization of Modern Society* (London: Longman, 1980), p.32.
[247] MacLaren, p.24.

access to the truth. The possibility that submission to an authoritative religious tradition may be a rational step to take is less easily acknowledged.[248]

Summarising the impact of the Enlightenment's ideas

MacLaren summarises the impact of these seven Enlightenment ideas as follows:

> Summarising the above, a range of consequences emerge. Christian beliefs are treated as a second rate form of knowledge, or fail to count as knowledge at all. God is reduced to a plausible hypothesis - one more object in a crowded world of objects that we can doubt and ultimately ignore. We no longer seek any pattern or meaning in the accidental events of history or in our lives: success and suffering alike have no meaning. At the same time, we believe things are getting better all the time and that human ingenuity has replaced the need for God. Religious conversation is taboo, resulting in wide ignorance of Christian content and vocabulary. Christianity is perceived to be largely irrelevant to everyday problems. And, if someone is going to be religious, they will be more inclined to mix and match a creed for themselves then to submit to the authority of historic Christianity.[249]

The rise of science

MacLaren explains that the rise of modern science from the seventeenth to the nineteenth centuries has been seen to have contributed to the development of secularism in two ways.

First, it led to a distinction between religious knowledge and the secular knowledge represented by science, with the latter being seen as replacing the former. This was because 'science cultivated a field of human awareness in which religious consciousness was epistemologically irrelevant' (for example, you don't need to be a religious believer to study biochemistry or astrophysics) and because

---

[248] MacLaren, p.25.
[249] MacLaren, p.25.

'science formulated hypotheses to explain aspects of human experience hitherto only explicable in supernaturalistic terms.' The theory of evolution as developed by Charles Darwin provides the classic example of the latter point. Since the mid nineteenth century the theory of evolution has been widely seen as providing an explanation for the development of life on earth which excludes the need to invoke the action of God.[250]

Secondly, the two points just mentioned mean that in popular consciousness religion has become increasingly marginalised as science has come to replace theology as the most prestigious way to understand the world. That which is 'scientific' is regarded as reliable and authoritative, which is why the opinions of a scientist are generally given more weight than those of a religious leader. The prestige now attached to science is shown in the British context, for example, by the way in which the BBC constantly runs prime time television series on science but has never in living memory run a similar series on theology.

This means that 'scientism,' the idea that science alone can provide a satisfactory explanation of the world, is the 'cognitive style' which has come to dominate the modern world.

To quote Maclaren again, whereas:

> Christian faith once enjoyed the prestige now conferred on science; today it no longer does. It once provided the lens through which people made sense of their world; it now represents a deviant cognitive style. We expect our doctor to apply her medical knowledge to our ailments in attempts to heal them - we do not expect to benefit from her theological wisdom. Theology has precious few footholds in the modern world.[251]

---

[250] For an influential modern re-statement of this idea see Richard Dawkins, *The Blind Watchmaker* (London: Penguin, 2006).
[251] MacLaren, p.29.

The rise of ideology

The growth of scientism is an example of the third reason for the displacement of religion in the realm of ideas, the development of alternative non-religious ideologies. In MacLaren's words:

> As John Milbank and others have argued, a secular society did not simply emerge as a blank space left by a retreating church: the secular sphere had to be imagined every bit as much as the sacred cosmos that preceded it, and ideological systems functioned to conceive of that sphere, and to bar the door to the church's re-entry.[252]

In addition to scientism, other examples of such ideologies are Marxism, secular humanism, romanticism, nihilism and existentialism, each of which in their own way provide Western society with alternatives to Christian belief.

b. Social processes

As MacLaren goes on to remind us, although the ideas generated by the Enlightenment have been important contributors to secularization, 'ideas do not float freely in the ether.'[253] As he explains:

> It is too simple to imagine that a grand philosopher of the Enlightenment thinks a new thought, and that this new thought is somehow gossip down through the ranks until it settles as an unexamined assumption in the consciousness of the plough-boy. Ideas do not simply float down through the intellectual strata like flakes of snow. Instead, ideas are carried and ideas are driven. They are embodied in brains and books and social structures, and these in turn are influenced by flows of capital, power, or personnel. In other words, ideas must be carried within social institutions of one sort or another, and they are subject to the forces at work within those institutions. A sociological explanation for religious decline

---

[252] MacLaren, p.29 referring to John Milbank, *Theology and Social Theory* (Oxford: Blackwell, 1990).
[253] MacLaren, p.31.

will therefore have to go beyond the history of ideas to consider both the processes or *catalysts* - of change in modernity, and the *institutional carriers* of change.[254]

Those who have studied the social processes that have acted as the catalysts of secularization are agreed that they can be traced back to the growth of industrial societies as a result of the Industrial Revolution, first in Britain and then in the Western world as a whole.

The social changes brought about by industrialization

As MacLaren explains, the process of industrialization led to a whole series of related social changes:

Apart from the obvious process of the *industrialization* of production, and the development of technology, the Industrial Revolution brought with it a range of associated processes. Industrialization required labour to be concentrated in one place, and so required the growth of cities. In other words, *urbanization* went hand in hand with it. The city, in turn, facilitated the specialization of roles and institutions. There is no point in everyone baking their own bread when a single baker can supply the local community more cheaply and efficiently. Roles and institutions therefore became *differentiated* from one another: in place of the rural home as a centre of production, products and services came to be increasingly supplied but a growing number of specialised agencies: the butcher, the baker, the candlestick maker, and so forth. Differentiation along class lines also took place. These different spheres of work encouraged the proliferation of different sub-cultures, which in turn fostered a growing variety of lifestyles and beliefs. The process by which institutions and lifestyles proliferated has been termed *pluralization*. Furthermore, as roles and institutions became increasingly differentiated, society became more complex, more interdependent, and more in need of some form of overarching organization. Two additional processes flowed

[254] MacLaren, pp.31-32.

out of this need for overall coordination: one is the process of *societalization* in which life became increasingly organised not at the level of a local community, but of a whole society, and chiefly of the nation state; the other was the process of *bureaucratization* in which local, face-to -face relationships were replaced by structured encounters within a bureaucratic framework. In such encounters people meet within prescribed roles (doctor/patient, consultant/client, waitress/diner) and typically observe set rules of engagement. The expansion of a rationalised bureaucratic sphere of relations threw into stark relief the kind of local personal relationships that belong between friends and relatives. One is personal and private, the other impersonal and public. (Sociologists call them 'mechanical' and 'organic' solidarity, respectively.) In this way, modernity brings with it one further process: *privatization*. Human friendships, domestic life, feelings, leisure, marriage, children and religious faith belong in the private sphere. Impersonal roles, work, and a range of public institutions, including those of politics, economics, health, welfare, education and law belong in the public sphere.[255]

Each of the seven changes italicised in this quotation can be seen as having contributed in different ways to the overarching process of secularization.

- *Industrialization* involved the increasing use of technology which in turn contributed to a growing indifference towards God: 'Why ask God to do something that he may or may not do (such as heal a sick person) when the technology that has been developed that will do it for certain?' [256]

- *Urbanization* 'seems to have disrupted local Christian communities, fostered alternatives, and disseminated A cognitive style that is antagonistic to traditional believing.' It

---

[255] MacLaren, pp.31-32.
[256] MacLaren, p.35.

acted as 'an incubator in which the consequences of the other process could rapidly multiply and disseminate.'[257]

- *Differentiation* led to the diminishment of the social importance of the clergy as aspects of their traditional roles such as, for example, teachers, doctors, magistrates, social workers, academics and counsellors were taken on by other secular figures. It further led to the emergence of a working class that was often either indifferent or hostile to religion (which was seen as reflecting the tastes and interests of the middle and upper classes). It also led to people's identities being increasingly linked with the technology involved in the means of production and hence to the displacement of God by technology noted above. [258]

- *Societalization:* 'upset the local organization of human life and, in so doing, disrupted the soil in which religion most readily flourished. To put it another way 'the intimacy of local relationships within a stable universe of meaning provided a settled soil for Christian faith to flourish.' The shift in the organization of social life from the local community to the mass society tore up this soil.' [259]

- *Pluralization* has contributed to secularization because it 'greatly increases the options available to modern people, and the psychological impact of this increase continues to undermine the plausibility of religious beliefs and, in particular, their absolute overarching claims.' [260]

- *Privatization* resulting from *Bureaucratization* has meant the evacuation of religion from the public sphere -from politics, economy, law, education, welfare and health provision -to the

[257] MacLaren, pp.38-39.
[258] MacLaren, pp.40-41.
[259] MacLaren, p.43.
[260] MacLaren, p.46.

private sphere of leisure and family life.' The consequence has been that 'Christian practice ceased to be the shared way of life for the majority of people, and was demoted to the status of a private preference or interest for those who like that sort of thing.' [261]

c. Institutional carriers

Building on the work of James Hunter in his 1996 article 'What is modernity?' [262] MacLaren identifies three institutional carriers of secularism, 'industrial capitalism,' 'the nation state' and 'the knowledge sector.'

Industrial capitalism

MacLaren defines industrial capitalism as 'the particular marriage of technology and capital which characterizes the economies of modern, industrialized nations.' [263] It was this marriage of capital and technology that led to the Industrial Revolution and the development of modern industrial societies, which in turn led to the social processes resulting in secularization that were outlined in the previous section of this chapter. Without the marriage of capital and technology these social processes would not have occurred.

The nation state

According to MacLaren the modern Western nation state has become a carrier of secularization in two ways.

First, the modern nation state takes a stance of religious neutrality, with its role being to act as a 'guardian of fair play between religions.' This is because any attempt to 'enforce the claims of one religion' would 'constitute an attack on the highly rationalized and specialized nature' of the economic order on which the modern nation state depends.[264] To

---

[261] Maclaren, p.47.
[262] James Hunter, 'What is Modernity?' in P Sampson, V Samuel and C Sugden (eds), *Faith and Modernity* (Oxford: Regnum/Lynx, 1996), pp.12-28.
[263] MacLaren, p.49.
[264] MacLaren, p.50.

put it simply, the modern nation state depends on people being able to fulfil their economic roles regardless of their religion or lack of it. This religious neutrality of the state can be seen as a good thing in terms of allowing freedom of religion, but it also reduces the social importance of religion, contributing to its privatization as discussed above.

Secondly, the modern nation state has ceased to base its legitimacy on religious grounds. MacLaren quotes the observation that in the modern world there has been a: 'shift in the location of decision making in human groups from elites claiming special access to supernatural ordinances to elites legitimating their authority by references to other bases of power.' [265] Thus, in contemporary Western nation states governments claim legitimacy on the basis of the will of the people as reflected in election results, rather than on the basis of appointment by God. As before, there is here an elimination of the importance of religion in the public sphere.

The knowledge sector

MacLaren uses the term 'the knowledge sector' to refer to 'any institution that disseminates 'knowledge,' such as schools or universities.'[266] Because the knowledge sector is a rather abstract concept, MacLaren focusses on the impact of the 'mass media' which he uses as a 'convenient term to describe a range of communications media as diverse as billboard advertising, film, newspapers, magazines, radio and television' (and today we would have to add the internet).[267]

In Maclaren's view the impact of the mass media has contributed to secularization in three ways.

[265] MacLaren, p.50 quoting Bryan Wilson, 'Secularization: The Inherited Model' in Phillip Hammond (ed), *The Sacred in a Secular Age* (Berkeley: University of California Press, 1985), p.12.
[266] MacLaren, p.51.
[267] MacLaren, p.51.

First, it has led to an increasing cultural homogenization in which the norms of a secular urban elite are spread across the country and throughout society. [268]

Secondly the influence of the mass media has led to a 'communal passivity' in which 'people less and less frequently engage in communal activities, which includes churchgoing.' [269]

Thirdly the mass media has major influence on pluralization by encouraging cultural relativism:

The mass media are the primary means by which alternative options for lifestyle, purchases beliefs, and so on, are disseminated, and it is arguably through the mass media that the relativising of beliefs and norms most effectively it takes place. [270]

Summarizing the importance of the institutional carriers of secularization, MacLaren writes:

In sum, the narrative of secularisation would be incomplete without taking into account the impact of three institutional carriers of modernity. Industrial capitalism has acted as a powerful catalyst, able to generate powerful processes that have been corrosive of religious life in Britain. The nation state has jettisoned its former alliance with religious forms of legitimation and looked elsewhere for justification. And the knowledge sector – pre-eminently the mass media -have disseminated secular, urban norms, discouraged communal activity (Including churchgoing), and streamlined attention away from eternal realities to the mundane. These three have carried the processes identified at the start of this chapter,

---

[268] MacLaren, p.51.

[269] McLaren, p.51.

[270] MaClaren, p.52. Os Guinness reinforces this last point when he notes that: 'The heightened awareness of the presence of others leads automatically to a sense of the possibilities for oneself. Modern people scan the cultural smorgasbord and say: *Their* cuisine, *their* customs, *their* convictions all become *our* choices, *our* options, *our* possibilities. '(Guinness, p.100).

ensuring that the flow of secularising ideas is not progressed merely in books and brains and speeches, but also through being embodied in the very structures of social life.[271]

While MacLaren focuses in this quotation on what has taken place in Britain, what he says in it is true across the Western world in general. The institutional carriers of modernity have had the same effect in Helsinki, Auckland, or Toronto as they have had in London or Edinburgh.

2. A new understanding of what it means to be human

What has gone hand in hand with the secularisation of the Western world has been the emergence, in what is known as 'post modernity,' of a new understanding of what it means to be human. This understanding has at its heart the notion of absolute personal autonomy. In the absence of God, human beings become their own creators and so to live well means to live according to our own vision of who we are and how we feel we should live.

As the Church of England Doctrine Commission report *The Mystery of Salvation* puts it:

In our postmodern culture self-fulfilment has become a matter of individually self-chosen goals. Freedom - in the sense of the absolute autonomy of the individual - must become the single, overarching ideal to which all other goals are subordinated. I must be free to be whoever I choose to be and to pursue whatever good I define for myself. There must be no normative goals, models, or ideals for which I should aim. The point is not simply that there *are* no such normative goals, but that there *must* be none, if I am to be truly free to be myself - to be the self I choose to make myself. Needless to say this contentless freedom is much more of an ideology than a reality. Most of us in fact seek fulfilment in goals presented enticingly to us by society, not least by commercial interests, as those normally thought desirable - in specially in

271 MacLaren, p.52.

sexual relationships, work and an affluent lifestyle. But these are ideologically packaged as a means to a freely chosen, non-normative path of self-creation. This ideological packaging is seductive. It leads people to set great value on, for example, freedom to buy things (consumer choice) and freedom from long term commitment in relationships - understanding these things as important to their self-fulfilment. [272]

As the report goes on to say, this ideology of self-fulfilment necessarily involves the rejection of God:

The roots of this particular ideology of self-fulfilment lie in the rejection of God and it requires the rejection of God. This is because it envisages freedom as absolute autonomy. The freedom it desires is not freedom to discover and to embrace truth and goodness for oneself, but freedom to create one's own truth and goodness for oneself. 'God' Is only conceivable as a kind of function of one's freedom, and is some debased forms of contemporary religion 'God' becomes a mere means to the religious persons self-fulfilment -a genie in their lamp. [273]

A similar account of the dominant anthropology of the Western world has been offered by a range of other writers such as, for example, Richard Bauckham, John Webster and Jonathan Grant.

Richard Bauckham writes:

Much of the modern age, with its distinctive aspirations and achievements, has been inspired by a vision of human beings as the sovereign subjects of history, capable of transcending all limits and mastering all the conditions of their life. Freedom is conceived as radical independence. Nothing is received, who is to be freely

---

[272] The Doctrine Commission of the Church of England, *The Mystery of Salvation* (London: CHP, 1995), p.34. Italics in the original.
[273] The Doctrine Commission, p.34.

chosen. Freedom is the freedom to make of oneself what one chooses. Human beings aspire to be, in effect, their own creators.[274]

John Webster likewise declares that according to the contemporary Western account of what it means to be human, to be human is to be entirely self-legislating:

Being human is not a matter of having a certain nature or being placed within an ordered reality of which I am not the originator; rather, the distinguishing feature of humankind is at last resort, the will. The agent is characterised, above all, not as a sort of substance, but as enacted intention. The subject is agent, and in her action is demonstrated her capacity for the self-determination which is freedom: in free action, the human subject is self-positing.

Making self-constitution from humanly fundamental is, in the end, erratically constructivist. Accordingly, freedom is inseparable from self-government. The freedom which the agent realizes in voluntary act of self-constitution is to be understood as autonomy. The agent id free in so far as she is autonomous, literally, a law to herself. 'Law' – that is to say, the norms by which we govern action, make discriminations between policies and hold up practices for evaluation – is thus radically internalized. Classically conceived, law is the structure of given reality ('nature') and the imperative force of that reality. To say that reality is law is to say that it presents itself to us as an order which requires me to be shaped by and to act in accordance with its given character. On a modern (and a postmodern) account of freedom, by contrast, 'law' is not an externally derived norm, but rather a corollary of my most fundamental activity of self -projection or self-constitution. It bears upon me only as the object of my choice (political, economic,

---

[274] Richard Bauckham, *God and the Crisis of Freedom* (Louisville and London: John Knox Press, 2002), p.32.

religious, sexual). And so only as a self legislator can I be said to be free.[275]

In his book *Divine Sex*, Jonathan Grant further declares that what the Canadian writer Charles Taylor has called the 'culture of authenticity':

'...encourages us to create our own beliefs and morality, the only rule being that they must resonate with who we feel we really are. The worst thing we can do is to conform to some moral code that is imposed on us from outside - by society, our parents, the church, or whoever else. It is deemed self-evident that any such imposition would undermine our unique identity.

Ultimately, this form of expressive individualism, with each person doing his or her own thing, leads to a form of soft moral relativism: we should not criticise each other's values because each person's right is to live as they wish. The only thing we cannot tolerate is intolerance.'...The authentic self believes that personal meaning must be found within ourselves or at least must resonate with our one-of-a-kind personality, we must as we often hear, 'be true to ourselves.'[276]

The development of this new understanding
If this is the new understanding of what it means to be human that has come to the fore in contemporary, secularized, Western society, the question that arises is how this understanding arose. This question is addressed in Carl Trueman's important study *The Rise and Triumph of the Modern Self*.[277]

In this book Trueman addresses the question of why it is that in contemporary Western society it has come to be regarded as meaningful for someone who identifies as transgender to say 'I am a

---

[275] Webster, p.217.
[276] Jonathan Grant, *Divine Sex* (Grand Rapids: Brazos Press, 2015), p.30.
[277] Carl Trueman, *The Rise and Triumph of the Modern Self* (Wheaton: Crossway, 2020).

woman trapped in a man's body' (and unacceptable to question this statement) when previous generations would have dismissed this statement as completely absurd.

Trueman's answer to this question is that the reason the statement is now regarded as meaningful is because a number of interrelated developments that have taken place across the Western world since the second half of the eighteenth century have together led to a radical shift in what Trueman calls the 'social imaginary'—that is, the way most people understand the world and how to behave within it.

These developments have been as follows:

First, the secularisation of Western society and the consequent loss of the sense of the world as God's creation, means that there has been a shift in people's views of the world from *mimesis* (from the Greek for 'imitation') to *poesis* (meaning 'creating). As Trueman explains:

> A *mimetic* view regards the world as having a given order and a given meaning and thus sees human beings as required to discover that meaning and conform themselves to it. *Poiesis*, by way of contrast, sees the world as so much raw material out of which meaning and purpose can be created by the individual.[278]

Secondly, there has been the related loss of the idea of 'sacred order'. The widespread acceptance of the idea that we live in a Godless, mechanistic and therefore amoral universe means that In Western culture today most people no longer believe that there is fixed moral order which has been set in place by God and which all human beings therefore need to respect.

Thirdly, as a result, Western culture lacks an agreed basis for ethics. So, as Alasdair MacIntyre has argued, the basis of ethical decision-making

---

[278] Trueman, p.740.

has, by default, become mere emotivism—that is, ethics based on personal feeling and preference. [279]

Fourthly, there has also been a change in the way in which most people view the purpose of human existence—the good to which human beings should aspire. What has emerged is what Taylor calls a 'culture of authenticity'. This is an understanding of life that says:

> ...that each of us has his/her own way of realizing our humanity, and that it is important to find and live out one's own way—as against surrendering to conformity with a model imposed on us from outside, by society, or by the previous generation, or religious or political authority.'[280]

Fifthly, there has been the development of what Philip Rieff calls the 'therapeutic society'—a society in which the purpose of social institutions is viewed as being to foster the individual's sense of psychological well-being as they live out their unique authentic existence.[281]

Sixthly, since the work of Sigmund Freud, it has come to be widely believed that 'humans, from infancy onward, are at core sexual beings. It is our sexual desires that are ultimately decisive for who we are.' [282] The acceptance of Freud's ideas has been facilitated by the huge growth in pornography fuelled by the desire of pornographers to make money, but also by the many developments in modern medicine which make the results of sexual activity less serious by separating sex from childbirth and by providing more effective treatment for sexually-transmitted diseases.

Finally, the work of twentieth century Neo-Marxist scholars such as Wilhelm Reich and Herbert Marcuse has led to the idea that the

---

[279] Alastair MacIntyre, *After Virtue* (London: Duckworth, 1983).
[280] Taylor, p.475.
[281] Philip Rieff, *The Triumph of the Therapeutic* (Chicago: Chicago University Press, 1966).
[282] Trueman, p.27.

traditional view of the family (consisting of a married couple and their children), together with the traditional sexual morality linked to this, are inherently oppressive and need to be overthrown.

A new social imaginary

As Trueman argues, the result of these seven developments has been to create a 'social imaginary,' the way 'the way that people think about the world, how they imagine it to be, how they act intuitively in relation to it,[283] that is based on *poiesis* rather than *mimesis*: we live in a world of our creating. In such a world the idea of being a woman trapped in a man's body begins to make sense. On the one hand, there is no fixed order of things, and no fixed pattern for human existence or behaviour; thus, there is no yardstick against which one can measure whether the idea is wrong. On the other, it becomes perfectly natural for an individual to say something such as:

'The purpose of my existence is to live as authentically as possible in accordance with what I perceive to be my true self. If this then involves seeing myself as a woman, even though I have a man's body, then that is what I should do.

Furthermore, society should support me in so doing because only then will I achieve psychological well-being. Thinking otherwise is immoral because it involves damaging my psychological well-being through a refusal to give recognition to who I believe myself to be.'

The same factors create a social imaginary in which the acceptance of same-sex relationships and the claim to a gay or lesbian identity also makes sense. Again, there is no fixed order of things and no fixed pattern for human behaviour, and thus no yardstick against which one can say same-sex relationships are wrong. And so, the individual may often justify an action as follows:

'The purpose of my existence is to live as authentically as possible in accordance with what I perceive to be my true self. If this involves

[283] Trueman, p.37.

having sex with someone of my own sex, then that is what I should do. In addition, because, as Freud has taught us, sexual desire is at the core of human identity, my desire for sex with someone of my own sex defines who I am. I am gay or lesbian.'

As Trueman goes on to say, within this worldview:

'...mere tolerance of homosexuality is bound to become unacceptable. The issue is not one of simply decriminalizing behaviour; that would certainly mean that homosexual acts were tolerated by society, but the acts are only part of the overall problem. The real issue is one of recognition, of recognizing the legitimacy of who the person thinks he actually is. This requires more than mere tolerance, it requires equality before the law and recognition by the law and in society. And that means that those who refuse to grant such recognition will be the ones who find themselves on the wrong side of both the law and emerging social attitudes.

The person who objects to homosexual practice is, in contemporary society, actually objecting to homosexual identity. And the refusal by any individual to recognize an identity that society at large recognizes as legitimate is a moral offense, not simply a matter of indifference.'[284]

This is why LGBTQI+ campaigners react so strongly against the idea that those Christians who object to same-sex sexual relationships can speak of 'hating the sin but loving the sinner'. Within a post-Freudian worldview sexual identity and sexual behaviour cannot be separated. Hence to hate the sin is also to hate the sinner.

An additional but related aspect of modern Western culture is the central place given to personal experience. If there is no fixed moral order, how should individuals decide how they should live? As The answer increasingly is that they should simply 'try it and see'. In other

[284] Trueman, pp.68-69.

words, as they proceed through life they should decide, on the basis of their personal experience, what pattern of life, and what pattern of sexual identity and activity, gives them that sense of psychological well-being which is the proper goal of life.

As Trueman points out, this idea of experience as normative can be found in one of the seminal works of modern Western thought, Jean-Jacques Rousseau's *Confessions*. [285] According to Rousseau, life should be lived on the basis of one's own understanding of one's own individual experience. This approach stands in contrast to the earlier *Confessions* of Augustine.[286] For Augustine what is normative is not his personal experiences, but the teaching of Scripture, since it is only through the witness of Scripture that he is able to make sense of his experiences.

What all this means is that Western society has now reached a place where human beings are playing the role of their own creator, constructing identities for themselves, and testing everything at the solitary bar of their own subjective experience. I am who I think I am on the basis of my unique experience and everybody else must accept this fact and how I choose to live on the basis of it.

Two further aspects of this emphasis on personal autonomy are the demand for what has come to be known as 'reproductive rights,' and the demand that people should be allowed to end their own lives at the moment of their own choosing with medical assistance to do so if that is what they desire.

As Human Rights Watch explains on their website, 'reproductive rights' 'include prenatal services, safe childbirth, and access to contraception. They also include access to legal and safe abortion.' These rights are seen as vital to give women freedom to 'make the best choices for their lives, including around the number of children they have, if any, and the

---

[285] Jean-Jacque Rousseau, *Confessions* (Oxford: OUP, 2008).
[286] Augustine, *The Confessions* (Oxford: OUP, 2008).

spacing between their children's births.' [287] People's freedom to end their lives at the time and in the manner of their choosing is also seen as integral to the right of human beings to exercise personal autonomy. As the mother of the paralyzed rugby player Dan James, who committed suicide at the Dignitas clinic in Zurich in 2008, wrote about his case:

> Whilst not everyone in Dan's situation would find it as unbearable as Dan, what right does any human being have to tell any other that they have to live such a life, filled with terror, discomfort and indignity, what right does one person who chooses to live with a particular illness or disability have to tell another that they should have to...Our son could not have been more loved and had he felt that he could live his life this way he would have been loved just the same but this was his right as a human being, nobody but nobody should judge him or anyone else.[288]

The Western social imaginary and attacks on Christian religious freedom

The development of the social imaginary described by Trueman and in the preceding quotations from the Doctrine Commission, and from Bauckham, Webster and Grant provides the context for the attacks on Christian religious freedom in contemporary Western society described in chapter 4. This is because of the way that the social imaginary has come to be reflected in the master narrative of twenty-first century Western secular society. As Glynn Harrison suggests in his book *A Better Story*, this narrative (which is constantly reinforced by governments, by the media and by the 'knowledge sector' in general) runs as follows:

> For centuries traditional morality had us -all of us - in its suffocating grip. Year after year the same old rules, chained to the past, heaped

---

[287] Human Rights Watch, 'Reproductive Rights and Abortion' at:
https://www.hrw.org/topic/womens-rights/reproductive-rights-and-abortion.
[288] Julie James, 'Rugby Suicide: The Unedited Emails of His Mother,' the *Daily Telegraph*, 18 October 2008, quoted in Sean Doherty, *The Only Way is Ethics – Part 2: Life and Death* (Milton Keynes: Authentic Media, 2016), p.70.

shame on ordinary men and women (and boys and girls) whose only crime was being different. Enemies of the human spirit, these bankrupt ideologies befriended bigots and encourage the spiteful. They nurtured a seedbed of hypocrisy and offered safe havens to perpetrators of abuse.

No more, change is here. We are breaking free from the shackles of bigotry and removing ourselves from under the dead hand of tradition. Our time has come. A time to be ourselves. A time to be truly who we are. A time to celebrate love wherever we find it. A time for the human spirit to flourish once again. And if you people won't move out of our way, we are going to push you out of our way.[289]

From the perspective of this narrative, traditional Christians are, as McAlpine says, the bad guys. Not only do they persist in holding on to a set of theological beliefs that the development of Western thought since the Enlightenment has shown to be outdated, but in so far as they reject the idea of human autonomy and oppose sexual freedom, the right to choose one's own gender identity, reproductive rights, and the right of people to end their lives in a time and a manner of their choosing, they are advocates of an oppressive morality and as such deserve to be pushed out of the way so that freedom may triumph.

Furthermore, in addition to the issues of sexual freedom, freedom of gender identity, reproductive rights and the right to die, there are a set of other historic issues which the Christian Church is seen as having taken the wrong side. These issues are sexism, racism, imperialism, slavery, ableism (taking a negative attitude to disabled people), the oppression of indigenous people and the sexual abuse children and vulnerable adults. What is seen to be the historic guilt of the Church in relation to all these issues means, it is argued, that Christians have no

---

[289] Glynn Harrison, *A Better Story* (London: Inter-Varsity Press, 2016), Kindle edition, p.51.

grounds to claim to be moral arbiters in today's society, or to claim protection for their beliefs and practices when these come under attack.

As Stephen McAlpine writes in his book *Being the Bad Guys*, in much of the Western world Christians are viewed:

> ...as angry, entitled, sticking our noses in where we are not wanted, and constantly grumbling about us loss of status and influence. Even our call for religious freedom is viewed as self-interest. Whose freedoms were we advocating for when we called the shots? Without needing to reach back as far as the Crusades, Christians have been accused of being slow off the blocks when dealing with systemic racism and all too silent when homosexuals were mistreated and imprisoned. And there's always the spectre of institutional child abuse hanging over the church. So when the cultural, legal and political forces corner and curtail us they're simply doing their job of protecting everyone else from us, aren't they? [290]

There are three reasons why the 'cultural, legal and political forces' in the Western world would seek to 'corner and curtail' Christian religious freedom in the way to which McAlpine refers.

The first reason is that these forces generally accept a liberal world view that is secular in nature for the reasons described by McLaren and that accepts as a given the master narrative described by Harrison.

The second reason is that they want the liberal world view to be reflected in all areas of the life of society. This is a point emphasised by Stephen Carter in his 2002 essay 'Liberalism's Religion problem' in which he warns of the tendency of Western liberal democratic political regimes, like other political regimes throughout history, to seek to impose their views on society in a hegemonic or totalitarian fashion.

---

[290] Stephen McAlpine, *Being the Bad Guys – How to Live for Jesus in a World That Says You Shouldn't* (Epsom: The Good Book Company, 2012) Kindle edition, p.17.

Carter notes that the response of modern liberal political regimes to what he calls 'serious religion' is to:

>...try to speak words that seem to celebrate it (as a part of the freedom of belief, or conscience, or the entitlement to select one's own version of the good) while in effect trying to domesticate it— or, if that fails, to try to destroy it.[291]

The reason this is the cases, he explains, is because modern secular liberalism and religion are in competition as sources of meaning in society:

>This accusation might sound overstated, but it should be unsurprising. Liberalism is a theory of the state in its relationship with individuals, but not just a theory of the organization or output of the state; liberalism also seeks to explain how the state should both stimulate and regulate the search for meaning. Religions, too, seek to provide meanings to their adherents, meanings of a deep and transcendent sort. What is religion, after all, but a narrative a people tells itself about its relationship with God, usually over an extended period of time? And if the narrative is truly about the meaning God assigns to the world, as Christianity's narrative is, the follower of the religion, if truly faithful, can hardly select a different meaning simply because the state says so. If a religionist believes that God's love does not allow some human beings to enslave others, no amount of teaching by the merely mortal agency of the state should cause the religionist to change. Quite the contrary: the religionist, if he believes that the state is committing great evil, has little choice but to try to get the state to change.[292]

As Carter goes on to write, what history teaches us is that 'every state seeks to restrict or eliminate competing centers of meaning.' The liberal state, he declares:

---

[291] Stephen Carter, 'Liberalism's Religion problem', *First Things*, March 2002, at https://www.firstthings.com/article/2002/03/liberalisms-religion-problem.
[292] Carter, 'Liberalism's Religion problem.'

...is no exception to the general rule. Liberalism, too, tends toward hegemony. Not content to serve as a theory of organization of the state, it has grown into a theory of organization of private institutions in the state. If the state itself cannot discriminate among its citizens on the basis of race or sex or religion, then private institutions, it seems, should not do so either. One need not support any of these forms of discrimination to see the obvious conceptual difficulty: a theory that developed in order to explain the organization of the state (from which there is no simple exit for dissenters or subjects of discrimination) becomes a theory about the organization of everything. And that, I think, is the true source of the supposed conflict between liberal theory on one side and religion on the other.[293]

Carter gives as an example of the hegemonic tendency of the liberal state, the attempt to do away with male only institutions in the United States:

There are in the United States of America a number of private colleges that accept only women as students. As of this writing, there is but one that accepts only men. A few decades ago there were significant numbers of both. The change in numbers is an artifact of the liberal idea that private organizations should follow the lead of public ones. (The democracy that the theorists of pluralism celebrated in the fifties and sixties believed exactly the opposite, but that is a rather moot point.) If it is wrong for public organizations to discriminate on the basis of sex (specifically, against women), then it is wrong for private organizations to do so. This idea is often dressed up in plausible theoretical garb—private male–only organizations may be conceptualized, for example, as supporting bulwarks for women's oppression—but no matter how it is dressed, it remains the same animal. That animal is hegemony. Its enemy is diversity.

[293] Carter, 'Liberalism's Religion problem.'

I have no particular brief for male-only colleges. I would never have dreamed of attending one and would not wish it for my son. But I am not prepared to say that no rational, public-spirited parents could ever decide that such a school would be better for their son than a sexually integrated campus would be. Certainly, enough parents think that way for the choice to be one that the market would support. But it is the tendency of liberalism, as for all successful theories of the state, to find danger in competing systems of meaning, and so to strive to eliminate them. Consequently, male-only colleges, male-only private clubs, and (on many campuses, including my own) male-only bathrooms have all died, or are on the way to dying, sacrificed to the public virtue of sexual equality. One may celebrate the public virtue and, at the same time, mourn the death of private diversity.

Democracy needs diversity because democracy advances through dissent, difference, and dialogue. The idea that the state should not only create a set of meanings, but try to alter the structure of institutions that do not match it, is ultimately destructive of democracy because it destroys the differences that create the dialectic. Yet the idea is a popular one—and religions, precisely because the meanings they offer can be so radically different from those proposed by the state, often bear the brunt of hegemony.[294]

According to Carter, the basic problem is that an increasing number of modern liberals see the state's duty as being to promote a particular world view, the world view in question being the belief we have looked at in this chapter that each individual must decide for themselves the best way for them to live. If this is the state's role, it necessarily brings the liberal state in conflict with those, such as traditional Christians, who believe that individuals need to live according to the external authority of the will of God as mediated by an authoritative religious tradition.

---

[294] Carter, 'Liberalism's Religion problem.'

To illustrate this point Carter gives the example of the differing views of modern liberals and Christians over the issue of the education of children:

Many contemporary theorists—I have in mind, for example, Stephen Macedo and William Galston—seem willing to discard the solid post–Rawlsian liberal tenet that the state must be neutral among competing conceptions of the good. In order to create a world in which citizens are able to pursue their own answers to basic question two—What is best for me?—it is important, evidently, to develop citizens who themselves see the pursuit of basic question two as important. Education for democracy, or for liberal citizenship, is the way the proposition is sometimes put: children must be trained, from the time they are young, to accept liberal precepts, including the central importance of basic question two. That is why so many liberal theorists are so scathing in their attacks on Wisconsin v. Yoder, a 1972 decision in which the Supreme Court allowed the Old Order Amish to remove their children from school after the eighth grade. The Amish, and the Supreme Court, saw further formal education as a threat to the Amish tradition, which is based in the terrible suffering of the Anabaptist experience and thus quite understandably preaches separation from the world. The critics, led by Justice William Douglas, argued that the refusal of Amish parents to send their children to school for ninth grade and beyond harmed the children—by denying them the tools they would need to lead lives in pursuit of the answer to basic question two.

Contemporary liberalism has constructed a worldview that exalts the individual self as a bundle of desires, the fulfilment of those desires in turn protected by rights. This criticism of liberalism is hardly new, and many theorists would not consider it a criticism at all. But Christianity, almost by its nature, must reject the liberal edifice, for Christianity constructs a worldview exalting not the individual but the connection—connection to other humans and, ultimately, to God. The Christian tradition teaches that the believer must die to self in order to live in Christ, and must reject the world for Christ's sake. Christianity, in short, is more about duty than choice. Parents who raise their children to understand their lives this way are training them to be other than what liberal theory says they should be; but a liberal state that tries to interfere is one that many committed Christians are likely to see as the enemy.[295]

To put Carter's argument another way, modern liberal Western democracies have the same totalitarian tendency as other forms of political organisation. Just as, for example, Communist regimes seek to impose a Marxist ideology upon their citizens, so also modern Western democracies are increasingly seeking to impose acceptance of a secular and individualistic world view upon their citizens and this necessarily leads to a conflict with Christians who are unable to accept this worldview and who instead advocate, and seek to live out, an alternative worldview in their teaching and practice.

The third reason, is because many modern liberals, seeing Christians as 'the bad guys,' feel that Christianity (or at least non-liberal versions of Christianity) must be severely restricted to prevent their return to power within society. Christians are a potential threat to liberalism and this threat must be contained.

The Polish writer and prominent political figure Ryszard Legutko makes this point in his book *The Demon in Democracy*. Referring to the situation in contemporary Europe he writes:

An anti-Christian rhetoric in the media and in politics and anti-Christian art, including paintings, installations, plays, novels, films, articles, and slogans, fills the public space today, making the Christian religion, its institutions, and its articles of faith objects of endlessly multiplying derisions and accusations. Homosexual activists see Christianity as the original source of homophobia and feminists as the foundation of patriarchy. Countless intellectuals accuse it of totalitarianism, reactionary sexual ethics, paedophilia,

---

[295] Carter, 'Liberalism's Religion problem.'

an inquisition -like - mentality, witch hunts, anti-semitism and the Holocaust, intellectual infantilism, a morbid fascination with guilt, and numerous other sins. On the one hand, there is an ever-present feeling of satisfaction that Christianity has been in retreat for some time, being driven back by a victorious wave of secularization; on the other, it is inevitably seen as an evil that miraculously resurrects itself and continues to cast its ominous shadow over Western civilization. The participation of Christians in public life - even as paltry as it is now - revives the usual suspicions and resuscitates the old anti-Christian stereotypes.[296] The crusade against Christianity verges on the absurd: liberals continue to make new conquest and to colonize more and more areas of human life, leaving more practically no territory outside their control, and the more they grab, the louder they rant against Christianity, flogging it with new accusations, invectives and blasphemies.[297]

As he goes on to say, reflecting on the Polish experience:

The analogy to what was happening under the communist rule seems irresistible. In the countries where, as result of brutal repressions by the communist regime, sometimes induced by historical and cultural peculiarities, Christianity was believed to be on the wane, and where the forces of secularism triumphed to the satisfaction of the apostles of the communist ideology, the anti-Christian warriors did not lay down their arms: they continued to fight, as if fearing that Christianity's death was temporary and that the religion, re born again, was soon to resume its sinister role as a major obstacle to the march of modernity. In a sense, the communists were right: much of the resistance that finally led the

---

[296] This point is illustrated by the attacks made on the Scottish Christian politician Kate Forbes during her recent attempt to become leader of the Scottish National Party. See 'Free Church criticise 'anti-Christian' attacks on Kate Forbes, *The Herald*, 22 February 2023 at: https://www.heraldscotland.com/politics/23338967.free-church-criticise-anti-christian-attacks-kate-forbes/.
[297] Ryszard Legutko, *The Demon in Democracy* (New York and London, Encounter Books, 2018) Kindle edition, p.159.

disintegration of the communist system came from religious groups and from religion itself. At the end of the day it turned out that the fear of religion was justified: the Pope had indeed far more troops than the communist dictators.[298] It is quite possible that the anti-Christian crusaders of today are haunted by a similar fear. [299]

Western liberalism and the right to freedom of religion

At this point someone might object that any attempt by Western liberals to restrict freedom of religion is surely limited by the international and national legal commitments to freedom of religion that we looked at in chapter 3.

The answer to this objection is that the argument is increasingly being advanced that the right to freedom of religion has to be balanced against the rights of other groups in society and may legitimately be restricted if it unduly infringes upon them.

The cases of Päivi Räsänen and Juhana Pohjola and Felix Ngole referred to chapter 4 illustrate this point. In both cases it was argued that their right to the exercise of freedom of religion had to be subordinated to the rights of gay and lesbian people, in the case of Räsänen and Pohjola the right not to be subject to 'derogatory and discriminatory' language and in the case of Ngole the right to access counselling without becoming subject to the risk of suicide.

Two further illustrations are provided by the court case involving Catch the Fire Ministries in Australia and the recent report to the United Nations Human Rights Council on *Freedom of religion or belief, and freedom from violence and discrimination based on sexual orientation and gender identity.*

---

[298] Legutko is referring to the question allegedly asked by Joseph Stalin in 1943. 'The Pope. How many divisions has he?'
[299] Legutko, p.159.

The case of Catch the Fire Ministries was about whether the right of Christians to express a particular view of Islam should be restricted in order to protect the right of Muslims not to have their religion vilified.

In his article 'The Vulnerability of Religious Liberty in Liberal States,' Rex Adhar explains that the case concerns the ruling by a tribunal in the Australian state of Victoria:

...that two Pentecostal pastors, and their evangelical organisation, Catch the Fire Ministries, had engaged in religious vilification of Muslims in the statements they had made at a seminar in 2002 and in the Ministries' website article and newsletter. The seminar was called 'Insight into Islam: What is holy Jihad?' and the speaker was a Pastor Daniel Scot, an Assemblies of God pastor. Pastor Scot had been born and raised in Pakistan and had fled that country when accused under Pakistan's blasphemy law. Ironically, he was to become the catalyst for major public controversy in his adopted country. The purpose of the seminar, conducted at a Melbourne Pentecostal church attended by some 200 to 250 people, was 'to encourage Christians to testify to Muslim people about the Christian faith, and for that purpose to equip Christians with a knowledge of Muslim beliefs.'

Three converts to Islam attended the seminar and lodged a complaint, claiming that it incited hatred against Muslims. The Islamic Council of Victoria also became involved. Following unsuccessful attempts at reconciliation, the Victorian Civil and Administrative Tribunal ruled, in 2004, that there had been a breach of the Racial and Religious Tolerance Act 2001. Unfortunately for Pastor Scot, he had given what was, in the Tribunal's view, an 'unbalanced' discussion of Muslim religious beliefs and conduct. He had supposedly 'made fun' of Muslim beliefs and practices, presenting them in a fashion that was 'essentially hostile, demeaning and derogatory of all Muslim people.'[300]

Adhar notes that:

...there is no doubt that the speaker did not mince his words and the seminar contained controversial assertions about Muslims' attitude to women and to people of other faiths and many blunt quotations from the Qur'an that suggested Islam was not such a peaceful religion as its followers claimed.

However, 'All the statements critical of Muslim teachings were, nonetheless, accompanied with constant exhortations by Pastor Scot to accept and love Muslim people.'[301]

In addition to what was said at the seminar:

The newsletter written by a Pastor Daniel Nalliah and website article were also found to infringe the Act and both pastors were ordered to publicly apologize in the form of a specified statement of apology. The pastors stubbornly refused to comply. The saga continued and in 2006 the Court of Appeal of the Supreme Court of Victoria found the Tribunal had erred on a number of interpretive points and remitted the matter back to be re-heard. The orders requiring a public apology were set aside.

The proceedings were finally resolved without the need for a rehearing. After mediation between the parties, an agreement was reached in June 2007 to end the long-running five-year battle—one that had cost the defendants more than $500,000. Hands were shaken and a joint statement was issued whereby each side

[300] Rex Adhar, 'The Vulnerability of Religious Liberty in Liberal States,' *Religion and Human Rights* 4 (2009), p.190-191.
[301] Adhar, p.191.

affirmed the dignity of each other and the rights of each to 'robustly debate religion.' [302]

As Adhar argues, the case of Catch the Fire ministries shows: 'how hegemonic liberalism seeks to refashion serious religion into something fit for liberal society.' It does this in four ways:

First, there is the state penetration into the private sphere. The seminar, although advertised to the public, was given at a church and was essentially an 'in house' exercise to educate believers so they could reach out to other believers. Yet the state's interest in its citizens' having 'right' attitudes to people of other faiths extended into this forum.

Second, there was the emphasis the trial judge placed upon the need for a 'balanced' presentation of Islamic beliefs. While one judge did point out that it was not for a secular tribunal to evaluate the theological accuracy or propriety of what was said, such an exercise is hard to avoid. It seems wrong to require an evangelist or other religious preacher to become a sort of impartial, 'open minded' purveyor of information—in other words to squeeze them into the liberal ideal.

Third, the truth of the statements about Islam was, the Tribunal ruled, no defence to a breach of the Act, which is concerned with whether upset or hatred is stirred up. But for the devout believer, truth is primary. One cannot fail to proclaim the truth because feelings are hurt or liberal sensibilities ruffled.

Fourth, in deciding whether the defence set out in s 8 of the Act was met, the court unerringly voices the liberal attitude to religion. The speaker is protected where the conduct complained of is 'engaged in reasonably and in good faith.' What is 'reasonable', said the court, is what would be so regarded 'by reasonable persons in general judged by the standards of an open and just multicultural society.'

[302] Adhar, pp.191-192.

When those given the freedom to express their religious views do so in a manner that the hypothetical reasonable and tolerant person considers excessive, the limit has been reached. Unacceptable religious expression is that which the tolerant find intolerable. Open multicultural societies can tolerate some criticism by adherents of one religion of another. But there is a limit, namely: 'when what is said is so ill-informed or misconceived or ignorant or so hurtful as to go beyond the bounds of what tolerance should accommodate that it may be regarded as unreasonable.'

As a practical guide to the operation and scope of the law, these broad statements about the limits of tolerance are entirely circular and vacuous. We might learn the limits of religious criticism after a tribunal has discerned the reactions of the hypothetical tolerant citizen, but not before then.

The message behind this is clear though. Public religious sentiment must satisfy the liberal litmus test of being 'reasonable'. And what is 'reasonable' seems to be a tamed, soft-edged version of the faith.[303]

Adhar's conclusion is that the case of Catch the Fire Ministries:

> ...illustrates that a law to promote religious tolerance can do the opposite and increase religious friction and suspicion. It may be used to effectively 'chill' religious speech, to muzzle religious people from bearing public witness or tempt them to either abandon the more inconvenient truths of scripture or at least water-down the message to make it inoffensive. The New Testament may teach that the preaching of the cross brings offence, but that is no answer in modern multicultural society.

Evangelism is an integral part of exercising one's religious liberty. For instance, in the Christian faith, it is not just as a suggestion but a duty to 'witness' and to preach the Gospel to all nations. But such speech, especially where it advances strong truth claims and

---

[303] Adhar, pp.193-194.

indirectly points to the falsity of other beliefs, may be seen as an instance of religious intolerance. For a secular tribunal, operating on the unspoken assumptions of liberal thought, it may represent nothing less than illegitimate religious hate speech.' [304]

The report to the United Nations Human Rights Council in June 2023 by the Independent Expert on protection against violence and discrimination based on sexual orientation and gender identity, is summarized as follows by the Center for Family and Human Rights (C-Fam):

> The report calls on governments to threaten and punish religious leaders and organizations that do not comply with LGBT orthodoxy, and, in a novel and unprecedented way, it calls on government to destabilize religions from within by supporting pro-LGBT factions within religious denominations.

The UN independent expert on sexual orientation and gender identity, Victor Madrigal-Borloz, the nominal author of the report, does not hide his intention to create 'a new normative space' where governments impose acceptable LGBT standards for religion.

'The limits established in the very design of Freedom of Religion and Belief – including the fundamental rights and freedoms of LGBT persons – are the key to full compatibility of Freedom of Religion and Belief and all actions that are necessary to combat violence and discrimination against them,' he concludes at the end of the report:

> Clergy and other faith-based actors should be threatened to comply with the official LGBT-friendly religious standards or face the consequences, according to the conclusions of the report. Governments should 'encourage religious institutions to consider the ways in which representatives will be held responsible in cases in which they promote discrimination against LGBT and other gender diverse persons.'

[304] Adhar, p.194.

When religions teach that homosexual conduct is a sin or that sex is an immutable biological reality they run afoul of human rights law.

'There are dark corners where LGBT people are regarded as sinners and second-class citizens who should be scorned and abused,' the report says.

Madrigal-Borloz urges UN member states to use favourable religious leaders and institutions to promote homosexual and transgender ideology. He expressly endorses several dissident religious groups: Catholics for Choice, which promotes abortion, and Muslims for Progressive Values, which promotes homosexual and transgender issues. He also praised the views of non-religious humanists about sex as 'an evolved trait, with no intrinsic meaning.'

Madrigal-Borloz argues that individuals who identify as homosexual or transgender have a 'right to access spirituality on equal terms with everyone else.' He concludes therefore that unless all religions endorse pro-LGBT ideas, individuals who identify as such will be alienated and excluded, causing them pain, mental health issues, and potentially leading them to suicide, and ultimately violating their human rights.

'For many individuals, their religion is part of the foundation of their sense of self, the source of truth,' he explains.

At the heart of the report is the belief that sexuality and gender identity are fundamental rights on the same plane, if not higher, than freedom of religion.

'All believers, including religion and belief leaders, have a sexual orientation and a gender identity, and all LGBT persons have beliefs,' the report states.

The report makes pronouncements regarding scriptural interpretation and theology. It disparages interpretations of Judeo-Christian scripture that condemn homosexuality as 'dogmatic' and modern 'homo-colonialist' inventions and asserts that the morality of homosexuality is a 'matter of theological debate.'

The report denies that religious health workers and institutions may object to providing abortions or transgender 'affirming' treatments and surgeries, including to children. It also denies that providers of services and goods, such as bakers and florists, can deny service to persons and events based on their conscientious objection. It claims that parochial schools may not fire teachers based on their sexual orientation and gender identity.

Ultimately, Madrigal-Borloz promotes homosexual marriage as a higher right than religious freedom. He even hints at forcing clergy to conduct homosexual marriages at the cost of losing their privilege to conduct legally recognized marriages.

'A human-rights-based approach directly challenges family conceptions that are exclusionary of LGBT persons,' he explains.[305]

The full text of the report can be found at the link below.[306] As the summary by C-Fam indicates, the problem is that Madrigal-Borloz sets the rights of LGBT people over against the rights of religious believers who take a traditional approach to questions of sexual conduct and identity, and proposes subordinating the rights of the latter in a way that would potentially restrict freedom of religion of to a serious extent.

This point is made by Wissam al-Saliby, Director of the World Evangelical Alliance office in Geneva in answers to questions published on the website *Evangelical Focus*:

---

[305] Stefano Gennarini, 'Religious freedom ends where LGBT rights begin.' C-Fam, June 21, 2023 at https://c-fam.org/friday_fax/un-attempts-to-impose-lgbt-orthodoxy-on-all-religions/?inf_contact_key=4e8d67307858c899074b9c8bcdfeae0dd18a532c4142cb79caf2b269de1401fa

[306] Victor Madgrigal-Borloz, *Freedom of religion or belief, and freedom from violence and discrimination based on sexual orientation and gender identity* at: https://view.officeapps.live.com/op/view.aspx?src=https%3A%2F%2Fwww.ohchr.org%2Fsites%2Fdefault%2Ffiles%2Fdocuments%2Fhrbodies%2Fhrcouncil%2Fsessions-regular%2Fsession53%2Fadvance-versions%2FA_HRC_53_37_AUV.docx&wdOrigin=BROWSELINK

Question. Does the report of the SOGI IE [Independent Expert on Sexual Orientation and Gender identity] in the 53rd session of the Human Rights Council challenge the autonomy of churches and religious organisations?

A. The World Evangelical Alliance supports the right to life, dignity, and freedom from violence for all people including those identifying as LGBT. We also support the right to enjoyment of Freedom of Religion or Belief (FoRB) for all.

Because religion is practiced collectively, the autonomy of religious organisations is part of FoRB. The autonomy of churches and religious organisations is two-fold: institutional and doctrinal. Autonomy includes defining our own doctrine and values, and the right to require adherence to the religious group's doctrines as part of institutional life, including employment.

The report claims that religious communities' institutions employing non-LGBT people or relationships to LGBT people could lead to violence and harm. But these claims are not supported by facts and a proper explanation.

Q. What worries you in Madrigal-Borloz's approach to what religions teach?

A. The report makes several references to 'sin' and to exclusionary teachings. The report blurs the lines between religious doctrines and the relationship with God on the one hand and presumed or real violations of human rights on the other hand.

Under international law, the State has the right to restrict religious freedom if the manifestation of religion amounts to a threat to public safety, order, health and life. However, the Independent Expert does not make the case that traditional Christian teachings about sin and sexuality would fall under the scope of restriction clauses in international law.

The report confuses non-discrimination obligations of the State in the provision of public services and in the treatment of minorities, and private actors which are not bound to the same under international law.

The report and its recommendations invite State intervention in Christian doctrine. Such an intervention would amount to an attack on the doctrinal autonomy of Christian communities and would violate the core protection of the forum internum or the non-negotiable internally held beliefs stemming from the God's revealed Word.

Q. The report talks of "dark corners where LGBT people are regarded as sinners and second-class citizens who should be scorned and abused" (paragraph 69). Is this description problematic?

A. God loves everyone - including LGBT people. And the failure of many people, including Christians, to echo this love to LGBT people is something we need to grapple with as Christian community.

International human rights law prohibits hate speech in accordance with the Rabat Plan of Action,[307] and we support the Rabat Plan of Action. Article 18 of the International Covenant on Civil and Political Rights allows for limited, proportional, and necessary restrictions on some forms of the manifestation of religion.

Beyond this, States cannot interfere in the internal affairs of religious communities' doctrine and teachings. And without a thorough justification for restriction of some religious teachings, the Independent Expert is expressing theological or doctrinal preferences which go beyond his mandate. [308]

---

[307] The Rabat Plan of Action is a United Nations document which sets out the circumstances in which it may be right for states to limit freedom of expression in order to prevent incitement to hatred and Violence. It can be found at: https://www.ohchr.org/sites/default/files/Documents/Issues/Opinion/SeminarRabat/Rabat_draft_outcome.pdf
[308] Joel Forster, 'Risk of 'state intervention in Christian doctrine if recommendations of UN expert on LGBT issues are followed, warns WEA,'

Conclusion

In this chapter we have traced the development across the Western World of a secular social imaginary in which the absence of God is generally assumed. We have also seen that one of the results of the development of this social imaginary is the emergence of a view of what it means to be human which emphasises the right of each individual to determine for themselves the best way for them to live, including in the areas of sexual identity and sexual expression. In addition, we have also noted that in Western liberal societies there is tendency for those with power to seek to impose the tenets of this social imaginary upon the whole of society in a totalitarian fashion.

In the context just described Christians have increasingly come be seen as the 'bad guys' because of their refusal to accept or live by this social imaginary and restrictions of religious activity have been justified on the grounds that the freedom of religious believers to exercise their faith may justifiably limited in order to protect the rights of others in society, these rights being increasingly understood in terms of the prevailing secular social imaginary.

In the remainder of this book, we shall look at how Christians who believe in the importance of freedom of religion should respond to this situation and to the increasing attacks on Christianity in the Western world noted in chapter 4.

In the next chapter we shall begin by asking how the emergence of secular Western Society and the social imaginary associated with it are to be understood theologically from the standpoint of the Christian faith. This is because it is only when we have understood them from a theological perspective that we can start to think in an informed fashion about how we can respond properly to them.

Evangelical Focus, 23 June 2023 at https://evangelicalfocus.com/world/22512/un-risks-state-intervention-in-christian-doctrine-if-recommendations- of-un-independent-expert-on-lgbt-issues-are-followed.

Chapter 6
A Christian theological account of the modern Western world

Why secularisation is the poisoned fruit of the success of Christianity in the Western world

In the previous two chapters we have seen that the attacks on Christian religious freedom that are now taking place in the Western world have as their background the new 'social imaginary' which has emerged because of the secularisation of Western society. We have also seen that the process of secularisation has had as its background an emphasis on the free exercise of human reason, which has led to developments in science and technology, which have in turn led to increasingly industrialised and urbanised societies in which Christian belief and practice, which were once central, have now become marginalised.

What is paradoxical about this process of secularisation is that it is a *result* of the success of Christianity in the Western world. This because the way that Western society has developed has been a result of the influence of Christian belief upon it. Without that influence the modern Western world would simply not exist.

This point is argued in detail by the American sociologist and historian Rodney Stark in his 2005 book *The Victory of Reason.* In this book he seeks to ask the question of why Western civilisation has become predominant in the contemporary world. His answer is that:

> ...the rise of the West was based on four primary victories of reason. The first was the development of faith in progress within Christian theology. The second victory was the way that faith in progress translated into technical and organisational innovations, many of them fostered by monastic estates. The third was that, thanks to Christian theology, reason influenced both political philosophy and practise to the extent that responsive states, sustaining a substantial degree of personal freedom, appeared in mediaeval Europe. The final victory involved application of reason to

commerce, resulting in the development of capitalism within the safe havens provided by responsive states. These were the victories by which the West won.[309]

Stark reiterates this answer in his book's conclusion, declaring:

Christianity created Western civilization. Had the followers of Jesus remained an obscure Jewish sect, most of you would not have learnt to read and the rest of you would be reading from hand copied scrolls. Without a theology committed to reason, progress, and moral equality, today the entire world and would be about where non -European societies were, in, say, 1800. A world with many astrologers and alchemists but no scientists. A world of despots lacking universities, banks, factories, eyeglasses, chimneys, and pianos. A world where most infants do not live to the age of five and many women die in childbirth - a world truly living in 'dark ages.'

The modern world arose only in Christian societies. Not in Islam. Not in Asia. Not in a 'secular' society there having been none. And all the modernization that has since occurred outside Christendom was imported from the West, often bought by colonisers and missionaries.[310]

He closes his book with the words of a leading Chinese scholar:

One of the things that we were asked to look into was what accounted for the success, in fact, the pre-eminence of the West all over the world. We studied everything we could from the historical, political, economic and cultural perspective. At first we thought it was because you had more powerful guns than we had. Then we thought it was because you had the best political system. Next we focused on your economic system. But in the last twenty years, we have realized that the heart of your culture is your religion: Christianity. That is why the West is so powerful. The Christian

---

[309] Rodney Stark, *The Victory of Reason* (New York: Random House, 2005), p. xiii.
[310] Stark, p.233.

moral foundation of social and cultural life was what made possible the emergence of capitalism and then the successful transition to democratic politics. We don't have any doubts about this.[311]

In his book Stark evaluates the success of Western civilization from a secular perspective. The same is also true of the Chinese scholar whom he quotes. They see the West as having been successful because it has developed a technologically advanced, economically successful, free and democratic society. However, the rise of Western civilization can also be seen as a success story from the perspective of Christian theology.

This is because a key implication of God's creation of human beings as creatures who are his image and likeness, as described in Genesis 1:26-28, is that human beings have been given both the ability and the responsibility to act as sub-creators who develop that latent potential of the world that God has created in new ways.

This truth is emphasised by Tim Keller in his book *Center Church*. In this book Keller notes that the city of God described in Revelation 21-22, the final home of redeemed humanity, is the same garden described in Genesis 2. However:

> ...it has been expanded and remade into the Garden City of God. *It is the garden of Eden*, yet faithfully cultivated - the fulfilment of the purposes of the Eden of God. Indeed, the very word used for 'garden' in Genesis 2 describes not a wilderness but a 'park,' a well-tended plot of land one would find in a city or near a royal palace.
> [312]

[311] Stark, p.235 citing David Aikman, *Jesus in Beijing: How Christianity is transforming China and changing the global balance of power* (Washington DC: Regnery, 2003), p.5.
[312] Tim Keller, *Center Church* (Grand Rapids: Zondervan, 2012), p.150.

According to Keller, the reason this is important is because the 'cultural mandate' to 'rule over' the earth given to the first human beings in Genesis 1:28:

> ...is a call for them to 'image God's work for the world by taking up our work in the world.' It is a call to develop a culture and build a civilization that honours God. Gardening (the original human vocation) is a paradigm for cultural development. A gardener neither leaves the ground as is, nor does he destroy it. Instead, he rearranges it to produce food and plants for human life. He cultivates it. (The words *culture* and *cultivate* come from the same root.) Every vocation is in some way a response to and an extension of, the primal Edenic act of cultivation. Artists, for example, take the raw material of the five senses and human experience to produce music and visual media; literature and painting; dance and architecture and theatre. In a similar way, technologists and builders take the raw material of the physical world and creatively rearrange it to enhance human productivity and flourishing. Because we are called to create culture in this way, and because the cities are the places of greatest cultural production, I believe that city building is a crucial part of fulfilling the mandate...God's intention for human endeavour is that it raise up civilizations – cities – that glorify him and steward the endless wonders and riches that God puts into the created world. [313]

Viewed in this light, the development of Western industrial, urban civilization has to be viewed in a positive light. Shaped by Christianity in the way we have noted, it has been at least a partial fulfilment of the cultural mandate given by God to humankind. However, like all human achievements since the Fall, it is also flawed. As we have become increasingly aware in recent decades, Western civilization has done serious damage to the natural world, and as we noted in the last chapter it has also done serious spiritual damage by being the catalyst for secularization.

---

[313] Keller, p.150 -151.

To put the same thing another way, the development of modern Western civilization has been a positive development in so far as it has been a way of fulfilling the cultural mandate given to humanity. On the other hand, it has been harmful in so far as the result of its development since the Enlightenment has been to lead people to turn away from God and from living the kind of lives he created them to live. The success of Christianity in the Western world has borne poisoned fruit.

Two quotations, one from the work of C S Lewis, the other from the work of Tom Holland, illustrate this point.

In his book *The Screwtape Letters* Lewis recounts how an experienced devil called Screwtape gives advice to a more junior devil about how to prevent people from turning to the 'Enemy' (i.e. God) and ensuring that they end up in 'Our Father's House (i.e. are damned). In the extract below Screwtape warn against the use of arguments to turn people from God:

> By the very act of arguing, you awake the patient's reason; and once it is awake, who can foresee the result? Even if a particular train of thought can be twisted so as to end in our favour, you will find that you have been strengthening in your patient the fatal habit of attending to universal issues and withdrawing his attention from the stream of immediate sense experiences. Your business is to fix his attention on the stream. Teach him to call it 'real life' and don't let him ask what he means by 'real.'

> Remember, he is not, like you, a pure spirit. Never having been a human (Oh that abominable advantage of the Enemy's!) you don't realise how enslaved they are to the pressure of the ordinary. I once had a patient, a sound atheist, who used to read in the British Museum. One day, as he sat reading, I saw a train of thought in his mind beginning to go the wrong way. The Enemy, of course was at his elbow in a moment. Before I knew where I was, I saw my twenty years' work beginning to totter. If I had lost my head and begun to attempt a defence by argument I should have been undone. But I was not such a fool. I struck instantly at the part of the man which I

had best under my control and suggested that it was just about time he had some lunch. The Enemy presumably made the counter - suggestion (you know how one can never *quite* overhear what He says to them?) that this was more important than lunch. At least I think that must have been His line for when I said 'Quite. In fact much *too* important to tackle at the end of the morning,' The patient brightened up considerably; and by the time I had added 'Much better to come back after lunch and go into it with a fresh mind,' he was already halfway to the door. Once he was in the street the battle was won. I showed him a newsboy shouting the midday paper, and a No. 73 bus going past, and before he reached the bottom of the steps I had got into him an unalterable conviction that, whatever odd ideas might come into a man's head when he was shut up alone with his books, a healthy dose of real life (by which he meant the bus and the news boy) was enough to show him that all that sort of thing just couldn't be true. He knew he had a narrow escape and in later years was fond of talking about 'that inarticulate sense for actuality which is our ultimate safeguard against the aberrations of mere logic.' He is now safe in our father's house.

You begin to see the point? Thanks to processes which we set at work in them centuries ago, they find it all but impossible to believe in the unfamiliar while the familiar is before their eyes.[314]

The truth that Lewis is seeking to get across in this extract is that Western civilization has developed a focus on the knowledge of the everyday material world mediated by direct sense experience. This focus has its roots in the Christian belief in the reality of the material world as God's creation, and it has helped people in the Western world fulfil the 'cultural mandate' by engaging in scientific enquiry and the development of technology. However, it has borne poisoned fruit in that it has also resulted in a social imaginary which has increasingly come to see the familiar everyday material world as the whole of reality, and

---

[314] C S Lewis, *The Screwtape Letters* (London: Fount, 1998), pp.2-3.

has therefore come to ignore God since he does not form part of it. For many in the contemporary Western world a No.73 bus or someone selling newspapers are seen as unquestionably real whereas God is not, even if philosophical logic might perhaps suggest otherwise.

In his book *Dominion – The Making of the Western Mind*, Tom Holland writes that the belief that:

> ...the great battles in America's culture war were being fought between Christians and those who had emancipated themselves from Christianity was a conceit that both sides had an interest in promoting. It was no less of a myth for that. In reality, Evangelicals and progressives were recognizably bred of the same matrix. If opponents of abortion were the heirs of Macrina, who had toured the rubbish tips of Cappadocia looking for abandoned infants to rescue, then those who argued against them were likewise drawing on a deeply rooted Christian supposition: that every woman's body was her own, and to be respected as such by every man. Supporters of gay marriage were quite as influenced by the Church's enthusiasm for monogamous fidelity as those against it were by the biblical condemnations of men who slept with men. To install transgender toilets might indeed seem an affront to the Lord God, who had created male and female; but to refuse kindness to the persecuted was to offend against the most fundamental teachings of Christ. In a country as saturated in Christian assumptions as the United States, there could be no escaping their influence – even for those who imagined that they had. [315]

Holland is undoubtedly right to claim that the 'culture wars' that have taken place in America (and in other parts of the Western world) in recent years have been conflict between sets of people who both influenced by the Christian faith. As we have noted, Western civilization as whole has been fundamentally shaped by Christianity and therefore

---

[315] Tom Holland, *Dominion – The Making of the Western Mind* (London, Little, Brown, 2019), p.514.

the beliefs of everyone in the Western world, whether believers or unbelievers, liberals or progressives, have been shaped to a greater or lesser degree by the tenets of Christianity.

However, what he fails to note is that in the three examples that he gives the Christian influences to which he refers have actually led those on the progressive side of the debate to turn away from key Christian principles.

Holland is correct to say that the Western belief that men do not have the right to do what they like with women's bodies is a belief that is Christian in origin. It goes back to the twin Christian convictions that, as those made in God's image and likeness, women have equal intrinsic dignity alongside men and that sexual activity should always be an act of love undertaken within the context of a marriage into which a woman has freely consented to enter. However, in the modern conflict over abortion the influence of the modern Western idea of absolute personal autonomy has meant that the belief that men cannot do what they want with women bodies has morphed into the idea that women should be allowed to decide to kill their unborn children if they wish to do so. This idea violates the Christian prohibition of infanticide going back to the earliest day of the Church[316] and the Christian conviction that:

> The foetus is neither a growth in the mother's body, nor even a potential human being, but already a human life who, though not yet mature, has the potentiality of growing into the fulness of the individual humanity he already possesses. [317]

---

[316] As the early second century *Epistle of Barnabas puts* it, the Christian rule was 'Never do away with an unborn child, or destroy it after its birth' (*Epistle of Barnabas* 19:2 in Maxwell Staniforth, *Early Christian Writings* (Harmondsworth: Penguin, 1978), p.217.

[317] John Stott, *Issues Facing Christians Today* (Basingstoke: Marshall, Morgan and Scott, 1984), p.288.

Holland is also correct when he says that support for gay marriage reflects influence of the Christian tradition. It is because the Christian belief in monogamous marriage has been such an important part of Western civilization for thousands of years that gay and lesbian people and their straight allies have wanted to expand the institution of marriage to include same-sex couples. This is because some gay and lesbian people simply like the idea of marriage and want to be part of it, because some gay and lesbian people want the social respectability that the marriage label gives to their relationships (which is why Civil Partnerships were deemed insufficient), and in the case of some gay and lesbian activists because of a belief that the legalisation of same-sex marriage will provide the opportunity to completely re-define what marriage means.[318]

However, by seeking a redefinition of marriage to include same-sex couples, those who support gay marriage have rejected the basic Christian belief that, because marriage is not a human invention but a divine ordinance, human beings cannot redefine marriage in way that goes against the marital pattern that God established at creation, namely that marriage is a permanent and exclusive relationships between one man one woman.

In the words of Oliver O'Donovan:

Christian have classically believed that in the ordinance of marriage there was given an end for human relationships, a teleological structure which was a fact of creation and therefore not negotiable. The dimorphic organisation of human sexuality, the particular attraction of two adults of the opposite sex and of different parents,

---

[318] In relation to the last reason for wanting same-sex marriage the American gay rights activist Michelangelo Signorile declares, for example, that same-sex couples should 'fight for same-sex marriage and its benefits and then, once granted, redefine the institution of marriage completely, because the most subversive activity lesbians and gay men can undertake...is to transform the notion of 'family' entirely.' (Michelangelo Signorile. 'Bridal Wave,' *Out*, December 1993/January 1994, p.161.

the setting up of a home distinct from the parental home and the uniting of their lives in a shared life (from which Jesus concluded the unnaturalness of divorce): these form a pattern of human fulfilment which serves the wider end of enabling procreation to occur in a context of affection and loyalty. Whatever happens in history, Christians have wished to say, this is what marriage really is. Particular cultures may have distorted it; individuals may fall short of it. It is to their cost in either case; for it reasserts itself as God's creative intention for human relationships on earth; and it will be with us in one form or another, as our natural good until (but not after) the kingdom of God shall appear. [319]

Finally, Holland is correct to say that a key reason for the support given to transgender people by those who are socially progressive is a deep rooted belief that those who are persecuted should be supported, a belief that has its roots in the Christian belief that we should show loving care for our neighbour in their need, whoever they are, as taught by Jesus in the parable of the Good Samaritan (Luke 10:25-37). However, the idea that this means that Christians should simply affirm transgender identities both in theory and practice goes against the Christian belief (which is also supported by what science tells us about human biology) that God has created human beings as a dimorphic species consisting of men and women, that being male or female is a matter of biology, and that a key part of the human vocation is to say to God 'thy will be done' by accepting the sex that God has given us.

To quote O'Donovan again, on the basis of Christian anthropology:

...we cannot and must not conceive of physical sexuality as a mere raw material with which we can construct a form of psychosexual self-expression which is determined only by the free impulse of our spirits. Responsibility in sexual development implies a

---

[319] Oliver O'Donovan, *Resurrection and Moral Order*, 2nd edition (Leicester and Grand Rapids: Apollos/Eerdmans, 1994), p.69.

responsibility to nature – to the ordered good of the bodily form which we have been given.[320]

In all these three examples, then, what we see is that the Christian inheritance of Western civilization has become distorted into a motive for acting in ways that are actually contrary to key aspects of the Christian faith. As before, the influence of Christianity has borne poisoned fruit.

The influence of Satan

Lewis' account in *The Screwtape Letters* of someone being tempted by a senior demon is a literary conceit. He is not intending to suggest that a particular individual was actually led away from God by a particular demon in the way he describes. However, his literary conceit was a serious one in that Lewis really did believe in the existence of Satan and of demons under his control.

Lewis makes this clear in his book *Mere Christianity*. In a chapter entitled 'The invasion', Lewis considers the notion of 'dualism,' the idea that there are: 'two equal and independent powers at the back of everything, one of them good and the other body and that this universe is the battlefield in which they fight out an endless war.'[321]

Lewis concludes that this idea will not work because in order for the bad power to be bad:

...he must exist and have intelligence and will. But existence, intelligence and will are in themselves good. Therefore, he must be getting them from the Good Power: even to be bad he must borrow or steal from his opponent. And do you now begin to see why Christianity has always said that the Devil is a fallen Angel? That is not a mere story for the children. It is a real recognition of the fact that evil is a parasite, not an original thing. The powers which enable evil to carry on are powers given it by goodness. All the

[320] Oliver O'Donovan, *Begotten or Made?* (Oxford: OUP, 1984), p.29.
[321] C S Lewis, *Mere Christianity* (Glasgow: Fount, 1984), p.44.

things which enable a bad man to be effectively bad are in themselves good things - resolution, cleverness, good looks, existence itself. That is why Dualism, in a strict sense, will not work.[322]

However, he then goes on to say that:

I freely admit that real Christianity (as distinct from Christianity-and-water) goes much nearer to Dualism than people think. One of the things that surprised me when I first read the New Testament seriously was that it talked so much about a Dark Power in the universe - a mighty evil spirit who is held to be the power behind death and disease, and sin. The difference is that Christianity thinks this Dark Power was created by God, and was good when he was created, and went wrong. Christianity agrees with Dualism that this universe is at war. But it does not think that this universe is a war between independent powers. It thinks it is a civil war, a rebellion, and that we are living in a part of the universe occupied by the rebel. [323]

In giving this account of the devil, Lewis is giving expression to a part of what his book calls 'mere Christianity,' the basic faith held in common down the centuries by Christians of many different traditions. We can see this if we look at the following three extracts taken from John of Damascus' *Exposition of The Orthodox Faith*, John Calvin's *Institutes of the Christian Religion* and the *Catechism of the Catholic Church*.

John of Damascus

John of Damascus' *Exposition of the Orthodox Faith* was written at the beginning of the eighth century. As its title suggests, it is an exposition of the Chistian faith as this was understood by the Eastern Church of his day.

[322] Lewis, *Mere Christianity,* pp.46-47.
[323] Lewis, *Mere Christianity*, p.47.

Chapter 4 of Book II of this work is concerned with 'the devil and demons.' It declares:

He who from among these angelic powers was set over the earthly realm, and into whose hands God committed the guardianship of the earth, was not made wicked in nature but was good, and made for good ends, and received from his Creator no trace whatever of evil in himself. But he did not sustain the brightness and the honour which the Creator had bestowed on him, and of his free choice was changed from what was in harmony to what was at variance with his nature, and became roused against God Who created him, and determined to rise in rebellion against Him: and he was the first to depart from good and become evil. For evil is nothing else than absence of goodness, just as darkness also is absence of light. For goodness is the light of the mind, and, similarly, evil is the darkness of the mind. Light, therefore, being the work of the Creator and being made good (for God saw all that He made, and behold they were exceeding good Genesis 1:31) produced darkness at His free-will. But along with him an innumerable host of angels subject to him were torn away and followed him and shared in his fall. Wherefore, being of the same nature as the angels, they became wicked, turning away at their own free choice from good to evil.

Hence they have no power or strength against anyone except what God in His dispensation has conceded to them, as for instance, against Job (Job 1:12) and those swine that are mentioned in the Gospels. (Mark 5:13) But when God has made the concession they do prevail, and are changed and transformed into any form whatever in which they wish to appear.

Of the future both the angels of God and the demons are alike ignorant: yet they make predictions. God reveals the future to the angels and commands them to prophesy, and so what they say comes to pass. But the demons also make predictions, sometimes because they see what is happening at a distance, and sometimes merely making guesses: hence much that they say is false and they should not be believed, even although they do often, in the way we have said, tell what is true. Besides they know the Scriptures.

All wickedness, then, and all impure passions are the work of their mind. But while the liberty to attack man has been granted to them, they have not the strength to over-master anyone: for we have it in our power to receive or not to receive the attack. Wherefore there has been prepared for the devil and his demons, and those who follow him, fire unquenchable and everlasting punishment (Matthew 25:41).[324]

John Calvin

John Calvin's *Institutes of the Christian Religion*, which reached its final form in 1559, is a guide to Christian theology written from the standpoint of the sixteenth century Reformed tradition. In Chapter XIV of Book I of the *Institutes*, Calvin writes about the devils by whom Christians are attacked as follows:

...the Scripture declares that the enemies who war against us are not one or two, or few in number, but a great host. Mary Magdalene is said to have been delivered from seven devils by which she was possessed; and our Saviour assures us that it is an ordinary circumstance, when a devil has been expelled, if access is again given to it, to take seven other spirits, more wicked than itself, and resume the vacant possession. Nay, one man is said to have been possessed by a whole legion. By this, then, we are taught that the number of enemies with whom we have to war is almost infinite, that we may not, from a contemptuous idea of the fewness of their numbers, be more remiss in the contest, or from imagining that an occasional truce is given us, indulge in sloth. In one Satan or devil being often mentioned in the singular number, the thing denoted is that domination of iniquity which is opposed to the reign of righteousness. For, as the Church and the communion of saints has

---

[324] John of Damascus, *Exposition of the Orthodox Faith*, Bk2, Ch.4 in *The Nicene and Post-Nicene Fathers*, Vol. IX (Edinburgh and Grand Rapids: T&T Clark, Eerdmans, 1997), p.20.

Christ for its head, so the faction of the wicked and wickedness itself, is portrayed with its prince exercising supremacy. Hence the expression, 'Depart, ye cursed, into everlasting fire, prepared for the devil and his angels,' (Mt.25:41)

But as the devil was created by God, we must remember that this malice which we attribute to his nature is not from creation, but from depravation. Everything damnable in him he brought upon himself, by his revolt and fall. Of this Scripture reminds us, lest, by believing that he was so created at first, we should ascribe to God what is most foreign to his nature. For this reason, Christ declares (John 8:44), that Satan, when he lies, 'speaketh of his own,' and states the reason, 'because he abode not in the truth.' By saying that he abode not in the truth, he certainly intimates that he once was in the truth, and by calling him the father of lies, he puts it out of his power to charge God with the depravity of which he was himself the cause. But although the expressions are brief and not very explicit, they are amply sufficient to vindicate the majesty of God from every calumny...

One thing which ought to animate us to perpetual contest with the devil is, that he is everywhere called both our adversary and the adversary of God. For, if the glory of God is dear to us, as it ought to be, we ought to struggle with all our might against him who aims at the extinction of that glory. If we are animated with proper zeal to maintain the Kingdom of Christ, we must wage irreconcilable war with him who conspires its ruin. Again, if we have any anxiety about our own salvation, we ought to make no peace nor truce with him who is continually laying schemes for its destruction. But such is the character given to Satan in the third chapter of Genesis, where he is seen seducing man from his allegiance to God, that he may both deprive God of his due honour and plunge man headlong in destruction. Such, too, is the description given of him in the Gospels (Mt. 13:28), where he is called the enemy, and is said to sow tares in order to corrupt the seed of eternal life. In one word, in all his actions we experience the truth of our Saviour's description, that he was 'a murderer from the beginning, and abode not in the truth,' (John 8:44). Truth he assails with lies, light he obscures with darkness. The minds of men he involves in error; he stirs up hatred, inflames strife and war, and all in order that he may overthrow the kingdom of God, and drown men in eternal perdition with himself. Hence it is evident that his whole nature is depraved, mischievous, and malignant. There must be extreme depravity in a mind bent on assailing the glory of God and the salvation of man. This is intimated by John in his Epistle, when he says that he 'sinneth from the beginning,' (1 John 3:8), implying that he is the author, leader, and contriver of all malice and wickedness.

With regard to the strife and war which Satan is said to wage with God, it must be understood with this qualification, that Satan cannot possibly do anything against the will and consent of God. For we read in the history of Job, that Satan appears in the presence of God to receive his commands, and dares not proceed to execute any enterprise until he is authorised. In the same way, when Ahab was to be deceived, he undertook to be a lying spirit in the mouth of all the prophets; and on being commissioned by the Lord, proceeds to do so. For this reason, also, the spirit which tormented Saul is said to be an evil spirit from the Lord, because he was, as it were, the scourge by which the misdeeds of the wicked king were punished. In another place it is said that the plagues of Egypt were inflicted by God through the instrumentality of wicked angels. In conformity with these particular examples, Paul declares generally that unbelievers are blinded by God, though he had previously described it as the doing of Satan. It is evident, therefore, that Satan is under the power of God, and is so ruled by his authority, that he must yield obedience to it. Moreover, though we say that Satan resists God, and does works at variance with His works, we at the same time maintain that this contrariety and opposition depend on the permission of God. I now speak not of Satan's will and endeavour, but only of the result. For the disposition of the devil being wicked, he has no inclination whatever to obey the divine will, but, on the contrary, is wholly bent on contumacy and rebellion. This much, therefore, he has of himself, and his own iniquity, that he eagerly, and of set purpose, opposes God, aiming at those things which he deems most contrary to the will of God. But as God holds him bound and fettered by the curb of his power, he executes those things only for which permission has been given him, and thus, however unwilling, obeys his Creator, being forced, whenever he is required, to do Him service.[325]

The Catechism of the Catholic Church

The Catechism of the Catholic Church is a 'catechism or compendium of all Catholic doctrine regarding both faith and morals'[326] that was published by the Roman Catholic Church in 1994. Its account of the Devil and the other demons forms part of its account of the Fall in its exposition of the Apostles Creed. In this account we are told:

> The Church teaches that Satan was at first a good angel, made by God: 'The devil and the other demons were indeed created naturally good by God, but they became evil by their own doing.'

> Scripture speaks of a *sin* of these angels. This 'fall' consists in the free choice of these created spirits, who radically and irrevocably rejected God and his reign. We find a reflection of that rebellion in the tempter's words to our first parents: 'You will be like God.' (Genesis 3:5) The devil has sinned from the beginning;' (1 John 3:8) he is 'a liar and the father of lies.' (John 8:44)

> It is the irrevocable character of their choice, and not a defect in the infinite divine mercy, that makes the angels' sin unforgivable. 'There is no repentance for the angels after their fall, just as there is no repentance for men after death.'

> Scripture witnesses to the disastrous influence of the one Jesus calls 'a murderer from the beginning,' (John 8:44) who would even try to

---

[325] John Calvin, *Institutes of the Christian Religion,* Vol.1, Bk 1, Ch XIV.14-17 (Grand Rapids: Eerdmans, 1975), pp.151-153.
[326] *The Catechism of the Catholic Church* (London: Geoffrey Chapman, 1994), p.3.

divert Jesus from the mission received from his Father. 'The reason the Son of God appeared was to destroy the works of the devil.' (1 John 3:8) In its consequences the gravest of these works was the mendacious seduction that led man to disobey God.

The power of Satan is, nonetheless, not infinite. He is only a creature, powerful from the fact that he is pure spirit, but still a creature. He cannot prevent the building up of God's reign. Although Satan may act in the world out of hatred for God and his kingdom in Christ Jesus, and although his action may cause grave injuries - of a spiritual nature and, indirectly, even of a physical nature - to each man and to society, the action is permitted by divine providence which with strength and gentleness guides human and cosmic history. It is a great mystery that providence should permit diabolical activity, but 'we know that in everything God works for good with those who love him.' (Romans 8:28) [327]

Taken together, what is said in these three passages, and in the previous passage from *Mere Christianity* gives a coherent picture of the existence and activity of the devil or Satan to use the other name given to him is Scripture) and the demonic powers that are under his leadership.

First, the devil and the large number of other demons are fallen angels. They are spiritual beings who have irrevocably turned against God through the abuse of their free will.

Secondly, since the beginning of human history these fallen angels have engaged in a spiritual assault of human beings, seeking to lead them away from God so that they will eventually join the angels in eternal perdition.

Thirdly, they have a limited ability to predict the future and the ability to cause human beings grave spiritual and even physical harm.

---

[327] *The Catechism of the Catholic Church,* 391-395, pp.88-89.

Fourthly, in spite of the powers they possess, the devil and the other demonic beings can be resisted by human beings and they can only act with the permission of God and within the limits set by God's providence.

Demonic powers, idolatry, and the development of secular Western society

The significance of the existence of the devil and the other demons for our understanding of contemporary Western society is that means that the poisoned fruit of secularisation that we have noted in this chapter has not occurred by accident. It has been the result of the action of human beings, but it has also been the result of the influence on human beings of the devil and the other demonic powers subject to him seeking to lead people away from God.

As Helmut Thielicke explains in his essay 'The Reality of the Demonic' it is important to note that this demonic activity has generally been anonymous rather than overt. In his words:

Anonymity is an indispensable mark of the demonic power. The New Testament expresses this anonymity by speaking of powers which exert their influence as spirits of the air from out of the dark, hidden background of the world (Eph.2:2, 6:12). Hence they are as life-determining as the atmosphere and just as imperceptible. An example is the so-called 'Zeitgeist' the spirit of the times. Who can determine where he himself ceases and the *Zeitgeist* starts! The *Zeitgeist is* so much in the atmosphere around us that we think it is we ourselves who hold its opinions and prejudices. It is true that we as subjects help to sustain the *Zeitgeist*, but it is also true that here we are being held under the spell of an anonymous power which is not ourselves but only acts as if it were ourselves and were expressing our own thoughts. Its anonymity lies precisely in the fact that it cannot be objectively grasped, but rather surrounds us in a nonobjective way. Therefore this power is also fond of using the instrument of *propaganda*, that is, the nonobjective suggestion for the purpose of 'forming the will (*Willensbildung*) The very phrase 'forming the will' is characteristic. For it indicates that propaganda does address itself to man as the bearer of a will, but never less influences this will in such a secret and insinuating way that it is almost unconsciously changed and then accepts and carries out secretly imposed and suggested decisions as if they were its own.

Once more then, the demonic is not an opponent who becomes objectively tangible like flesh and blood - Paul says we are not contending with flesh and blood! - but rather works through us non objectively and retreats into invisibility behind us. To use Paul's terminology this constitutes his principality his power, and his invisible atmospheric character.[328]

Because the influence of the demonic has been anonymous and invisible in the way Thielicke describes, most writers who have traced the development of the modern, secular Western world have left the influence of the devil and other demons out of the picture. However, this has been a mistake because it results in a seriously incomplete picture of what has taken place. It is truer that that formation of the modern world has been the result of the activity of human beings along the lines described in the previous chapter.

However, it has also been the result of human beings influenced by the activity of the devil and other demonic powers who have led people into idolatry.

The nature of idolatry

To understand this point we have to begin by understanding the nature of idolatry, and a helpful introduction to the nature of idolatry is provided by Martin Luther in his *Large Catechism* of 1529.

In this work Luther expounds the first of the Ten Commandments, 'You shall have no other gods before me,' in the following terms:

---

[328] Helmut Thielicke, 'The Reality of the Demonic' in Helmut Thielicke, *Man in God's World* (Cambridge: Lutterworth Press, 2016), pp.184-185. Italics in the original.

Thou shalt have [and worship] me alone as thy God. What is the force of this, and how is it to be understood? What is it to have a god? or, what is God?

Answer: A god is that whereto we are to look for all good and to take refuge in all distress; so that to have a god is to trust and believe him from the whole heart; as I have often said that the confidence and faith of the heart alone make both God and an idol. If your faith and trust be right, then is your god also true. And, on the other hand, if your trust be false and wrong, then you have not the true God; for these two belong together, viz. faith and God. That now, I say, upon which you set your heart and put your trust is properly your god. Therefore, it is the intent of this commandment to require such true faith and trust of the heart as regards the only true God, and rest in him alone. That is as much as to say: 'See to it that you let me be your God, and you never seek another,' i.e. 'Whatever you lack in good, seek it of me, and look to me for it, and whenever you suffer misfortune and distress, lay hold of me and cling fast to me. I verily will give you enough and help you out of every necessity; only let not your heart cleave to or rest in any other.'

This I must unfold somewhat more plainly, that it may be understood and perceived by ordinary examples of the contrary. Many a one thinks that he has God and everything in abundance when he has money and possessions, in which he trusts and boasts so arrogantly as to care for no one. Lo, such a man also has a god, Mammon by name, i.e. money and possessions, on which he sets all his heart, and which is also the most common idol on earth. He who has money and possessions feels secure, and is as joyful and undismayed as though he were in the midst of Paradise. On the other hand, he who has none doubts and is despondent, as though he knew of no God. For very few are to be found who are of good cheer, and who neither mourn nor complain if they have not Mammon.

This [care and desire for money] adheres and clings to our nature, even to the grave.

So too, whoever trusts and boasts in the possession of great skill, prudence, power, favour, friendship and honour has also a god, but not the only true God. This appears again when you notice how presumptuous, secure and proud people are because of such possessions, and how despondent when without them or deprived of them. Therefore I repeat that the true explanation of this point is that to have a god is to have something upon which the heart entirely trusts.

Besides, consider what, in our blindness, we have hitherto been doing under the Papacy. If any one had toothache, he fasted and honoured St. Apollonia [macerated his flesh by voluntary fasting to the honour of St. Apollonia]; if he were afraid of fire, he sought St. Laurence as his deliverer; if he dreaded pestilence, he made a vow to St. Sebastian or Rachio, and a countless number of such abominations, where everyone selected his own saint whom he worshiped and invoked in distress. Here belong those also whose idolatry is most gross, and who make a covenant with the devil, in order that he may give them plenty of money or help them in love-affairs, preserve their cattle, restore to them lost possessions, etc., as e.g. sorcerers and necromancers. For all these place their heart and trust elsewhere than in the true God, and neither look to him for any good nor seek anything from him. Thus, you can easily understand what and how much this commandment requires, viz. that man's entire heart and all his confidence be placed in God alone, and in no one else. For to have God, you can easily perceive, is not to lay hold of him with our hands or to put him in a bag [as money], or to lock him in a chest [as silver vessels]. But he is said to be apprehended when the heart lays hold of him and depends upon him. But to depend upon him with the heart is nothing else than to trust in him entirely. For this reason he wishes to withdraw us from everything else, and to attract us to himself, viz. because he is the only eternal good. As though he would say: Whatever you have heretofore sought of the saints, or for which you have trusted in Mammon, as well as all else, expect of me, and regard me as the one who will help you and endow you richly with all good things.

Lo, you have here the true honour and service of God, which pleases God, and which he commands under penalty of eternal wrath, viz. that the heart know no other trust or confidence than in him, and do not suffer itself to be torn from him, but, for him, risk and disregard everything upon earth. On the other hand, you can easily see and judge how the world practices only false worship and idolatry. For no people has ever been so godless as not to institute and observe some sort of divine service. Thus every one has set up as his own god whatever he looked to for blessings, help and comfort.

When, for example, the heathen who aimed at power and dominion elevated Jupiter as the supreme god, the others, who were bent upon riches, happiness, or pleasure and a life of ease, venerated Hercules, Mercury, Venus, or others. Women with child worshiped Diana or Lucina. Thus everyone makes that to which his heart is inclined his god. So that even in the mind of the heathen to have a god is nothing but to trust and believe. But their error is this, that their trust is false and wrong; for it is not placed in the only God, beside whom there is truly no other in heaven or upon earth. Wherefore the heathen really form their self-invented notions and dreams of God into an idol, and put their trust in that which is altogether nothing. Thus is it with all idolatry; for it consists not merely in erecting an image and worshiping it, but rather in the heart, which is intent on something else, and seeks help and consolation from creatures, saints or devils, and neither accepts God, nor looks to him for good to such an extent as to believe that he is willing to help; neither believes that whatever good it experiences comes from God.[329]

What Luther makes clear in this extract is that the key issue in relation to idolatry is not the veneration of material images such as the golden calf created by the people of Israel in Exodus 32:1-7 or the images of the Greek gods seen by Paul in Athens Acts 17:16-31. Such images may become the focus of idolatry (which is why they are prohibited in the second of the Ten Commandments in Exodus 20:4-6), but the key issue is that all forms of activity are idolatry if they involve putting trust and faith for our well-being in anyone (or anything) other than God himself. As Luther emphasises, it is misplaced faith and trust that is the thing that is really important.

What the Bible tells us is that idolatry in this comprehensive sense of putting trust and faith in that which is not God has been a problem throughout human history.

Idolatry and the Fall
According to the Bible the very first act of idolatry was the Fall of Adam and Eve, the parents of the human race. Their Fall is described in Genesis 3:1-6:

Now the serpent was more subtle than any other wild creature that the Lord God had made. He said to the woman, 'Did God say, 'You shall not eat of any tree of the garden'?' And the woman said to the serpent, 'We may eat of the fruit of the trees of the garden; but God said, 'You shall not eat of the fruit of the tree which is in the midst of the garden, neither shall you touch it, lest you die.' But the serpent said to the woman, 'You will not die. For God knows that when you eat of it your eyes will be opened, and you will be like God, knowing good and evil.' So when the woman saw that the tree was good for food, and that it was a delight to the eyes, and that the tree was to

---

[329] Martin Luther, *Large Catechism*, pp.16-18 at:
https://www.lutheranlibrary.org/pdf/194-jacobs-luther-large-catechism.pdf

be desired to make one wise, she took of its fruit and ate; and she also gave some to her husband, and he ate.

There are three elements in this account of their Fall which shed light on the nature of idolatry.

First, there is activity of the devil seeking to lead human beings away from God. In the context of the Bible as a whole it is clear that the serpent in the Garden of Eden is a physical form taken by the devil (described in Revelation 12:9 as 'that ancient serpent, who is called the devil and Satan') and in this form, he tempts Eve, and through her Adam, to rebel against God. This pattern of the devil tempting people to rebel against God is one that is then repeated again and again among the descendants of Adam and Eve. Idolatry is the result of people saying 'yes' to this temptation by deciding to put their faith and trust in someone or something other than God.

Secondly, the temptation presented to Eve by the devil takes the form of a 'noble lie' by the Devil. According to Genesis, the claim made to Eve by the devil is that if she eats the fruit of the forbidden tree 'you will be like God, knowing good and evil.' To understand the what the devil is suggesting, we need to understand that what 'knowing good and evil' means is to act like God by deciding for oneself what is good and what is evil.[330] As Chris Wright notes, 'It is the prerogative of God, in the supreme goodness of his own being, to decide and define for ourselves what constitutes goodness and therefore conversely what is evil.' For a human being to decide for themselves what they will deem good and evil is therefore to 'usurp the prerogative of God in rebellious moral autonomy.' [331]

The pitch made by the devil to Eve is that to be like God in this way is something desirable.

---

[330] For a helpful discussion of the meaning of the phrase see Karl Barth, *Church Dogmatics* III.1 (London and New York: T&T Clark, 2004), pp.257-288.
[331] Chris Wright. *Here are your Gods!'* (London: Inter-Varsity Press, 2020), Kindle edition, p.49.

In the words of Christopher Watkin this pitch:

> ...is the origin of what has come to be called the 'noble lie,' a falsehood told by an individual or group in power with the aim of manipulating those under their power into doing what otherwise they would not do, often with the veneer of a noble purpose. Such is the case here: on the surface Satan wants Eve to 'reach her full potential,' not to be held back by the 'artificial constraints' of God's nannying. She was 'made for greater things,' and it is time for her to start making her own decisions, time to take on the world on her own terms, time to be 'everything that she can be.' Like a monarch preaching to his or her subjects that it is sweet and fitting to die for one's country, Satan feeds Eve a false dream and encourages her to follow her dreams. In thinking that she's acting her own best interests, Eve is in fact slavishly doing the bidding of Satan and violating her own best interests: that is the devilish genius of the satanic noble lie.[332]

Every act of idolatry post Eden is the result of some similar form of the 'satanic noble lie.' Behind every act of idolatry is the voice of the devil suggesting that if we want to truly flourish we need to put our trust and faith in someone or something other than God for our well-being.

Thirdly, we learn from Genesis 3 that after having listened to the voice of the devil Eve usurps the place of God. Watkin notes that in Genesis 3:6 there is an echo what has been said in Genesis 1:

> Eve 'saw' that the tree was good for food, just as God repeatedly 'saw that it was good' in the creation narrative. Eve is putting herself in the place of God, deciding what is good and evil. In so doing, she tries to upturn the order of creation. Imagine a triangle, with God the creator as the topmost point, and even the serpent, both creatures, as the two bottom points. Eve has rearranged the pieces called: now she is at the apex of the triangle, sitting in

---

[332] Christopher Watkin, *Biblical Critical Theory* (Grand Rapids: Zondervan Academic, 2022), Kindle edition, p.113.

judgement over what God and the serpent have said to her, weighing up their alternative truths.[333]

What then happens is that Eve decides to act upon the 'truth' suggested to her by the devil, eating the forbidden fruit herself and giving some of it to Adam who eats also.

Every act of idolatry follows this same pattern. It involves a human being, led astray by the Devil, deciding that they can stand in the place of God, determining what is good and evil, and then opting for what they think is good, but is in fact evil, and acting upon that choice. Furthermore, the individual who opts for idolatry then all too frequently, as in the case of Eve, leads someone else into idolatry as well. According to Genesis 2:16-17 it was Adam who was originally given the command by God not to eat the fruit of the tree of the knowledge of good and evil, but following Eve's lead he does it anyway. Idolatry is contagious.

Fourthly, we learn from Genesis 3 that idolatry does not deliver what it promises. Eve (and then presumably Adam) act in a way that they think will benefit them. The forbidden fruit looks good to eat and they have the Devil's assurance that if they eat it, they will not die as God has said, but will achieve something desirable, the ability to be like God. However, the Devil's assurance is a lie in two ways.

a. Eve and Adam do not actually become gods. The power to determine good and evil still eludes them. As Wright notes, it is not 'that humans have now *become* gods, but that they have chosen to act *as though they were* – defining and deciding for themselves what they will regard as good and evil.'[334]

b. God's declaration that eating of the forbidden fruit will lead to death turns out to be true. God expels them from Eden, thus barring them from access to the 'tree of life' (Genesis 3:22-23) and they subsequently

---

[333] Watkin, p.113.
[334] Wright, p.49, italics in the original.

die. In the light of the biblical witness as a whole, the death penalty imposed by God on Adam and Eve can be seen as an act of paradoxical mercy. It means that they are not doomed to life for ever in their fallen state and it opens the way for God to redeem mankind through the death and resurrection of Christ. Nevertheless, for Adam and Eve death was not what they desired. What they wanted, and what the devil promised them was immortal life in this world and this did not happen.

This aspect of the Genesis account points us to the wider truth that idolatry never delivers what it promises. Human beings engage in idiolatry because, being misled by the devil, they believe that they will receive some form of good by so doing. However, this belief is always mistaken. All that is good ultimately comes from God, the sole good creator, and so any good that human beings may appear to receive as a result of idolatry actually comes from God and the ultimate good which all humans desire, the fulfilment of their human potential in a life without end will always elude them except if they put their faith and trust in him.

Idolatry as the worship of false gods
The biblical account of the beginning of the human story tells us that the original religion of humanity was the worship of the one creator God described in Genesis 1 and 2, the God who subsequently revealed himself to Israel as *Yahweh*, or in English versions of the Bible 'the Lord.' Thus, in Genesis 4:26, which is intended to give a description of what Gerhard von Rad calls 'the primeval religion of mankind in general,'[335] we are told that in the time of Seth the son of Adam 'men began to call upon the name of the Lord' ('call upon' meaning worship).

The God who created the world had made himself known by means of personal revelation to the first ancestors of the human race (Genesis 1:26-30, 2:15-24, 3:8-19, 4:1-7) and it was this same God, Genesis says, who was worshipped when corporate worship was instituted in the time of Seth (Genesis 4:26).

[335] Gerhard von Rad, *Genesis* (London: SCM, 1972), p.113.

The evidence of historical, ethnographic, and linguistic study confirms the biblical idea that the original religion of mankind was the worship of one creator God who had revealed himself personally to the earliest ancestors of the human race. To quote the great German student of early religion, Willhelm Schmidt:

> The bottom line is that the reports we have from the adherents of the oldest religions themselves are not only merely disinclined towards the supposition that the religions were created by seeking and searching human beings; rather, worse yet, they do not even mention it with a single word. All their affirmative responses are directed to the side of divine revelation: it is God Himself Who taught humans what to believe about Him, how to venerate Him, and how they should obey the expression of His will.[336]

Once again in accordance with the biblical account, the evidence gathered by Schmidt and other scholars tells us that polytheism was a later development. Even when the early direct revelation ceased the existence of the one creator God was revealed through creation (Romans 1:19-20), but in spite of this fact monotheism gradually came to be replaced by various forms of polytheism with the creator God being subsumed into a pantheon of different divine beings. Thus, Zeus, the divine father, was still worshipped, but becomes only one among a range of Greek deities and the same was true of the Norse creator God Tyr who ends up as a fairly minor Norse deity. Alongside this development both people (such as the Egyptian Pharaohs), and created objects such as statues, came to be seen as the places where the gods manifested themselves on earth, and therefore became the objects of worship In their own right.[337]

---

[336] Schmidt, *Der Ursprung der Gottesidee*, Vol. VI (Munster: Aschendorff, 1935), p.480.

[337] For the evidence for this development see Winfried Corduan, *In the beginning God – A fresh look at the case for original monotheism* (Nashville: B&H Academic, 2013).

In biblical terms this development was another development of idolatry. Rather than putting their faith and trust in the one creator God for their well-being, people put their faith and trust instead in the gods of polytheism and the material idols who represented them. This point is made in graphic fashion by the prophet Hosea who compares the people of Israel to an unfaithful wife who says: I will go after my lovers, who give me my bread and my water, my wool and my flax, my oil and my drink.' (Hosea 2:5).

As Derek Kidner explains, what lies behind the sexual imagery employed by Hosea is that:

> The gods of Canaan were largely patrons of fertility. To get the best results of farming one would be tempted to enlist their help, imagining that Yahweh must be somewhat out of his depth in such a realm ('And she did not know,' the Lord exclaims, 'that it was I who gave her the grain, the wine, and the oil...', verse 8). More than that, these gods were Baals, meaning Lords or husbands, and while some of their rituals were a re-enacting of their wars and victories, or vegetation's death and resurrection, which would supposedly ensure the progress of the seasons and the crops, other rituals were sexual acts with cultic prostitutes, whereby the coitus at the sanctuary would magically induce fertility in the flocks and herds and farm produce.[338]

As time went on, and different groups with different gods merged, what happened was that the number of gods multiplied into the thousands and because people desired supernatural help not just in agricultural matters but in all areas of life, the result was that, in the words of Augustine, the 'functions of the gods' were 'portioned out in penny packets, with instructions that each of these divinities should be supplicated for his special responsibility.' [339] He gives the example of

[338] Derek Kidner, *Love to the Loveless* (Leicester: Inter-Varsity Press, 1981), pp.29-30.
[339] Augustine, *The City of God,* Bk.6, Ch.9 (Harmondsworth: Penguin, 1981), pp.243-244.

the Roman gods Educa and Potina who were responsible for infant children receiving solid food and drink respectively.

Furthermore, as Augustine also explains, the gods did nothing to ensure moral behaviour. Religion had to do with ritual not ethics. As Augustine puts it:

> ...It was responsibility of the gods as counsellors, not to conceal the instructions for a good life from the people who worship them. They should have presented and proclaimed them plainly; they should have confronted and convicted sinners by their prophets, threatening punishments to evil-doers and promising rewards to those of upright life. Yet the temples of these gods never rang with any such clearly and emphatically uttered exhortations. [340]

Indeed, not only did the gods not discourage moral behaviour, they were held to positively support it in its most depraved form as in the case of alleged requirement of the gods for ritual prostitution and child sacrifice. As a result, the fruit of idolatry was the moral breakdown described by Paul in Romans 1:26-32.

What the Bible also indicates is that behind the gods there were Satan and his demons. Thus, in Deuteronomy 32:16-18 Moses declares concerning the people of Israel:

> They stirred him to jealousy with strange gods;
>> with abominable practices they provoked him to anger.
> They sacrificed to demons which were no gods,
>> to gods they had never known,
> to new gods that had come in of late,
>> whom your fathers had never dreaded.
> You were unmindful of the Rock that begot you,
>> and you forgot the God who gave you birth.

---

[340] Augustine, Bk. II, Ch.4, p.51.

Here the pagan gods to whom the people of Israel offered worshipped are specifically identified as demons.

In similar fashion the Psalmist declares in Psalm 106:35-38 that the people of Israel:

> ...did not destroy the peoples,
> > as the Lord commanded them,
> but they mingled with the nations
> > and learned to do as they did.
> They served their idols,
> > which became a snare to them.
> They sacrificed their sons
> > and their daughters to the demons;
> they poured out innocent blood,
> > the blood of their sons and daughters,
> whom they sacrificed to the idols of Canaan;
> > and the land was polluted with blood.

According to the Psalmist the idols to whom the Israelites sacrificed their children were in reality demons.

Moving on to the New Testament, in Acts 26:18 Paul tells Agrippa that the commission given to him by Christ to convert Gentiles from the worship of the pagan gods and their idols to Christianity was so that 'they may turn from darkness to light and from the power of Satan to God.' The implication here is clear, worship of the gods and their idols is subjection to the power of Satan.

In 1 Corinthians 10:19-21, after he has warned the Christians in Corinth to shun the worship of idols, Paul goes on to say:

> What do I imply then? That food offered to idols is anything, or that an idol is anything? No, I imply that what pagans sacrifice they offer to demons and not to God. I do not want you to be partners with

demons. You cannot drink the cup of the Lord and the cup of demons. You cannot partake of the table of the Lord and the table of demons.

What Paul is saying here is clear. The worship of idols is the worship of demons and it is for that reason that Christians must not participate in it.

Finally, in Revelation 9:20 we are told:

The rest of mankind, who were not killed by these plagues, did not repent of the works of their hands nor give up worshiping demons and idols of gold and silver and bronze and stone and wood, which cannot either see or hear or walk.

Here again the worship of idols and the worship of demons is said to be one and the same thing.

To quote Chris Wright again, although there are only a few verses in the Old and New Testaments that specifically identify gods, idols and demons, nevertheless in these passages: 'The connection is clear: to worship other gods is to worship satanic demons that infest the very statues that represent them.' [341]

This identification of gods, idols and demons was accepted by the Early Fathers. For example, in the *Divine Institutes* Lactantius states:

When they are adjured, those most wicked spirits confess they are demons. Yet, when they are worshipped, they falsely say they are gods, in order to lead men into errors and call them away from the knowledge of the true God, by which alone eternal death can be escaped. [342]

This makes perfectly good theological sense. If the purpose of Satan and the demons under his control is to lead people away from God, then

[341] Wright, p.28.
[342] Lactantius p.130.

what better way to do so than by presenting themselves as gods and making themselves the objects of human worship? In accordance with the principle of demonic anonymity noted by Thielicke, the demons conceal themselves behind the idols who act as their public face.

Idolatry today

The result of the long process of the conversion of Europe to Christianity was that the pagan gods and their idols eventually ceased to be worshiped. To give one example, in his *History of the English Church and People* Bede gives an account of the conversion to Christianity of King Edwin of Northumbria and his Chief Priest Coifi. In this account Bede records that when King Edwin asked Coifi:

> ...who should be the first to profane the altars and shrines of the idols, together with the enclosures that surrounded them, Coifi replied: 'I will do this myself; for now that the true God has granted me knowledge, who more suitably than I can set a public example and destroy the idols that I worshipped in ignorance?' So he formally renounced his empty superstitions and asked the king to give him arms and a stallion - for hitherto it had not been lawful for the chief priest to carry arms or to ride anything but a mare -and, thus equipped, he set out to destroy the idols. Girded with a sword and with a spear in his hand, he mounted the king's stallion and rode up to the idols. When the crowd saw him, they thought he had gone mad; but without hesitation as soon as he reached the temple, he cast into it the spear he carried and thus profaned it. Then, full of joy at his knowledge of the worship of the true God, he told his companions to set fire to the temple and its enclosures and to destroy them. The site where these idols once stood is still shown, not far East of York, beyond the river Derwent and is known today as Goodmanham. Here it was that the Chief Priest, inspired by the

true God, desecrated and destroyed the altars that he had himself dedicated. [343]

This abandonment of the old gods and their idols has become a permanent state of affairs. The decline of Christianity in the Western world has not been accompanied by a widespread return to the worship of the old gods.

This does not mean however, that idols have ceased to exist in our modern secularised society. There are just as many idols as there ever were. It is just that in the lapsed Christian world that exists in the West today these idols are no longer linked to supernatural gods in the way that they used to be. To put the point another way, what we now have is a new set of secular idols.

This is a point that is well made by Tim Keller in his book *Counterfeit Gods*. Like Luther before him Keller gives a functional account of idolatry, declaring that an idol is whatever takes the place of God in our lives.

He writes:

> What is an idol? It is anything more important to you then God, anything that absorbs your heart and imagination more than God, anything you seek to give you what only God can give.

> A counterfeit God is anything so central and essential to your life that, should you lose it, your life would feel hardly worth living. An idol has such a controlling position in your heart that you can spend most of your passion and energy, your emotional and financial resources, on it without a second thought. It can be family and children, or career and making money, or achievement and critical acclaim, or saving face and social standing. It can be romantic relationship, peer approval, competence and skill, secure and

[343] Bede, *History of the English Church and People,* Bk II.14 (Harmondsworth: Penguin, 1977), p.128.

comfortable circumstances, your beauty or your brains, a great political or social cause, your morality and virtue, or even success in the Christian ministry. When your meaning in life is to fix someone else's life we may call it co-dependency but it's really idolatry. An idol is whatever you look at inside, in your heart of hearts, 'If I have that, then I'll feel my life has meaning, then I'll know I have value, then I'll feel significant and secure.' There are many ways to describe that kind of relationships to something but perhaps the best one is *worship*.

The old pagans were not fanciful when they depicted virtually everything as a god. They had sex gods, work gods, war gods, money gods, nation gods - for the simple fact but anything can be a god that rules and serves as a deity in the heart of a person or in the life of a people. For example, physical beauty is a pleasant thing, but if you 'deify' it, if you make it the most important thing in a person's life or a culture's life, then you have Aphrodite, not just beautiful. You have people, and an entire culture, constantly agonising over appearance, spending inordinate amounts of time and money on it, and foolishly evaluating character on the basis of it. If anything becomes more fundamental than God to your happiness, meaning in life, and identity, then it is an idol.

The biblical concept of idolatry is an extremely sophisticated idea, integrating intellectual, psychological, social, cultural, and spiritual categories. There are personal idols, such as romantic love and family: or money, power, and achievement; or access to particular social circles; or the emotional dependence of others on you; or health, fitness, and physical beauty, many look to these things for the hope, meaning, and fulfilment that only God can provide.

There are cultural idols such as military power, technological progress and economic prosperity. The idols of traditional societies include family, hard work, duty, and moral virtue all those of Western cultures are individual freedom, self-discovery, personal affluence and fulfilment All these good things can and do take on a disproportionate size and power within a society. They promise safety, peace, and happiness if only we base our lives on them. [344]

If we accept this account of idolatry, then what follows is that there are just as many gods in our modern Western secular society as there were in the ancient Roman world described by Augustine. However, it needs to be noted that not all gods are equal. In the ancient world some gods were more important than others and the same is true today. Two gods in particular have special importance in our society.

The first is the god of 'individual freedom' and 'self-discovery' noted by Keller. As we saw in chapter 5 one of the key reasons that Christian freedom is under attack in the Western world is because Christians will not conform to contemporary emphasis on personal autonomy by for example, affirming the acceptability of abortion, same-sex sexual activity, or gender transition.

The problem for Christians is that to participate in the cult of personal autonomy, as Western society wants them to do, is to participate in idolatry. This point is well made by Matthew Roberts in his book *Pride, Identity and the Worship of Self*. Roberts comments that the new understanding of the autonomous self that has come to dominate Western culture:

> ...has a powerfully religious aspect to it, even if that is not how it was (and is) conceived by those who developed it and live by it. The Self, and the freedom to be ourselves, is not just an idea but an object of devotion. The freedom to create myself according to my own desires has become the highest and final authority. And we cannot establish a new authority without coming to worship it, to lavish on devotion upon it, to willingly prostrate ourselves before it as our god.

[344] Tim Keller, *Counterfeit Gods*, (London: Hodder and Stoughton, 1979), Kindle edition. loc. 116-126.

All sin is a form of pride: the exalting of self above God. Every choice to disobey God does this; every idol carved by us in our image implicitly does the same. But to make the Self and its Freedom the very idol that we worship would seem to be pride expressed in a particularly pure form.

This explains the towering significance that feelings and choices have come to have in our world. To worship liberty is to worship the Self; and so the choices that the Self makes are no longer simply moral choices but have become moral imperatives. What the Self chooses is right by definition, for the self is god. What is more, the desires that underly those choices are not subject to any external moral norms but have become *the* moral norm: they are aspects of the divine will which must be obeyed. Freedom, autonomy, the self, and the self's desires form a nexus which functions in western society as a kind of modern pantheon, the thing which is worshipped with the love and willing service due to God alone. [345]

Those commentators who have seen the holding of Pride marches and the now ubiquitous flying of LGBTQI+ flags by public institutions as being emblematic of a new form of religion have therefore been right. These are indeed expressions of a new form of religion whose god is the autonomous self and its desires.

Furthermore, as we noted in chapter 5 this new religion has a hegemonic tendency. It wants to be, if not the only, certainly the dominant, form of religion in Western society and consequently other forms of religion, such as traditional Christianity, which will not accept its dominance must be controlled or suppressed. However, for Christians to accept its dominance, for them to bow down to this new god, would be for them to break the first and second commandments and that is something that they may not do.

---

[345] Matthew Roberts, *Pride, Identity and the Worship of Self* (Fearn: Christian Focus, 2023), Kindle edition, pp.40-41.

The other god that has become dominant in Western society is the god of identity politics. Modern identity politics is an offshoot of Marxist thought. In traditional Marxism the thing that had the highest value, the good to which all else was subject, was the revolutionary liberation of the working class. The achievement of this goal was the Marxist god, and the Marxist revolutionaries were its acolytes.

In modern identity politics the basic idea of the revolutionary liberation of the oppressed remains but the oppressed now tend to be defined not as the working class, but as particular oppressed groups within society, women, sexual minorities, racial minorities,[346] indigenous peoples and people with disabilities. In identity politics the highest good, the god to which all else must be subject, is the liberation of these groups through the overthrow of the political power exercised by their oppressors and the assumption of political power by the oppressed. [347]

Like the cult of personal autonomy, identity politics is a form of religion for a secular age. As Tara Burton notes, identity politics, what she calls 'Modern social justice culture' has created:

...a fairly compelling, a shadow logically focused account of a meaningful world, in which every human being has a fundamental purpose in a cosmic struggle, all without including, well, God...The social justice movement is so successful because it replicates the

---

[346] For the purposes of identity politics, being Muslim counts as an ethnic identity, which is why 'Islamophobia' forms part of its lexicon and why attacks on Islam are generally treated more seriously than attacks on other religious groups, as exemplified by the case in New Zealand reported in chapter 5.

[347] For helpful introductions to identity politics from a Christian perspective see Scott David Allen, *Why social Justice is not Biblical Justice* (Grand Rapids: Credo House, 2020), Ben Chang, *Christ and the Culture Wars* (Fearn: Christian Focus, 2023) and Edward Feser, *All One in Christ- A Catholic Critique of Racism and Critical Race Theory* (San Franciso: Ignatius Press, 2022.

cornerstones of traditional religion -meaning, purpose, community and ritual. [348]

To put it another way, people in Western society may have turned their back on the Christian God, but a God-shaped gap remains and, like Communism before it, identity politics helps to fill this gap by giving people without God the meaning and purpose for which they are looking.

In the world of identity politics neutrality is seen as impossible. You are either a member of an oppressed group, or an 'ally' of an oppressed group (such as white people supportive of anti-racist politics), or are an oppressor exercising some form of 'ism' or 'phobia.' This means that Christianity is only seen as a positive force in so far as it gives support to the struggle against the various forms of oppression recognised by identity politics.

Thus Ibram X. Kendi, writing from a black anti-racist perspective, contrasts 'liberation theology' and 'savior theology' (i.e. the traditional Christian account of salvation from sin) insisting that only the former is acceptable from an anti-racist standpoint:

Jesus was a revolutionary, and the job of the Christian is to revolutionise society...To liberate society from the powers on Earth that are oppressing humanity...that's liberation theology in a nutshell. Savior theology is a different type of theology. The job of the Christian is to go out and save these individuals who are behaviourally deficient. In other words, we are to bring them into the church, these individuals who are doing all these evil, sinful things, and heal them. And save them. And then, once we've saved them, we've done our jobs... Anti racists fundamentally reject savior

[348] Tara Burton, *Strange Rites: New Religions for a Godless World* (New York: Public Affairs, 2020).

theology (which) goes right in line with racist ideas and a racist theology.[349]

The reason that Christians, with the exception of those who sign up to the agenda of identity politics in the way described by Kendi, are seen as being in McAlpine's words 'the bad guys,' is because Christians are seen as having historically supported the oppression of women, sexual minorities, ethnic minorities, indigenous peoples, and people with disabilities[350] and because, they are seen as still being supportive of their oppression today (hence the common claims that churches are sexist, homophobic, racist etc.).

Furthermore, just as the Communist governments of the twentieth century took action against the Christian churches for their alleged 'anti-revolutionary' attitudes and activities, so supporters of identity politics support governmental action against what they see as oppressive attitudes and activities by the churches today – the calls for a legal ban on 'conversion therapy' being a case in point. Christians have offended against the god of identity politics and should be prevented from doing so in future.

Where all this leaves us

What we have seen in chapters 5 and 6 is the that the increasing attacks on Christian freedom of religion in the Western world today are not occurring by accident. They are the result of the secularisation of Western Society, and the alternative social imaginary that has emerged as a result. These developments are paradoxically the poisoned fruit of the success of Christianity in shaping Western Society and its values and the production of this poisoned fruit has to be seen theologically as a continuation of the attack on God's human creatures undertaken by the devil and other fallen angels working with him which has taken place ever since the world was first created.

---

[349] Ibram X. Kendi, 'How to Be Anti-Racist,' cited in Feser, Kindle edition, p.84
[350] This is reflected, for instance, in the report on chaplaincy in the Canadian armed forces we looked at in chapter 4.

The instrument that the devil and the other demons have used to turn people away from obedience to God throughout human history has been various forms of idolatry and this continues to be the case today, although the idols that now exist and through which the demonic now operates are ones which fit in with the contemporary Western social imaginary. Two of the dominant gods that are worshipped in modern Western idolatry are the god of personal autonomy and the god of identity politics. The current attacks on Christianity in the Western world can be seen as the result of the refusal of those who hold to traditional Christian beliefs to bow down and worship these new gods.

The question that we shall explore in the next three chapters is how Christians in the western World should respond to this situation. We shall begin in chapter 7 by exploring the freedoms that Christians in the West still have in spite of the contemporary attacks on their freedom that we have noted.

Chapter 7
Why Western Christians are free to live by the truth and not by lies

1. The need to live by the truth and not by lies

In 1978 the Czech dissident Vaclav Havel published a book called *The Power of the Powerless* which became a manifesto for dissent against Soviet Communism in Czechoslovakia, Poland and other countries in the Soviet bloc.

In chapter III of this book Havel writes as follows about the actions of a Greengrocer in a Communist regime:

> The manager of a fruit-and-vegetable shop places in his window, among the onions and carrots, the slogan: 'Workers of the world, unite!' Why does he do it? What is he trying to communicate to the world? Is he genuinely enthusiastic about the idea of unity among the workers of the world? Is his enthusiasm so great that he feels an irrepressible impulse to acquaint the public with his ideals? Has he really given more than a moment's thought to how such a unification might occur and what it would mean?

> I think it can safely be assumed that the overwhelming majority of shopkeepers never think about the slogans they put in their windows, nor do they use them to express their real opinions. That poster was delivered to our greengrocer from the enterprise headquarters along with the onions and carrots. He put them all into the window simply because it has been done that way for years, because everyone does it, and because that is the way it has to be. If he were to refuse, there could be trouble. He could be reproached for not having the proper decoration in his window; someone might even accuse him of disloyalty. He does it because these things must be done if one is to get along in life. It is one of the

thousands of details that guarantee him a relatively tranquil life 'in harmony with society,' as they say. [351]

Havel goes on to note that the ideology of the Communist state, as reflected in the slogan that the greengrocer has been asked to display, provides him with a cover from having to admit that he has displayed the slogan simply to protect himself from trouble. In Havel's words:

> Let us take note: if the greengrocer had been instructed to display the slogan 'I am afraid and therefore unquestioningly obedient,' he would not be nearly as indifferent to its semantics, even though the statement would reflect the truth. The greengrocer would be embarrassed and ashamed to put such an unequivocal statement of his own degradation in the shop window, and quite naturally so, for he is a human being and thus has a sense of his own dignity. To overcome this complication, his expression of loyalty must take the form of a sign which, at least on its textual surface, indicates a level of disinterested conviction. It must allow the greengrocer to say, 'What's wrong with the workers of the world uniting?' Thus the sign helps the greengrocer to conceal from himself the low foundations of his obedience, at the same time concealing the low foundations of power. It hides them behind the facade of something high. And that something is *ideology*.

> Ideology is a specious way of relating to the world. It offers human beings the illusion of an identity, of dignity, and of morality while making it easier for them to *part* with them. As the repository of something 'supra-personal' and objective, it enables people to deceive their conscience and conceal their true position and their inglorious modus vivendi, both from the world and from themselves. It is a very pragmatic but, at the same time, an apparently dignified way of legitimizing what is above, below, and on either side. It is directed toward people and toward God. It is a

---

[351] Vaclav Havel, *The Power of the Powerless* (London: Vintage Classics, 2018), Kindle edition, p.21.

veil behind which human beings can hide their own fallen existence, their trivialization, and their adaptation to the status quo. It is an excuse that everyone can use, from the greengrocer, who conceals his fear of losing his job behind an alleged interest in the unification of the workers of the world, to the highest functionary, whose interest in staying in power can be cloaked in phrases about service to the working class. The primary excusatory function of ideology, therefore, is to provide people, both as victims and pillars of the post-totalitarian system, with the illusion that the system is in harmony with the human order and the order of the universe.[352]

In chapter VII Havel imagines what would happen if the greengrocer decided to rebel:

Let us now imagine that one day something in our greengrocer snaps and he stops putting up the slogans merely to ingratiate himself. He stops voting in elections he knows are a farce. He begins to say what he really thinks at political meetings. And he even finds the strength in himself to express solidarity with those whom his conscience commands him to support. In this revolt the greengrocer steps out of living within the lie. He rejects the ritual and breaks the rules of the game. He discovers once more his suppressed identity and dignity. He gives his freedom a concrete significance. His revolt is an attempt to live within the truth.

The bill is not long in coming. He will be relieved of his post as manager of the shop and transferred to the warehouse. His pay will be reduced. His hopes for a holiday in Bulgaria will evaporate. His children's access to higher education will be threatened. His superiors will harass him and his fellow workers will wonder about him.[353]

According to Havel, the reason that the Communist authorities will react in this way is because, by showing it is possible to live within the

---

[352] Havel, pp.21-22.
[353] Havel, p.34.

truth, the greengrocer threatens the whole Communist system which is based on people being willing to live by lies.

Thus, the power structure, through the agency of those who carry out the sanctions, those anonymous components of the system, will spew the greengrocer from its mouth. The system, through its alienating presence in people, will punish him for his rebellion. It must do so because the logic of its automatism and self-defence dictate it. The greengrocer has not committed a simple, individual offence, isolated in its own uniqueness, but something incomparably more serious. By breaking the rules of the game, he has disrupted the game as such. He has exposed it as a mere game. He has shattered the world of appearances, the fundamental pillar of the system. He has upset the power structure by tearing apart what holds it together. He has demonstrated that living a lie is living a lie. He has broken through the exalted facade of the system and exposed the real, base foundations of power. He has said that the emperor is naked. And because the emperor is in fact naked, something extremely dangerous has happened: by his action, the greengrocer has addressed the world. He has enabled everyone to peer behind the curtain. He has shown everyone that it is possible to live within the truth. Living within the lie can constitute the system only if it is universal. The principle must embrace and permeate everything. There are no terms whatsoever on which it can coexist with living within the truth, and therefore everyone who steps out of line *denies it in principle and threatens it in its entirety.*

This is understandable: as long as appearance is not confronted with reality, it does not seem to be appearance. As long as living a lie is not confronted with living the truth, the perspective needed to expose its mendacity is lacking. As soon as the alternative appears, however, it threatens the very existence of appearance and living a lie in terms of what they are, both their essence and their all-inclusiveness. And at the same time, it is utterly unimportant how large a space this alternative occupies: its power does not consist in its physical attributes but in the light it casts on those pillars of the system and on its unstable foundations. After all, the greengrocer was a threat to the system not because of any physical or actual power he had, but because his action went beyond itself, because it illuminated its surroundings and, of course, because of the incalculable consequences of that illumination. In the post totalitarian system, therefore, living within the truth has more than a mere existential dimension (returning humanity to its inherent nature), or a noetic dimension (revealing reality as it is), or a moral dimension (setting an example for others). It also has an unambiguous *political* dimension. If the main pillar of the system is living a lie, then it is not surprising that the fundamental threat to it is living the truth. This is why it must be suppressed more severely than anything else.[354]

Although Havel was writing about the actions of a Communist state, what he writes is still relevant to Christians living in the West today. This is because as we noted in chapters 5 and 6, it is not only the regimes of the old Communist bloc that have sought to ensure that their ideology is accepted as the only accepted truth. The same is also true of Western liberal democratic regimes today.

To echo what was said in chapters 5 and 6, modern liberal Western democracies have the same totalitarian tendency as other forms of political organisation. Just as Communist regimes sought to impose a Marxist ideology upon their citizens, so also modern Western democracies are increasingly seeking to impose acceptance of the idolatrous word-views of personal autonomy and identity politics upon their citizens,[355] and this necessarily leads to a conflict with Christians who, like Havel's greengrocer, are unwilling to accept these prevailing worldviews and who instead advocate, and seek to live out, an alternative worldview in their teaching and practice.

As Rod Dreher notes in his book *Live not by Lies,* in the days of the old Soviet Union there were Christians who were willing to do in practice

---

[354] Havel, pp.34-35.
[355] As Thielicke notes 'there is in the state the demonic tendency to become overweening; the beast from the abyss [Revelation 13] lies in wait within it.' (Thielicke, pp.182-183).

what Havel's greengrocer did only in fiction. Dreher records the testimony of the retired Baptist pastor Yuri Sipko:

In his village classroom in the 1950s in Siberia, Sipko and his classmates were given a badge with a portrait of Lenin. At age eleven, the children were given the red scarf of the Young Pioneers, A kind of Boy Scouts and Girl Scouts for communist youth. Teachers drilled the children in the slogan of the Pioneers: 'Be ready, Always be ready.'

'I didn't wear the pin with Lenin's face, nor did I wear the red scarf. I was a Baptist. I wasn't going to do that,' recalls Sipko.' I was the only one in my class. They went after my teachers. They wanted to know what they were doing wrong that they had a boy in their class who wasn't a Pioneer. They pressured the director of the school too. They were forced to pressure me to save themselves.'

To be a Baptist in Soviet Russia was to know that you were a permanent outsider. They endured it because they knew the truth was embodied in Jesus Christ, and that to live apart from him would mean living a lie. For the Baptists, to compromise with lies for the sake of a peaceful life is to bend the knee to death.

'When I think about the past, and how our brothers were sent to prison and never returned, I'm sure that this is the kind of certainty they had,' says the old pastor.' 'They lost any kind of status. They were mocked and ridiculed in society. Sometimes they even lost their children. Just because they were Baptists, the state was willing to take away their kids and send them to orphanages. Believers were unable to find jobs. Their children were not able to enter universities. And still, they believed.' [356]

The choice before Christians in the West today is the same basic choice that was faced in fiction by Havel's greengrocer and in real life by the Baptists recalled by Yuri Sipko. Are they going to live by lies for the

[356] Rod Dreher, *Live not by Lies* (New York: Sentinel, 2020), pp.102-103.

sake of a quiet life, or are they going to 'live within the truth' and face the consequences?

For any Christian who understands the reality of the human situation there can be only one answer to this question. In Matthew 10:26-33 Jesus declares:

So have no fear of them; for nothing is covered that will not be revealed, or hidden that will not be known. What I tell you in the dark, utter in the light; and what you hear whispered, proclaim upon the housetops. And do not fear those who kill the body but cannot kill the soul; rather fear him who can destroy both soul and body in hell. Are not two sparrows sold for a penny? And not one of them will fall to the ground without your Father's will. But even the hairs of your head are all numbered. Fear not, therefore; you are of more value than many sparrows. So every one who acknowledges me before men, I also will acknowledge before my Father who is in heaven; but whoever denies me before men, I also will deny before my Father who is in heaven.

In the words of J C Ryle, what Jesus is saying here is that:

Man can hurt the body, but there his enmity must stop: he can go no further. God 'is able to destroy both body and soul in hell.' We may be threatened with the loss of character, property, and all that makes life enjoyable, if we go on in the path of religious duty: we must not heed such threats, when our course is plain. Like Daniel and the three children, we must submit to anything rather than displease God, and wound our consciences. The anger of men may be hard to bear, but the anger of God is much harder; the fear of man does indeed bring a snare, but we must make it give way to the expulsive power of a stronger principle, even the fear of God.[357]

---

[357] J C Ryle, *Expository Thoughts on St. Matthew* (London: William Hunt, 1883), p.103.

What Jesus' saying means for Christians in the West today is that, motivated by godly fear, they have to live within the truth that has been made known to them by God rather than living by the lies that have become prevalent in modern Western culture. Furthermore, as we shall see in the rest of this chapter, Christians have the freedom to live in this way because of the freedom granted by human law and the freedom given to them by God. The only question is whether they are willing to make use of it.

2. The freedom granted by human law

First of all, as we saw in chapter 3, Christians in the West have the legal right to exercise freedom of religion as this has been laid down in the Article 18 of the United Nations' Covenant on Civil and Political Rights and adopted by states into their own codes of national law.

This means that they have the legal right 'to freedom of thought, conscience and religion' which includes 'freedom to have or to adopt a religion or belief of his choice, and freedom, either individually or in community with others and in public or private, to manifest his religion or belief in worship, observance, practice and teaching.'

Although, as we have seen, this legal freedom is now beginning to be restricted in practice, it nevertheless remains the case that Christians in the West have the right to adopt the Christian faith, to attend Christian worship, to observe Christian religious practices. to hear the Christian faith taught, and to teach the Christian faith to others. These are vitally important freedoms and Christians need to take every opportunity to make use of them.

In specific terms this means the following.

First, Christians must be proactive in seeking to persuade people to adopt the Christian faith by accepting the Christian message, repenting of their sins, receiving catechetical instruction, being baptised, and becoming part of a Christian church.

Secondly, they must take heed of the exhortation in Hebrews 10:25 that they should 'not neglect to meet together' and must instead be faithful in attending services of Christian worship both on Sundays and on other days of the week as well. The pressures on Christians to neglect this duty are increasing as social support for church attendance declines in the West and as Sunday has increasingly become a day for sleeping in late, shopping, sport or spending time with family and friends. However, it is vital that this pressure is rejected both because publicly going to church is in itself an important witness in a secular society and because worshipping God and receiving from him in word and sacraments are important goods in themselves.

As well as recognising the importance of coming together to worship Christians also need to recognise the importance of the liturgy that takes place when they do. The term liturgy refers to 'the form of service or regular ritual of a church'[358] and in the words of the Church of England's *Book of Common Prayer* it provides the framework within which Christians can 'acknowledge our sins before God...render thanks for the great benefits that we have received at his hands...set forth his most worthy praise...hear his most holy Word and...ask those things which are requisite and necessary, as well for the body as the soul.'[359]

In a world that emphasizes freedom and spontaneity it can be easy for Christians to disparage set liturgy as a restriction on their liberty to worship God in the way that they see fit, but they need to realize that the importance of a well-crafted form of liturgy is that it will ensure that all of the essential components of Christian worship set out above are included, and also take on board C S Lewis' point that that a familiar form of liturgy is helpful precisely because it is familiar:

> Every service is a structure of acts and words through which we receive a sacrament, or repent, or supplicate, or adore. And it enables us to do these things best - if you like, it 'works' best - when, through long familiarity, we don't have to think about it. As long as you notice, and have to count, the steps, you are not dancing but

---

[358] 'Liturgy', *The Chambers Dictionary* (Edinburgh: Chambers Harrap, 2003), p.867
[359] *The Book of Common Prayer*, 'The Order for Morning Prayer.'

only learning to dance. A good shoe is a shoe you don't notice. Good reading becomes possible when you need not consciously think about eyes, or light, or print, or spelling. The perfect church service would be one that we were almost unaware of; all attention would have been on God.[360]

Thirdly, Christians must continue to observe other Christian religious practices such as having regular times of personal prayer and Bible study, confessing their sins to priests or other believers, holding family prayers, saying grace before meals going, and marking the seasons of the Christian year. These things matter because over time they create an ingrained habit of Christian observance that helps to combat the incessant cultural pressure of secular modernity and because they bear witness to others that there are still Christians around who take their faith seriously.

In her book *Surprised by Oxford* the Canadian writer Carolyn Weber notes that what struck her about the Christians she met in her early days as a post-graduate student in Oxford, and what eventually led her to take the Christian faith seriously and eventually become a Christian herself, was that in contrast to those around them:

> These Christian people were *deliberate*. They were pursuing despite being persecuted. They were deliberate in discerning and knowing their own hearts, confessing their own faults, desiring forgiveness, and being grateful for grace. They were then deliberate in exercising the same forgiveness that had been granted to them, deliberate in at least trying to sidestep the continuous trap of self-reference and judgement. Most of us would baulk at being called 'evil.' But it takes a lot of courage to be self-evaluative before other-judgemental, to be conscious rather than oblivious, to be actively loving rather than apathetic. [361]

---

[360] C S Lewis, *Prayer: Letters to Malcom* (Glasgow: Fountain Books, 1977), p.6.
[361] Carolyn Weber, *Surprised by Oxford* (Nashville: Thomas Nelson, 2011), Kindle edition pp.250-251.

The sort of deliberate Christian behaviour noted by Weber is not something that develops accidentally. It is the fruit of divine grace, but, humanly speaking, it is also the fruit of a rule of life marked by the sort of habits of Christian observance noted above. Habits, whether good or bad, make us the kind of people we are and that is why we need to maintain the good habits of Christian observance.

Finally, Christians must teach the Christian faith to others. This means teaching those who are not yet Christians through books, online content, and live courses such as Alpha and Christianity Explored. However, prior to, and as the basis of that, it means the deliberate catechesis of children, young people and new believers and the continuing high quality religious instruction of adult believers. As we have seen in the course of the previous chapters, there is an ideological battle going on Western culture in which Christianity is under attack from an alternative non-Christian worldview. If that attack is to be resisted Christians have to take religious instruction with absolute seriousness. Like the habits of life previously mentioned, Christian habits of thought don't happen accidentally. They need to be taught and if Christians don't do it no one else will.

Christians in the West today still have the legal freedom to do all the things just mentioned. They need to exercise that freedom.

3. The freedom granted by God
a. The free choice to believe

It is important that Christians should acknowledge, be grateful for, and make use, of the hard-won legal freedoms that they have, freedoms which, as we have seen in this book, are the fruit of the work of previous generations of Christians going all the way back to Tertullian and Lactantius.

However, it is even more important that Christians should understand that the freedom that they have to be Christians and to live as Christians is not at root a freedom granted to them by human law. If this were the case, then Christians would be dependent on other human beings to be able to be Christian believers and practice their faith. However, this is not in fact the case.

As we saw in the first two chapters of this book, the teaching of Scripture, echoed by Christian advocates for religious freedom down the centuries, is that the freedom to believe and to live accordingly is in reality something given by God. Individuals and governments can choose to whether to acknowledge this freedom or deny it, but they can neither grant it, nor can they abolish it, any more than they can grant or abolish the orbit of the earth around the sun.

What we saw in chapter 1 is that the freedom to believe the Christian faith possessed by human beings has two foundations, both of which are the free gift of the Triune God who is free in himself and freely decides to grant freedom to his human creatures.

The first foundation is the freedom of choice which God has given to all human beings as part of their creation in his image and likeness. God created men and women to be people who would share in the relationship of love that exists within the Trinity and so that this would be the case he granted them to freedom to choose, freedom being the necessary condition for love.

To repeat the quotation from Kallistos Ware given in chapter 1:

> As a Trinity of love, God desired to share his life with created persons made in his image, who would be capable of responding to him freely and willingly in a relationship of love. Where there is no freedom, there can be no love. Compulsion excludes love; as Paul Evdokimov used to say, God can do everything except compel us to love him. God, therefore – desiring to share his love – created, not robots who would obey him mechanically, but angels and human beings endowed with free choice. [362]

---

[362] Ware, pp.74-75.

As we saw in chapter 1, this capacity for free choice is something that we see exercised by human beings throughout the biblical record, including by Jesus in his human nature. Jesus was not a divinely controlled robot, but was instead someone who made genuine choices in the course of his incarnate life and ministry.

Hebrews 12:2 exhorts Christians to look to Jesus 'the pioneer and perfecter of our faith, who for the joy that was set before him endured the cross, despising the shame and is seated at the right hand of the throne of god.' The word 'pioneer' in this passage is significant. A pioneer is someone who makes a way for others to follow and what the writer to the Hebrews is doing is to encourage Christians facing the threat of persecution to follow the example of Jesus who freely chose to embrace the shame and suffering of the cross for the sake of the joy that he understood would follow. However, this only makes sense if Christians have a like freedom to choose to believe in the joy that God has promised to his faithful people and to act accordingly.

Furthermore, as the context of this quotation from Hebrews also reminds us, this freedom of choice is something which human beings continue to possess even when they are threatened with extreme consequences for being believers. Even if Christians face the prospect of death for being believers they still have the choice of whether or not to go on believing and face the penalty for so doing.

It is also important to note that it is the exercise of our free choice that will determine our eternal destiny. As we also saw in chapter 1, this is the message set out with unmistakeable clarity in John 3:16-18:

> For God so loved the world that he gave his only Son, that whoever believes in him should not perish but have eternal life. For God sent the Son into the world, not to condemn the world, but that the world might be saved through him. He who believes in him is not condemned; he who does not believe is condemned already, because he has not believed in the name of the only Son of God.

Those who have eternal life and who will live joyfully with God for ever in his everlasting kingdom are those who have freely chosen to believe, whereas those who are condemned now, and who will be separated from God for ever unless they repent, are those who have freely chosen to disbelieve. Furthermore, these verses do not include a caveat which says that the ability to exercise saving faith only exists when Christian belief is something permitted by human law. The ability (and therefore responsibility) to believe in the Son is something that exists without qualification.

What we likewise saw in chapter 1 is that the second foundation of human freedom to believe the Christian faith is divine grace. In the history of Christian theology there has been a recurring tendency to play freedom of choice and divine grace off against each other. Theologians have sometimes so emphasised human freedom that they have left no place for divine grace and, conversely, they have sometimes so emphasised divine grace that they have left no room for the exercise of human freedom of choice. However, if we are to be faithful to the teaching of Scripture we have to reject both these approaches. We have to say that the reason we can believe is not because we possess freedom of choice *or* because of divine grace, but as a result of both freedom of choice *and* divine grace. To quote again the words of Oliver O'Donovan cited in chapter 1:

Must we not say that it is up to men whether they believe or not? Plainly in one sense we must say this, since belief is a decision of man for which he is responsible, as he is for all his other acts. We would be wrong to suggest that human beings come to believe in Christ only by the *suspension* of a capacity which they otherwise exercise. In that case, as we would now say, belief would be 'inauthentic.' So much may reasonably be said - but it is possible to be too impressed by this power of human decision and to forget the context within which it must be exercised. For the act of belief, too, can occur only as God evokes it: no one can say 'Jesus is Lord' says Saint Paul, accept through the Holy Spirit (1 Corinthians 12:3).[363]

The necessary conjunction of human free choice and divine grace can be clearly seen in John's Gospel. We have already noted that John 3:16-18 highlights the reality and eternal significance of the free choice of human beings to believe or not to believe. In John 6:37-40 we also find an emphasis on belief being the result of the prior gracious initiative of God the Father:

All that the Father gives me will come to me; and him who comes to me I will not cast out. For I have come down from heaven, not to do my own will, but the will of him who sent me; and this is the will of him who sent me, that I should lose nothing of all that he has given me, but raise it up at the last day. For this is the will of my Father, that every one who sees the Son and believes in him should have eternal life; and I will raise him up at the last day.

In the words of William Barclay, according to the words of Jesus in this passage what underlies the whole process of human beings coming to believe in Jesus and feed on him as the bread of life is the antecedent action of God:

It is those whom God has given to him who come to Christ. God not only provides the goal: he moves in the human heart to awaken desire for him; and he works in the human heart to take away the rebellion and pride that would hinder the great submission. We could never even have sought him unless he had found us.[364]

Thomas Scott comments similarly:

...the Father who sent the Son into the world to save sinners, must draw them to the Son to be saved by him; or they will universally neglect his salvation. The gospel finds none *willing* to be saved in

[363] O'Donovan, *p.*74.
[364] William Barclay, *The Gospel of John* Vol.1 (Edinburgh: The St Andrew Press, 1982), p.217.

the humbling holy manner revealed therein: none are saved against their will; but the Lord by his grace disposes, allures and draws sinners to Christ; and his drawing is the cause of their activity and diligence. He cures as it were the fever of the soul, he creates the appetite, he sets the provisions before the sinner; he satisfies him that they are wholesome and pleasant, and that he is welcome: and thus the man is drawn to come and eat, and live for ever. [365]

Because the freedom to believe in Christ rests upon these two foundations freely given to human beings by God, no human being can shrug off the responsibility to believe. All the necessary conditions for belief have been put in place by God and therefore it is the responsibility of the sinner to decide whether or not to make use of the opportunity that he or she has been given. He or she will not be able to claim at the last judgement that they would have believed if only God had made it possible. He did.

The converse of this is that no matter how repressive the legal system of particular society is with regard to the Christian faith, however much it may seek to restrict or forbid Christian belief, the possibility of belief still exists, and human beings still have the responsibility to act on this possibility.

This means that it is even more the case that Christians in the West today, where freedom to believe is still available without legal restriction, have the responsibility to continue believing themselves and to continue to call other human beings to do the same.

This may seem obvious in theory, but Christians do not always realise the implications of this truth. What they often fail to realise is that belief in God means acceptance of the whole truth that God has revealed about himself through the two books of creation and Scripture and through the orthodox teaching of the Church based on these twin

---

[365] Thomas Scott, *Commentary on the whole Bible*, Vol. III (London: Jordan and Maxwell, 1803) on John 6:41-46.

sources, and that the failure of such acceptance is itself a form of unbelief.

That is why the *Athanasian Creed*, one of the three classic statements of faith recognised by the Western Christian tradition as a whole declares in its first two verses:

> Whosoever will be saved; before all things it is necessary that he hold the Catholic Faith. Which Faith except every one do keep whole and undefiled: without doubt he shall perish everlastingly.

From the end of the seventeenth century exception has been taken to what is said in these two verses (what are sometimes referred to as the 'damnatory clauses') on the grounds that what they say is unduly harsh and unduly restricts the possibility of salvation. However, in spite of the opposition that has been expressed to them, what is said in these verses should be accepted (as it has been for most of the history of the Western Church) because they are firmly based on the responsibility for belief that has just been outlined.[366]

The link between what is said in these verses and this responsibility lies in the fact that belief in Jesus leading to salvation means belief in the teaching of the apostles. Because Christ has ascended to the right hand of the Father, he no longer presents himself directly to us as the object of our belief as was the case during the years of his earthly ministry. Instead, he is presented to us in the form of the teaching of the Apostles. As Paul says, the apostles are the 'ambassadors' of Christ (2 Corinthians 5:20) appointed by him to speak and act on his behalf. This means that our belief or unbelief in the Apostles' teaching is our belief or unbelief in Christ himself.

The 'Catholic faith' to which opening verse of the Athanasian Creed refer is the teaching of the apostles as this is expounded in the New

---

[366] What is said about the teaching of the *Athanasian Creed* in the following paragraphs is an adapted version of material first published in Martin Davie, *The Athanasian Creed* (London: Latimer Trust, 2019), pp.45-47.

Testament and has been handed down in the Church. It follows that belief or unbelief in the Catholic faith is also belief or unbelief in Christ and that if we wish to be saved rather than condemned we have the responsibility to believe what the Catholic faith teaches. Furthermore, we have to go on believing it even when, like the Christians in Gaul and Spain in the fifth and sixth centuries for whom the *Athanasian Creed* was first written, we face pressure to do otherwise. As the parable of the sower (Mark 4:1–20) makes clear, it is persistence in the faith that brings salvation.

We must also go on believing the faith in its entirety, 'whole and undefiled' as the *Athanasian Creed* puts it. This is because we cannot legitimately choose to believe some bits of the faith and reject others. It is the Catholic faith as a whole that has been presented to us by God to be the object of our belief and if we decide not to believe parts of it then we enter into a state of unbelief and therefore become subject to condemnation unless and until we repent.

Ever since the seventeenth century, part of the Satanic attack on the Church described in the previous chapters of this book has been an attempt to persuade Christians to do precisely what the *Athanasian Creed* warns us against, namely taking a pick and mix attitude to adherence to the apostolic faith. Thus, Christians have been tempted to deny the truths of the Trinity and the divinity of Christ, the historicity of the biblical miracles, God's activity in human history more generally, the separation between the saved and the lost at the last judgement, and at the end of the twentieth century even the objective reality of God himself.[367] At the moment the most pressing temptation in the West is to deny the existence and/or applicability of the biblical teaching about God's creation of human beings as male and female, about marriage and about sexual ethics.

[367] For this last temptation see, for instance Thomas Altizer, *The Gospel of Christian Atheism* (Philadelphia: Westminster Press, 1966.

Christians have the freedom to reject this current temptation just as previous generations of Christians have had the freedom to reject the other temptations mentioned in the last paragraph. Paul reminded the Christians in Corinth, who were tempted by the idolatry of their day:

> No temptation has overtaken you that is not common to man. God is faithful, and he will not let you be tempted beyond your strength, but with the temptation will also provide the way of escape, that you may be able to endure it. (1 Corinthians 10:13)

This reminder also applies to Christians in the West today. God gives the freedom to resist the temptation to dispense with those parts of the apostolic faith that do not fit in with the prevailing ideology of our day. With this freedom comes the responsibility to act accordingly, that is to continue to adhere to the apostolic faith 'whole and undefiled.'

b. The freedom to live in obedience to God

As J I Packer writes:

> The disobedience of Adam, the first representative man, and the perfect obedience of Christ, are decisive factors in the destiny of everyone. Adam's lapse from obedience plunged mankind into guilt, condemnation and death (Romans 5:19; 1 Corinthians 15:22). Christ's unfailing obedience 'unto death' (Philippians 2:8; cf. Hebrews 5:8, 10:5-10) won righteousness (acceptance with God) and life (fellowship with God) for all who believe in him (Romans 5:15-19) (J I. Packer 'Obedience' in J D Douglas (ed), *The New Bible Dictionary* (Leicester: Inter-Varsity Press, 1962), p.904.)

Furthermore, one of the key features of the new covenant brought about through the obedience of Christ is that those who are accepted by God and enter into fellowship with him begin to become like Christ through the work of the Holy Spirit (as Paul puts it in Romans 8:29 they are 'conformed to the image of his son'). A key part of this is that they receive the gift of being able to live in obedience to God, the gift promised by God in Jeremiah 31:33 and 32:40 and Ezekiel 36: 26-27 and 37:23-26).

The first act of obedience is making the free choice to believe the Christian faith explored in the previous section of this chapter. This free choice is an act of obedience because when the faith is proclaimed God asks us to accept who he is and what he has done (and will do) for us and for the world as whole, and so saying 'yes' to the faith is to be obedient to him.

We see this form of obedience in Acts 6:7 where Luke's statement that 'many of the priests were obedient to the faith' means that priests concerned accepted the faith (it is an expansion of the statement in the previous clause that 'the number of the disciples multiplied greatly in Jerusalem). We also see it in Romans 1:5 where Paul declares that the purpose of his missionary work is bring about 'the obedience of faith' (i.e., the obedience which consists in the acceptance of the faith) among all the nations, and in Hebrews 5:9 where 'all who obey him' are those who believe the gospel message.

However, obedience means more than simply believing the Christian faith. It also means living rightly in accordance with this belief. As Charles Cranfield comments on Romans 1:5, it is right to say: 'that to make the decision of faith is an act of obedience to God,' and also right to say 'that true faith by its very nature includes in itself the sincere desire and will to obey God in all things.' [368]

This is the truth that is emphasised in what is arguably the earliest writing in the New Testament, the letter written by James to the leaders of the Jewish churches in Judaea and Samaria.[369] In James 2:14-26 James writes:

What does it profit, my brethren, if a man says he has faith but has not works? Can his faith save him? If a brother or sister is ill-clad and in lack of daily food, and one of you says to them, 'Go in peace,

[368] Charles Cranfield, *Romans, Vol.1* (Edinburgh: T&T Clark, 1987), pp.66-67.
[369] For the date and recipients of James see David Scaer, *James the Apostle of Faith* (Eugene: Wipf and Stock, 2004).

be warmed and filled,' without giving them the things needed for the body, what does it profit? So faith by itself, if it has no works, is dead.

But someone will say, 'You have faith and I have works.' Show me your faith apart from your works, and I by my works will show you my faith. You believe that God is one; you do well. Even the demons believe—and shudder. Do you want to be shown, you shallow man, that faith apart from works is barren? Was not Abraham our father justified by works, when he offered his son Isaac upon the altar? You see that faith was active along with his works, and faith was completed by works, and the scripture was fulfilled which says, 'Abraham believed God, and it was reckoned to him as righteousness'; and he was called the friend of God. You see that a man is justified by works and not by faith alone. And in the same way was not also Rahab the harlot justified by works when she received the messengers and sent them out another way? For as the body apart from the spirit is dead, so faith apart from works is dead.

Because of the polemical use made of the letter of James in the disputes between Protestants and Roman Catholics at the Reformation it is still sometimes suggested that what James writes in these verses contradicts the teaching about justification by faith taught by Paul. However, to say this is to misunderstand what both Paul and James are saying. When Paul writes in Galatians 2:16 'we have believed in Jesus Christ in order to be justified by faith in Christ and not by works of the law, for by works of the law shall no man be justified' what he is rejecting is the idea that obedience to the Jewish law by someone without faith in Jesus Christ could make someone righteous in the eyes of God. By contrast, what James is saying is that the reality of faith in Jesus Christ is shown by the works done in obedience to the will of God that are its result. A living faith is shown in what it does.

Exactly the same point is made by Jesus himself at the end of the Sermon on the Mount when he declares:

'Not everyone who says to me, 'Lord, Lord,' shall enter the kingdom of heaven, but he who does the will of my Father who is in heaven. On that day many will say to me, 'Lord, Lord, did we not prophesy in your name, and cast out demons in your name, and do many mighty works in your name?' And then will I declare to them, 'I never knew you; depart from me, you evildoers.' (Matthew 7:21-23)

'Everyone then who hears these words of mine and does them will be like a wise man who built his house upon the rock; and the rain fell, and the floods came, and the winds blew and beat upon that house, but it did not fall, because it had been founded on the rock. And everyone who hears these words of mine and does not do them will be like a foolish man who built his house upon the sand; and the rain fell, and the floods came, and the winds blew and beat against that house, and it fell; and great was the fall of it.' (Matthew 7:21-27)

In these words of Jesus, as in the letter of James, we learn that the reality of faith is shown not just by words but by obedient deeds.

The words we say that show our faith are important. That is why Peter is blessed by Jesus when he confesses 'You are the Christ, the Son of the Living God' (Matthew 16:16). That is why Paul joins together belief and confession in Romans 10:10 when he writes 'For man believes with his heart and so is justified, and he confesses, with his lips and so is saved.' It is also why from the earliest times a verbal profession of faith was required of those wishing to be baptised.

However, a profession of faith that goes no further than words and that is not backed up by obedient actions has no reality. Why? Because of the point noted by Cranfield 'that true faith by its very nature includes in itself the sincere desire and will to obey God in all things.' If we truly have a sincere desire and will to obey God in all things then actions done in obedience to God will necessarily follow.

Paul emphasises this point in Romans 6:15-23 where he rejoices in the fact that the Christians in Rome have ceased to be 'slaves of sin' who 'yielded your members to impurity and to greater and greater iniquity' (vv.17 & 19) and are now instead 'slaves of God' who are yielding 'your members to righteousness for sanctification' (vv.22 & 19). The image here is of someone acting in accordance with the instructions of their master, which used to be sin, but is now God. Christians, says Paul, are people who act in the way that God wants.

In this same passage Paul also indicates that the obedience that the Roman Christians are now offering to God takes the form of being 'obedient from the heart to the standard of teaching to which you were committed.' (v18). What Paul is saying here is that there is body of authoritative teaching which has been handed on to the Christians in Rome, possibly as part of their preparation for baptism and it is this authoritative teaching that forms the basis for their Christian obedience.

We can see this same idea of corpus of authoritative teaching in a number of other places in Paul's letters as well. For example, in Colossians 2:7 he exhorts the Colossians to be 'established in the faith as you have been taught it', in 2 Thessalonians 2:15 he tells the Thessalonians to 'stand firm and hold to the traditions which you were taught by us, either by word of mouth or by letter' and in Titus 1:9 he lays down that a bishop 'must hold fast to the sure word as taught, so that he may be able to give instruction in sound doctrine and also confute those who contradict it.'

The same idea is also put forward by a range of other New Testament writers. Thus in Hebrews 10:23 the writer to the Hebrews refers to 'the confession of our faith' to which he wants his readers to hold fast without wavering, in 1 Peter 1:25 Peter talks about 'the good news which was preached to you,'[370] in Jude 3 and 20 Jude refers to 'the faith once delivered to the saints' and 'your most holy faith' and 1 John 2:24

---

[370] In context this appears to refer to some form of baptismal catechesis.

John's readers are exhorted 'let what you have heard from the beginning abide in you.'[371]

If we ask where this authoritative teaching came from, the answer that the New Testament gives us is that it was given to the Church by the apostles and those associated with them such as Jesus' brothers James and Jude. This is made clear by Luke in his two-part account of the origins of Christianity in Luke and Acts. In Luke and at the start of the first chapter of Acts Jesus instructs the Apostles and from then onwards it is the Apostles and those associated with them who give instruction to those who subsequently become Christians. It is this 'teaching of the Apostles' (Acts 2:42) that is the standard of faith for the Church. Although Paul is not part of the original group of apostles he is commissioned as an additional apostle by Jesus himself and his teaching is in line with the teaching of the other apostles.

This last point is also made by Paul himself in the opening chapters of Galatians. He emphasises his own independent commissioning as an a apostle ('Paul an apostle – not from men nor through man, but through Jesus Christ and God the Father, who raised him from the dead' Gal 1:1), but he also notes that what he preached as an Apostle was 'the faith he once tried to destroy', the faith that was believed by the Church in its earliest days (Galatians 1:23) and that it was recognised by the leaders of the Church in Jerusalem that he had been appointed to preach to the Gentiles the same gospel that they had been appointed to preach to the Jews (Galatians 2:6-10). His subsequent argument with Peter was not because he and Peter had a different understanding of what the gospel was but because St Peter was unwilling to behave in a way that was consistent with the gospel (Galatians 2:11-21). There were not two different gospels, a Pauline gospel and a Petrine one, but a single agreed

---

[371] For a further discussion of the passages referred to in these two paragraphs and other similar passages see J N D Kelly, *Early Christian Creeds* 3ed (Harlow: Longman, 1972), pp.8-11. New Testament scholars have suggested that elements of the sort of teaching referred to in these verses can be found in the speeches in Acts and embedded in the Epistles in passages such as 1 Cor 15:3-8, 11:23-25, Phil 2:5-11, 1 Tim 3:16 and 1 Pet 3:18 and 20.

gospel, one agreed understanding of the Christian faith, which Peter had failed to live out adequately.

Throughout the New Testament it is this one common understanding of the Christian faith, the 'apostolic faith' referred to in the previous section of this chapter in relation to what is said in Athanasian Creed, that forms the template for what it means for Christians to live in obedience to God. The reason for the emergence of the New Testament Canon was because of the conviction that Christians needed a continuing authoritative guide to Christian obedience and that this was provided by the books included in the Canon, in which the apostolic understanding of the Christian faith was preserved in written form under the guidance of the Holy Spirit

In summary, the obedience of Christ creates the freedom for Christians to exercise the 'obedience of faith' an obedience which consists in accepting the apostolic faith intellectually, but also then living it out in accordance with the authoritative teaching given by the apostles and those associated with them and preserved in written form in the New Testament.

c. The Freedom to reject idolatry

At the beginning of his first letter to the Thessalonians Paul gives thanks for the Christians in Thessalonica in the following terms:

We give thanks to God always for you all, constantly mentioning you in our prayers, remembering before our God and Father your work of faith and labour of love and steadfastness of hope in our Lord Jesus Christ. For we know, brethren beloved by God, that he has chosen you; for our gospel came to you not only in word, but also in power and in the Holy Spirit and with full conviction. You know what kind of men we proved to be among you for your sake. And you became imitators of us and of the Lord, for you received the word in much affliction, with joy inspired by the Holy Spirit; so that you became an example to all the believers in Macedo'nia and in Acha'ia. For not only has the word of the Lord sounded forth from you in Macedo'nia and Acha'ia, but your faith in God has gone forth everywhere, so that we need not say anything. For they themselves report concerning us what a welcome we had among you, and how you turned to God from idols, to serve a living and true God, and to wait for his Son from heaven, whom he raised from the dead, Jesus who delivers us from the wrath to come. (1 Thessalonians 1:2-10).

What we see in these verses is once again that the freedom to believe and to act accordingly is given not by human beings but by God. It is God who has chosen that the Thessalonians should believe the gospel preached by Paul and made that choice effective through the work of the Holy Spirit.

What we also see in these verses is that accepting the Gospel meant turning to God from idols. This highlights the point that according to the New Testament belief in God and worshipping idols are always seen as incompatible. You can be a believer in God, or you can choose to worship idols. What you may not do as both. There is a binary choice between one and the other.

Three other New Testament examples further illustrate this point.

First, there is the account of the ministry of Barnabas and Paul at Lystra as recorded in Acts 14:11-18. This account tells us that after Paul healed a man who had never been able to walk, the crowds who had seen what Paul had done:

> ...lifted up their voices, saying in Lycao'nian, 'The gods have come down to us in the likeness of men!' Barnabas they called Zeus, and Paul, because he was the chief speaker, they called Hermes. And the priest of Zeus, whose temple was in front of the city, brought oxen and garlands to the gates and wanted to offer sacrifice with the people. But when the apostles Barnabas and Paul heard of it, they tore their garments and rushed out among the multitude, crying, Men, why are you doing this? We also are men, of like nature with you, 'and bring you good news, that you should turn from these vain things to a living God who made the heaven and the earth and the

sea and all that is in them. In past generations he allowed all the nations to walk in their own ways; yet he did not leave himself without witness, for he did good and gave you from heaven rains and fruitful seasons, satisfying your hearts with food and gladness.' With these words they scarcely restrained the people from offering sacrifice to them.

The reason that Barnabas and Paul refuse to accept idolatrous worship from the people of Lystra as the embodiment of the Greek gods is because the good news which they have been sent to proclaim is precisely that people should turn from such 'vain things' (i.e. the worship of idols) to the worship of the ' living God who made the heaven and the earth and the sea and all that is in them.' What they want to bring about is people ceasing to worship idols and worshipping the true God instead. It should also be noted that Barnabas and Paul assume that the people in Lystra are free to do this, even in a culture where idolatry is normal. They can cease to be idolaters if they want to.

Secondly, in 1 Corinthians 10:14-22, a passage from which we quoted in the previous chapter, Paul tells the Corinthians:

Therefore, my beloved, shun the worship of idols. I speak as to sensible men; judge for yourselves what I say. The cup of blessing which we bless, is it not a participation in the blood of Christ? The bread which we break, is it not a participation in the body of Christ? Because there is one bread, we who are many are one body, for we all partake of the one bread. Consider the people of Israel; are not those who eat the sacrifices partners in the altar? What do I imply then? That food offered to idols is anything, or that an idol is anything? No, I imply that what pagans sacrifice they offer to demons and not to God. I do not want you to be partners with demons. You cannot drink the cup of the Lord and the cup of demons. You cannot partake of the table of the Lord and the table of demons. Shall we provoke the Lord to jealousy? Are we stronger than he?

As we saw in the previous chapter, the point that Paul emphasises here is that the worship of idols is the worship of demons, and it is for that reason that Christians must not participate in it. In the words of David Prior: 'Paul is not prepared to put any ifs or buts into his rejection of idolatry.'[372] The Corinthians are to simply 'shun the worship of idols.' Once again it needs to be noted that Paul thinks that in spite of the cultural pressure in Corinth to do otherwise, the Corinthians do have the freedom to act in line with his instructions. They are 'sensible men' who have the ability to judge for themselves that what Paul is saying is correct and act accordingly.

Thirdly, in 1 John 5:20-21 John concludes his first epistle by declaring:

> And we know that the Son of God has come and has given us understanding, to know him who is true; and we are in him who is true, in his Son Jesus Christ. This is the true God and eternal life. Little children, keep yourselves from idols. (1 John 5:20-21)

In these verses John begins by reminding his readers that through Jesus Christ we come to know 'him who is true,' that is the one true God, and that because Christ not only points us to the true God, but is himself the true God, when we are united to him, we possess eternal life. In the words of Calvin:

> The meaning is that when we have Christ, we enjoy the true and ternal God, for nowhere else is he to be sought; and, secondly, that we thus become partakers of eternal life, because it is offered to us in Christ, though his in the Father. The origin of life is, indeed, the Father; but the fountain from which we are to draw it, is Christ. [373]

---

[372] David Prior, *The Message of 1 Corinthians* (Leicester: Inter-Varsity Press, 1985), p.17.
[373] John Calvin on 1 John 5:20 in *The Complete Biblical Commentary Collection of John Calvin*, Kindle edition, Loc 520409.

To quote B F Westcott:

> From the thought of 'Him that is true' St John turns almost of necessity to the thought of the vain shadows which usurp His place. In them the world asserted its power. They forced themselves into notice on every side in innumerable shapes and tempted believers away from the perfect simplicity of faith. One sharp warning therefore closes the Epistle of which the main scope has been to deepen the fellowship of man with God through God with man.[374]

Westcott goes on to note that although the term idol is used literally in verses such as 1 Thessalonian 1:9 to refer to an image of one of the pagan gods, idolatry also has a 'wider sense' in verses such as Colossians 3:5 and Ephesians 5:5. In the former Paul writes of covetousness, which is idolatry' and in the latter he likewise refers to 'one who is covetous (that is, an idolator). ' The context in 1 John 5:21 he argues also: 'seems to require a corresponding extension of the meaning of the term. An 'idol' is anything that takes the place of God.'[375]

The exhortation 'keep yourself from idols' emphasises 'the duty of personal effort'[376] but by so doing it also makes clear that duty is one that can be fulfilled. John is not asking the impossible. Christians have the responsibility to expend effort to keep themselves from idolatry because this is something that they have capacity to do. As those who belong to the one true God through Jesus Christ, they have the freedom to reject all forms of idolatry if they want to do so.

The fact that for John an idol is anything that takes the place of God, as when the object of their desire takes the place of God in the life of the person who is covetous, means that the idols that Christians are free to reject include not just the idols of classical paganism, but the idols of the modern world that we noted in chapter 6. The story of the young Yuri Sipko cited at the beginning of this chapter illustrates this point.

---

[374] B F Westcott, *The Epistles of John* (London: Macmillan 1883), p.188.
[375] Westcott, p.188.
[376] Westcott, p.188.

Even at a time when Soviet Communism was at its hight he exercised his God given Christian freedom by refusing to wear a Lenin lapel badge or the red scarf of the Pioneers, both of which functioned as material idols, symbols of the idolatrous worship given to Communist ideology and the Communist state. The calling of Christians in the West today is to exercise their freedom in similar way.

d. The freedom to serve

According to the New Testament, a key part of the freedom of the Christian to live in obedience to God is the freedom to serve.

The importance of service is emphasised by Jesus in Matthew 20:26-28:

> But Jesus called them to him and said, 'You know that the rulers of the Gentiles lord it over them, and their great men exercise authority over them. It shall not be so among you; but whoever would be great among you must be your servant, and whoever would be first among you must be your slave; even as the Son of Man came not to be served but to serve, and to give his life as a ransom for many.'

These verses are response by Jesus to the attempt by James and John to secure for themselves the preeminent places in Jesus' coming kingdom and the annoyance of the other disciples at their doing so. As Barclay explains:

> Jesus knew what was going on in their minds; and he spoke to them words which are the very basis and foundation of the Christian life. Out in the world, said Jesus, it is quite true that the great man is the man who controls others; the man who is master; the man who with a wave of his hand can command service, and have his slightest need supplied. Out in the world there was the Roman governor with his retinue; the eastern potentate with his slaves; the man of affairs with his staff of attendant slaves. The world counts then great. But in the Christian assessment service alone is the badge of greatness; greatness does not consist in commanding others to do things for us; greatness consists in doing things for

others; and the greater the service, the greater the honour. Jesus uses a kind of gradation. 'If you wish to be *great*,' He says, 'be a *servant*, if you wish to be first of all be a *slave*.' Here is the Christian revolution; Here is the complete reversal of all the world standards. Here a complete new set of values has been brought into life. [377]

Jesus further emphasises the importance of service in the words he speaks to his disciples after he has washed their feet at the Last Supper:

When he had washed their feet, and taken his garments, and resumed his place, he said to them, "Do you know what I have done to you? You call me Teacher and Lord; and you are right, for so I am. If I then, your Lord and Teacher, have washed your feet, you also ought to wash one another's feet. For I have given you an example, that you also should do as I have done to you. Truly, truly, I say to you, a servant is not greater than his master; nor is he who is sent greater than he who sent him. If you know these things, blessed are you if you do them.' (John 13:12-17).

To quote Barclay:

[Jesus] Himself did what none of them was prepared to do. And then he said to them: 'You see what I have done. You call me your master and your Lord; and you are quite right; for so I am; I need I'm prepared to do this for you; and surely you don't think that the pupil deserves more honour than teacher, or servant than a master. Surely if I do this, you ought to prepared to do it. I am giving you this example of how you ought to behave towards each other.'[378]

As Barclay goes on to say: 'Here is the lesson and the proof that there is only one kind of greatness, and that is the greatness of service.'[379]

---

[377] William Barclay, *Gospel of Matthew*, Volume 2 (Edinburgh: St Andrew Press, 1963), p.256.
[378] William Barclay, *The Gospel of John, Volume 2* (Edinburgh: St Andrew press, 963), p.162.
[379] Barclay, *The Gospel of John, Volume 2*, p.162.

The fact that Jesus taught the disciples about the importance of service in this way only makes sense if Jesus thought that his followers had, and would have, the freedom to offer the kind of service to which he refers. Saying that his disciples will be blessed if they put his teaching about service into practice must mean that the possibility of doing so is open to them.

Furthermore, in Galatians Paul specifically says that Christians should use the spiritual freedom which is God's gift to all those who have faith in Christ as an opportunity to serve one another in love. In his words:

> For you were called to freedom, brethren; only do not use your freedom as an opportunity for the flesh, but through love be servants of one another. For the whole law is fulfilled in one word, 'You shall love your neighbour as yourself.' (Galatians 5:13-14)

To quote John Stott, what Paul is saying here is that the freedom Christian's possess is not:

> ...freedom to do as I please in the indulgence of my flesh. It is freedom to approach God without fear, not freedom to exploit my neighbour without love.

> Indeed, so far from having liberty to ignore, neglect or abuse our fellow men, we are commanded to love them, and through love to serve them. We are not to use them as if they were *things* to serve us; we are to respect them as *persons* and give ourselves to serve them. We are even through love to become each other's slaves...' Not to be one master with a lot of slaves, but each to be one poor slave with a lot of masters,' sacrificing our good for theirs, not theirs to ours. Christian liberty is service not selfishness.

It is a remarkable paradox. For from one point of view Christian freedom is a form of slavery, - not slavery to our flesh, but to our neighbour. We are free in relation to God but slaves in relation to each other. [380]

e. The freedom to suffer

Not only does Christian freedom involve the freedom to serve, but it also involves the freedom to suffer.

One of the counterintuitive things about the teaching of the New Testament is the way in which it not only sees suffering as inevitable but sees it in a positive light. Suffering is viewed as something which Christians are able to experience and this is regarded as a good thing because suffering is used by God to achieve his good purposes in their lives.

In 2 Corinthians 1: 3-7 for example, Paul gives thanks for the suffering he and the Corinthians are enduring because the suffering of the afflicted Christian believer is something that results in them being comforted by God and being able to comfort others in their turn.

Blessed be the God and Father of our Lord Jesus Christ, the Father of mercies and God of all comfort, who comforts us in all our affliction, so that we may be able to comfort those who are in any affliction, with the comfort with which we ourselves are comforted by God. For as we share abundantly in Christ's sufferings, so through Christ we share abundantly in comfort too. If we are afflicted, it is for your comfort and salvation; and if we are comforted, it is for your comfort, which you experience when you patiently endure the same sufferings that we suffer. Our hope for you is unshaken; for we know that as you share in our sufferings, you will also share in our comfort.

For a second example, James writes:

---

[380] John Stott, *The Message of Galatians* (Leicester: Inter-Varsity Press, 1988), pp.141-142.

Count it all joy, my brethren, when you meet various trials, for you know that the testing of your faith produces steadfastness. And let steadfastness have its full effect, that you may be perfect and complete, lacking in nothing. (James 1:2-4)

The point that James is making here is that reason why the various trials which Christians suffer are to be viewed as something joyful is because if they are met with patient endurance they are the means by which God makes us the 'perfect and complete' people he wants us to be. To put it another way: 'they are God's designed way forward. It is only by meeting and passing its tests that faith grows into strong constancy.'[381]

A similar point is made by Peter in his first epistle. In it he tells the Christians to whom he is writing:

...for a little while you may have to suffer various trials, so that the genuineness of your faith, more precious than gold which though perishable is tested by fire, may redound to praise and glory and honour at the revelation of Jesus Christ. (1 Peter 1:6-7)

As Edmund Clowney explains, what Peter is saying is that:

If our faith is to endure, it must be purified and stress-tested. Like gold it must pass through the furnace (verse 7). Trials should not surprise us, or cause us to doubt God's faithfulness. Rather, we should actually be glad for them. God sends trials to strengthen our trust in him so that our faith will not fail. Our trials keep us trusting; they burn away self our self-confidence and drivers to our Saviour. The fires of affliction or persecution will not reduce our faith at ashes. *Fire* does not destroy gold: it only removes combustible impurities. Yet even gold will at last vanish with the whole of this created order. Faith is infinitely more precious and more enduring. Like a jeweller putting his most precious metal in the crucible, so

---

[381] Alec Motyer, *The Message of James* (Leicester: Inter-Varsity Press, 1985), p.32.

God proves us in the furnace of trial and affliction. The genuineness of our faith shines from the fire to his praise.[382]

f. Free to hope

A final form of freedom which Christians are free to enjoy is the freedom to hope, a hope grounded in the resurrection of Jesus in the past and the promise of his coming in glory at the end of time.

Thus, Peter writes at the beginning of his first epistle:

Blessed be the God and Father of our Lord Jesus Christ! By his great mercy we have been born anew to a living hope through the resurrection of Jesus Christ from the dead, and to an inheritance which is imperishable, undefiled, and unfading, kept in heaven for you, who by God's power are guarded through faith for a salvation ready to be revealed in the last time. (1 Peter 1:3-5)

As Clowney notes, what Peter reminds the Christians to whom he is writing is that:

Christ's resurrection spells hope for us not just because he lives, but because by God's mercy, we live...By the resurrection of Christ, God has given life, not only to him, but to us. We are given new birth by God; he fathers us by the resurrection of his Son. In Christ's triumph God makes all things new, beginning with us.[383]

Furthermore:

The salvation that was sealed by Christ's resurrection and planted in our hearts by the seed of the Word will be revealed when Christ comes again in glory. Our hope is anchored in the past: Jesus rose!

---

[382] Edmund Clowney, *The Message of 1 Peter* (Leicester: Inter-Varsity Press, 1988), p.52.
[383] Clowney, p.45.

Our hope remains in the present: Jesus lives! Our hope is completed in the future: Jesus is coming! [384]

It is important to highlight Clowney's point that in the triumph of Christ 'God makes all things new.' The Christian hope is not just for the future of individual human beings, but for the future of the whole world. Paul emphasises this point in Romans 8: 18-21 where he writes:

I consider that the sufferings of this present time are not worth comparing with the glory that is to be revealed to us. For the creation waits with eager longing for the revealing of the sons of God; for the creation was subjected to futility, not of its own will but by the will of him who subjected it in hope; because the creation itself will be set free from its bondage to decay and obtain the glorious liberty of the children of God.

As Tom Wright explains, the point that Paul is making in these verses is that:

The world as it is, though still God's good creation, and pregnant with his power and glory (1.20), is not at present the way it should be. God's 'covenant faithfulness' was always about his commitment that, through the promises to Abraham, he would one day put the whole world to rights. Now at last we see what this meant. The human race was put in charge of creation (as so often, Paul has Genesis 1-3 not far from his mind). When humans rebelled and worship parts of creation instead of God himself (1:21-23) creation fell into disrepair. God allowed this state of slavery to continue, not because the creation wanted to be like that but because he was determined eventually to put the world back to right according to the original plan (just as, when Israel let him down, he didn't change the plan, but sent at last a faithful Israelite). The plan had called for human beings to take their place under God and over the world, worshipping the creator and exercising glorious stewardship over the world. The creation isn't waiting to *share* the freedom of

---

[384] Clowney, p.46.

God's children as some translations imply. It is waiting to benefit wonderfully when God's children are glorified. It is waiting -on tiptoe with expectation, in fact -for the particular freedom it will enjoy when God gives to his children that glory, that wise rule and stewardship, which was always intended for those who bear God's glorious image.[385]

To quote Cranfield in his commentary on 1 Peter:

Unlike their pagan neighbours the early Christians were men of hope, who could look steadily into the future without fear, not with mere resignation, but with eager anticipation. A new dimension has been given to their lives – the dimension of the future, of eternal life. [386]

What was true of the first Christians is also true for Christians today. They are people who are free to hope that because of the saving action of God in Christ, 'all shall be well, and all shall be well, and all manner [of] thing shall be well '[387] both for they themselves and for creation as a whole.

The fact that they have this hope means that it makes sense for Christians to 'live in the truth' by exercising the freedom to believe, to live in obedience to God, to reject idolatry, to serve, and to suffer which they also possess. This is because it is as they exercise these freedoms that they begin to share in the present, and will fully share in the future, in that eternal renewal of all things by God to which the Christian hope points.

A final point to note about the six forms of freedom we have just looked at is that they are all God given. God gives human being the freedom to choose to believe the gospel and with it the freedom to live in

[385] Tom Wright, *Romans Part 1: Chapters 1-8* (London and Louisville: SPCK/Westminster John Knox Press, 2004), pp.151-152.
[386] Charles Cranfield, *I and II Peter and Jude* (London: SCM, 1960), p.37.
[387] Julian of Norwich, *Revelations of Divine Love* (Grand Rapids: Christian Classics Ethereal library), p.57.

obedience to God, to reject idolatry, to serve, to suffer and to have hope. Because these freedoms are God given, they cannot be taken away by human beings. Human beings can make the exercise of these freedoms more difficult and unpleasant, but they cannot cause them to cease to exist. Even if government or society were to seek to forbid Christians from believing, obeying, rejecting idolatry, serving, suffering and hoping they could not stop Christians from doing these things should they choose to do so.

In summary

What we have seen in this chapter is that Christians are faced with the same basic choice faced by Vaclav Havel's greengrocer in fiction and Yuri Sipko in real life. Are they going to live by lies for the sake of a quiet life, or are they going to 'live within the truth' and face the consequences?

Christians are called to be people who 'live within the truth' and this means that they need to be people who make the deliberate choice to exercise the freedom granted to them by law to seek to persuade people to accept the Christian faith, to be faithful in attending Christian worship and observe other Christian practices such as having regular times of prayer and Bible study, saying grace before meals and marking the seasons of the Christian year. They also need to be people who make the deliberate choice to exercise the freedom given to them by God to believe, obey, reject idolatry, suffer, serve and live in hope.

In the next chapter we shall go on to explore how Christians are called to 'live within the truth' by saying 'No' to forms of conduct that are contrary to the will of God as summarised in the Ten Commandments even when such forms of conduct are demanded by those in positions of power in contemporary Western society.

Chapter 8
A Christian life of conscientious objection

In chapter 2 of this study we saw the importance that the Christian tradition since the Middle Ages has attached to the principle that one should act according to one's conscience even when civil or religious authorities told one not to.

In chapter 3 we saw that as a result of the influence of this aspect of the Christian tradition freedom of religion has been legally recognised to include the freedom to refuse to perform certain actions which a person's conscience, informed by their religion, declares to be wrong. Such actions have been recognised as including, among other things, participation in military service, performing or assisting in abortions, and officiating at same-sex marriages.

In this chapter I shall explore the concept of conscientious objection further. I shall argue that Christians need to exercise their God given freedom by conscientiously objecting to taking part in *any* kind of action which they have reason to believe it is contrary to the will of God. To put the same point another way, the freedom to obey God which we noted in the last chapter includes the obligation to say 'No' to all actions that we have reason to believe go against God's will. This involves not only intellectually acknowledging them to be wrong, but also not doing them, even when the church, society, or the state, expects or requires us to and by being willing to say 'No' when they are done by others.

Heroic acts of conscientious objection
In the history of the Church particular honour has been given to those Christians who have refused to go against their religiously informed conscience even when faced with the prospect of imprisonment, torture, or death for so doing.

In the Protestant tradition, for instance, Martin Luther's refusal to recant his teachings even when facing the prospect of execution as a heretic has been seen been seen as a particularly notable example of this tradition of heroic conscientious objection, but there are numerous other examples that could be cited from across the centuries and from across the range of Christian traditions. I shall cite four examples to illustrate this point.

Polycarp's refusal to reject Christ in favour of Caesar
The first is the account of the martyrdom of Bishop Polycarp of Smyrna in 155, one of the classic accounts of early Christian martyrdom This contemporary account tells us that after Polycarp, at this stage a very old man, had been arrested and brought to the stadium in Smyrna:

> ...the proconsul asked him whether he was Polycarp. On his confessing that he was, [the proconsul] sought to persuade him to deny Christ, saying, 'Have respect to your old age,' and other similar things, according to their custom, such as, 'Swear by the fortune of Cæsar; repent, and say, Away with the Atheists.' But Polycarp, gazing with a stern countenance on all the multitude of the wicked heathen then in the stadium, and waving his hand towards them, while with groans he looked up to heaven, said, 'Away with the Atheists.' Then, the proconsul urging him, and saying, 'Swear, and I will set you at liberty, reproach Christ;' Polycarp declared, 'Eighty and six years have I served Him, and He never did me any injury: how then can I blaspheme my King and my Saviour?'

> And when the proconsul yet again pressed him, and said, 'Swear by the fortune of Cæsar,' he answered,

> 'Since you are vainly urgent that, as you say, I should swear by the fortune of Cæsar, and pretend not to know who and what I am, hear me declare with boldness, I am a Christian. And if you wish to learn what the doctrines of Christianity are, appoint me a day, and you shall hear them.'

> The proconsul replied, 'Persuade the people.' But Polycarp said,

> 'To you I have thought it right to offer an account [of my faith]; for we are taught to give all due honour (which entails no injury upon ourselves) to the powers and authorities which are ordained of

God. [Romans 13:1-7; Titus 3:1] But as for these, I do not deem them worthy of receiving any account from me.'

The proconsul then said to him, 'I have wild beasts at hand; to these will I cast you, unless you repent.'

But he answered, 'Call them then, for we are not accustomed to repent of what is good in order to adopt that which is evil; and it is well for me to be changed from what is evil to what is righteous.'

But again the proconsul said to him, 'I will cause you to be consumed by fire, seeing you despise the wild beasts, if you will not repent.'

But Polycarp said, 'You threaten me with fire which burns for an hour, and after a little is extinguished, but are ignorant of the fire of the coming judgment and of eternal punishment, reserved for the ungodly. But why do you tarry? Bring forth what you will.'

While he spoke these and many other like things, he was filled with confidence and joy, and his countenance was full of grace, so that not merely did it not fall as if troubled by the things said to him, but, on the contrary, the proconsul was astonished, and sent his herald to proclaim in the midst of the stadium thrice, 'Polycarp has confessed that he is a Christian.' This proclamation having been made by the herald, the whole multitude both of the heathen and Jews, who dwelt at Smyrna, cried out with uncontrollable fury, and in a loud voice, 'This is the teacher of Asia, the father of the Christians, and the overthrower of our gods, he who has been teaching many not to sacrifice, or to worship the gods.' Speaking thus, they cried out, and besought Philip the Asiarch to let loose a lion upon Polycarp. But Philip answered that it was not lawful for him to do so, seeing the shows of wild beasts were already finished. Then it seemed good to them to cry out with one consent, that Polycarp should be burnt alive. For thus it behoved the vision which was revealed to him in regard to his pillow to be fulfilled, when, seeing it on fire as he was praying, he turned about and said prophetically to the faithful that were with him, 'I must be burnt alive.'

This, then, was carried into effect with greater speed than it was spoken, the multitudes immediately gathering together wood and fagots out of the shops and baths; the Jews especially, according to custom, eagerly assisting them in it. And when the funeral pile was ready, Polycarp, laying aside all his garments, and loosing his girdle, sought also to take off his sandals—a thing he was not accustomed to do, inasmuch as every one of the faithful was always eager who should first touch his skin. For, on account of his good behaviour he was, even before his martyrdom, adorned with every kind of good. Immediately then they surrounded him with those substances which had been prepared for the funeral pile. But when they were about also to fix him with nails, he said, 'Leave me as I am; for He that gives me strength to endure the fire, will also enable me, without your securing me by nails, to remain without moving in the pile.'

They did not nail him then, but simply bound him. And he, placing his hands behind him, and being bound like a distinguished ram [taken] out of a great flock for sacrifice, and prepared to be an acceptable burnt-offering unto God, looked up to heaven, and said,

'O Lord God Almighty, the Father of your beloved and blessed Son Jesus Christ, by whom we have received the knowledge of You, the God of angels and powers, and of every creature, and of the whole race of the righteous who live before you, I give You thanks that You have counted me, worthy of this day and this hour, that I should have a part in the number of Your martyrs, in the cup of your Christ, to the resurrection of eternal life, both of soul and body, through the incorruption imparted by the Holy Ghost. Among whom may I be accepted this day before You as a fat and acceptable sacrifice, according as You, the ever-truthful God, have foreordained, have revealed beforehand to me, and now have fulfilled. Wherefore also I praise You for all things, I bless You, I glorify You, along with the everlasting and heavenly Jesus Christ, Your beloved Son, with whom, to You, and the Holy Ghost, be glory both now and to all coming ages. Amen.'

When he had pronounced this amen, and so finished his prayer, those who were appointed for the purpose kindled the fire. And as the flame blazed forth in great fury, we, to whom it was given to witness it, beheld a great miracle, and have been preserved that we might report to others what then took place. For the fire, shaping itself into the form of an arch, like the sail of a ship when filled with the wind, encompassed as by a circle the body of the martyr. And he appeared within not like flesh which is burnt, but as bread that is baked, or as gold and silver glowing in a furnace. Moreover, we perceived such a sweet odour [coming from the pile], as if frankincense or some such precious spices had been smoking there.

At length, when those wicked men perceived that his body could not be consumed by the fire, they commanded an executioner to go near and pierce him through with a dagger. And on his doing this, there came forth a dove, and a great quantity of blood, so that the fire was extinguished; and all the people wondered that there should be such a difference between the unbelievers and the elect, of whom this most admirable Polycarp was one, having in our own times been an apostolic and prophetic teacher, and bishop of the Catholic Church which is in Smyrna. For every word that went out of his mouth either has been or shall yet be accomplished.[388]

George Fox's refusal to take an oath

One of the distinctive beliefs of George Fox, the founder of Quakerism, was that the teaching of Jesus (Matthew 5:33-37) and of James (James 5:12) meant that Christians were absolutely forbidden to take oaths of any kind, including oaths of loyalty to the crown and oaths in court.

In 1664 Fox refused to take an oath declaring allegiance to King Charles II and declaring acceptance of the king as supreme governor of the

---

[388] 'Epistle Concerning the Martyrdom of Polycarp,' in *The Ante-Nicene Fathers*, Vol.1 (Edinburgh and Grand Rapids: T & T Clark/Eerdmans, 1996), pp.4142.

Church of England. In his *Journal* he records what happened when because of this refusal he was brought to trial at the Lancaster Assizes knowing that a continuing refusal to take the oath would result in imprisonment:

> I, George Fox, being called before the judge, was put among the murderers and felons, and there stood among them above two hours, people, and the justices, and judge gazing upon me. And there they tried many things before the judge. And then the judge caused me to be brought, and they called me to the bar. And then he caused the jury to be called. And he asked the justices whether they had tended me the oath at the Sessions, and they said that they had. And the judge caused the book to be given to the justices for them to swear they tended me the oath according to the indictment, and some of them refused it. And the judge said he would do it to take away occasion, that there might be no occasion, and the justices swore that they had tendered me the oath according to the indictment.
>
> And when then and the jury were sworn, the judge asked me whether I had refused the oath, the last Assizes.
>
> And I said that I never took an oath in my life, and Christ the saviour and judge of the world saith 'Swear not at all.'
>
> And the judge seemed not to take notice of my answer but asked me whether or not I had not refused to take the oath, the last Assizes.
>
> And I said the words that I said to them were that if either priest, or teacher, or the justices could prove that after Christ and the apostles had forbidden swearing, they after commanded men to swear, I would swear.
>
> The judge said he was not at that time to dispute whether it was lawful to swear, but to inquire whether I did refuse to take the oath or no.

I told him those things as concerning plots, and the Pope's and foreign power contained in the oath, I utterly denied.

The judge said I said well in that.

I said again to them, as I had said before, but if they could prove that after Christ and the apostles forbade swearing, again they commanded to swear, I would swear; but Christ and the apostle commanded not to swear, therefore I would show forth Christianity for I was a Christian.[389]

Franz Jägerstätter's refusal to fight in the German army

Franz Jägerstätter was an Austrian Roman Catholic who was executed in 1943 because his Christian conscience would not allow him to agree to serve in the German army. After the war he was beatified by the Catholic church for his stand against Nazism and the Vatican website contains the following account of his life and death:

Franz Jägerstätter was born on 20 May 1907 in St Radegund, Upper Austria, to his unmarried mother, Rosalia Huber, and to Franz Bachmeier, who was killed during World War I. After the death of his natural father, Rosalia married Heinrich Jägerstätter, who adopted Franz and gave the boy his surname of Jägerstätter in 1917.

Franz received a basic education in his village's one-room schoolhouse. His step-grandfather helped with his education and the boy became an avid reader.

It seems Franz was unruly in his younger years; he was, in fact, the first in his village to own a motorcycle. However, he is better known as an ordinary and humble Catholic who did not draw attention to himself.

After his marriage to Franziska in 1936 and their honeymoon in Rome, Franz grew in his faith but was not extreme in his piety.

---

[389] John Nickalls (ed), *Journal of George Fox,* (London: Religious Society of Friends, 1975), pp.474-475.

Besides his farm work Franz became the local sexton in 1936 and began receiving the Eucharist daily. He was known to refuse the customary offering for his services at funerals, preferring the spiritual and corporal works of mercy over any remuneration.

In the mid to late 1930s, while much of Austria was beginning to follow the tide of Nazism, Franz became ever more rooted in his Catholic faith and placed his complete trust in God.

While carrying out his duties as husband and breadwinner for his wife and three daughters, this ordinary man began thinking deeply about obedience to legitimate authority and obedience to God, about mortal life and eternal life and about Jesus' suffering and Passion.

Franz was neither a revolutionary nor part of any resistance movement, but in 1938 he was the only local citizen to vote against the "Anschluss" (annexation of Austria by Germany), because his conscience prevailed over the path of least resistance.

Franz Jägerstätter was called up for military service and sworn in on 17 June 1940. Shortly thereafter, thanks to the intervention of his mayor, he was allowed to return to the farm. Later, he was in active service from October 1940 to April 1941, until the mayor's further intervention permitted his return home.

He became convinced that participation in the war was a serious sin and decided that any future call-up had to be met with his refusal to fight.

"It is very sad", he wrote, "to hear again and again from Catholics that this war waged by Germany is perhaps not so unjust because it will wipe out Bolshevism...But now a question: what are they fighting in this Country - Bolshevism or the Russian People?

'When our Catholic missionaries went to a pagan country to make them Christians, did they advance with machine guns and bombs in order to convert and improve them?...If adversaries wage war on another nation, they have usually invaded the country not to improve people or even perhaps to give them something, but usually to get something for themselves...If we were merely fighting Bolshevism, these other things - minerals, oil wells or good farmland - would not be a factor.'

Jägerstätter was at peace with himself despite the alarm he could have experienced witnessing the masses' capitulation to Hitler. Mesmerized by the National Socialist propaganda machine, many people knelt when Hitler made his entrance into Vienna. Catholic Churches were forced to fly the swastika flag and subjected to other abusive laws.

In February 1943 Franz was called up again for military service. He presented himself at the induction centre on 1 March 1943 and announced his refusal to fight, offering to carry out non-violent services: this was denied him.

He was held in custody at Linz in March and April, transferred to Berlin-Tegel in May and subject to trial on 6 July 1943 when he was condemned to death for sedition. The prison chaplain was struck by the man's tranquil character...

On 9 August, before being executed, Franz wrote: 'If I must write...with my hands in chains, I find that much better than if my will were in chains. Neither prison nor chains nor sentence of death can rob a man of the Faith and his free will. God gives so much strength that it is possible to bear any suffering...People worry about the obligations of conscience as they concern my wife and children.

But I cannot believe that, just because one has a wife and children, a man is free to offend God.'

Franz Jägerstätter, who would not bow his head to Hitler, bowed his head to God, and the guillotine took care of the rest. He was obviously called up to serve a higher order. [390]

[390] 'Bl. Franz Jägerstätter (1907-1943) Layman and martyr' at: https://www.vatican.va/news_services/liturgy/saints/ns_lit_doc_20071026_jagerstatter_en.html

Nien Cheng's refusal to confess to spying

Nien Cheng was Chinese woman from a wealthy landowning family who converted to Christianity from Buddhism as a teenager. After the Communist revolution in China in 1949, she and her husband decided to remain in mainland China rather than flee to Taiwan and she worked for the Shell oil company in China until Shell's holdings in China were nationalized by the Chinese government in 1966.

In that same year she was arrested during the Cultural Revolution and accused of having conspired with the British government to undermine the Chinese government. As she later wrote, in spite of her arrest and the accusations against her 'I was not afraid. I believed in a just and merciful God, and I thought he would lead me out of the abyss.' [391]

The Chinese authorities pressured Nien Cheng to confess to having been a British agent, but her Christian conscience would not allow her to do so, and she maintained that refusal even in the face of torture. An account of her ordeal is given by Charles Colson in his book *The Good Life*:

> The People's Government did not have truth - or evidence - on its side, but it possessed power in abundance over Nien Cheng's life. One day Nien was taken to an interrogation where five people swarmed around her. Male and female guards pushed her from one to another. 'You are the running dog of the imperialists,' they shouted. 'You are a dirty exploiter of workers and peasants.'

> A male guard then picked up Nien by the lapels of her jacket and threw her against the wall. Before she collapsed, he grabbed her once more and threw her even harder against the wall. He repeated this again and again.

[391] Nien Cheng, *Life and Death in Shanghai*, quoted in Charles Colson, *The Charles Colson Collection* (Carol Stream: Tyndale House Publishers 2005), Kindle edition, Loc1122.

Nien was finally allowed to collapse into a chair. The guards kept raining blows on her, slapping her face. They screamed, 'Are you going to confess? Confess!'

When Nien refused yet again, the guards slapped handcuffs on her. 'These handcuffs are to punish you for your intransigence. You will wear them until you are ready to confess. Only then will we take them off. If you confess now, we will take them off now. If you confess tomorrow, we will take them off tomorrow. If you do not confess for a year, you will have to wear them for a year. If you never confess, you will have to wear them to your grave.'

Just before Nien was led out of the room, a female guard ratcheted the handcuffs several notches tighter. She then took Nien into a five - foot - by-five - foot windowless torture cell. There Nien spent a sleepless night as her manacled hands began to swell and burn furiously. Guards came at random intervals to ask her whether she was ready to confess.

After twenty-four hours in the torture cell, Nien underwent another round of interrogation, where her accusers confirmed that the hard edged handcuffs she was wearing could do serious long term damage to her hands. 'You are worried about your hands. That's quite right,' they said. 'Hands are very important to everybody but especially to an intellectual who must write. You should try to protect your hands and not let them be hurt. You can do that easily by just agreeing to confess.'

The guard took Nien back to her regular cell but kept the handcuffs on. Soon they began to wear through her skin toward the bone. She felt only a small measure of relief from the swelling and burning by propping her hands on a rolled blanket as she tried to sleep sitting up. In the morning the blanket was covered with puss and blood. She began to run a high fever.

The handcuffs all but prevented her from eating and drinking. She was able to take in only a little nourishment by spilling her cup of rice and cabbage out onto a towel, then eating the food like an animal.

The guards' attempts to extract a confession from her never ceased. Their commands grew more distant, however, ask her strength ebbed.

One day she came back to consciousness after fainting to find a group of guards standing above her. 'Get up! Get up!' a man shouted at her. 'You are feigning death! You won't be allowed to get away with it.'

Nien's head cleared a little, and she found that her hands, although still bent behind her back, were no longer handcuffed.

'Get up! Get up!' A female guard shouted.

Nien had been manacled for eleven days.[392]

Heroic acts of conscientious objection such as the four examples we have just looked at have been rightly honoured in the history of the Church because they exemplify the principle that a Christian must always refuse to act in a way that their conscience tells them is contrary to God's will, even if this refusal leads to imprisonment, torture or even death. As Jägerstätter said, whatever the consequences a Christian is not 'free to offend God.' To put it another way, they remind us that we need to take seriously the words of Jesus '...do not fear those who kill the body but cannot kill the soul; rather fear him who can destroy both body and soul in hell' (Matthew 10:28).

What would be a mistake, however, would be to think that the call to Christians to engage in conscientious objection should be seen as only being a call to engage in the sort of acts of heroic virtue that we have just considered. Similarly, it would be a mistake to think that acts of conscientious objection can be confined to the sort of acts of conscientious objection that have specific legal recognition, such as not performing military service, or assisting with abortions.

What needs to be understood is that conscientious objection, understood as the exercise of that freedom of conscience historically

---

[392] Colson, Loc 1276-1299 quoting *Life and Death in Shanghai.*

recognised by the Christian tradition and subsequently recognised by the Universal Declaration of Human Rights, the European Convention on Human Rights, and other similar statements concerning human rights,[393] must be viewed as a normal part of everyday Christian life. The faithful Christian life is one long practice of conscientious objection.

In all areas of their lives, and at all times, Christians are under an obligation to refuse to do whatever their conscience tells them will 'offend God.' This applies just as much to refusing to take part in ungodly workplace banter, for example, as it does to refusing to renounce faith in Christ, or refusing to take part in an unjust war.

The Ten Commandments as a guide to Christian conscientious objection

A problem raised by the necessity for the Christian to refuse to do what their conscience tells them will offend God is that the conscience is capable of being misled. This can happen in two ways. The first is when people come to believe that something is contrary to God's will when in fact it is not. An example of this is the belief held by some in the early days of the Church that it was always wrong to eat meat that was a result of sacrifices made to pagan idols (1 Corinthians 8:1-13). The second is when people come to believe that that something is acceptable to God when in fact it is not. An example of this is the way in which the Christians in the church in Corinth apparently saw no problem with a man living with his father's wife (which is why Paul had to remind the Corinthians that such behaviour was deeply immoral and needed to be met with firm disciplinary action - 1 Corinthians 5:1-5).

In order to avoid both of these situations, it is important for Christians to be aware of what God commands and forbids so that their consciences will prompt them to do what God commands and not do what he forbids.

---

[393] It is important to note in that in these recent statements concerning human rights the right to exercise freedom of conscience is s general freedom which is not confined to those cases where the right to conscientious objection is specifically laid down in national law.

Down the centuries the Ten Commandments recorded in Exodus 20:2-17 have been seen by Christians of all traditions as the starting point for learning what God commands and forbids. In the Catechism in the Church of England's *Book of Common Prayer,* for example, the Ten Commandments are seen as providing Christians with a guide to what it means to fulfil their baptismal promise 'to keep God's holy will and commandments and walk in the same all the days of my life.'

The reason why Christians have been right to see the Ten Commandments as having this significance is helpfully explained by Peter Leithart in his study of the Ten Commandments, what calls the 'Ten Words'.

Leithart raises the question of why the Ten Words are addressed in 'the masculine singular of the second person' ('Thou shalt...).[394] The answer, writes Leithart, is that they are addressed collectively to Israel as God's son (a son who is made up of men and women equally):

> God gave his first command to Adam, his first son. At Sinai, he speaks to his son, the new Adam. The Ten Words are imperatives, but not merely imperatives. When Father Yahweh speaks to son Israel, he discloses his likes and dislikes. The Ten Words are 'a personal declaration' that reveals *Yahweh's* character. Like Proverbs, they're Father-son talk. The ten new-creative words are designed to form Israel into an image of his Father.
>
> The Decalogue is about Israel's mission. When Israel obeys the Ten Words, his common life becomes a living filial icon of the heavenly Father among the nations of the earth. Hearing the voice from Sinai, Israel takes up Λdam's vocation of imitating and imaging his Father.[395]

---

[394] Peter Leithart, *The Ten Commandments* (Bellingham: Lexham Press, 2020), Kindle edition, p.10.
[395] Leiithart, p.10.

Leithart goes on to explain that although the Ten Words can appear to impose a new form of slavery on Israel, what they in fact do is enable Israel to become free:

> Many complain about the negativity of the Ten Words. There are two positive commandments – remember the Sabbath day, honor your father and mother. Mostly, it's one 'Don't' after another. God says he brought Israel from slavery, but it may seem he just imposed a different slavery.
>
> According to Scripture, Torah is the 'perfect law of liberty' (James 1:25; 2:12). A community dominated by disrespect for parents, workaholism, violence, envy, theft and lies isn't free. Besides, absolute freedom is impossible. In the world that God made, the world that actually exists, things aren't free to do or be anything they please. They're free when they become what they are. An acorn is free to become an oak, not an elephant. The Ten Words guide Israel to grow up to be what he is, the son who rules in his Father's house (see Gal 4:1-7). [396]

Leithart also notes that the Ten Words need to be understood Christologically. That is to say, we need to understand them both as having been perfectly fulfilled by Christ, God's perfect son, and as being fulfilled by in us by Christ through his Spirit:

> Israel cannot listen to the Lord's voice. He asks Yahweh to speak through Moses (Exod 20:18-21). At Sinai, the son's heart is too hardened to hear his Father. But Israel isn't left hopeless. Yahweh *will* have a son who conforms to the Ten Words. The Father does have such a Son, the eternal Son who became Israel to be and do what Israel failed to be and do.
>
> The Ten Words are a character portrait of Jesus, the Son of God. The Ten Words lay out the part of *imitatio Dei* because they lay out the path of *Imitatio Christi*. As Israel kept the commandments, Augustine wrote 'the life of that people foretold and foreshadowed Christ.' As Irenaeus said, *Christ* fulfils the law that he spoke from

[396] Leithart, p.10.

355

Sinai. The law exposes our sin, restrains the unruly, provides a guide to life. But Jesus is the heart and soul of the Decalogue. The first use of the law is Christological.

Many centuries after Sinai, God returned in the third month, in rushing wind and fire, to pour out his Spirit. At that completed Pentecost, the Spirit began to write 'not on stone but on the heart' (see 2 Cor 3:3). He forms a new Israel, a company of sons who share Jesus's Spirit of sonship. By that Spirit, the Father fulfils his ten new-creative words, *in us*.

Is the Decalogue for us? We might as well ask, is *Jesus* for us.[397]

In summary, the Ten Commandments of the Decalogue are given to us as Christians to provide the guidance we need in order to live in free filial obedience to God the Father and thus bear witness to him among the nations of the earth. We can live in this way because Jesus's perfect fulfilment of the Commandments is being reproduced in us through the Holy Spirit, the Spirit of Sonship.

What follows from this is that we need to allow our consciences to be formed by an awareness of what is required of us in the Ten Commandments and then begin to live accordingly seeking the assistance of God through the Spirit to enable us to do so. Furthermore, as we shall see as we consider each of the Commandments individually, what us is required of us by the Ten Commandments is (as previously suggested) a permanent state of conscientious objection, a permanent refusal to do anything which is contrary to our heavenly Father's will for us as his children.

What each of the Commandments tells us about the form Christian conscientious objection needs to take

Commandment 1: 'I am the LORD your God, who brought you out of the land of Egypt, out of the house of bondage. You shall have no other gods before me.' (Exodus 20:2-3)

[397] Leithhart, pp.10-11.

From the perspective of the biblical witness as a whole, the Lord God of Israel who is the subject of the first commandment is the not only the God who delivered Israel from Egypt at the Exodus. He is also the creator God who called the whole world into being and continues to sustain it, the God who became incarnate as Jesus Christ to deliver not only Israel but the human race as a whole from the power of sin and death and the God who is going to bring in a new creation in which all who are his children through Christ will live and reign with him forever.

Furthermore, he is a God who has revealed a triune identity. He is the God who is, from all eternity to all eternity, Father, Son and Holy Spirit. In the words of the Athanasian Creed:

...there is one Person of the Father, another of the Son, and another of the Holy Ghost. But the Godhead of the Father, of the Son, and of the Holy Ghost, is all one: the Glory equal, the Majesty co-eternal.

Obedience to the first commandment means acknowledging this God alone as the only true God (and worshipping him alone). Such obedience will involve faithful Christians engaging in three forms of conscientious objection.

First, they must refuse to acknowledge the existence of, or engage in the worship of, any alleged god or supernatural being alongside the one true God.

As Larry Hurtado notes in his book *Destroyer of the Gods*, from the earliest days of the Church one of the things that made Christians distinctive was that they: 'were expected to avoid taking part in the worship of any other deity other than the one God of the biblical tradition.'[398] As he goes on to write:

This refusal to reverence the many gods that was demanded of early Christians would have included refusing to offer worship to

---

[398] Larry Hurtado, *Destroyer of the Gods* (Waco: Baylor University Press, 2016), p.49.

household divinities, to the tutelary deities of cities, to the traditional gods of the various cities and peoples of the Roman world, and even to the deities that represented the empire itself, such as the goddess Roma, and that conferred legitimacy to Roman rule. [399]

As the account of the martyrdom of Polycarp given above makes clear, this refusal led to Christians being branded as 'atheists' in the sense of being those who denied the gods and being regarded as being religiously, socially and politically subversive as a result.

What following the example of the early Christians means today is not only a refusal to join in the worship of other gods at non-Christian places of worship, or in rites offering worship to the gods in household settings (such as the worship offered in Hindu household shrines), but arguably also refusing to take part in inter-faith religious or social activities which involve worship being offered to other gods, or that could be seen to imply that such worship is religiously legitimate (see 1 Corinthians 10:28-29). Such refusal will lead to accusations that Christians are guilty of an intolerant rejection of religious equality and diversity, but it is nonetheless demanded by the first commandment.

Where such refusal will be particularly challenging will be in settings such as hospitals, prisons or universities where there are inter-faith chaplaincies. The issue here will be how Christians can engage in chaplaincy work in such settings without implying that the religions supported by other chaplains are equally legitimate.

Secondly, Christians must be equally careful to also avoid worshipping other non-religious gods, such as the idols of the modern Western world noted in chapter 6. As Packer observes in his commentary on the Ten Commandments, even if we reject the worship of the gods of other religions:

---

[399] Hurtado, p.49.

...there are still the great gods Sex, Shekels and Stomach (an unholy trinity constituting one god, self), and the other enslaving trio, Pleasure, Possessions and Position, whose worship in described in 1 John 2:16 as 'the desires of the flesh and the desire of the eyes and pride in possessions.' Football, the Firm, Freemasonry and the Family are also gods for some, and indeed the list of other gods is endless, for anything than anyone allows to run his life becomes his god, and the claimants for this prerogative are legion. In the matter of life's basic loyalty temptation is a many-headed monster. [400]

What the conscientious refusal to worship any of these other gods involves is the refusal to make any of them in practical terms the most important thing in our life, so that the thing we actually care about most in life is, for example, our career, or our family, or our sporting activities. It also involves refusing to allow the demands of other gods to undermine our service and obedience to God, by, for instance, spending time working, engaging in sporting activities, or engaging in family activities, rather than worshipping God in church. Such refusal can be costly as it can potentially damage our careers or our relationships with friends or family members, but it is a necessary consequence of obedience to the first commandment.

Thirdly, Christians must be diligent in refusing to make a god out of their religion. There are three dangers to be avoided in this regard.

The first is that religious activity, like all forms of human activity, can become all absorbing with the result that the things we do for God in the service of the Church can become more important to us than our relationship with God himself. In practical terms, for example, this can mean that we spend our time and energy in doing those things and the result is that we squeeze out time spent studying the Bible, praying, or engaging in spiritual self-examination.

---

[400] J I Packer, *Keeping the 10 Commandments* (Wheaton: Crossway, 2007), Kindle edition, p.48.

The second is that the desire to be well regarded by other members of our church, or to progress in our career if we work for it, can become more important to us than what God wants with the result that we compromise our obedience to him in what we say or do so that we are well regarded or get a new job or a promotion. An example would be compromising what we say about issues of human sexuality so as to avoid conflict with others or to gain a new church appointment.

The third danger is if we begin to trust in our religion as the basis for our salvation. As Thomas Watson notes in his commentary on the first commandment, we are apt either to neglect our religious duties or to idolize them by thinking that they by themselves will make God look favourably upon us.[401] To avoid the latter danger we must constantly remind ourselves that we are righteous in the eyes of God simply and solely because of what Christ has done for us and not because of anything that we do.

> **Commandment 2:** You shall not make for yourself a graven image, or any likeness of anything that is in heaven above, or that is in the earth beneath, or that is in the water under the earth; you shall not bow down to them or serve them; for I the Lord your God am a jealous God, visiting the iniquity of the fathers upon the children to the third and the fourth generation of those who hate me, but showing steadfast love to thousands of those who love me and keep my commandments. (Exodus 20:4-6)

As Packer explains, the key issue underlying the second commandment is how to think rightly about God:

> How should we form thoughts of God? Not only can we not imagine him adequately, since he is at every point greater than we can grasp – we dare not trust anything our imagination suggests about him, for the built-in habit of fallen minds is to scale God down. Sin began as a response to the temptation, 'You will be like God' (Genesis 3:5),

---

[401] Thomas Watson, *The Ten Commandments* (London: Banner of Truth, 1962), p.42.

and the effect of our wanting to be on God's level is that we bring him down to ours. This is unrealistic, not to say irreverent, but it is what we do when imagination is in the saddle.

Hence the second commandment, 'You shall not make for yourself a carved image, or any likeness of anything...' This forbids, not worshipping many gods (the first commandment covered that) but imagining the true God as like yourself or something lower. God's real attack is on mental images, of which metal images are more truly the consequence than the cause. When Israelites worshipped God under the form of a golden bull calf, they were using their imagination to conceive him in terms of power without purity; that was their basic sin. And if imagination leads our thoughts about God we too shall go astray. No statement starting, 'This is how I like to think of God' should ever be trusted. An imagined God will always be quite imaginary and unreal. [402]

If this is how we are to understand the second commandment, the question that follows is on what basis we should think about God. If the use of our imagination is ruled out, what is the alternative? Leithart helps us here by pointing to the importance in the Bible of the distinction between seeing and hearing. He writes that the second commandment:

...implies a distinction between sight and hearing, eye and ear. In Deuteronomy 4, Moses reminds Israel that they didn't see any form on Sinai but heard a voice. When Yahweh tells Moses to carve new tablets, he uses the verb form of 'graven image' (Exod 34:1): Moses 'graves' tablets. But these graven stones contain *words*, not pictures. Yahweh declares, commands, writes on the tablets. Yahweh does not show himself. Yahweh is the unseen God who speaks. He is Word.

Eyes are the organs of scrutiny and judgement (see Ps 11:4). God sees and judges the creation good (Gen 1:31). Eve sees and

---

[402] Packer, p.54.

evaluates the tree (Gen 3:6), Adam and Eve's eyes are opened after they eat (Gen 3:7). With visible things, we assume a stance of criticism, command and control. But God is not under our control. We don't judge him, but he us.

Hearing has a different phenomenology. In Scripture, hearing is virtually identical to obedience. To hear is to receive commands. Listening puts us in the position of being judged. Hearing opens up an uncontrollable future. Someone says, for the first time, 'I love you,' and the world shifts beneath your feet.

Since Sinai, God *has* been seen: The Word tabernacled in flesh and we saw his glory (John 1:14). Seeing Jesus, we see the Father (John 14:9). Some Christians say that Jesus' advent changed the Second Word so that we are now permitted to serve images. But Jesus ascended and is no longer visibly present. We *don't* see his glory as the apostles did. He's with us by his Spirit, the wind who blows where he will, the Spirit whom we hear but cannot see. The Spirit comes to us in sensible forms -in audible words, tangible water, and edible food and drink. Someday we will see Jesus face-to -face. But not yet. To live by the eyes to reach ahead of our time. It immanentizes the eschaton. After the incarnation, we *still* live by ear (2 Cor 5:7), until he comes again. [403]

If we further ask which are the words to which we are to listen to in order to hear God the Word, the answer is that we are to listen to the Spirit inspired words of the Old and New Testament Scriptures. Jesus Christ is the Word who makes God known (John 1:18) and we hear about Jesus through the words of Holy Scripture. The Father is revealed by the Son who is himself revealed by the Spirit through the words of Scripture.

This means that the *Barmen Declaration* of 1934 was right to declare that:

---

[403] Leithart, p.25.

Jesus Christ as he is testified to us in Holy Scripture is the one Word of God, whom we are to hear, whom we are to trust and obey in life and in death.

We repudiate the false teaching that the church must recognize yet other happenings and powers, images and truths as divine revelation alongside this one Word of God, as a source for her preaching. [404]

To obey the Second Commandment is to follow Barmen by conscientiously refusing to put our trust in life and in death in anyone, or anything, else other than Jesus the Word testified to in Scripture.

We can see what this means in practice if we consider Philip Turner's account of a standard Episcopal Church Sermon in his essay 'ECUSA's God and the idols of Liberal Protestantism.' Turner writes that:

The standard Episcopal sermon, at its most fulsome, begins with a statement to the effect the Incarnation is to be understood (in an almost exhaustive sense) as a manifestation of divine love. From this starting point, several conclusions are drawn. The first is that God is love pure and simple. Thus, one is to see in Christ's death no judgement upon the human condition. Rather, one is to see an affirmation of creation and the persons we are. The great news of the Christian gospel is this. The life and death of Jesus revealed the fact that God accepts and affirms us. From this revelation, we can draw a further conclusion. God wants us to love one another, and such love requires of us both acceptance and affirmation of the other. From this point we can't arrive yet another. Accepting love requires a form of justice that is inclusive of all people, particularly those who in some way have been marginalised by oppressive social practice. The mission of the church is, therefore, to see that those have been rejected are included and that justice as inclusion defines public policy. The result is a practical equivalence between the gospel of the Kingdom of God and this form of social justice. The

---

[404] *The Barmen Declaration*, section I, text in Leith, p.520.

statements 'It's a matter of the gospel' and 'It's a justice issue' stand on all fours with one another.[405]

What we see reported in this quotation is a distortion both of the Gospel and of the Church's calling. It reduces God's love to affirmation without judgement and the Church's mission to supporting a particular (and problematic) understanding of the nature of social justice.[406]

In Packer's terms, those who preach like this have imagined both what God is like and what he requires of his people, rather than listening to what the Word witnessed to by Scripture tells us about these matters. Faithful Christians must refuse to go down this route. Instead, they must hold fast to what the Scriptural Word says, and conscientiously refuse to depart from it in what they say, or what they do, even if this makes them unpopular with those both outside and inside the Church. To do anything else is to violate the second commandment.

> **Commandment 3:** 'You shall not take the name of the Lord your God in vain; for the Lord will not hold him guiltless who takes his name in vain.' (Exodus 20:7)

The basic meaning of the prohibition contained in the third commandment is helpfully summarised in *To be a Christian*, the catechism produced by the Anglican Church in North America, as follows:

Why is God's Name sacred? God's Name reveals who he is—his nature, his character, his power, and his purposes. All forms of God's Name are holy. (Exodus 3:1–15; 34:5–7; Psalms 8; 54:1; 79:9; Isaiah 57:15; Luke 1:46–49)

---

[405] Philip Turner, ''ECUSA's God and the idols of Liberal Protestantism,' in Ephraim Radner and Philip Turner, *The Fate of Communion* (Grand Rapids: Eerdmans 2006), p.245.

[406] For the reason why this understanding of social justice is problematic from a Christian perspective see Scott Allen, *Why Social Justice is not Biblical Justice* (Grand Rapids: Credo, 2020).

What does it mean to take God's Name "in vain"? "Vain" means empty, meaningless, and of no account. To take God's Name in vain is to treat it as such. (Leviticus 24:10–16; Romans 2:23–24).[407]

The catechism goes on to explain that not treating God's name in this way involves avoiding using it profanely or carelessly:

How can you avoid taking God's Name in vain? Because I love him, I should use God's Name with reverence, not carelessly or profanely. (Deuteronomy 28:58–59; Psalms 86:11–12; 99:1–5; Revelation 15:2–4)

How might you use God's Name profanely? By the unholy use of God's holy Name, especially through perjury, blasphemy, and attributing to God any falsehood, heresy, or evil deed, as if he had authorized or approved them. (Deuteronomy 18:20–22; Proverbs 30:7–9; Jeremiah 34:15–16; Ezekiel 36:16–23; Amos 2:6–7; Jude 5–13)

How might you use God's Name carelessly? Cursing, magic, broken vows, false piety, manipulation of others, and hypocrisy all cheapen God's Name. These treat God's Name as empty of the reality for which it stands. (Leviticus 5:4–6; 19:26b, 31; Psalm 10:2–7; Malachi 1:6–14; Matthew 5:33–37; James 3:5–12; Articles of Religion, 39). [408]

As Joy Davidman notes in her book on the Ten Commandments, *Smoke on the Mountain*, one key way in which both individual Christians and whole nations and churches have broken the third commandment by treating God's name in profane and careless ways is by using God's name as an instrument of their own self-justification. In her words:

---

[407] The Anglican Church in North America, *To be a Christian*, paragraphs 284-285 at: https://anglicanchurch.net/wp-content/uploads/2020/06/To-Be-a-Christian.pdf
[408] *To be a Christian*, paragraphs 286-288.

Nor can we limit ourselves to condemning the sins of the outer world. We of the churches often gather our robes away from contamination, and thank God that we are not as other men. *We* don't despise God's name; in fact, we call upon it constantly to justify ourselves. How few parents, annoyed past bearing by young child, can resist the facile, 'God will punish you!' How few straight-laced church women, outraged by the shamelessness (and popularity) of the town's bad girl, can keep from secret satisfaction at the thought of the divine judgement awaiting her! if we object to meat eating, we declare that God is vegetarian; if we abhor war we proclaim a pacifist Deity. He who turned water into wine to gladden a wedding is now accused by many of favouring of that abominable fluid grape juice.

There can hardly be a more evil way of taking God's name in vain than this way of presuming to speak in it. For here is spiritual pride, the ultimate sin, in action - the sin of believing in one's own righteousness. The true prophet says humbly, 'To me, a sinful man, God spoke.' But the scribes and Pharisees declare, 'When we speak, God agrees.' They feel no need of a special revelation coma for always, in their own view, infallible. It is this self-righteousness of the pious that most breeds atheism, by inspiring all decent ordinary men with loathing of the enormous lie. [409]

As she goes on to write:

Nor is Pharisaism in confined to individuals. Whole nations practise it; many a campaign of looting has been proclaimed as a holy war. And whole churches, indeed all the churches, have fallen victim to it at one time or another; From the pathetic backwoods' sect of hysterics to the pomp and majesty of Rome, all have at one time or other claimed to hold a monopoly in God. The Protestants who are at times over eager to see the mote in the Roman Catholic eye might

---

[409] Joy Davidman, *Smoke on the Mountain* (London: Hodder and Stoughton, 1959), p.45.

do well to look up with their own ecclesiastical history; they will find there such things as the seventeenth-century century Kirk of Scotland calling for the massacre of women and children in God's name.

'Many will say to me in that day, Lord, Lord... and then I will profess unto them, I never knew you: depart from me, ye that work iniquity.' There has been only one who always spoke for God.[410]

What Davidman's words remind us is that while Christian conscientious objection to breaking the third commandment has to involve avoiding acquiescing in the sort of careless and profane use of God's name found in modern secular society (such as the use of the name of Jesus as a swear word, or the mockery of God and Christianity in general found in so much of the modern media) it also has to involve taking great care not to use God's name carelessly or profanely ourselves in the way that we speak or behave as God's people.

In Leithart's words:

God binds his Name and reputation to us. Whether his name is praised or blasphemed depends on whether we bear his name with the weight it deserves. It is a weighty responsibility to bear the weighty Name of the living God before the world.

Commandment 4: 'Remember the sabbath day, to keep it holy. Six days you shall labour, and do all your work; but the seventh day is a sabbath to the Lord your God; in it you shall not do any work, you, or your son, or your daughter, your manservant, or your maidservant, or your cattle, or the sojourner who is within your gates; for in six days the Lord made heaven and earth, the sea, and all that is in them, and rested the seventh day; therefore the Lord blessed the sabbath day and hallowed it.' (Exodus 20:8-11)

---

[410] Davidman, pp.45-46.

Although the sabbath day referred to Exodus 20 is the seventh day of the week, as *To be a Christian* explains:

> The earliest Christians came to observe Sunday as 'the Lord's Day' (Revelation 1:10) for their primary day of worship in remembrance of Jesus' resurrection on the first day of the week. (Luke 24:1–7; Acts 20:7; 1 Corinthians 16:2; Didache 14.1; Ignatius of Antioch, Letter to the Magnesians 9).[411]

In line with this transference of the primary day of worship, the majority Christian tradition, with the notable exception of the Seventh Day Adventists, has seen the fourth commandment as still in force, but as applying as far as Christians are concerned to Sunday rather than to the Jewish sabbath. In the words of the *Westminster Confession*:

> As it is of the law of nature, that, in general, a due proportion of time be set apart for the worship of God; so, in his word, by a positive, moral, and perpetual commandment, binding all men in all ages, he hath particularly appointed one day in seven for a Sabbath, to be kept holy unto him: which, from the beginning of the world to the resurrection of Christ, was the last day of the week; and from the resurrection of Christ, was changed into the first day of the week, which in Scripture is called the Lord's day, and is to be continued to the end of the world, as the Christian Sabbath.[412]

As Leithhart notes, when understood as referring to the Christian as well as the Jewish Sabbath, the fourth commandment given to Israel 'teaches us how to live, what we do and don't do.'[413] There are five aspects to this.

---

[411] *To be a Christian*, paragraph 297.
[412] *The Westminster Confession*, Chapter XXI in Leith, p.218. For a detailed study of the move from the Jewish to the Christian Sabbath see Don Carson (ed), *From Sabbath to Lord's Day: A Biblical, Historical and Theological Investigation* (Eugene: Wipf and Stock, 1999).
[413] Leithhart, p.33.

First, 'God requires that we 'interrupt' our work to acknowledge him as Lord, as a public confession that our authority over creation is a derived authority. Sabbath pauses life's noise. It's the silence that tunes our ears to Yahweh's word.' [414]

Secondly, we are to set aside the Sabbath as holy time:

Holy time is time claimed by God. The Sabbath is God's day as the tabernacle is God's space. On the Sabbath Israel is on the Lord's time. If they use Yahweh's time for their own projects, they commit sacrilege and trespass a holy boundary. We're always on the Lord's time, but the Sabbath embeds that truth in weekly habit.[415]

Thirdly, we are to set aside Sabbath as a day of worship:

Israel consecrates the day by worship. At the sanctuary, priests offered extra offerings (Num 28) and throughout Israel the people gathered in local 'synagogues' for praise, study of the Torah, and prayer. Israel consecrated the day be gathering in the presence of the Sabbath-keeping God (Lev 23:3). [416]

Fourthly, we are not only to take rest ourselves, but also ensure that rest is available for others:

Israel mimics Yahweh by mimicking Yahweh's *gift* of rest: Yahweh brings Israel from restless slavery; therefore, Israel gives rest to slaves. Most of Exodus 20:10 is a list of seven (!) categories of people who are *granted* rest. Each Israelite takes rest, and each also gives rest. Like Father, like son.

The Sabbath is unparalleled in the ancient world. It spreads out from the seventh day to fill the nooks and crannies of Israel's life. Indentured servants are held for six years, released in the seventh. Debt isn't allowed to become a permanent burden. Land could be sold for fifty

---

[414] Leithart, p.34.
[415] Leithart, p.35.
[416] Leithart, p.35.

years (7 Sabbath years +1) but reverted to the original owners at Jubilee (Lev 25). At the center of the calendar in Leviticus 23, the Lord reminds Israel to care for the needy (23:22). Torah calls Israel, to justice, mercy, and faithfulness, a Sabbath way of life (Isa. 58). From this, it is clear that Jesus never broke Sabbath, or made exceptions. Jesus keeps Sabbath by giving relief to the distressed. Pulling an ox from a ditch isn't an exception to Sabbath rules (Luke 14:5). It fulfils Sabbath by giving rest to a suffering ox.

...Sabbath redistributes and equalizes rest. It treats slaves as persons, not machines. It guards Israel from organising his time for 24/7 production, and so defies the reign of Mammon. [417]

Fifthly, by ceasing from work and keeping Sabbath we share in the rest of God:

By ceasing, son Israel *shares* his Father's Sabbatical. For Israel, this is sheer gift. Yahweh stops working because he's finished (Gen 2:1-4). Israel *hasn't* finished, and neither have we. After rest, we go back to work, but we work with the Sabbath satisfaction of a job done. By keeping Sabbath, we express confidence that the Lord will bring his work to completion and give *us* time to finish. Sharing Sabbath, we participate *already* in the divine pleasure of bringing things to an end, long before things come to their end. We enjoy what Thomas Aquinas calls 'all future blessings.' The Lord opens up his day of ceasing to include us, so that we share in his rest, like Father, like son.

...By extending Sabbath to Israel and to us, Yahweh raises his son to kingship. We work, but aren't slaves to work. We sit now in heavenly places (Eph 2:6), sharing Jesus' lordship over all. Enthroned in Sabbath glory, we with Israel participate in our Father's rest, and his rest giving.[418]

---

[417] Leithart, p.35.
[418] Leithart, pp.36-37 quoting Thomas Aquinas, *Summa Theologiae* I-II, q.100, art 5.

These five aspects of Sabbath observance constitute a call to conscientious objection by Christians in Western Society.

This is because in Western secular society as a whole God is no longer recognised as Lord, and as the one who will enable us to bring our work to completion, Sunday is no longer seen as holy time, and the obligation to engage in Christian worship on Sunday is neither understood nor accepted by the majority of the population. Furthermore, the worship of Mammon in Western society has led to an emphasis on the need for 24/7 economic activity which has undermined a right balance between work and rest, with adequate leisure time becoming increasingly the preserve of the economically well off, and the poor often having to work multiple jobs simply to make ends meet. In addition, there are also multiple forms of modern-day slavery with those caught up in them having no opportunity for proper rest and no opportunity to escape from their captivity.

In the face of this situation, Christians are called to say 'No!' and the primary way they do this is by going to church to worship on a Sunday rather than turning up for work. This point is emphasised by Stanley Hauerwas and William Willimon in their study of the Commandments, *The Truth about God*. In their chapter on the fourth commandment, they link the Christian Sabbath to the Texas institution of 'Juneteenth:'

> One of us was raised in Texas, where there is a wonderful institution known as Juneteenth. On June 19 news of the Emancipation Proclamation reached Texas. June 19 became the day on which African Americans, with no legal recourse, simply refused to show up for work. Whites might not have liked it, but there was nothing they could do about it. They simply accepted 'Juneteenth' as a holiday.

> The Christian Sabbath is Juneteenth. It is when Christians perform one of our most radical, countercultural, peculiarly defining acts - we simply refuse to show up for work. It is how we put the world in its place. It is how we take over the world's time and help to make it God's time. It is how we get over our amnesia and recover our memory of how we got here, who we are, and in whose service we

are called. Memory is hard for us not because we have got to resuscitate in memory a dead Jesus, but rather because we become distracted from the joyful truth that Jesus is resurrected, present among us in time, for all time.

Thus Calvin speaks of the Sabbath as a model of civil order, the time when we are trained for our true service to God. 'And what is this order? It is to assemble ourselves in the name of God.' (*Sermons*, 108). We need to take time to separate ourselves from the world's disorder so that the world might see true order.[419]

Obviously, there are some Christians who have to work on the Sabbath because of the nature of the calling that God has given them, but as a rule Christians need to 'refuse to show up' by setting aside Sunday as a day for worship, rest, time spent with family, friends, and neighbours and for performing acts of loving service for those in need. They are to do this even if this makes it difficult to obtain employment or to advance in the employment they have and even if it causes difficulties with family members or friends who want to spend Sunday differently. This can be a very difficult discipline to follow, but it is one that Christians need to follow if they are serious about obeying the fourth commandment.

A long-standing question is exactly what kind of activity it is legitimate for Christians to undertake on the Sabbath. There are no hard and fast rules on this issue, but in general terms it can be argued that as far as possible Christians ought to avoid taking part in their normal paid employment in order to have time to do the other things that they are called to do on the Sabbath. Hauerwas and Willimon suggest as a rule of thumb that apart from worship Christians ought only to undertake 'activity for the upbuilding of the community' and activity which is a

---

[419] Stanley Hauerwas and William Willimon, *The Truth about God – The Ten Commandments in Christian Life* (Nashville: Abingdon Press, 1999), Kindle edition, p.64.

joy. 'If planting bulbs in the yard is work, then it must wait until Monday. If it is a joy, then it is Sabbath work.'[420]

This also means that Christians need to think carefully about what they expect others to for them on the Sabbath, for example delivery drivers and those who work in shops or restaurants. It is not legitimate to ask others to do for us on the Sabbath what we do not think it would be right for us to do ourselves. In addition, Christians need to be proactive in working with others in society to try to ensure that no-one who does not wish to do so has to work on the Sabbath, to try to eradicate modern day slavery and to ensure all workers have the opportunity for adequate times of rest.

Commandment 5: 'Honour your father and your mother, that your days may be long in the land which the Lord your God gives you.' (Exodus 20:12)

While the primary focus of Exodus 20:12 is on the honour due to parents, in the history of the Christian Church it has also come to be understood as also referring by extension to the biblical teaching that honour is due to all those who hold various forms of authority in society.

Two examples will serve to illustrate this point.

The first is what is said about the fifth commandment in the Reformed *Heidelberg Catechism* of 1563:

Question 104. What does God require in the fifth commandment?

That I show honour, love, and faithfulness to my father and mother and to all who are set in authority over me; that I submit myself with respectful obedience to all their careful instruction and

---

[420] Hauerwas and Willimon, pp.63-64.

discipline; and that I also bear patiently their failures, since it is God's will to govern us by their hand. [421]

The second is what is said about this commandment in the 1994 *Catechism of the Catholic Church* (in line with the Roman Catholic numbering of the Ten Commandments it is referred to as the fourth commandment):

The fourth commandment is addressed expressly to children in their relationship to their father and mother, because this relationship is the most universal. It likewise concerns the ties of kinship between members of the extended family. It requires honour, affection, and gratitude toward elders and ancestors. Finally, it extends to the duties of pupils to teachers, employees to employers, subordinates to leaders, citizens to their country, and to those who administer or govern it. This commandment includes and presupposes the duties of parents, instructors, teachers, leaders, magistrates, those who govern, all who exercise authority over others or over a community of persons.

Observing the fourth commandment brings its reward: 'Honour your father and your mother, that your days may be long in the land which the LORD your God gives you.' Respecting this commandment provides, along with spiritual fruits, temporal fruits of peace and prosperity. Conversely, failure to observe it brings great harm to communities and to individuals.[422]

If we ask what it means in practical terms to obey the fifth commandment, a classic answer is provided by the Church of England bishop Thomas Ken in his exposition of this commandment in his 1685 work *The Practice of Divine Love.*

---

[421] *The Heidelberg Catechism*, 1563, Q.104, text in Mark Noll, *Confessions and Catechisms of the Reformation* (Vancouver: Regent College Publishing, 2004), p.159.
[422] *The Catechism of the Catholic Church*, paras 2199-2200, text in *Catechism of the Catholic Church*, p.475.

Let thy reverential Love, O my God, teach and incline me, to shew respectful Love to all my superiors, in my inward esteem, in my outward speech and behaviour. [1 Peter 2:17]

Glory be to thee, O Lord, who hast comprehended all that are above me, under the tender and venerable Names of Father and Mother, that I looking on them as Resemblances and Instruments of thy Sovereign Power and Paternal Providence to me, may be the more effectually engaged for thy sake to reverence and love them.

O my God, give me grace to imitate thy Paternal Goodness, and for the sake of thy Love; to love and cherish, and provide for; to educate and instruct, and pray for my Children [Deuteronomy 6:6-7, Ephesians 6:4, Colossians 3:21, 2 Corinthians 12:14] ; to take conscientious care to give them medicinal correction and good example, and to make them thy children, that they may truly love thee.

O my God, give me grace for the sake of thy love, to Honour my Father and Mother, to render them all love, and reverence, and thankfulness, and all that regard which is due from a Child [Ephesians 6:1-3, Colossians 3:20], that I may pay obedience to their commands, submission to their corrections, attention to their instructions, and succour to their necessities {Matthew 16:4 etc.], and may daily pray for their welfare.

Thou, O Lord, hast set our most Gracious King over us [Proverbs 8:13], as our Political Parent, as thy Supreme Minister, to govern and protect us, and to be a terror to those that do ill: O grant Him a long and happy Reign, that we may all live a peaceable and quiet life under Him, in all godliness and honesty [1 Timothy 2:1-2]. Defend Him from all His Enemies; let Him be ever beloved by thee, and let Him ever love thee, and ever promote thy love.

Multiply, O Lord God, the blessings of thy love on our most Gracious Queen Mary, Catharine the Queen Dowager, their Royal Highnesses Mary Princess of Orange, and the Princess Anne of Denmark, and on all the Royal Family: Give them grace to exceed others, as much in Goodness as in Greatness, and make them signal instruments of thy Glory, and examples of thy Love.

O my God, give grace to me and all my fellow-subjects, next to thy own infinite self, to love and honour, to fear and obey our Sovereign Lord the King, thy own Vicegerent, for Conscience sake [Romans 13:1 etc. 1 Peter 2:3, Titus 3:1], and for thy own sake, who hast placed Him over us; O may we ever faithfully render Him his due tribute; O may we ever pray for His prosperity, sacrifice our fortunes and our lives in His defence, and be always ready rather to suffer than resist.

Glory be to thee, O Lord, who hast ordained Pastors, and hast given them the Power of the Keys; to be our Ecclesiastical Parents; to watch over our Souls; to instruct us in saving Knowledge [Malachi 2:7] ; to guide us by their Examples; to pray for, and to bless us; to administer spiritual discipline in thy Church, and to manage all the conveyances of thy Divine Love.

O my God, for thy Love's sake, let me ever honour and love the Ministers of thy Love, the Ambassadors thou dost send in thy stead, to beseech us sinners to be reconciled to thee [2 Corinthians 5:20], to offer thy Enemies conditions of Love, of love eternal; O may I ever hear them attentively, practise their heavenly doctrine, imitate their holy examples, pay them their dues, and revere their censures! [Hebrews 13:7,17, 1 Timothy 5:17]

O my God, for the sake of thy love, grant I may ever love, and provide for my Servants [servant,] and may treat them like Brethren; let me never exact from them immoderate work; O may I always give them just wages, and equitable commands, and good example, and merciful correction: Grant, Lord, I may daily allow them time for their prayers, indulge them due refreshments, and may take care of their souls, and persuade them to love thee; remembering, that I also have a Master in Heaven. [Colossians 4:1, Ephesians 6:19]

Give me grace, O my God, for the sake of thy Love, to honour, and love, and obey my Master [and Mistress] and to serve him [her] with diligence and faithfulness, and readiness to please [1 Timothy 6:1-2, Colossians 3:22-24, Ephesians 6:5-8], and to pray for him [her] them; and whatever I do, to do heartily as to thee, O Lord, and not to him, [her] [them.]

O my God, let thy love incline me to love, and to honour all whom thou hast any way made my superiors, suitably to their quality [Leviticus 19:32, 1 Timothy 5:1-3 1 Peter 5:5], or age, or gifts, or learning, or wisdom, or gravity, or goodness.

O my God, grant that for thy sake, I may ever love and honour all that are, or have been, instruments of thy love to me, in doing me good; O may I reverence my teachers [Galatians 6:6] be grateful to my benefactors and may I have always a peculiar respect to my particular Pastor.

O my God, let thy love engage me to love those whom thou hast obliged to love me; to shew constancy, and fidelity, and sympathy, and love, and communicativeness to my Friend; to be affectionate to my Brethren and Sisters; to be kind and affable to my Equals; condescending[423] to my Inferiors; to be all the possible ways I can, universally helpful and obliging, and loving to all. [424]

The specific examples of proper Christian behaviour contained in this quotation are now dated, but what it teaches us is that obedience to the fifth commandment involves thinking how to give appropriate honour to all those people in whatever walk of life that God has placed in positions of authority over us. God does not make mistakes. God has

---

[423] In seventeenth century English 'condescend' does not mean treat patronisingly, but rather to 'voluntarily waive ceremony or dignity proper to one's superior position or rank and willingly assume equality with inferiors.' (https://www.etymonline.com/word/condescend).
[424] Thomas Ken, *The Practice of Divine Love* (London: 1685) at http://anglicanhistory.org/ken/divine_poor.html. The spelling has been updated and the biblical references have been added from another version of the text.

placed them in authority over us for a reason and honouring him means seeking his help to honour them. What also needs to be noted is that in line with the teaching of the New Testament, Ken insists that being given authority by God involves exercising the particular responsibilities that the role we have been given appropriately and treating those under our authority with appropriate love, dignity and respect. Christian authority does not involve self-indulgence or tyranny.

In relation to Christian conscientious objection, what we have noted about the meaning of the fifth commandment means three things.

First, it means that Christians need to say 'No' to the widespread contemporary belief that human beings should be answerable to no one except themselves and to nothing beyond their own personal preferences and desires.

As Luther argues in his *Larg Catechism,* such rejection of the authority given by God brings with it its own appropriate punishment:

> Why, think you, is the world now so full of unfaithfulness, disgrace, calamity and murder, but that everyone desires to be his own master and subject to no authority, to care nothing for anyone, and do what pleases him? Therefore, God punishes one knave by means of another, so that when you defraud and despise your master, another comes and deals the same with you, yea in your household you must suffer ten times more from wife, child or servants.[425]

In the words of Hauerwas and Willimon:

> Though written in the sixteenth century, how well Luther's description of a world where there is no valid authority and hierarchy describes our own day. If we will not honour our mothers and fathers, we will still obey someone, who too often turns out to

---

[425] Martin Luther, *Large Catechism*, p.30 at:
https://www.lutheranlibrary.org/pdf/194-jacobs-luther-large-catechism.pdf.

be the state or 'the business.' Fearing no rightful authority results in our fearing everyone and most particularly ourselves. [426]

Secondly, Christians need to say 'No' to any form of authority in which the person with authority refuses to acknowledge the superior authority of God and which involves self-indulgence or tyranny. It is the calling of Christians to remind both themselves and anyone else exercising any form of rule that they have been given their rule by God and that they will be answerable to God if they fail to exercise their rule in an appropriate manner.

Thirdly, Christians need to say 'No' to any form of political totalitarianism. The only one who should exercise total Lordship is God himself. All human rulers have been given a limited authority and need to respect the other forms of authority that God has established in society.

As the *Catechism of the Catholic Church* explains:

> God has not willed to reserve to himself all exercise of power. He entrusts to every creature the functions it is capable of performing, according to the capacities of its own nature. This mode of governance ought to be followed in social life. The way God acts in governing the world, which bears witness to such great regard for human freedom, should inspire the wisdom of those who govern human communities.

What this means in our situation is that any attempt by the state, including the liberal democratic state, to impose its authority on the Church or on the family in the way that denies church leaders or parents the freedom to exercise the authority given to them by God in accordance with God's will, is illegitimate and something that Christians must reject. For example, the state has no authority to prevent either the Church or Christian parents teaching their church members or their children the truths of the Christian faith,

---

[426] Hauerwas and Willimon, p.76.

including traditional forms of Christian sexual ethics. If it attempts to do so, the principle enunciated by Peter and the other apostles in Acts 5:29 comes into play: 'We must obey God rather than men.' [427]

Commandment 6: You shall not kill (Exodus 20:13).

In the mainstream Christian tradition, the sixth commandment has not been understood as an absolute prohibition of the taking of all life. Instead, it has been seen as forbidding both the unjustified killing of another human being ('murder') and the ungodly anger against another human being that leads to such killing. It has also been understood to witness to the value of all life created by God and hence both to the need both to avoid all forms of unwarranted harm to other human beings and to other living things, and, in positive terms, to promote the flourishing of human beings and of God's creation as a whole.

This comprehensive understanding of the sixth commandment is illustrated, for example, by the teaching on the sixth commandment in in *To Be a Christian* which runs as follows:

307. What is the sixth commandment?

The sixth commandment is 'You shall not murder.' (Exodus 20:13; Deuteronomy 5:17)

308. What is murder? Murder is the wilful and unjust taking of human life. (Genesis 4:1–10; Deuteronomy 19:4–13; Acts 7:54–8:3)

309. Why does God prohibit murder? Because every human being is made in God's image, all human life is sacred, from conception to natural death. Therefore, I may not take the life of others unjustly. (Genesis 9:6; Deuteronomy 19:4–13; Psalm 94:1–7; Isaiah 46:3–4; Romans 12:19–21)

---

[427] *The Catechism of the Catholic Church*, Paragraph 1184, p.414. It is also important to note the reciprocal truth that the Church should not seek to arrogate total power in society to itself. It too must recognise that God has established multiple forms of social authority.

310. What other actions are considered murder? Genocide, infanticide, abortion, suicide, and euthanasia are all forms of murder. Sins of murderous intent include physical and emotional abuse, abandonment, wilful negligence, and wanton recklessness. (Exodus 1:15–22; 21:28–30; 2 Kings 17:16–18; Psalm 139:13–16; Amos 1:13–15; Acts 9:1–2; Didache 2.2)

311. How did Jesus extend the law against murder? Jesus taught that this commandment also forbids the vice of un-godly anger. A murderous heart can lead to hatred, threatening words, violent acts, and murder itself, and is counter to God's life-affirming love. (Leviticus 19:17–18; Matthew 5:21–22, 43–45; 15:18–20; 1 John 3:15)

312. Is anger always sinful? While godly anger is a just response to wickedness and injustice, we are more often led into ungodly anger by fear, pride, and revenge. We should therefore be slow to anger and quick to forgive.

(Psalm 103:8–9; Proverbs 15:18; 16:32; 19:11; Micah 7:18; John 2:13–17; Ephesians 4:26–27, 31–32; James 1:19–20)

313. Is it always wrong to harm or kill another? There are circumstances in which justice, the protection of the weak and defenceless, and the preservation of life may require acts of violence. It is the particular task of government to uphold these principles in society. However, our Lord calls us to show mercy and to return evil with good. (Numbers 35:9–34; Matthew 5:43–45; Romans 12:17–21; 13:1–4; Articles of Religion 37)

314. How should Christians understand the value of life? All life belongs to God. Human life is especially sacred because we are created in God's image, and because Jesus came to give us new and abundant life in him. Christians, therefore, should act with reverence toward all living things, and with special regard for the sanctity of human life. (Genesis 1:26–27; 2:5–8; Psalm 104:24–30; Matthew 6:26; John 10:10; Acts 17:24–29; Colossians 1:15–20)

315. How did Christ cause life to flourish? Jesus sought the well-being of all who came to him: he healed the sick, fed the hungry, cast out demons, raised the dead, preached good news, forgave his enemies, and offered his life to redeem ours. (Isaiah 53:4–5; Matthew 4:13–17; Luke 4:17–21; 7:20–22; 23:32–34; Acts 10:34–42)

316. How else can you obey this commandment? As a witness to the Gospel and a follower of Christ, I can also keep this commandment by forgiving those who wrong me, patiently refraining from ungodly anger and hateful words; defending the unborn, vulnerable, and oppressed; rescuing those who harm themselves; and seeking the well-being of all. (Psalm 37:5–11; Zechariah 7:8–14; Matthew 5:38–48; Ephesians 4:25–5:2; James 1:27).[428]

The implications of this understanding of the sixth commandment for Christian conscientious objection are that Christians must not only refuse to engage in acts of deliberate murder, but they must also refuse to engage in, and take appropriate action against, all other actions which constitute an unwarranted attack on the life that God has created.

For example, because torture is 'contrary to respect for the person and for human dignity'[429] it is a breach of the sixth commandment even if it does not result in death. For this reason, Christians have an obligation to refuse to engage in torture themselves and to advocate against its use by others.

Similarly, a business might not deliberately murder people, but it might decide to dispose of chemicals in a way that resulted environmental damage and the poisoning of human beings. Christians aware of this activity would need to refuse to be involved in it and to seek to bring it to an end.

---

[428] *To be a Christian,* paragraphs 307-16.
[429] *The Catechism of the Catholic Church*, Paragraph 2297, p.497.

Down the centuries a minority of Christians, such as for example the Church of the Brethren, the Quakers, and the Mennonites (what are known as the historic 'peace churches'), have held that the sixth commandment forbids all forms of armed conflict and therefore rules out Christian participation in war. Today an increasing number of churches and individual Christians would also say that capital punishment is also forbidden by this commandment.

The majority Christian tradition has not, however, historically taken either of these positions. While holding that individual Christians must not kill or take vengeance against wrongdoing on their own authority, those who have been given public authority by God to uphold justice by restraining and punish wrongdoing (Romans 13:1-7, 1 Peter 2:13-14) may, if necessary, take human life as part of their exercise of this function, what has traditional been called the state's 'use of the sword.'

As Karl Barth put it in his *Letter to Great Britain from Switzerland* in 1941:

Where the life of men will not be governed by the preaching of the Gospel nor by prayer, nor by Baptism or the lord's supper – in other words, where the bounds of the Church stop – there begins the realm within whose bounds God's fatherly care, which does not fail even there, must be maintained and imposed, if necessary, by the threat of the sword, and, in the last resort, by its use. We have no right to revolt against or to ignore this ordering of human affairs. And indeed, is there any order conceivable other than this so long as human life is not controlled by Faith, Love and Hope? We must be grateful to God that He has given us this order, which is certainly stern but which has proved itself to be effective. Whatever we may say about it, it is an order which sets up a barrier not indeed against sin, but against the chaos into which sin would inevitably plunge us if God had not instituted the State, and if He had not entrusted it with the sword. The State would lose all meaning and would be failing in its duty as an appointed minister of God, and it would be depriving men of the benefit which God, by its function, had intended for them, if it failed to defend the bounds between Right and Wrong by the threat, and by the actual use of, the sword. [430]

For this reason, Christians may be involved in the infliction of capital punishment[431] and may take part in war. It should be noted, however, that the very grounds on which the majority Christian tradition declares that Christians may on occasion take life at the command of the civil authorities also mean that Christians may not take part in either the infliction of capital punishment or in war if these conditions have not been met.

[430] Karl Barth, *A Letter to Great Britain from Switzerland* (London: Sheldon Press, 1941), p.13-14.

[431] Barth himself was opposed to the infliction of capital punishment, but his position in this regard was inconsistent because, as Oliver O'Donovan has argued, it is impossible to separate the state's right to take life in time of war from its right to take life in general and hence to inflict some form of capital punishment if it is necessary for it to do so. To quote O'Donovan:

'There are basic conditions for any penal system, and they can be derived from the words of Genesis 9:6 promulgating the Noachic covenant: 'Whoever sheds the blood of man, by man shall his blood be shed.' This is not the formulation of the lex talionis as a determination of penalty; it is, rather, an expression of the basis of retributive practice itself. We are all mortal, and our life has a limited expectancy. That fact gives all crime and all punishment its meaning. Two years in prison are 'two good years of my life'; if we were immortal, they would count for nothing. A heavy fine is a drain on resources needed for food, clothing, and shelter. Corporal punishment weakens the bodily constitution. Every serious injury is an assault, directly or indirectly, on the victim's life; so every punishment, too, is an assault on the victim's life.

What we are looking for in a system of punishment is a flexible range of intermediate punishments that hedge that infringement of life around with alternatives, so that we are not driven too quickly back upon the ultimate resort of taking life directly. The art of penal development is the multiplication of a carefully differentiated range of intermediate assaults. Yet its horizon is the ultimate penalty of death itself. Even if a society formally abolishes the death penalty from its criminal sanctions, it does not abolish death as its ultimate recourse, for when crime become uncontrollable by normal means, resorts to making war upon it. The armed patrol takes the place of the hangman.' (Oliver O'Donovan, *The Ways of Judgement* (Grand Rapids: Eerdmans, 2005), pp.122-123).

This means, firstly, that Christians must not take part in the infliction of capital punishment themselves, and must protest against its infliction by others, when they believe an execution to be unjust, either because someone has been wrongly convicted of a capital offence, or because the death penalty would be an excessive punishment for a crime that someone has committed. It also means, that like Franz Jägerstätter, Christians must refuse to take part in any war that they believe to be unjust, and that they must also likewise refuse to take part in any unjust action which they are ordered to perform in the context of war.

In order to help Christians determine whether a particular war Is just, and whether acts performed within it are also just, the Christian tradition has developed a number of criteria for both the right to go to war and for right conduct in war.

The traditional criteria for the right to go to war are:

Proper authority - war must be declared and waged by the properly constituted political authorities in a particular state.

Just cause – those who are attack must deserve to attacked on account of some serious wrong they have done or to prevent some wrong that they are planning to do.

Right intention – the purpose of going to war must be to establish a just peace by preventing, correcting or punishing wrongdoing.

Necessity – going to war must be the only way prevent, correcting or punishing wrongdoing.

A reasonable hope of success - If the justification for going to war is to try to correct a wrong and bring about a just peace then there is no point in the exercise if there is no hope that this end can be obtained.

The traditional criteria for right conduct in war are:

Discrimination or non-combatant immunity – this means that we should attack only enemy combatants, which in turn means that non-combatants should never be killed or harmed intentionally.

Proportionality – this means that the amount of force used must be limited to that necessary to achieve a legitimate military objective, and that while it may be impossible to avoid harming or killing non-combatants, all reasonable steps must be taken to avoid them being killed or harmed when there are ways in which this could be avoided. [432]

When they judge that these criteria are not met, Christians have to conscientiously refuse to take part in a given war, or in particular actions within a war, even when this war, or these actions, are undertaken at the command of those with legitimate political and military authority, and they must also seek to prevent such a war and such actions from taking place.

Although there are Christians today who support abortion, suicide and euthanasia, the Christian tradition down the centuries has always held that all three actions are contrary to the sixth commandment.

In the case of abortion, which is currently by far the largest cause of human death,[433] the early Christian writing known as the *Didache*, dating from the second half of the first century, declares specifically 'you shall not abort a child or commit infanticide' [434] and this is the position that has been generally accepted by Christians until recent times. As the *Catechism of the Catholic Church* explains this is because human life begins at the moment of conception and therefore:

Human life must be respected and protected absolutely from the moment of conception. From the first moment of his existence, a

---

[432] For studies of the Christian just war tradition see Darrell Cole, *When God says war is right* (Colorado Springs: Waterbrook Press, 2002) and Oliver O'Donovan, *The just war revisited* (Cambridge: CUP, 2003).
[433] See *Care*, 'Abortion the leading cause of death in 2023, at: https://care.org.uk/news/2024/01/abortion-the-leading-cause-of-death-in-2023.
[434] *Didache* 2.2, J B Lightfoot, J R Harmer and Michael Holmes, The Apostolic Fathers (Leicester Apollos, 1989), p.150.

human being must be recognized as having the rights of a person – among which is the inviolable right of every human being to life.[435]

In the case of suicide, Christian thinking going at least as far back as Augustine has rightly held that the prohibition of unjustified killing in the sixth commandment rules out suicide. This thinking is once again summarised by the *Catechism of the Catholic Church*, which declares:

> Everyone is responsible for his life before God who has given it to him. It is God who remains the sovereign master of life. We are obliged to accept life gratefully and preserve it for his honour and the salvation of our souls. We are stewards, not owners, of the life that God has entrusted to us. It is not ours to dispose of.

> Suicide contradicts the natural inclination of the human being to preserve and perpetuate his life. It is gravely contrary to the just love of self. It likewise offends love of neighbour because it unjustly breaks the ties of solidarity with family, nation and other human societies to which we continue to have obligations. Suicide is contrary to love for the living God.[436]

As the *Catechism* goes on to say: 'Grave psychological disturbances, anguish or grave fear of hardship, suffering or torture can diminish the responsibility of the one committing suicide' and 'We should nor despair of the eternal salvation of persons who have taken their own lives.'[437] Nevertheless, the fact remains, that for the reasons previously given suicide does have to be judged as a grave sin against God and neighbour.

Euthanasia must also be judged as contrary to the sixth commandment. If it is what is known as 'assisted dying,' when someone helps another person to end their own life, it is a form of suicide which is impermissible for the reasons already given. If it is the killing of those

---

[435] *Catechism of the Catholic Church*, Paragraph 2270, p.489.
[436] *Catechism of the Catholic Church*, Paragraphs 2280-2281, p.491.
[437] *Catechism of the Catholic Church*, Paragraphs 2282-2283, p.491.

judged physically or mentally unfit to live, then it is an act of murder based on the mistaken belief that a particular life created by God lacks value and should therefore be brought to an end. To quote the *Catechism of the Catholic Church* once more, from a Christian perspective 'Those whose lives are diminished or weakened deserve special respect. Sick or handicapped persons should be helped to live a life as normal as possible.'[438]

Because abortion, suicide and euthanasia thus have to be regarded as breaches of the sixth commandment, Christians are under an obligation to refuse to engage in all three acts themselves, and to refuse to assist other people in performing them, in the same way that they would refuse to engage in other acts of unjustified killing. In addition, they must do what they can to avoid them taking place, which means not simply declaring that they are wrong, or trying to ensure that they are illegal, but in compassionately helping people tempted to engage in them to understand that they are not necessary because God's way provides a better alternative. [439]

Commandment 7: You shall not commit adultery (Exodus 20:14).

Just as the Christian tradition has understood the sixth commandment as forbidding more than just murder, so also it has understood the seventh commandment as prohibiting more than simply having sex with someone if you, or they, or both of you, are married to someone else. Following the teaching of Jesus in the Sermon on the Mount (Matthew 5:27-30), it has also understood the commandment as prohibiting any indulgence in the lustful thoughts that lead to adultery. In addition, it has seen the commandment as prohibiting any form of sexual activity outside marriage, any involvement in activities that are

---

[438] *Catechism of the Catholic Church*, Paragraph 2276, p.290.
[439] For further studies of abortion see Niggel Biggar, *Aiming to Kill: The Ethics of Suicide and Euthanasia* (London: DLT: 2004) Sean Doherty, *The Only Way is Ethics – Part 2: Life and Death* (Authentic Media, Milton Keynes, 2016) and Jonathan Jeffes, *Abortion, Breaking the Silence* (Chichester: Lean Press 2013).

likely to incite illicit sexual desires, and finally any form of ungodly conduct within marriage itself.

This approach to the seventh commandment is illustrated by the following two quotations from *The Heidelberg Catechism* and from Thomas Ken's *The Practice of Divine Love.*

Questions 108 and 109 of *The Heidelberg Catechism* run as follows:

Question 108. *What does the seventh commandment teach us?*

That all unchastity is condemned by God, and that we should therefore detest it from the heart, and live chaste and disciplined lives, whether in holy wedlock or in single life.

Question 109. *Does God forbid nothing more than adultery and such gross sins in this commandment?*

Since both our body and soul are a temple of the Holy Spirit, it is his will that we keep both pure and holy. Therefore, he forbids all unchaste actions, gestures, words, thoughts, desires, and whatever may excite another person to them.[440]

The term 'chastity' used in *The Heidelberg Catechism* has dropped out of common use today, and when it is used it is often seen as synonymous with the term 'celibacy.' However, the two terms, although overlapping, are distinct. Celibacy means accepting a calling from God to permanently refrain from entering into marriage and permanent abstinence from sexual activity as a result. In biblical terms it means becoming a eunuch for the sake of the kingdom of heaven (Matthew 19:12). Chastity, by contrast, simply means appropriate sexual conduct depending on whether or not one is married. It means adhering to the Christian rule of sexual conduct summarised by C S Lewis in his book *Mere Christianity*: "Either marriage with complete faithfulness to your partner, or else total abstinence.'[441] What *The Heidelberg Catechism*

---

[440] *The Heidelberg Catechism*, Q.108-109, in Noll, p.160.
[441] C S Lewis, *Mere Christianity* (Glasgow: Fount, 1984), p.86.

teaches is that any breach of this rule in action or in thought is a breach of the seventh commandment.

In his exposition of the seventh commandment in *The Practice of Divine Love* Ken declares that obedience to it means rejecting:

All adultery and violations of my neighbour's bed, in the gross act, robbing him of that he loves best. (Matthew 5:29)

All adultery and unchastity of the eye or the hand.

All the kinds and degrees of lust, fornication, pollution of our own bodies, and works of darkness, which it is a shame to mention. (Ephesians 5:11-12, 4:19)

All things that provoke, or feed lust, impure company, discourse, songs, books or pictures. (Ephesians 4:19)

All lascivious dresses (Ephesians 5:3-5, 1 Timothy 2:9, 1 Peter 3:3), or dances, or plays; all idleness or luxurious diet. (Romans 13:13-14, 1 Peter 4:3)

All the excesses or abuses of lawful Marriage, all unreasonable jealousies, and all things that lessen the mutual kindness, or alienate the affections of those that are married. (I Timothy 2:12, Matthew 19:6).

All the least tendencies to any of these impurities.[442]

In this exposition Ken sees the seventh commandment as prohibiting any form of activity that involves or encourage sexual activity outside marriage as well as any form of behaviour that undermines the kindness and love that ought to exist between husband and wife. The reference to a 'luxurious diet' reflects the fact that in the seventeenth

---

[442] Ken, *The Practice of Divine Love*, spelling modernised and references added from another edition.

century it was believed that certain kinds of food could inflame lust (in the same way that certain foods today are seen as aphrodisiacs).

In both *The Heidelberg Catechism* and *The Practice of Divine Love* it is taken for granted that marriage will be between two people of the opposite sex. In the Christian tradition which they reflect the idea that marriage could be between two people of the same sex has never been entertained. In the same way although neither of them specifically mentions homosexual activity, it is implicitly included in their rejection of unchastity. This is because for them, and for the universal Christian tradition which they represent, chastity involved the rejection of what the Church of England's *First Book of Homilies* calls 'all unlawful use of those parts which be ordained for generation,' a category which embraces homosexual as well as heterosexual sexual activity. [443]

If we ask why marriage should be viewed as exclusively a relationship between two people of the opposite sex and why sex outside marriage, whether heterosexual or homosexual in form, should always be seen as wrong the answer is twofold.

The first answer is that the Bible declares that God created marriage and that he created it as a marriage between two people of the opposite sex (Genesis 2:18-25, Matthew 19:3-9). Because human beings are creatures rather than the creator, they do not have the power to change the nature of marriage. They cannot change marriage so that it includes relationships between two people of the same sex any more than they can make the sun cold. They can, if they wish, call a relationship between two people of the same sex a marriage, but this does not make it so.

The second answer is that God created marriage and sex within marriage as an image of the faithful covenant relationship God wants to have his people. As Leithart puts it:

---

[443] *The First Book of Homilies*, 'A Sermon against whoredom and uncleanness,' text in Ian Robinson, *The Homilies* (Bishopstone: The Brynmill Press, 2006), p.88.

Sex and marriage are theological realities from top to bottom. Paul wasn't imposing a Christ-and - church paradigm on the neutral natural phenomenon of sexual difference (Eph 5). Sex is created as a sign of God's love for his bride. That's what it's *for*. That's why Paul quotes from Genesis 2: The great mystery is that God created man male and female, a differentiated unity and a unified differentiation as a living sign of his covenant bond with his people.[444]

As he goes on to say, all forms of non-marital sexual activity distort:

...the created design of marriage. Adultery, Clement of Alexandria says, is like the betrayal of idolatry. We seek sexual pleasure without a commitment to a shared life, and so defy the faithful covenant God. We try out multiple sexual partners, and thus live a lie about the God who loves *one* bride. Homosexual acts shatter the union-in-difference at the heart of God's relation to his people. Sexual sin lies about the Creator. The created order is to be a manifestation all the Lord of the covenant.

This is the logic of the prophetic imagery all the sexual unfaithfulness. At times, the prophets condemned the sexual behaviour of individuals in Judah. More often unfaithful Judah is the adulterous wife. Jesus uses the same imagery when he condemns the evil and adulterous generation (Matt 12:39; 16:4) that rejects him. James warns his readers not to be 'adulteresses.' friends of the world who are faithless to the divine husband (Jas 4:4).

Once we see marriage and adultery in this theological perspective, the 'Do nots' fall into place. All are rooted in the fundamental 'Do': Be what you are as male and female. As a *married* husband and wife, be the living image of the God of creation and covenant.

Sexual faithfulness in marriage and sexual purity outside of marriage aren't mere demands of law. Sexual faithfulness preaches

---

[444] Leithart, p.50.

the gospel. When a husband and wife are faithful to one another, sexually and otherwise, they become a created symbol of a covenant God who keeps his vows to Israel and the new Israel. By keeping the Seventh Word, we dramatize the good news of Jesus, the Bridegroom of the church, who gives himself in utter fidelity two and for his Bride. [445]

The call that some Christians have to celibacy fits in with this understanding of the nature of sex and marriage in two ways.

First, by being sexually abstinent as part of their call to remain unmarried, those who are celibate witness to the truth that sex is designed by God to be confined to marriage.

Secondly, by being unmarried and sexually abstinent those who are celibate point forward to the truth that in God's eternal kingdom sex and marriage as we know them will be no more (Matthew 22:23-33). The reason will be the case is that sex and marriage as we know them will no longer be needed because in the world to come God's faithful people will enjoy the perfect, intimate, relationship with God of which sex and marriage in this world are only a sign and foretaste. The reality will have come and so the sign of that reality will no longer be needed.

Because the seventh commandment points to the need to live in accordance with God's creation of human beings as men and women it also rules out adopting a transgender identity. This because God has created all human beings as one of two distinct biological identities, male or female (Genesis 1:26-27, 5:1-2)[446] and submitting to the goodness of God's creative decision involves being willing to accept his

---

[445] Leithart pp.51-52.

[446] So called 'intersex' conditions in which people have unusual biological characteristics do not negate this truth. This is because there is no evidence that any of these conditions have resulted in an individual who is a true hermaphrodite, i.e. able to produce both eggs and sperm. As far as we know all human beings are biologically ordered to produce either eggs (and hence are female) or sperm (and hence are male). For this point see Abigail Favele, *The Genesis of Gender* (San Francisco: Ignatius Press, 2022), pp.122-129.

decision even if, like those suffering from gender dysphoria, we find it painfully difficult to accept. In the words of Oliver O'Donovan:

> ...we cannot and must not conceive of physical sexuality as a mere raw material with which we can construct a form of psychosexual self-expression which is determined only be the free impulse of our spirits. Responsibility in sexual development implies a responsibility to nature – to the ordered good of the bodily form we have been given. [447]

In terms of conscientious objection what the seventh commandment means is that, first, Christians may not enter into same-sex marriages (since this would imply acceptance of the idea that a relationship between two people can be a marriage) or engage in any form of sexual activity outside of marriage, whether heterosexual or homosexual.

It also means that they may not adopt a sexual identity that is at odds with their biological identity as a man or a woman, whether that is a transgender identity, or some form of alternative 'non-binary' sexual identity.

It further means that they must say no to activities in the Church or in wider society that give support either to same-sex marriage, or to sex outside marriage, or to the acceptance of transgender or non-binary identities.

This means, for example, refusing to officiate at, or participate in, same-sex marriages or same-sex civil partnership celebrations,[448] or the blessing of same-sex relationships, and objecting to the use of educational material that suggests that either same-sex relationships, or any form of sexual relationship outside marriage is morally acceptable.

---

[447] Oliver O'Donovan, *Begotten or Made?* (Oxford: OUP, 1984), pp,28-29.
[448] See Carl Trueman, 'Can Christians Attend Gay Weddings?' *First Things*, 25.1.24 at: https://www.firstthings.com/web-exclusives/2024/01/can-christians-attend-gay-weddings.

It also means, as far as possible, avoiding participating in gender transition, objecting to material that suggests that sex is not binary and/or that people can have an identity which is at odds with their biological sex, and where possible avoiding the use of language that indicates acceptance of transgender or non-binary identities. [449]

Finally, it means that Christians must be willing to explain why they object to same-sex marriage, sex outside marriage and the adoption of transgender and non-binary identities and do all that they can to help those who wish to do so to cease engaging in these forms of behaviour. [450]

Commandment 8: You shall not steal (Exodus 20: 15).

As in the case of the previous two commandments, the Christian tradition has seen the eighth commandment as very broad in scope. It has viewed it as a prohibition of any form of activity that involves depriving one's neighbour of what rightly belongs to them.

This view of the breadth of the eight commandment becomes clear, for example, in Thomas Aquinas' commentary on this commandment in his *Catechetical Instructions*. He begins his commentary by declaring:

The Lord specifically forbids injury to our neighbour in the Commandments. Thus, 'Thou shalt not kill' forbids us to injure our neighbour in his own person; 'Thou shalt not commit adultery' forbids injury to the person to whom one is bound in marriage; and now the Commandment, 'Thou shalt not steal,' forbids us to injure our

---

[449] See Rosaria Butterfield, 'Why I no longer use Transgender Pronouns—and Why You shouldn't, either,' *Reformation 21,* 3 April 23 at:
https://www.reformation21.org/blog/why-i-no-longer-use-transgender-pronouns-and-why-you-shouldnt-either.
[450] For helpful first-hand accounts of Christians acting in this way see Rosaria Butterfield, *The secret thoughts of an unlikely convert* (Pittsburgh: Crown and Covenant, 2014) and Walt Heyer, *A Transgender's Faith* (Walt Heyer 2015)

neighbour in his goods. This Commandment forbids any worldly goods whatsoever to be taken away wrongfully.[451]

He then outlines five different ways in which theft can take place:

First, by taking stealthily: 'If the goodman of the house knew at what hour the thief would come.' [Matthew 24:42] This is an act wholly blameworthy because it is a form of treachery. 'Confusion...is upon the thief.' [Ecclesiasticus 5:17]

Secondly, by taking with violence, and this is an even greater injury: 'They have violently robbed the fatherless.'[Job 24:9] Among such that do such things are wicked kings and rulers: 'Her princes are in the midst of her as roaring lions; her judges are evening wolves, they left nothing for the morning.'[Wisdom 3:3] They act contrary to God's will who wishes a rule according to justice: 'By Me kings reign and lawgivers decree just things.'[Proverbs 8:15] Sometimes they do such things stealthily and sometimes with violence: 'Thy princes are faithless companions of thieves, they all love bribes, they run after rewards.'[Isaiah 1:23] At times they steal by enacting laws and enforcing them for profit only: 'Woe to them that make wicked laws.'[Isaiah 8:1] And St. Augustine says that every wrongful usurpation is theft when he asks: 'What are thrones but forms of thievery?'[*The City of God* 4:4]

Thirdly, theft is committed by not paying wages that are due: 'The wages of him that hath been hired by thee shall not abide by thee until the morning.' [Leviticus 19:13] This means that a man must pay everyone his due, whether he be prince, prelate, or cleric, etc.: 'Render therefore to all men their dues. Tribute, to whom tribute is due, custom, to whom custom.' [Romans 13:7] Hence, we are bound to give a return to rulers who guard our safety.

---

[451] Joseph Collins and Rudolph Bandas, *The Catechetical Instructions of St Thomas Aquinas* (Baltimore, 1939) p.81 at: https://www.documentacatholicaomnia.eu /03d/1225-1274,_Thomas_Aquinas_Catechismus,_EN.pdf.

The fourth kind of theft is fraud in buying and selling: 'Thou shalt not have divers weights in thy bag, a greater and a less.' [Deuteronomy 25:13] And again: 'Do not any unjust thing in judgment, in rule, in weight, or in measure.'[Leviticus 19:35-36] All this is directed against the keepers of wine-shops who mix water with the wine. Usury is also forbidden: 'Who shall dwell in Thy tabernacle, or who shall rest in Thy holy hill?...He that hath not put his money out to usury.' [Psalm 14:1-5] This is also against money-changers who commit many frauds, and against the sellers of cloth and other goods.

Fifthly, theft is committed by those who buy promotions to positions of temporal or spiritual honour. 'The riches which he hath swallowed, he shall vomit up, and God shall draw them out of his belly,' [Job 20:15] has reference to temporal position. Thus, all tyrants who hold a kingdom or province or land by force are thieves, and are held to restitution. Concerning spiritual dignities: 'Amen, amen, I say to you, he that entereth not by the door into the sheepfold but climbeth up another way is a thief and a robber.' [John 10:1] Therefore, they who commit simony are thieves. [452]

Aquinas sees rulers taking bribes, or enacting laws to make a profit, as forms of theft because the result is justice being stolen from those who cannot afford to pay.

By 'usury' Aquinas means charging interest on a loan. In the words of John Finnis, for Aquinas:

To make any further charge in respect of the loan of money is unjust, and the name for this sort of charge—this sort of wrong—is usury. [453]

[452] Collins and Bandas, pp.81-82.
[453] John Finnis, *Aquinas* (Oxford: OUP, 1998), pp.205-206.

Because charging interest is unjust, acquiring money in this way is theft.

The reason why Aquinas sees purchasing promotions to positions of honour in the state or in the Church, or taking hold of territory by force, as forms of theft is because those who do this are taking that position or that territory from someone else to whom it rightly belongs.

The breadth of the eighth commandment is likewise made clear by Ken in his exposition of the commandment in *The Practice of Divine Love*. Ken writes:

O my God, O my Love, I renounce, &c.

All kinds of stealing, by open Robbery, Violence, or Invasion (Ephesians 4:28, 1 Peter 4:15).

All Oppression, or Extortion, or Rapine (1 Corinthians 6:9-10), vexatious Law-suits, or griping Usury.

All fraud in Trade and Contracts, false Weights, and Measures, and Coin (1 Thessalonians 4:6, Amos 8:5).

All concealing the defects of our own Goods or depreciating those of our neighbour (Proverbs 20:14).

All making haste to be rich or taking advantage of the ignorance or necessity of the persons we deal with.

All withholding our neighbours' Dues or detaining the hire of the Labourer (James 5:4).

All borrowing and not paying, injurious keeping the Goods of other (Psalm 37:21), and refusing to make restitution (Luke 19:8).

All breach of trust or removing Landmarks (Proverbs 22:22-23, 28), wasteful prodigality, avaricious gaming, or idle begging.

All outrages to the Fatherless, the Widow and the Stranger (Jeremiah 7:6).

All the least tendencies to any of these acts of injustice.

From all these and the like hateful violations of thy Love, and of the Love of my neighbour, and from the vengeance they justly deserve, O my God, O my Love, deliver me and all faithful people.[454]

The breadth of the eighth commandment is also emphasised by Packer. He declares that the principle that it is wrong to steal which is expressed in the commandment:

...reaches further than perhaps we realize.

There is, for instance, theft of *time*, perhaps the most common form of theft today. Employees contract to do so many hours work for so much pay and fail to do it. We start late, finish early, stretch coffee, lunch, and tea breaks, and waste time in between. This is theft.

It is theft too when a tradesman fails to give *value for money*. The Old Testament damns false weights and measures (Deuteronomy 25:13-15, Amos 8:5); the modern equivalent is overpricing goods and services, cashing in on another's need. Profiteering and all forms of overcharging are theft.

Again, it is theft when *debts* are left unpaid, thus robbing the person owed of the use of money to which he is morally entitled. Letting debts hang on is a way of life for some, but Scripture condemns it. 'Owe no one anything, accept to love each other,' says Paul (Romans 13:8). If we really love our neighbour, we shall not try to postpone paying him.

Finally, it is theft to steal a *reputation*, destroying someone's credit by malicious gossip behind his back. 'Who steals my purse, steals trash,' wrote Shakespeare, '...but he that filches for me my good name...makes me poor indeed.' Thus, gossip is a breach of the ninth commandment; its effect will be a breach of the eighth.[455]

---

[454] Ken, spelling modernised and references added from another edition.
[455] Packer, p.91.

In terms of conscientious objection, the traditional Christian understanding of the broad scope of the eight commandment, which we have seen illustrated by Aquinas, Ken and Packer, means that Christians need to think constantly about what kind of behaviour deprives other people of that which rightly belongs to them. They then need to act upon the result of this thinking by not only refraining from this kind of behaviour themselves, but also by openly objecting when any such behaviour is engaged in by individuals or groups within society and seeking to bring such behaviour to an end. This will be a never-ending battle because theft in all its various forms is endemic in human society, but it is a battle which Christians must be willing to fight.

An issue relating to the eighth commandment which Christians today tend to ignore, but which they do need to consider with care, is the issue of usury mentioned by Aquinas. Lending money at interest is specifically forbidden in biblical passages such as Leviticus 25:36-37 and Ezekiel 18:8-17. During most of the history of the Church the biblical material was understood to prohibit absolutely the charging of interest, but since the Reformation it has become increasingly argued that what is forbidden is charging exorbitant interest in a way that harms one's neighbour rather than charging interest as such.

Christians today need to be aware of this change of approach and decide whether charging interest is absolutely forbidden (and therefore something to which they must conscientiously object) or whether it is only charging exorbitant interest that is wrong (and if so, how one decides what counts as exorbitant because harmful). [456]

[456] For good starting points for such thinking see Thomas Renz, 'Do we ignore the biblical teaching on usury?' *Psephizo*, 25 January 2024 at https://www.psephizo.com/biblical-studies/do-we-ignore-the-biblical-teaching-on-usury./ and Philip Booth, 'Pope Francis condemns usury, but what is it?' *Transatlantic Blog*, 12 February 2018 at https://www.acton.org/publications/transatlantic/2018/02/12/pope-francis-condemns-usury-what-It.

Commandment 9: You shall not bear false witness against your neighbour (Exodus 20:16).

As in the case of the previous commandments, the Christian tradition has seen the ninth commandment as having both a basic and an extended meaning. The basic meaning is that it is forbidden to harm one's neighbour by giving false evidence against them in a court of law. The extended meaning is that we are forbidden to engage in any kind of speech, in any context, whether legal, religious, social, or familial, that contains falsehood and either does harm to others, or wrongly benefits us, what the catechism in the *Book of Common Prayer* calls 'evil-speaking, lying and slandering.'

This dual understanding of the commandment can be seen, for example, in what is said about the ninth commandment in Luther's *Large Catechism* and in *To be a Christian*.

In his comments on this commandment Luther states:

And in the first place we take the most manifest meaning of this commandment according to the words (Thou shalt not bear false witness), as pertaining to courts of justice, where a poor innocent man is accused and oppressed by false witnesses in order to be punished in his body, property or honor. This appears indeed little to concern us now, but with the Jews it was a common and ordinary matter. For the people were organized under an excellent and regular government; and where such a government is, it is not administered without cases of this sin. The cause of it is, that where judges, magistrates, princes or others in authority sit in judgment, it cannot in the course of the world be otherwise but that men will be unwilling to give offence, will flatter and speak with regard to favor, money, hope or friendship; and in consequence a poor man and his cause must be oppressed and be subject to wrong and punishment. And it is a common calamity in the world that those who sit in judgment are seldom godly men.

For a judge ought necessarily to be above all things a godly man, and not only godly, but also wise, modest, yea, a brave and fearless man. So also ought a witness to be fearless, but especially a godly man. For he who would judge all matters rightly and decide them by his verdict will often offend good friends, relatives, neighbours and the rich and powerful who can greatly serve or injure him. Therefore, he must be quite blind, closing eyes and ears, neither seeing nor hearing, but going straight forward in everything that comes before him, and deciding accordingly.

Therefore this commandment is given first of all that everyone shall help his neighbour to secure his rights, and not allow them to be hindered or violence to be done them, but to strictly maintain and promote them as God may grant, whether he be judge or witness, and let it affect what it will. And especially is a goal set up here for our jurists that they use all diligence in dealing truly and uprightly with every case, allowing right to be right, and neither perverting nor glossing it over or keeping silent concerning it, irrespective of money, possession, honor or power. This is one part and the most immediate sense of this commandment respecting all that takes place in court.

Afterwards, however, it extends much further, if we apply it to spiritual jurisdiction or administration; here it is a fact that everyone bears false witness against his neighbour. For wherever there are godly preachers and Christians, they must bear the judgment of the world, and be called heretics, apostates, yea seditious and desperately wicked miscreants. And besides the Word of God must be subjected to the most shameful and virulent persecutions, blasphemies, contradictions, perversions and false explanations and applications. But that we will let pass; for it is the way of the blind world that she condemns and persecutes the truth and the children of God, and yet esteems it no sin.

In the third place, what concerns us all, this commandment forbids all sins of the tongue whereby we can injure or molest our neighbour. For to bear false witness is nothing else but a work of the tongue. Whatever therefore is done with the tongue against a fellow-man is hereby forbidden by God; whether it be false preachers with their doctrine and blasphemy, false judges and witnesses with their unjust verdicts, or outside of court by lying and evil-speaking. Here belongs particularly the detestable vice of gossip and slander, with which the devil instigates us, and of which there is much to be said. For it is a common evil plague that everyone prefers hearing evil to hearing good of his neighbor; and although we ourselves are ever so bad, we cannot suffer that any one should say anything bad about us, but everyone would much rather that all the world should speak of him in terms of gold; and yet we cannot bear that only the best be said of others. [457]

In similar fashion, *To be a Christian* expounds the meaning of the commandment as follows:

339. What is the ninth commandment? The ninth commandment is "You shall not bear false witness against your neighbour." (Exodus 20:16; Deuteronomy 5:20)

340. What is bearing false witness against your neighbour? It is to wilfully communicate a falsehood about my neighbour, either in legal or in other matters, in order to misrepresent them. (Deuteronomy 19:16–19; Psalm 109; Proverbs 12:17; Matthew 26:57–61)

341. Why does God forbid such false witness? Because it defames and wounds my neighbour, erodes my love of truth, disobeys my Lord Jesus, and aligns me with Satan, the father of lies. (Psalm 52:1–5; Proverbs 25:18; Jeremiah 9:3–9; John 8:42–47)

342. How is false witness given in public life?

Any wilful misrepresentation of the truth in legal, civic, or business affairs bears false witness, rebels against God's will, and subverts

---

[457] Luther, *Large Catechism*, pp.51-53.

God's justice. (Exodus 23:1–3; Leviticus 6:1–7; Proverbs 11:1; 24:23–26, 28–29; Acts 6:8–15)

343. How is false witness given in respect to the teaching of the Church? All false or misleading teaching concerning the Christian faith bears false witness against the truth of God's Word and abuses the authority given by Christ to his Body. (Deuteronomy 13; Matthew 24:3–14; 2 Peter 2:1–3; 1 John 2:18–27)

344. What other acts are forbidden by this commandment? This commandment forbids all lying, slander, or gossip; all manipulative, deceitful, or insulting speech; and testifying falsely about myself for personal gain. (Leviticus 19:15–17; Psalm 12:2–3; Proverbs 10:18; 11:12; 16:28; Matthew 5:21–22; Romans 16:17–18;1 Peter 2:1). [458]

The converse of the fact that we are prohibited from harming our neighbours by telling lies to or about them is that we should be people who tell our neighbours the truth. As Leithart explains, such truth-telling:

...isn't necessarily nice. We learn to be truth tellers when we learn to see clearly and when we break the habit of covering our cowardice with a pious excuse of love. Immediately after Yahweh forbids Israelites to hate their countrymen (Lev 19:17) and immediately before he tells them to 'love your neighbour as yourself' (Lev 19:18), he tells them to 'reprove your neighbour' (Lev 19:17 NASB). Prophets like Nathan (2 Sam 12) and Elijah (1 Kgs 17-19) weren't nice. They really performed the cliche: they spoke truth to power. And their blistering words carried divine power, to pluck up and plan to, to diminish and build (cf. Jer 1:10). Truthful correction is an expression of love, not hate. If you tell the truth, you will create conflict, and then you are called to be a peacemaker. But true peace can be won only if the truth shatters the false peace of the lie.

[458] *To be a Christian*, paragraphs 339-344.

Here we stumble on the flipside of today's social disorder. War we gleefully spread gossip on social media, we tiptoe gingerly around the truth. We say we're tolerant and wants to avoid triggering. But we are cowards, and hateful cowards to boot. If we can't tell the truth, we cannot identify real evils. If we're forbidden to the problems, we cannot propose solutions.[459]

The point made by Leithart that we must not evade our obligation to speak the truth under the cover of love is also emphasised by Hauerwas and Wilimon who write:

We owe it to one another as creatures of a good God to tell one another the truth. That requires learning great skill since, confounded and confronted with this command, we find ourselves captured by falsehood.

There is no sin more precious to the devil than the lie, for the devil knows that we never lie more readily then when we do so in the name of a love that is undisciplined in the truth of Christ's cross and resurrection. Thus in John 8:44 we learn that the devil is a liar and the father of all lies. And from lies we die deadly death. Therefore as the witnesses to Christ's cross and resurrection we are called to speak the truth and thus disclose the lies that leads to violence and death.

For instance, many doctors and nurses, when asked why they did not tell the truth to a seriously ill patient, justify their lack of candour on the basis of love. 'I didn't think the patient really wanted to hear that he was dying.'

Such love is the source of our lies. Patients are given false hope, hope based not on the truth of Christ's death and resurrection, but hope based upon a lie. The patient is encouraged to live in a dream world, is denied the opportunity to put life in order in the face of death, is robbed of the joy that might come, in the last days of life,

[459] Leithart, p.60.

from reconciliation with family, friends, and God. Lawyers shaped by such undisciplined and malformed loves are among the most deadly. Such lies not only make us liars, but also act as if God lies, for to tell the truth, God has created us to be the sort of people who can hear the truth about our condition (that we are all 'terminal') without despair. [460]

The obligation of Christians to tell the truth emphasised by Leithart, Hauerwas and Wilimon, has led Christians throughout the history of the Church to discuss whether it is ever permissible to not tell the truth in order to achieve a morally good end, as when the Hebrew midwives did not tell the truth to Pharaoh about their failure to obey his command to kill Hebrew male babies (Exodus 1:15-20) or when Rahab did not tell the truth to the King of Jericho about the Israelite spies whom she had hidden (Joshua 2:1-7).

There is a major strand of Christian thought exemplified by Augustine in his work *On Lying* that holds that failure to tell the truth is never justified, under any circumstances, but is always a sin. In Augustine's words: 'whoever shall think there is any sort of lie that is not sin, will deceive himself foully, while he deems himself honest as a deceiver of other men.' [461] For those who hold this position, who alongside Augustine include Aquinas and Calvin, there is an absolute obligation to always tell the truth.

An alternative Christian view, however, argues that biblical examples such as that of the Hebrew midwives or Rahab show that there are circumstances in which it is permissible not to tell the truth. This approach is taken, for instance, by Packer who explains that:

> ...when one sets out to be truthful, new problems appear. There are people to whom it is clearly not right to tell the whole truth - invalids, not yet strong enough to take bad news, enemies in

---

[460] Hauerwas and Wilimon, p.119.
[461] Augustine, *On Lying*, 42 in *The Nicene and Post Nicene Fathers*, First series, vol. III (Edinburgh and Grand Rapids: T&T Clark/Eerdmans, 1998), p.477.

wartime to whom one should not give information, and from whom, like Rahab (Joshua 2) And Corrie ten Boom, one may have fugitives to hide; mad and bad folk, who would use what you tell them to harm others; the general public, when as a politician one is putting through a beneficent plan that depends for its effect on nobody anticipating it; and so on. Nobody doubts that in these cases responsible persons must dissemble. But does that square with the ninth commandment?

In principle yes, what is forbidden is false witness against your neighbour that is, as we said, prideful lying designed to do him down and exalt you at his expense. The positive command implicit in this negative is that we should seek our neighbor's good and speak truth to him and about him to this end. When the love that seeks his good prompt us to withhold truth that, if spoken, would bring him harm, the spirit of the ninth commandment is being observed. In such exceptional cases as we have mentioned, all courses of action have something of evil in them, and an outright lie, I like that of Rahab (Joshua 2:4-5; note the commendation of her in James 2:25) may actually be the best way, the least evil, and the truest expression of love to all the parties involved.

Yet a lie, even when prompted by love, loyalty, and an inescapable recognition that if telling it is bad, not telling it would be worse, remains an evil thing (unless, indeed, with old-style Jesuits and modern type situationists we hold that the end justifies the means). To bear false witness *for* one's neighbour is not so bad as bearing false witness *against* him; but the lie as such however necessary it appears, is bad, not good, and the right-minded man knows this. Rightly will he feel defiled; rightly will he seek fresh cleansing the blood of Christ and settle for living the only way anyone can live with our holy God - by the forgiveness of sins. [462]

---

[462] Packer, pp.97-98.

It is important to note Packer's point that even if a failure to tell the truth can be justified it remains something that is evil, even if a necessary evil. Under normal circumstances Christians are under an absolute obligation to speak the truth. Even if, contrary to Augustine, there are occasions on which it would be right to utter a falsehood, these occasions have to be viewed as exceptional. The norm is always to tell the truth rather than to lie.

A final point which needs to be considered in relation to the ninth commandment is the question of whether it is right to take oaths. There have been and are Christians, such as George Fox and the Quakers following him, who argue that swearing oaths is specifically forbidden by Jesus in Matthew 5:33-37 and by James in James 5:12 and that Christians should be such truthful people that it is unnecessary for them to be asked to swear to tell the truth.

However, the mainstream Christian position has been that what is forbidden is what Article XXXIX of the Church of England's *Thirty-Nine Articles* calls 'vain and rash swearing', that is, swearing detached from truth, whereas oaths may be sworn by someone who seriously intends to speak the truth and solely in order that truth may prevail.

This is the position taken, for example, in the comments on swearing an oath in court in the homily 'Against Swearing and Perjury' in the *First Book of Homilies,* which declares:

> God by the Prophet Jeremy saith, 'Thou shalt swear, The Lord liveth, in truth, in judgement, in righteousness' (Jeremiah 4.2). So that whosoever sweareth when he is required of a judge, let him be sure in his conscience that his oath have three conditions, and he shall never need to be afraid of perjury. First, he that sweareth, may swear truly, that is, he must (setting apart all favour and affection to the parties) have the truth only before his eyes, and for love thereof, say and speak that which he knoweth to be truth, and no further. The second is, he that taketh an oath, must do it with judgement, not rashly and unadvisedly, but soberly, considering what an oath is. The third is, he that sweareth, must swear in righteousness: that

is, for the very zeal and love which he beareth to the defence of innocency, to the maintenance of the truth, and of the righteousness of the matter or cause: all profit, disprofit, all love and favour unto the person for friendship or kindred laid apart.[463]

What all this means in terms of conscientious objection is that the ninth commandment requires that in all normal circumstances Christian must be people who tell the truth to and about their neighbours and that they must resist all pressure to do otherwise even if, as in the case of Nien Cheng, the pressure to do so is extreme. Only in exceptional circumstances may they fail to tell the truth, and then only in order to benefit their neighbour, and in the clear recognition that what they are doing is evil, even if it is necessary.

In addition, not only must Christians not tell lies themselves, but they must also be prepared to challenge the lies told by others, whether spoken, in print, or online, and whether by individuals, governments, lobby groups, commercial organisations, or even churches. They must not let lies prevail by reason of their silence.

Commandment 10: You shall not covet your neighbour's house; you shall not covet your neighbour's wife, or his manservant, or his maidservant, or his ox, or his ass, or anything that is your neighbour's (Exodus 20: 17).

During the history of the Church there have been some commentators who have seen the tenth commandment as having to do with people attempting to wrongly acquire that which belongs to their neighbour.

This is, for example, the understanding of the commandment put forward by Luther in his *Small Catechism*. Following medieval tradition, Luther divides the commandment into two parts (which he calls the ninth and tenth commandments) and he sees both as prohibiting taking action to deprive our neighbour of what belongs to them.

---

[463] 'Against Swearing and Perjury,' in *The Homilies*, p.53.

The Ninth 'You shall not covet your neighbour's house.'

What does this mean?

Answer: We should fear and love God, and so we should not seek by craftiness to gain possession of our neighbour's inheritance or home, nought obtain them under pretext of legal right, but be of service and help to him so that he may keep what is his.

The Tenth 'You shall not covet your neighbour's wife, or his manservant, or his maidservant, or his ox, or his ass, or anything that is your neighbours.'

What does this mean?

Answer: we should fear and love God, and so we should not obstruct, it's strange, or entice away our neighbour's wife servants, or cattle, but encourage them to remain and discharge their duty to him.[464]

The problem with this approach to understanding the tenth commandment is twofold. First, it makes the commandment superfluous since what it prohibits is already prohibited in the seventh commandment against adultery and the eighth commandment against stealing. Secondly, the term 'covet' in concerned with desire for something rather than the action taken to acquire it (even if that desire then leads to action).[465]

For these two reasons, the best understanding of the tenth commandment, and the majority understanding in the Christian tradition, is that the commandment prohibits wrongful desire. This is the view taken, for instance, in *To Be a Christian*:

---

[464] Martin Luther, *Small Catechism*, in Noll, p.67.
[465] See J P Hyatt, *Exodus* (Grand Rapids and London: Eerdmans/ Marshall Morgan & Scott, 1980), p.216 and J W Marshall, 'Decalogue' in T Desmond Alexander and David Baker (eds), *Dictionary of the Old Testament: Pentateuch* (Downers Grove and Leicester, Inter-Varsity Press, 2003) p.178.

349. What is the tenth commandment?

The tenth commandment is "You shall not covet...anything that is your neighbour's." (Exodus 20:17; Deuteronomy 5:21)

350. What does it mean to covet?

Coveting is the disordered desire for what belongs to another or what I am unable to have by law, by gift, or by right. (Joshua 7:1, 10–26)

351. What does the tenth commandment forbid you to covet? It forbids me to covet my neighbour's property, possessions, relationships, or status, or anything else that is my neighbour's. (Exodus20:17; Deuteronomy 5:21; Job 31:7–12, 24–28)

352. Why does God forbid coveting?

God forbids coveting because it breeds enmity with my neighbour, makes me captive to ungodly desire, and leads me into further sins. (Deuteronomy 7:25; Proverbs 12:12; Ephesians 5:5; James 4:2)

353. Why do you covet?

I covet because I do not trust God to provide what I need, and I do not remain content with what I have; rather, I persist in envy and desire. (Proverbs 14:30; 23:17–18; Luke 12:13–21; Galatians 5:17–21)

354. How can covetousness lead to other sins?

Covetousness begins with discontent and, as it grows in the heart, can lead to sins such as idolatry, adultery, and theft. (2 Samuel 11; 1 Kings 21:1–19; Proverbs 1:8–19; James 1:14–15)[466]

As Leithart explains:

---

[466] *To be a Christian*, paragraphs 349-354.

Desire is fundamental to biblical anthropology, its understanding of human existence. We think, but we aren't primarily thinking beings. We're *desiring* beings. Like the animals, Adam was made a 'living soul.' (Gen 2:7; cf. 1:20-21, 24, 30). Our souls move us to action and our souls move us by desire (1 Sam 23:20; Job 23:13; Eccl 6:2,9) Sexual desire is a longing of soul (Gen 34:8), hunger and thirst arise from the soul (Psalm 107:9), and the yearning for God's presence is a desire of the soul (Ps 42:1-2;63:1;84:2; 143:6; Isa 26:9). Dante was right: everything we do is motivated by a proper or distorted love. Desire is the combustible power that moves human life.

Desires are inseparable from evaluations of the desirability of the thing desired God made trees 'desirable to the eyes' (Gen 2:9), and eyes are organs of judgement and evaluation. Eve 'saw' the tree was desirable to make one wise, and so she ate (Gen 3:6). Desire moves us to take the object of desire - food, a sexually attractive person, our neighbours shiny Porsche - and to incorporate it into ourselves. [467]

As he goes on to say:

The Bible acknowledges the disruptive, dangerous power of desire, and Christians developed the notion of seven deadly sins to warn against disfigured desire. But desire isn't evil because it's strong. Desire becomes evil when it's fixed on the wrong objects. When we misevaluate the desirability of something. Eve covets the fruit and takes it, Shechem desires Dinah and seduces her (Gen 34) and Achan covets the treasure of Jericho and steals it from Yahweh (Josh 7:21). Evil desire lays traps (e.g. Deut 7:25), That is why Paul says covetousness is idolatry (Col 3). Our souls impel us to seek satisfactions in things that we *wrongly* judge to be satisfying.

The reason that our souls impel us to seek satisfaction in things that will never satisfy is because as, Aquinas notes in his *Catechetical Instructions*, 'man's desire has no limits, because desire itself is

[467] Leithart, p.64.

boundless.'[468] As Augustine famously puts it in his *Confessions*: 'Thou hast formed us for Thyself, and our hearts are restless till they find their rest in Thee.'[469] Human beings are created to find limitless satisfaction in communion with God and when, as a result of their fallen state, this does not happen, they seek for satisfaction in created things, even if these are things which they should not desire, which they have to sin to attain, and which even if attained will never bring them the satisfaction they are seeking.

What human beings need is not to desire less, but to desire better: 'Our desires are to *mature* so that our souls, brought to life by the Spirit, move us to pursue *real* treasure and eternal glory *with passion*.'[470] As in Jesus' parables of the hidden treasure and hidden pearl (Matthew 13:44-46) what we need to do is discover our true treasure (a right relationship with God) and then be prepared to set aside everything else to obtain it. In context the tenth commandment points us to this truth. It tells us that if we desire a right relationship with God as part of his people, we need to set aside our disordered desires for those things which God in his wisdom has given to others and be content instead with those things that he has chosen to give us in that station in life in which he has chosen to place us. To quote *To Be a Christian* again:

How can you keep this commandment? I can keep this commandment by learning contentment: seeking first the kingdom of God, meditating on God's provision in creation and in my life, cultivating gratitude for what I have and simplicity in what I want, and practicing joyful generosity toward others. (Exodus 35:20–29; 36:2–5; Psalms 104; 145:15–21; Ecclesiastes 5:10; 2 Corinthians 9:6–15; 1 Timothy 6:6–10; Hebrews 13:5). [471]

---

[468] Collins and Bandas, p.88.
[469] Augustine, *Confessions*, Bk 1.1, in *The Nicene and Post Nicene Fathers*, First series, vol. I (Edinburgh and Grand Rapids: T&T Clark/Eerdmans, 1994), p.45.
[470] Leithart, p.65.
[471] *To be a Christian*, paragraph, 356.

As many cultural commentators have pointed out, current Western culture is based on the twin ideas of unlimited desire and unlimited consumption to try to satisfy that desire. In the light of the tenth commandment, Christians need to conscientiously object to these ideas in two ways. First, by cultivating a desire for God that results in contentment with what God has given us rather an envy of what he has given to others and a desire to obtain it. Secondly, by being willing to be vocal about the fact that our consumer culture will never bring us genuine satisfaction because our restless hearts were made for something better.

In conclusion

What we have seen in this chapter is that Christians are called to exercise the freedom that God has given to them by living in a permanent state of conscientious objection, a permanent refusal to do anything which is contrary to God's will for his children. Conscientious objection is not just a calling for a few particularly heroic Christians. Rather it is a way of life that all Christians are called to at all times. Christians are people who need to say 'No.'

What we have also seen is that the Ten Commandments prove a basic framework for understanding what Christians need to say no to. They set out the parameters for what we need to reject in word and deed if we want to be people who love God all our heart, soul, mind and strength and love our neighbours as ourselves.

However, there is more to rightly exercising Christian freedom than simply rejecting things. We also need to provide a positive witness for God in the contemporary world and in the next chapter we will go on to consider what this positive witness should involve.

Chapter 9
Back to the Future - How Christians can provide a positive witness for God in today's world

In the previous chapter we considered how Christians should use their God given freedom by living a life marked by permanent conscientious objection to anything that is contrary to the will of God, with the Ten Commandments providing a basic framework for understanding what such conscientious objection should involve.

In this chapter we shall go on to consider how Christians should use their God given freedom to not only conscientiously object to things that are ungodly, but to provide a positive witness for God in today's world.

1. Christians need to argue for the principle of freedom of religion

The first thing that Christians need to do is to argue that the basic principle of freedom of religion, belief and conscience, which Christians have advocated over many centuries, and which since the Second World War has come to be enshrined in numerous national and international legal documents, needs to continue to be upheld and must not be curtailed unnecessarily.

To quote the words of Timothy Shah, the sort of thing that Christians need to be saying is that:

> The dignity and integrity of the human person require that all people everywhere enjoy the freedom to fulfil their duty to seek and embrace the truth about transcendent reality as best they can.

> Human beings are noble agents - agents with high worth and dignity. An integral aspect of these characteristics is that all persons have the great privilege and responsibility of freely forming their own judgments of reason and conscience about - and freely establishing their own relationship with - transcendent reality.

They have an intrinsic interest in forming their characters and lives -constituting themselves - into integrated wholes that fully reflect the demands and implications of transcendent truth as they grasp it. Anything less than full religious freedom fails to respect the dignity of persons as free truth - seekers, duty bound to respond to the truth (and only the truth) about the transcendent in accordance with their own judgements of conscience. Furthermore, anything less than the full religious freedom also fails to respect the proper integrity and authenticity of persons.

What persons gain, therefore, when they enjoy this freedom is the freedom to make judgments concerning religious truths in accordance with their own dictates of conscience, not in accordance with the dictates of some coercive, external authority. What they gain, as well, is the freedom to act on these judgments in the way they organise their personal lives and in the way they express themselves in their communities. What they gain is the full freedom to be persons.

Conversely, what they lose when they do not enjoy religious freedom is the freedom to make and act on their own judgments of religious conscience. In losing this freedom, they lose capacities that are essential to being complete human beings.

When people lose their religious freedom, in other words, they lose more than their freedom to be religious. They lose their freedom to be human. The dignity of human beings, then grounds the various dimensions of religious freedom: the freedom to explore the truth about an unseen order, the freedom to embrace it, and the freedom to express it.[472]

---

[472] The Witherspoon Institute Task Force on International Religious Freedom, *Religious Freedom: Why Now? – Defending an Embattled Human Right?* (Princeton: Witherspoon Institute, 2012), Kindle Edition, Loc. 625-636.

Furthermore, to quote Shah again, Christians need to explain that, properly understood, the principle of religious freedom needs to include at least four major dimensions:

First is the freedom of every person to use his reason to seek the truth about whatever unseen order of reality there may be - whether such an order exists and, if so, what its various dimensions might be and what they may say about human life. *It is the religious freedom of intellectual and spiritual inquiry.*

Second, religious freedom in full includes the freedom to engage one's conscience, intellect, and will in embracing whatever truth one can discover about an unseen order of reality. Which is the freedom to align one's life with the truth about an unseen order. *It is the religious freedom of practical reason.*

Third, religious freedom in full includes the freedom to engage all the aspects of one's physical being to practise and manifest the truth about the unseen order of reality, and to join with others of like mind and spirit. This is the freedom to speak and act - both individually and in community with others -in ways that express whatever truth one may possess about a transcendent order. *It is the religious freedom of human sociality.*

The fourth and final dimension of religious freedom in full is the right -both individually and as part of a larger rooted community - to express religious beliefs freely in civil society and political life on a basis no less favourable that is according to non-religious expression. This aspect of religious freedom encompasses the right of religious individuals and groups to own and sell property, or to establish and run religious schools, charitable organisations and other institutions of civil society. It includes the right to form political parties, or to make arguments in the public square, on the basis of religious teaching. *The is the religious freedom of political and legal expression.*[473]

2. Christians need to argue for the application of the principle of freedom of religion

The second thing that Christians need to do is to be prepared to argue the case for the application of the principle of freedom of religion in particular cases where it either has been violated or is in danger of being violated.

This means, for example, that when Christians such as Päivi Räsänen and Juhana Pohjola in Finland, Bernard Randall in Great Britain, Matthieu Raffray in France or Catch the Fire ministries in Australia are unjustly accused of wrongdoing because of their exercise of religious freedom other Christians need to be prepared to explain how the principle of freedom of religion is being violated and why it needs to be upheld.

In similar fashion, when it is proposed that undue restrictions should be placed upon religious activity, as in current proposals in the United Kingdon to ban conversion therapy, Christians need to explain why such restrictions would violate the principle of freedom of religion and to argue that they should therefore not be introduced.

For example, the private member's bill introduced in the British House of Lords by Baroness Jane Burt in November 2023 proposed the prohibition of conversion therapy in the following terms

> A person commits an offence if they practise, or offer to practise, conversion therapy.
>
> **(2)**
> In this Act, "conversion therapy" is any practice aimed at a person or group of people which demonstrates an assumption that any

---

[473] The Witherspoon Institute, Loc.416-428. Italics in the original.

sexual orientation or gender identity is inherently preferable to another, and which has the intended purpose of attempting to—

(a)

change a person's sexual orientation or gender identity, or

(b)

suppress a person's expression of sexual orientation or gender identity.

(3)

A person guilty of an offence under this section is liable on summary conviction to a fine not exceeding level 5 on the standard scale. [474]

The legal opinion of the human rights lawyer Jason Koppel on the proposed bill is that:

(1) The Bill is notably broad in scope. It applies both to practices which seek to 'change' sexual orientation or gender identity ("SO/GI") and practices which seek to 'suppress' the 'expression' of SO/GI; i.e., to change conduct. It would apply to acts which cause no injury or distress; and, indeed, to acts to which the person in question consents.1 It would apply across the whole range of life; including in religious settings, social settings, and in the home. No attempt has been made to craft exemptions or exceptions so as to ensure that any particular conduct, including conduct in domestic settings, or the practice of religion, is not prohibited.

(2) The Bill would, if enacted, interfere with a number of rights protected by the ECHR. It would (by way of example) restrict the ability of gender-critical persons to express their beliefs; the ability of religious organisations to express their beliefs (both to the wider world, and within their own communities); and the ability of

---

[474] *Conversion Therapy Prohibition (Sexual Orientation and Gender Identity) Bill* [HL] at https://bills.parliament.uk/bills/3512

parents to counsel and bring up children in the way they believe to be right. Such restrictions are likely to interfere with (at least) the right to respect for private and family life (Article 8 ECHR); the right to freedom of thought, conscience and religion (Article 9 ECHR); the right to freedom of expression (Article 10 ECHR); and the right to freedom of assembly and association (Article 11 ECHR).

(3) Any interference with such rights must be justified and proportionate in order to be lawful. It is very difficult to see how the wide-ranging interference with fundamental rights contemplate by the Bill could be justified. Put shortly, the Bill criminalises expressions of personal conviction even if they are made without expressions of hatred or intolerance, or improper purpose or coercion, or abuse of power. Such an approach runs contrary to the consistent case law of the European Court of Human Rights ("ECtHR").[475]

Because of the sort of issues raised by Koppel in his opinion, Christian bodies such as the Christian Institute have argued against Baroness Burt's Bill, as have individual Christians both in the House of Lords and elsewhere, and they have been right to do so.

It is important to note that Christians should not simply be arguing for the right of Christians to exercise freedom of religion. Because the right to exercise freedom of religion is something that is important for all human beings as such, Christians have an obligation to defend the religious freedoms of, for example, Jews, Muslims or Sikhs just as much as they should defend their own religious freedoms.

---

[475] Jason Koppel, *The Christian Institute, Private Member's Bill to prohibit Conversion Therapy, Advice*, at https://www.christian.org.uk/wp-content/uploads/Burt-CT-Bill-Coppel-Legal-Opinion.pdf. For a further legal opinion about the proposal for a ban on conversion therapy from a Christian perspective see Roger Kiska, 'Is a conversion therapy ban compatible with human rights?' at: file:///C:/Users/mbarr/Downloads/CC-Resource-Briefings-Conversion-Therapy-Ban-Opinion-Roger-Kiska-220407.pdf

In November 2023, for instance, the Court of Justice of the European Union made the following ruling in regard to a ban by the Belgian municipality of Ans on any employee wearing an outward sign of ideological or religious affiliation.

(1) Article 2(2)(a) of Council Directive 2000/78/EC of 27 November 2000 establishing a general framework for equal treatment in employment and occupation must be interpreted to mean that a provision of a public body's terms of employment which prohibits employees from wearing any visible sign of political, philosophical or religious belief in the workplace, with the aim of putting in place an entirely neutral administrative environment, does not constitute, with regard to employees who intend to exercise their freedom of religion and conscience through the visible wearing of a sign or an item of clothing with religious connotations, direct discrimination on the grounds of religion or belief, for the purposes of that directive, provided that that provision is applied in a general and undifferentiated way.

(2) Article 2(2)(b) of Directive 2000/78 must be interpreted to mean that a difference of treatment indirectly based on religion or belief arising from a provision of a public body's terms of employment which prohibits employees from wearing any visible sign of political, philosophical or religious belief in the workplace may be justified by that body's desire to put in place an entirely neutral administrative environment, provided, first, that that desire responds to a genuine need on the part of that body, which it is for that body to demonstrate; second, that that difference of treatment is appropriate for the purpose of ensuring that that desire is properly realised; and, third, that that prohibition is limited to what is strictly necessary.[476]

[476] The ruling can be found at:
https://curia.europa.eu/juris/document/document.jsf?text=&docid=273313&pageIndex=0&doclang=EN&mode=lst&dir=&occ=first&part=1&cid=3078169

This ruling could have particularly severe consequences for Sikhs and Muslims for whom the wearing of particular items of clothing such as a turban for Sikh men or a head scarf for Muslim women has deep religious significance. To say that they cannot dress in accordance with their religious beliefs when at work is a major infringement of their freedom of religion and Christians should support them in protesting against it even if the ban does not directly affect them because they do not feel that a particular form of dress is required by their Christian faith. Freedom of religion is a universal right, and Christians must support it for everybody.

Even though the courts and the political process have not been perfect, it is imperative that Christians continue to advocate for religious freedom both in the courts and in the political arena. Failure to do so will mean even more diminished freedoms; whereas a full-throated defence of religious freedom, especially if the call is widespread, can only yield positive results.

3. Christians need to work with others to promote the common good

It is a fundamental part of the Christian obligation to love their neighbours that they should do all that they can to help their fellow human beings to live together rightly before God.

This means that Christians need to do is to support forms of political and economic activity that promote what the Roman Catholic tradition has called the 'common good.' *The Catechism of the Catholic Church* defines the common good as 'the sum total of economic or social conditions which allow people, either as groups or individuals, to reach their fulfilment more fully and more easily.'[477]

Understood in this way, the common good can be seen to consist of a number of different aspects:

---

[477]*The Catechism of the Catholic Church*, para 1906, text in *The Catechism of the Catholic Church*, p.418.

- In order to live rightly before God people need the ability to exist ('the right to life') and therefore they need food and drink, clothing, shelter and medical care.

- In order to develop emotionally and to learn to exercise their God given abilities people need a loving and supportive family and they require education so as to be able to understand and appreciate the world in which they live and to cultivate their intellectual and physical skills.

- In order to act as responsible stewards of God's creation, using their God given abilities to provide for their own well-being and those of their families and neighbours, people need the opportunity to undertake fulfilling work.

- In order to exercise their responsibility for the welfare of their neighbours and of God's creation, people need the ability to participate in decisions which affect the way in which their society operates and how it relates to the natural world. This in turn means that they need to be able to participate in the political system at all levels and that they also need freedom of speech and freedom of assembly.

- In order for all the above to happen and for people to be able to relate to each other over distances a framework of transport and communication is also required.

- In order for people to live rightly together there needs to be a framework of law and order in which those things that are contrary to the common good are prevented or discouraged and those things which are conducive to the common good are supported and affirmed.

- Finally, in order for all the above to take place there needs to be economic activity. In order for the common good to flourish material resources need to be provided in the shape of goods, services and the finances to pay for them. In addition, in order to make proper provision for the future and give proper respect to the created order these material resources have to be provided in a way that is environmentally sustainable.

Christians need to do all that they can, working with people of good will of all faiths and none, to ensure that all these aspects of the common good are in place. For example, it is right for Christians to work with atheists, Muslims and Hindus to ensure that people in need have adequate supplies of food and drink and also clothing, shelter and medical care. Similarly, it is right for Christians to work with agnostics, Jews and Zoroastrians to help develop and maintain adequate transport and communication systems.

What Christians also need to be willing to do, however, when it is appropriate for them to do so, is to explain that they are undertaking these tasks in grateful obedience to the God who has created and redeemed them in his son Jesus Christ. The tasks they are doing may be the same as those of their non - Christian co-workers, but their motivation will be different, and they need to be willing to witness to the fact that this is the case.

In the rest of this chapter, we shall explore why this needs to be the case.

4. Christians need to be patient people whose lives reflect the patience of God

The calling that Christians have to live lives of conscientious objection, to contend for the principle of freedom of religion and its application, and to work together with non-Christians to promote the common good are all aspects of larger whole, which is the calling of Christians to live as patient people whose lives reflect the patience of God and by so doing take forward God's good purposes in the world.

The biblical witness to the patience of God and the patience called for from God's people in response

A central part of the biblical witness to the nature of God is its testimony that God is not only gracious and merciful, but also patient.

As Karl Barth notes:

There is a whole series of Old Testament texts (Ex 34:6; Joel 2:13; Jonah 4:2; Neh 9:17 Ps 86:15, 103:8, 145:8) in which, with variations of order, but obviously a certain necessity which has almost become a formula, these three - Yahweh's grace, mercy and patience (or longsuffering), usually completed by the comprehensive thought of his 'great faithfulness' – are described as the distinctive marks of the God revealed and active in Israel. [478]

As Barth goes on to say, God's patience is:

His will, deep-rooted in His essence and constituting His divine being and action, to allow to another – for the sake of His own grace and mercy and in the affirmation of His holiness and justice – space and time for the development of its own existence, thus conceding to this existence a reality side by side with His own and fulfilling His will towards this other in such a way that He does not suspend and destroy it as this other but accompanies and sustains it and allows it to develop in freedom. [479]

To quote J W L Hoad:

Such patience is characteristic of God's dealings with sinful men, who are fully deserving of His wrath (Is. xlviii:9; Ho. xi:9). His protecting mark on the murderer Cain (Gn.iv:15), His providential rainbow sign to a world that had forfeited its existence (Gn. Ix:11-17; cf. 1 Pet.iii:20), His many restorations of disobedient Israel (Ho.xi:8,9), His sparing of Nineveh (Jonah), His repeated pleadings with Jerusalem (Mk. xii:1-11; Lk.xiii:1-9, 34, Rom.ix.22), His deferment of His second coming (2 Pet. iii:9) – these are all expressions of His patience. [480]

---

[478] Karl Barth, *Church Dogmatics II.1* (London and New York: T&T Clark, 2004), p.407.

[479] Barth, pp.409-410.

[480] J W L Hoad, 'Patience,' in J D Douglas et.al *The New Bible Dictionary* (Leicester: Inter-Varsity Press, 1980), p938.

If we ask why God shows patience, the answer suggested by passages such as Ezekiel 18:21-23, Romans 2:4 and 9:22 and 2 Peter 3:9 is that God exercises patience in order to allow time for sinful human beings to come to repentance. However, as Barth notes, this explanation of God's patience raises the question '...is there anywhere or at any time a real act of human penitence for the sake of which it is worthwhile to God and to give them time and life?'[481]

If the answer to this question is 'No.' the further questions that then follow are: 'What, then is the meaning of the patience of God? Is it not the equivalent of weakness? Does it not mean that God allows himself to be mocked? For when and where will not both the actual and anticipated penitence prove a disappointment?'[482]

Alternatively, if there is no real penitence does this not mean that God's patience simply means judgement deferred so that; 'the kindness and grace of God have been only the affair of a moment, whereas His wrath is the constant and eternal factor and will necessarily have the last word?[483]

The answer to these questions, says Barth, is given in the biblical witness to Jesus Christ, who stands in the place of sinners 'and for them all has accomplished the genuine penitence which was expected from all.' [484] As Barth goes on to say:

> For the sake of this One, there is space and time for the many. It is not that they have deserved this or ever will or can deserve it by their ambiguous and in the last resort, insincere penitence. Nor is it, of course, that space and time have been granted to enable them to continue in their impenitence. It is rather that they have might have space and time to appropriate the life which has been secured for them by the sincere penitence of that One - space and time to

481 Barth, p.415.
482 Barth, p.415.
483 Barth, p.416.
484 Barth, p.416.

believe in him in whom as their Head their penitence becomes sincere and acceptable to God. Because there, in the One, the zeal of God is so powerful and attains its goal, therefore the others, the many who are summed up in Him, who in Him are conducted to the goal and have already attained it, can as the many be at their various times on the way - the way of faith on which their footsteps follow His, their freedom is an acknowledgement of His freedom, their time a sharing of His time, and therefore contemporary with Him. To go the way of faith is what God's patience leaves to them and concedes to them. Therefore, the meaning of the divine patience is a summons to have faith. We have only to think of the object of faith, of the one Jesus Christ to believe in whom the many are called by the patience of God, to realise that in the tarrying of the divine patience there can be no question of the indifference of God to his creature, but that this very tarrying of God is his decisive action and work in relation to it.[485]

Furthermore, declares Barth, once we understand God's patience in this way this will necessarily lead to us being patient in face of the sufferings that we still have to undergo in this world:

The only way open to us now is a way of gratitude for our life which has been undeservedly left to us; the way which will become and be of itself the way of the patience that we now have to show in suffering the judgments and punishments which strike us. The fact that, in spite of our infinite guilt we are permitted to suffer them in the fellowship and shadow of the innocent suffering of Christ, by which we have been spared the suffering of the eternal wrath and judgement of God, is sufficient reason for us to suffer them patiently and to allow them to serve the purpose which they have for us: the conversion from every illusion of our own worthiness; the return to the One who has made us worthy of God, to faith, therefore, in which we can give ourselves to the God who in His Son has taken our cause into his own hands. The relationship with Jesus Christ in

---

[485] Barth, pp.418-419.

which we must suffer is sufficient to overrule our suffering and the gift of our whole life for good (Rom 8:28). In this relationship the worst and harshest thing that we can encounter, and do encounter, is our inevitable death in time, with which we must finally profess this relationship. But even this, the imminent end of all things, is not only not unbearable – for in its unbearable reality it has all been borne for us in Jesus Christ – but is in fact the outwardly bitter, yet inwardly sweet, promise of the eternal life which has already been won for us.[486]

If we ask what living the way of gratitude and patience will mean in terms of our behaviour, the answer is that according to the teaching of the New Testament it will mean two things.

First, it will mean showing loving patience (μακροθυμία) towards other people, or as some translations put it, being 'longsuffering' towards them (Matthew 18:26-30, 1 Corinthians 13:4, 2 Corinthians 6:6, Galatians 5:22, Ephesians 4:2, Colossians 1:11, 2 Timothy 4:2).

Secondly, it will mean showing patient endurance (ὑπομονῇ), that is the endurance that is the fruit of patience and that enables the Christian to stand firm in the face of hardship, persecution and other difficulties they may encounter in this world (Luke 21:19, Romans 5:3-4, 15:4, 2 Corinthians 6:4, 1 Thessalonians 1;3, 1 Timothy 6:11, Hebrews 10:36, James 1:12).

Patient endurance is a particularly important theme in Revelation where John uses the term seven times (Revelation 1:9, 2:2, 2:3, 2:19, 3:10, 13:10, 14:12). In Revelation God shows patience by delaying the final coming of the kingdom in order to allow time for repentance before the final judgement. In the words of Richard Bauckham; 'the

---

[486] Barth, p.421.

logic of delay is that of God's patience and grace. He gives people time to repent.'[487]

This delay creates a situation where evil continues to flourish and in which Christians face hostility, persecution and the possibility of martyrdom as a result. Patient endurance is depicted as the appropriate Christian response to this situation.

As Ian Paul explains in his commentary on Revelation:

The rhetorical goal of John's writing – for his first readers as well as for subsequent generations – is that they should be motivated and equipped to live as mature disciples of Jesus. The central element of this is to be a 'faithful witness' as Jesus was, living a life of 'patient endurance' (1:9) in the face of opposition and difficulty, but motivated by a clearer understanding of the 'kingdom' that is ours in Jesus. It is this 'quietist' approach, involving non-violent resistance to the forces of imperial conformity, which constitutes true victory, trusting as it does in God's ultimate power and justice for vindication.' [488]

A final point about patient endurance in the New Testament is that it involves patient endurance in living a godly life. We can see this in Luke 8:15 where Jesus describes the seed that falls in good soil as referring to 'those who, hearing the word, hold it fast in a honest and good heart and bring forth fruit with patience.' We can also see it in Romans 2:7 where Paul declares that God will give eternal life 'to those who by patience in well-doing seek for glory and honour and immortality.'

[487] Richard Bauckham, *The Theology of the Book of Revelation* (Cambridge: CUP, 1993), p.158.
[488] Ian Paul, *Revelation* (London and Downers Grove: Inter-Varsity Press, 2018), Kindle edition, p.47.

Patience in the patristic period

If we look at texts from the first four centuries of the Church, we find that the early Christians followed the New Testament in continuing to emphasise the importance of patience.

The Apostolic Fathers

The earliest Christian writers outside the New Testament are collectively known as the Apostolic Fathers. If we look at their writings, we find a number of references to the importance of patience.

In the letter known as *1 Clement* which was written by Clement, Bishop of Rome, to the church in Corinth in 95-96 AD, Clement responds to a situation in which there was pride, anger, and division in the Corinthian church, by emphasising the importance of Jesus ethic of gentleness and patience:

> Most of all, let us remember the words of the Lord Jesus, which he spoke as he taught gentleness and patience. For he said this: 'Show mercy, that you may receive mercy; forgive that you may be forgiven. As you do, so shall it be done to you. As you give, so shall it be given to you. As you judge, so shall you be judged. As you show kindness, so shall kindness be shown to you. With the measure you use, it will be measured to you.' With this commandment and these precepts let us strengthen ourselves, that we may walk humbly in obedience to his holy words. [489]

The letter written by Ignatius, Bishop of Antioch, to the church in Rome in about 110 AD concludes with the words 'Farewell to the end, in the patient endurance of Jesus Christ.'[490] The meaning of these words is not immediately apparent in the English translation, but what they mean is

---

[489] *1 Clement* 13:1-3 in J B Lightfoot, J R Harmer and Michael Holmes, *The Apostolic Fathers* 2ed (Leicester: Apollos, 1989), p.35. Clement seems to be making a reference to Jesus' teaching in Matthew 5:7, 6:14, 7:1-2, Luke 6:31 and 36-38. Clements cites these texts in a rather loose fashion as he does in his citation of texts from the Old Testament.

[490] Ignatius, *To the Romans, 10*, in Lightfoot, Harmer and Holmes, p.106.

that Ignatius's hope for the Christians in Rome is that they will continue to do well ('fare well') until the end of their earthly course and that they will do so by sharing in the patient endurance in well doing that was pioneered by Jesus and is reproduced in his people by his Spirit.

The work known as the *Shepherd of Hermas* seems to have originated at the end of the first century and to have reached its final form by the middle of the second century. The second of three parts of which this work consists of twelve short homilies or 'mandates' on Christian behaviour which in the literary genre of the work are said to have been given to its author by an angel.

Mandate 5 declares that Christians must be people who are patient, and who reject all anger and bitterness, and that doing so is the basis for obedience to all the other commandments given by God.

> 'Be patient and understanding,' he [the angel] said, 'and you will overcome all evil deeds and will accomplish all righteousness. For if you are patient the Holy Spirit who lives in you will be pure, uncontaminated by some other evil spirit; living in a spacious room, it will rejoice and be glad with the vessel in which it lives, and will serve God with much cheerfulness, for it is at peace with itself. But if an angry temper approaches, immediately the Holy Spirit, which is very sensitive, is distressed because it does not have a clean place, and it seeks to leave the place. For it is choked by the evil spirit and does not have the room to serve the Lord the way it wants to, because it is polluted by the angry temper. For the Lord lives in patience, but the devil lives in an angry temper. So, if both spirits lived together, it is unfortunate and evil for that person in whom they live. For if you take a little wormwood[491] and pour it into a jar of honey, isn't all the honey spoiled? Such a large amount of honey spoiled by such a small amount of wormwood; it spoils the sweetness, and owner no longer cares for it, because it has become

---

[491] 'Wormwood' refers to the bitter tasting herb artemisia absinthium which was traditionally used for a variety of medicinal purposes.

bitter and lost its usefulness. But if the wormwood is not put into the honey the honey turns out to be sweet and is useful to its owner. You see then that patience is very sweet, even more so than honey, and is useful to the Lord, and he lives in it. But an angry temper is bitter and useless. So, if angry temper is mixed with patience, the patient is polluted, and the person's intercession is no longer useful to God.'

'...Have nothing to do, therefore, with an angry temper. Instead put on patience and resist an angry temper and bitterness, and you will be found in the company of the holiness that is loved by the Lord. So, take care that you never neglect this commandment if you master it, you will also be able to keep the rest of the commandments that I'm about to give you.'[492]

Justin Martyr's First Apology

From about 120-220 a number of Christian writers produced written defences of Christian belief and practice which have come to be known as 'apologies.' To quote the *Oxford Dictionary of the Christian Church* '[t]heir object was to gain a fair hearing for Christianity and to dispel popular slanders and misunderstandings' and '[t]heir method was to exhibit Christianity to emperors and to the public as politically harmless and morally and culturally superior to paganism.' [493]

The *Apology* by Tertullian quoted in chapter 2 was one of these apologies, and another was the *First Apology* by the Christian philosopher Justin Martyr which was written in 155-157. In chapter 16 of this work Justin explains how, in the light of the teaching of Jesus, patience was central to the life of the Christian community in Rome' Justin writes:

---

[492] *The Shepherd of Hermas*, Mandate 5:1-6 and 8 in Lightfoot, Harmer and Holmes, pp.219-221.
[493] 'Apologists' in F L Cross (ed) *The Oxford Dictionary of the Christian Church* (London: OUP, 1963), p.71.

And concerning our being patient of injuries, and ready to serve all, and free from anger, this is what He [Jesus] said: 'To him that smites you on the one cheek, offer also the other; and him that takes away your cloak or coat, forbid not. And whosoever shall be angry, is in danger of the fire. And every one that compels you to go with him a mile, follow him two. And let your good works shine before men, that they, seeing them, may glorify your Father which is in heaven.' For we ought not to strive; neither has He desired us to be imitators of wicked men, but He has exhorted us to lead all men, by patience and gentleness, from shame and the love of evil. And this indeed is proved in the case of many who once were of your way of thinking, but have changed their violent and tyrannical disposition, being overcome either by the constancy which they have witnessed in their neighbours' lives, or by the extraordinary forbearance they have observed in their fellow-travellers when defrauded, or by the honesty of those with whom they have transacted business.[494]

For Justin the task given to Christians by God is to lead people from 'shame and the love of evil' and the means he has given them to do this is through the kind of patient and gentle behaviour taught by Jesus. It is by living lives of patience goodness that their good works will 'shine before men' and the Father will be glorified.

Clement of Alexandria, *Exhortation to Endurance*, or, *To the newly baptized*

Clement of Alexandria was a Christian theologian who was head of the Catechetical School in Alexandria at the end of the second and the beginning of the third century AD. The Catechetical School gave Christian instruction to those preparing for baptism and others interested in Christianity and, as its name suggests his *Exhortation to Endurance* is a work which gives instruction to the newly baptized as to what it means to live out their new lives as Christians with patient endurance.

---

[494] Justin Martyr, *The First Apology*, 16, in *The Ante-Nicene Fathers*, vol. I (Edinburgh and Grand Rapids, T&T Clark/Eerdmans, 1996), p.168.

As can be seen below, for Clement a life of patient endurance means a distinctive lifestyle involving quietness and gentleness in word and deed, constant prayer (including prayer for those in distress), being disciplined in your eating, drinking and sleeping, rejecting anxiety about the things of this life, and showing fortitude when faced with disease:

Cultivate quietness in word, quietness in deed, likewise in speech and gait; and avoid impetuous eagerness. For then the mind will remain steady, and will not be agitated by your eagerness and so become weak and of narrow discernment and see darkly; nor will it be worsted by gluttony, worsted by boiling rage, worsted by the other passions, lying a ready prey to them. For the mind, seated on high on a quiet throne looking intently towards God, must control the passions. By no means be swept away by temper in bursts of anger, nor be sluggish in speaking, nor all nervousness in movement; so that your quietness may be adorned by good proportion and your bearing may appear something divine and sacred. Guard also against the signs of arrogance, a haughty bearing, a lofty head, a dainty and high-treading footstep.

Let your speech be gentle towards those you meet, and your greetings kind; be modest towards women, and let your glance be turned to the ground. Be thoughtful in all your talk, and give back a useful answer, adapting the utterance to the hearer's need, just so loud that it may be distinctly audible, neither escaping the ears of the company by reason of feebleness nor going to excess with too much noise. Take care never to speak what you have not weighed and pondered beforehand; nor interject your own words on the spur of the moment and in the midst of another's; for you must listen and converse in turn, with set times for speech and for silence. Learn gladly, and teach ungrudgingly; never hide wisdom for others by reason of a grudging spirit, nor through false modesty stand aloof from instruction. Submit to elders just as to fathers. Honour God's servants. Be first to practice wisdom and virtue. Do not wrangle with your friends, nor mock at them and play the buffoon. Firmly renounce falsehood, guile and insolence. Endure in silence, as a gentle and high-minded man, the arrogant and insolent.

Let everything you do be done for God, both deeds and words; and refer all that is yours to Christ; and constantly turn your soul to God; and lean your thought on the power of Christ, as if in some harbour by the divine light of the Saviour it were resting from all talk and action. And often by day communicate your thoughts to men, but most of all to God at night as well as by day; for let not much sleep prevail to keep you from your prayers and hymns to God, since long sleep is a rival of death. Show yourself always a partner of Christ who makes the divine ray shine from heaven; let Christ be to you continual and unceasing joy.

Relax not the tension of your soul with feasting and indulgence in drink, but consider what is needful to be enough for the body. And do not hasten early to meals before the time for dinner comes; but let your dinner be bread, and let earth's grasses and the ripe fruits of trees be set before you; and go to your meal with composure, showing no sign of raging gluttony. Be not a flesh-eater nor a lover of wine, when no sickness leads you to this as a cure. But in place of the pleasures that are in these, choose the joys that are in divine words and hymns, joys supplied to you by wisdom from God; and let heavenly meditation ever lead you upward to heaven.

And give up the many anxious cares about the body by taking comfort in hopes towards God; because for you He will provide all necessary things in sufficiency, food to support life, covering for the body, and protection against winter cold. For to your King belongs the whole earth and all that is produced from it; and God treats the bodily parts of His servants with exceeding care, as if they were His, like His own shrines and temples. On this account do not dread severe diseases, nor the approach of old age, which must be expected in time; for even disease will come to an end, when the whole-hearted purpose we do His commandments.

Knowing this, make your soul strong even in face of diseases; be of good courage, like a man in the arena, bravest to submit to his toils with strength unmoved. Be not utterly crushed in soul by grief, whether disease lies heavily upon you, or any other hardship befalls, but nobly confront toils with your understanding, even in the midst of your struggles rendering thanks to God; since His thoughts are wiser than Men's, and such as it is not easy nor possible for men to find out. Pity those who are in distress, and ask for men the help that comes from God; for God will grant grace to His friend when he asks, and will provide succour for those in distress, wishing to make His power known to men, in the hope that, when they have come to full knowledge, they may return to God, and may enjoy eternal blessedness when the Son of God shall appear and restore good things to His own.[495]

For Clement it is this kind of disciplined lifestyle that helps a Christian lead 'those he holds dearest' – his family and friends - to 'repentance and conversion' and also prepares Christians to bear witness to their faith by standing firm in the face of persecution and even martyrdom. [496]

Tertullian *Of Patience*

Tertullian's work *Of Patience*, which was the first treatise on a single virtue by a Christian writer, was written in 204, a few years after Clement of Alexandria's *Exhortation to Endurance*. To quote Alan Kreider, in this treatise

...Tertullian establishes a biblical and theological basis for the central role that patience had been playing and would continue to play in the life of the Christian communities. And he writes to help

---

[495] Clement of Alexandria, *Exhortation to Endurance,* text at:
https://catholiclibrary.org/library/view?docId=Synchronized-EN/anf.Clement ofAlexandria.ExhortationNewlyBaptized.en.html&chunk.id=00000001.
[496] Alan Kreider, *The Patient Ferment of the Early Church* (Grand Rapids, Baker Academic, 2016), Kindle Edition, pp.17-18 citing Clement, *Stromateis* 7.18.20 and 4.4.

the believers think Christianly about their lives so that they would differentiate themselves from their neighbours who did not grasp the power and profundity of a patient lifestyle, and even more from philosophers who were unwilling to recognise patience as a virtue.[497]

In Chapter II of his treatise Tertullian declares that Christians base their patient way of life on the patience shown by God himself in the way he deals patiently with the human race, even in the face of persistent human sinfulness:

> To us no human affectation of canine[498] equanimity, modelled by insensibility, furnishes the warrant for exercising patience; but the divine arrangement of a living and celestial discipline, holding up before us God Himself in the very first place as an example of patience; who scatters equally over just and unjust the bloom of this light; who suffers the good offices of the seasons, the services of the elements, the tributes of entire nature, to accrue at once to worthy and unworthy; bearing with the most ungrateful nations, adoring *as they do* the toys of the arts and the works of their own hands, persecuting His Name together with His family; *bearing with* luxury, avarice, iniquity, malignity, waxing insolent daily: so that by His own patience He disparages Himself; for the cause why many believe not in the Lord is that they are so long without knowing that He is angry with the world.[499]

He then goes on to explain that the patient nature of God is shown even more clearly in the patience shown by God in the incarnate life of Jesus Christ:

---

[497] Kreider, p.20.
[498] 'Canine' here means 'cynical.' The point Tertullian is making is that Christian patience is not shaped by a world-weary cynicism that has simply ceased to care about what occurs ('que sera, sera').
[499] Tertullian, *Of Patience*, Ch. II in *The Ante-Nicene Fathers*, Vol. III, p..707-708. Italics in the original.

And *this* species of the divine patience indeed being, as it were, at a distance, may perhaps be esteemed as among 'things too high for us;' but what is that which, in a certain way, has been grasped by hand [1 John 1:1] among men openly on the earth? God suffers Himself to be conceived in a mother's womb, and awaits the *time for birth*; and, when born, bears *the delay* of growing up; and, when grown up, is not eager to be recognised, but is furthermore contumelious to Himself, and is baptized by His own servant; and repels with words alone the assaults of the tempter; while from being 'Lord' He becomes 'Master,' teaching man to escape death, having been trained to the exercise of the absolute forbearance of offended patience. He did not strive; He did not cry aloud; nor did any hear His voice in the streets. He did not break the bruised reed; the smoking flax He did not quench: for the prophet—nay, the attestation of God Himself, placing His own Spirit, together with patience in its entirety, in His Son—had not falsely spoken. There was none desirous of cleaving to Him whom He did not receive. No one's table or roof did He despise: indeed, Himself ministered to the washing of the disciples' feet; not sinners, not publicans, did He repel; not with that city even which had refused to receive Him was He angry, [Luke 9:51-56] when even the disciples had wished that the celestial fires should be immediately hurled on so contumelious a town. He cared for the ungrateful; He yielded to His ensnarers. This were a small matter, if He had not had in His company even His own betrayer, and steadfastly abstained from pointing him out. Moreover, while IIe is being betrayed, while IIe is being led up 'as a sheep for a victim,' (for 'so He no more opens His mouth than a lamb under the power of the shearer,') He to whom, had He willed it, legions of angels would at one word have presented themselves from the heavens, approved not the avenging sword of even one disciple. The patience of the Lord was wounded in (the wound of) Malchus. And so, too, He cursed for the time to come the works of the sword; and, by the restoration of health, made satisfaction to him whom Himself had not hurt, through Patience, the mother of Mercy. I pass by in silence (the fact) that He is crucified, for this was the end for which He had come; yet had the death which must be undergone need of contumelies likewise? Nay, but, when about to depart, He wished to be sated with the pleasure of patience. He is spitted on, scourged, derided, clad foully, more foully crowned. Wondrous is the faith of equanimity! He who had set before *Him* the concealing of Himself in man's shape, imitated nought of man's impatience! Hence, even more than from any other trait, ought you, Pharisees, to have recognised the Lord. Patience of this kind none of men would achieve. Such and so mighty evidences—the very magnitude of which proves to be among the nations indeed a cause for rejection of the faith, but among us its reason and rearing— proves manifestly enough (not by the sermons only, in enjoining, but likewise by the sufferings of the Lord in enduring) to them to whom it is given to believe, that as the effect and excellence of some inherent propriety, patience is God's nature.[500]

Since God is patient, argues Tertullian, impatience cannot have come from him. So where has it come from? The answer is that it has come from the devil. In Tertullian's words:

I detect the nativity of impatience in the devil himself, at that very time when he impatiently bore that the Lord God subjected the universal works which He had made to His own image, that is, to man. For if he had endured (that), he would not have grieved; nor would he have envied man if he had not grieved. Accordingly he deceived him, because he had envied him; but he had envied because he had grieved: he had grieved because, of course, he had not patiently borne.[501]

Tertullian then argues that impatience was the cause of the Fall, and the subsequent murder of Abel by Cain, is the cause of not only murder but adultery ('Who *ever* committed adultery without the *impatience* of *lust?*'), and was the reason why the Israelities created the golden calf,

---

[500] Tertullian, *Of Patience*, Ch. III, p.708. Italics in the original.
[501] Tertullian, *Of Patience,* Ch. V. p.709.

complained about a lack of water in the wilderness and slew the prophets ('through impatience of hearing them').[502]

Conversely, the reason that Abraham was blessed an account of his faith was on account of the patience he showed when God asked him to sacrifice Isaac: 'Deservedly then was he 'blessed,' because he was 'faithful;' deservedly 'faithful,' because 'patient.' [503] Furthermore, the pre-eminent way in which the Christian faith amplifies and fulfils the Old Testament law is by calling for people to exercise 'the universal discipline of patience:'

> For men were of old wont to require eye for eye, and tooth for tooth and to repay with usury evil with evil; for, as yet, patience was not on earth, because faith was not either. Of course, meantime, impatience used to enjoy the opportunities which the law gave. That was easy, while the Lord and Master of patience was absent. But after He has supervened, and has united the grace of faith with patience, now it is no longer lawful to assail even with word, nor to say fool even, without danger of the judgment. Anger has been prohibited, our spirits retained, the petulance of the hand checked, the poison of the tongue extracted. The law has found more than it has lost, while Christ says, Love your personal enemies, and bless your cursers, and pray for your persecutors, that you may be sons of your heavenly Father. [Matthew 5:44-45] Do you see whom patience gains for us as a Father? In this principal precept the universal discipline of patience is succinctly comprised, since evil-doing is not conceded even when it is deserved.[504]

According to Tertullian Christians are called to practice patience when met with violence or 'malediction' [i.e. verbal abuse], in the face of bereavement (because of the hope of the resurrection), and when tempted by a desire for revenge. The reward for such patience is the happiness promised in the Beatitudes:

---

[502] Tertullian, *Of Patience,* Ch. V. p.710. Italics in the original.
[503] Tertullian, *Of Patience,* Ch. VI. p.710.
[504] Tertullian, *Of Patience,* Ch. V1, p.711.

For whom but the patient has the Lord called happy, in saying, 'Blessed are the poor in spirit, for theirs is the kingdom of the heavens?' [Matthew 5:3] No one, assuredly, is 'poor in spirit,' except he be humble. Well, who is humble, except he be patient? For no one can abase himself without patience, in the first instance, to bear the act of abasement. 'Blessed,' says He, 'are the weepers and mourners.' [Matthew 5:4] Who, without patience, is tolerant of such un-happinesses? And so to such, 'consolation' and 'laughter' are promised. 'Blessed are the gentle:' [Matthew 5:5] under this term, surely, the impatient cannot possibly be classed. Again, when He marks 'the peacemakers' [Matthew 5:9] with the same title of felicity, and names them 'sons of God,' pray have the impatient any affinity with 'peace?' Even a fool may perceive that. When, however, He says, 'Rejoice and exult, as often as they shall curse and persecute you; for very great is your reward in heaven,' of course it is not to the impatience of exultation that He makes that promise; because no one will 'exult' in adversities unless he have first learned to contemn them; no one will contemn them unless he have learned to practise patience.[505]

It is patience that enables Christians to practice the supreme Christian virtue of charity ('the highest sacrament of faith, the treasure house of the Christian name') as described by Paul in 1 Corinthians 13:

'Charity,' he says, 'is long suffering;' thus she applies patience: 'is beneficent;' Patience does no evil: 'is not emulous;' that certainly is a peculiar mark of patience: 'savours not of violence:' she has drawn her self-restraint from patience: 'is not puffed up; is not violent;' for that pertains not unto patience: 'nor does she seek her own' if, she offers her own, provided she may benefit her neighbours: 'nor is irritable;' if she were, what would she have left to Impatience? Accordingly he says, 'Charity endures all things; tolerates all things;' of course because she is patient. Justly, then, 'will she never fail;' for all other things will be cancelled, will have their consummation.

[505] Tertullian, *Of Patience*, Chs. VIII-XI, pp.712-714.

'Tongues, sciences, prophecies, become exhausted; faith, hope, charity, are permanent:' Faith, which Christ's patience introduced; hope, which man's patience waits for; charity, which Patience accompanies, with God as Master. [506]

In sum, write Tertullian, patience (personified in this quotation as a female figure):

...fortifies faith; is the pilot of peace; assists charity; establishes humility; waits long for repentance; sets her seal on confession; rules the flesh; preserves the spirit; bridles the tongue; restrains the hand; tramples temptations under foot; drives away scandals; gives their crowning grace to martyrdoms; consoles the poor; teaches the rich moderation; overstrains not the weak; exhausts not the strong; is the delight of the believer; invites the Gentile; commends the servant to his lord, and his lord to God; adorns the woman; makes the man approved; is loved in childhood, praised in youth, looked up to in age; is beauteous in either sex, in every time of life. Come, now, see whether we have a general idea of her mien and habit. Her countenance is tranquil and peaceful; her brow serene contracted by no wrinkle of sadness or of anger; her eyebrows evenly relaxed in gladsome wise, with eyes downcast in humility, not in unhappiness; her mouth sealed with the honourable mark of silence; her hue such as theirs who are without care and without guilt; the motion of her head frequent against the devil, and her laugh threatening; her clothing, moreover, about her bosom white and well fitted to her person, as being neither inflated nor disturbed. For Patience sits on the throne of that calmest and gentlest Spirit, who is not found in the roll of the whirlwind, nor in the leaden hue of the cloud, but is of soft serenity, open and simple, whom Elias saw at his third essay. For where God is, there too is His foster-child, namely Patience. When God's Spirit descends, then Patience accompanies Him indivisibly. If we do not give admission to her together with the Spirit, will (He) always tarry with us? Nay, I

---

[506] Tertullian, *Of Patience*, Ch XII, p.715.

know not whether He would remain any longer. Without His companion and handmaid, He must of necessity be straitened in every place and at every time. Whatever blow His enemy may inflict He will be unable to endure alone, being without the instrumental means of enduring.[507]

One important aspect of this final summary section of the treatise is Tertullian's assertion that patience 'invites the Gentile' or, as Kreider translates it 'attracts the heathen.'[508] What Kreider's translation makes clear is that Tertullian believed, just like Justin Martyr and Clement of Alexandria before him, that a patient Christian way of life possessed the ability to attract unbelievers to God.

Cyprian, *On the Good of Patience*

Cyprian, who was Bishop of Carthage in North Africa in the middle of the third century, was a great admirer of Tertullian who he used to refer to as 'the master,' and yet around 256 AD he decided to supplement Tertullian's existing treatise on patience with an additional one of his own. Kreider makes a number of plausible suggestions as to why he did this.

No doubt he knew that a new treatise by him *as bishop* would have more clout with the African Christians than to Italians earlier one. Perhaps he sensed that he could write more simply than Tertullian's earlier one. Certainly, he knew that the church was in a different place than it had been fifty years earlier. Especially in the decade prior to Cyprian's writing, Christians had been through severe testing: some believers were tired, some were losing hope, some were in danger of lapsing into impatient practises, even engaging in violent revenge against their enemies. In the face of these developments, Cyprian may have sensed that patience - the characteristic virtue of the church - was under pressure. But patience would help his people live as Christians in their pressure-

---

[507] Tertullian, *Of Patience,* Ch. XV, pp.716-717.
[508] Kreider, p.25.

filled situation. So Cyprian set out to renew their conviction that there was something *good* in patience. He followed in Tertullian's tradition by writing a treatise on patience, but he changed his title; instead of *On Patience* (*De patientia*), Cyprian's title was *On the Good of Patience* (*De bono patientiae*). Cyprian believed that patience was good; he had to show people what that good was and demonstrate why it mattered. [509]

Like Tertullian before him, Cyprian begins his treatise by explaining that the patience which Christians are called to exercise has its origins in God. In his words:

> From Him patience begins; from Him its glory and its dignity take their rise. The origin and greatness of patience proceed from God as its author. Man ought to love the thing which is dear to God; the good which the Divine Majesty loves, it commends. If God is our Lord and Father, let us imitate the patience of our Lord as well as our Father; because it behoves servants to be obedient, no less than it becomes sons not to be degenerate.[510]

God shows his patience, declares Cyprian, by maintaining the created order in place despite the rejection of God shown by human idolatry, in order to benefit the righteous and the unrighteous alike, and to give sinners time to repent before the final judgement.

> But what and how great is the patience in God, that, most patiently enduring the profane temples and the images of earth, and the sacrilegious rites instituted by men, in contempt of His majesty and honour, He makes the day to begin and the light of the sun to arise alike upon the good and the evil; and while He waters the earth with showers, no one is excluded from His benefits, but upon the righteous equally with the unrighteous He bestows His undiscriminating rains. We see that with undistinguishing equality

---

[509] Kreider, pp.25-26. Italics in the original.
[510] Cyprian, *On the Good of Patience*, 3 in *The Ante-Nicene Fathers*, Vol. V (Edinburgh and Grand Rapids: T&T Clark/Eerdmans, 1995), p.484.

of patience, at God's behest, the seasons minister to the guilty and the guiltless, the religious and the impious—those who give thanks and the unthankful; that the elements wait on them; the winds blow, the fountains flow, the abundance of the harvests increases, the fruits of the vineyards ripen, the trees are loaded with apples, the groves put on their leaves, the meadows their verdure; and while God is provoked with frequent, yea, with continual offenses, He softens His indignation, and in patience waits for the day of retribution, once for all determined; and although He has revenge in His power, He prefers to keep patience for a long while, bearing, that is to say, mercifully, and putting off, so that, if it might be possible, the long protracted mischief may at some time be changed, and man, involved in the contagion of errors and crimes, may even though late be converted to God, as He Himself warns and says, 'I do not will the death of him that dies, so much as that he may return and live.' And again, Return unto me, says the Lord. And again: 'Return to the Lord your God; for He is merciful, and gracious, and patient, and of great pity, and who inclines His judgment towards the evils inflicted.' [Joel 2:13] Which, moreover, the blessed apostle referring to, and recalling the sinner to repentance, sets forward, and says: 'Or do you despise the riches of His goodness, and forbearance, and long-suffering, not knowing that the patience and goodness of God leads you to repentance? But after your hardness and impenitent heart you store up unto yourself wrath in the day of wrath and of revelation of the righteous judgment of God, who shall render to every one according to his works.' [Romans 2:4-6].[511]

God shows his patience even more clearly, Cyprian continues, in Jesus' teaching and his deeds. In the Sermon on the Mount Jesus taught that the exercise of patient love to all, including those who persecute us, is an essential part of the Christian privilege of sharing in the perfection of God the Father:

---

[511] Cyprian, *On the Good of Patience,* 4, pp.484-485.

And that we may more fully understand, beloved brethren, that patience is a thing of God, and that whoever is gentle, and patient, and meek, is an imitator of God the Father; when the Lord in His Gospel was giving precepts for salvation, and, bringing forth divine warnings, was instructing His disciples to perfection, He laid it down, and said, 'You have heard that it is said, You shall love your neighbour, and have your enemy in hatred. But I say unto you, Love your enemies, and pray for them which persecute you; that you may be the children of your Father which is in heaven, who makes His sun to rise on the good and on the evil, and rains upon the just and on the unjust. For if you love them which love you, what reward shall you have? Do not even the publicans the same? And if you shall salute your brethren only, what do you do more (than others)? Do not even the heathens the same thing? Be therefore perfect, even as your Father in heaven is perfect.' [Matthew 5:43-48] He said that the children of God would thus become perfect. He showed that they were thus completed, and taught that they were restored by a heavenly birth, if the patience of God our Father dwell in us—if the divine likeness, which Adam had lost by sin, be manifested and shine in our actions. What a glory is it to become like to God! What and how great a felicity, to possess among our virtues, that which may be placed on the level of divine praises!

Furthermore, not only did Jesus teach the importance of patience, he also demonstrated patience in the whole course of his earthly ministry.

Nor, beloved brethren, did Jesus Christ, our God and Lord, teach this in words only; but He fulfilled it also in deeds. And because He had said that He had come down for this purpose, that He might do the will of His Father; among the other marvels of His virtues, whereby He showed forth the marks of a divine majesty, He also maintained the patience of His Father in the constancy of His endurance. Finally, all His actions, even from His very advent, are characterized by patience as their associate; in that, first of all, coming down from that heavenly sublimity to earthly things, the Son of God did not scorn to put on the flesh of man, and although He Himself was not a sinner, to bear the sins of others. His immortality being in the meantime laid aside, He suffers Himself to become mortal, so that the guiltless may be put to death for the salvation of the guilty. The Lord is baptized by the servant; and He who is about to bestow remission of sins, does not Himself disdain to wash His body in the laver of regeneration. For forty days He fasts, by whom others are feasted. He is hungry, and suffers famine, that they who had been in hunger of the word and of grace may be satisfied with heavenly bread. He wrestles with the devil tempting Him; and, content only to have overcome the enemy, He strives no farther than by words. He ruled over His disciples not as servants in the power of a master; but, kind and gentle, He loved them with a brotherly love.

...And moreover, in His very passion and cross, before they had reached the cruelty of death and the effusion of blood, what infamies of reproach were patiently heard, what mockings of contumely were suffered, so that He received the spittings of insulters, who with His spittle had a little before made eyes for a blind man; and He in whose name the devil and his angels is now scourged by His servants, Himself suffered scourgings! He was crowned with thorns, who crowns martyrs with eternal flowers. He was smitten on the face with palms, who gives the true palms to those who overcome. He was despoiled of His earthly garment, who clothes others in the vesture of immortality. He was fed with gall, who gave heavenly food. He was given to drink of vinegar, who appointed the cup of salvation. That guiltless, that just One—nay, He who is innocency itself and justice itself—is counted among transgressors, and truth is oppressed with false witnesses. He who shall judge is judged; and the Word of God is led silently to the slaughter.[512]

In addition, Jesus did not stop showing patience when he died. He continues to show patience after his resurrection and ascension:

[512] Cyprian, *On the Good of Patience*, 6-7, pp.485-486.

And after all these things, He still receives His murderers, if they will be converted and come to Him; and with a saving patience, He who is benignant to preserve, closes His Church to none. Those adversaries, those blasphemers, those who were always enemies to His name, if they repent of their sin, if they acknowledge the crime committed, He receives, not only to the pardon of their sin, but to the reward of the heavenly kingdom. What can be said more patient, what more merciful? [513]

As those who are in Christ, Christians are called to imitate Christ's patience:

But if we also, beloved brethren, are in Christ; if we put Him on, if He is the way of our salvation, who follow Christ in the footsteps of salvation, let us walk by the example of Christ, as the Apostle John instructs us, saying, 'He who says he abides in Christ, ought himself also to walk even as He walked.' [1 John 2:6] Peter also, upon whom by the Lord's condescension the Church was founded, [Matthew 16:18] lays it down in his epistle, and says, 'Christ suffered for us, leaving you an example, that you should follow His steps, who did no sin, neither was deceit found in His mouth; who, when He was reviled, reviled not again; when He suffered, threatened not, but gave Himself up to him that judged Him unjustly.' [1 Peter 2:21-23] [514]

It is patience that enables Christians to attain the salvation in which they believe, and for which they hope, and which enables them to defeat the power of evil:

We must endure and persevere, beloved brethren, in order that, being admitted to the hope of truth and liberty, we may attain to the truth and liberty itself; for that very fact that we are Christians is the substance of faith and hope. But that hope and faith may attain to their result, there is need of patience. For we are not following

[513] Cyprian, *On the Good of Patience,* 8, p.486.
[514] Cyprian, *On the Good of Patience*, 9, p.486.

after present glory, but future, according to what Paul the apostle also warns us, and says, 'We are saved by hope; but hope that is seen is not hope: for what a man sees, why does he hope for? But if we hope for that which we see not, then do we by patience wait for it.' [Romans 8:24-25] Therefore, waiting and patience are needful, that we may fulfil that which we have begun to be, and may receive that which we believe and hope for, according to God's own showing.

But patience, beloved brethren, not only, keeps watch over what is good, but it also repels what is evil. In harmony with the Holy Spirit, and associated with what is heavenly and divine, it struggles with the defence of its strength against the deeds of the flesh and the body, wherewith the soul is assaulted and taken. Let us look briefly into a few things out of many, that from a few the rest also may be understood. Adultery, fraud, manslaughter, are mortal crimes. Let patience be strong and steadfast in the heart; and neither is the sanctified body and temple of God polluted by adultery, nor is the innocence dedicated to righteousness stained with the contagion of fraud; nor, after the Eucharist carried in it, is the hand spotted with the sword and blood.[515]

What is more, argues Cyprian, patience is essential to 'charity' (i.e. Christian love):

Charity is the bond of brotherhood, the foundation of peace, the holdfast and security of unity, which is greater than both hope and faith, which excels both good works and martyrdoms, which will abide with us always, eternal with God in the kingdom of heaven. Take from it patience; and deprived of it, it does not endure. Take from it the substance of bearing and of enduring, and it continues with no roots nor strength.[516]

Finally, Cyprian sums up the argument of his treatise by exclaiming:

[515] Cyprian, *On the Good of Patience,* 13-14, pp.487-488.
[516] Cyprian., *On the Good of Patience*, 15, p.487.

...let us hold fast with full watchfulness the patience whereby we abide in Christ, that with Christ we may attain to God; which patience, copious and manifold, is not restrained by narrow limits, nor confined by strait boundaries. The virtue of patience is widely manifest, and its fertility and liberality proceed indeed from a source of one name, but are diffused by overflowing streams through many ways of glory; nor can anything in our actions avail for the perfection of praise, unless from this it receives the substance of its perfection. It is patience which both commends and keeps us to God. It is patience, too, which assuages anger, which bridles the tongue, governs the mind, guards peace, rules discipline, breaks the force of lust, represses the violence of pride, extinguishes the fire of enmity, checks the power of the rich, soothes the want of the poor, protects a blessed integrity in virgins, a careful purity in widows, in those who are united and married a single affection. It makes men humble in prosperity, brave in adversity, gentle towards wrongs and contempts. It teaches us quickly to pardon those who wrong us; and if you yourself do wrong, to entreat long and earnestly. It resists temptations, suffers persecutions, perfects passions and martyrdoms. It is patience which firmly fortifies the foundations of our faith. It is this which lifts up on high the increase of our hope. It is this which directs our doing, that we may hold fast the way of Christ while we walk by His patience. It is this that makes us to persevere as sons of God, while we imitate our Father's patience.[517]

Lactantius *The Divine Institutes*

As we saw in Chapter 2, Lactantius' *The Divine Institutes* was a systematic defence and exposition of Christian teaching in response to its pagan critics.

In this work Lactantius refers to patience (*patientia*) over 150 times, referring to it as the 'greatest of all the virtues.'[518] He defines patience

---

[517] Cyprian, *On the Good of Patience*, 20, pp.489-90.
[518] Lactantius, *The Divine Institutes,* VI: XVIII, p.184.

as 'the bearing with equanimity of the evils which are either inflicted or happen to fall upon us,'[519] and echoing Tertullian and Cyprian he declares that the reason why the 'supreme Father' ordered his Son 'to descend to the earth, and to put on a human body was that 'He might teach virtue and patience not only by words, but also by deeds.'[520]

According to Lactantius, patience is an integral part of the 'heavenly way' which Christians are called to walk. This way is:

...set forth as difficult and hilly, or rough with dreadful thorns, or entangled with stones jutting out; so that everyone must walk with the greatest labour and wearing of the feet, and with great precautions against falling. In this he [God] has placed justice, temperance, patience, faith, chastity, self-restraint, concord, knowledge, truth, wisdom, and the other virtues; but together with these, poverty, ignominy, labour, pain, and all kinds of hardship. For whoever has extended his hope beyond the present, and chosen better things, will be without these earthly goods, that, being lightly equipped and without impediment, he may overcome the difficulty of the way. For it is impossible for him who has surrounded himself with royal pomp, or loaded himself with riches, either to enter upon or to persevere in these difficulties.[521]

Walking this tough road with God's assistance, a Christian will therefore be:

...poor, humble, ignoble, subject to injury, and yet enduring all things which are grievous; and if he shall continue his patience unceasingly to that last step and end, the crown of virtue will be given to him, and he will be rewarded by God with immortality for

---

[519] Lactantius, *The Divine Institutes,* V: XXIII, p.159.
[520] Lactantius, *The Epitome of the Divine Institutes,* p.239.
[521] Lactantius, *The Divine Institutes,* VI: IV, p.165.

the labours which he has endured in life for the sake of righteousness.[522]

Lactantius goes on to say that Christians are called to be people who engage in mutual assistance, speak the truth, are content with what they have, do not engage in usury, act mercifully, and do not seek to revenge themselves when injury is done to them, preferring to leave their cause in the hands of God.

Such non-retaliation will lead Christians to be 'an object of contempt to all' on the grounds that they are slothful 'slothful and inactive.'[523] However, such non-retaliation is in fact the mark of a truly good man. The Roman writer Cicero did not go far enough when he stated that the 'good man ... injures no one, unless provoked by injury.'[524] What Cicero failed to see was that: 'he must necessarily lose the name of a good man from this very circumstance, if he shall inflict injury.' This is because:

> ...it is not the part of a wise and good man to wish to contend, and to commit himself to danger, since to conquer is not in our power, and every contest is doubtful; but it is the part of a wise and excellent man not to wish to remove his adversary, which cannot be done without guilt and danger, but to put an end to the contest itself, which may be done with advantage and with justice. Therefore, patience is to be regarded as a very great virtue; and that the just man might obtain this, God willed, as has been before said, that he should be despised as sluggish. For unless he shall have been insulted, it will not be known what fortitude he has in restraining himself. Now if, when provoked by injury, he has begun to follow up his assailant with violence, he is overcome. But if he shall have repressed that emotion by reasoning, he altogether has command over himself: he is able to rule himself. And this restraining of oneself is rightly named patience, which single virtue is opposed to all vices and affections. This recalls the disturbed and

[522] Lactantius, *The Divine Institutes*, VI: IV, p.165.
[523] Lactantius, *The Divine Institutes* VI: XVIII, pp.183-184.
[524] Lactantius, *The Divine Institutes,* VI: XVIII, p.184.

wavering mind to its tranquillity; this mitigates, this restores a man to himself. Therefore, since it is impossible and useless to resist nature, so that we are not excited at all; before, however, the emotion bursts forth to the infliction of injury, as far as is possible let it be calmed in time. God has enjoined us not to let the sun go down upon our wrath, [Ephesians 4:26] lest he should depart as a witness of our madness.[525]

A final point to note is that according to Lactantius one of the reasons that God allows Christians to be persecuted is that the perseverance shown by Christians in the face of persecution leads many who are not yet Christians to turn to God:

There is also another cause why He [God] permits persecutions to be carried on against us, that the people of God may be increased. Nor is it difficult to show why or how this happens. First of all, great numbers are driven from the worship of the false gods by their hatred of cruelty. For who would not shrink from such sacrifices? In the next place, some are pleased with virtue and faith itself. Some suspect that it is not without reason that the worship of the gods is considered evil by so many men, so that they would rather die than do that which others do that they may preserve their life. Someone desires to know what that good is which is defended even to death, which is preferred to all things which are pleasant and beloved in this life, from which neither the loss of goods, nor of the light, nor bodily pain, nor tortures of the vitals deter them. These things have great effect; but these causes have always especially increased the number of our followers. The people who stand around hear them saying in the midst of these very torments that they do not sacrifice to stones wrought by the hand of man, but to the living God, who is in heaven: many understand that this is true, and admit it into their breast. In the next place, as it is accustomed to happen in matters of uncertainty while they make inquiry of one another, what is the cause of this perseverance, many things which relate to religion,

<hr>

[525] Lactantius, *The Divine Institutes,* VI: XVIII, p.185.

being spread abroad and carefully observed by rumour among one another, are learned; and because these are good they cannot fail to please. [526]

The perseverance in the face of persecution that formed such a powerful witness did not occur accidentally. It was the fruit of the habit of patience endurance which Christians had previously cultivated in the course of their Christian lives. Tertullian made the famous statement that persecution is a benefit to the Church because: 'The oftener we are mown down by you, the more in number we grow; the blood of Christians is seed'[527] but the point we learn from Lactantius is that this seed flourished in the soil of a pre-existent patient Christian life. It was, as Lactantius said, that life's 'last step and end.'

5. Patience as the key to the growth of the Early Church

What we have seen in the patristic texts surveyed in the previous section is that the writers of the early patristic period followed the writers of the New Testament in insisting that just as God is patient so human beings need to be patient as well. They believed that God's good purposes would be fulfilled as God's people were patient in living the Christian way of life.

What we have also seen is that the early Christians believed that it was as they lived patiently in this way that God would draw unbelievers to faith.

If we ask how the Christians of the early centuries sought to bring about the 'obedience of faith' (Romans 1:5) in an unbelieving and idolatrous world, the first thing note is that there were a number of things they did not do.

First, they made no attempt to further God's kingdom by overthrowing the existing ruling authorities, either in the Roman Empire, or in the

---

[526] Lactantius, *The Divine Institutes*, V: XXIV, pp.160-161.
[527] Tertullian, Apology, Ch. XL in in *The Ante-Nicene Fathers*, Vol. III, p.55

other territories to which Christianity spread beyond the bounds of the Roman Empire and then replacing them with Christian rulers.

They believed that any such action would be wrong in principle because they took seriously the biblical injunction to honour existing authorities that we looked at in chapter 8, and because they believed that any injustice they suffered as a result would be rectified by God at the last judgement. This meant that they paid their taxes and submitted to and prayed for those in political authority.

Justin Martyr thus speaks for the Early Church as a whole when in his *First Apology* he tells the Roman Emperor Antoninus Pius and the members of the Senate:

And everywhere we, more readily than all men, endeavour to pay to those appointed by you the taxes both ordinary and extraordinary, as we have been taught by Him; for at that time some came to Him and asked Him, if one ought to pay tribute to Cæsar; and He answered, 'Tell Me, whose image does the coin bear?' And they said, 'Cæsar's.' And again He answered them, 'Render therefore to Cæsar the things that are Cæsar's, and to God the things that are God's.' [Matthew 23:17-21] Whence to God alone we render worship, but in other things we gladly serve you, acknowledging you as kings and rulers of men, and praying that with your kingly power you be found to possess also sound judgment. But if you pay no regard to our prayers and frank explanations, we shall suffer no loss, since we believe (or rather, indeed, are persuaded) that every man will suffer punishment in eternal fire according to the merit of his deed, and will render account according to the power he has received from God, as Christ intimated when He said, 'To whom God has given more, of him shall more be required.' [Luke 12:48]. [528]

---

[528] Justin Martyr, *First Apology*, Ch XVII, p.168.

When the rulers of Edessa and Armenia converted to Christianity in the early third and the early fourth centuries respectively[529] and when the Roman Emperor Constantine became a Christian later on in the fourth century, these conversions were something that Christians welcomed as acts of God, but these were not events that Christians had either planned or expected. Unlike in the case of early Islam, for early Christianity the spread of true religion was not linked to that religion taking political control of earthly kingdoms. Christ was already the king over all nations and that was enough.

Secondly, the Christians of the early centuries also made no attempt to change the existing practices of the lands in which they dwelt by means of political activity, however much they disapproved of those practices. When rulers such as the later Roman Emperors became Christians, the leaders of the Church were happy to use their influence to try to change the religious and social practices of the Roman Empire for the better, thus establishing a tradition of Christian political involvement that changed the Western world and eventually the world as a whole for the better, but this again was not something the Christians of the Early Church planned for, or expected to happen. Instead, they saw their role as being to live patiently godly lives in world which had a very different set of values. To use the later terminology of Augustine, they sought to live as citizens of the city of God within the city of this world.

The classic statement of this position is found in chapters 5-6 of the second century *Epistle to Diognetus.* These chapters declare that while Christians:

> ...live in both Greek and barbarian cities, as each one's lot was cast, and follow the local customs in dress and food and other aspects of life, at the same time they demonstrate their remarkable and admittedly unusual character of their own citizenship. They live in their own countries but only as aliens; they participate in

[529] The story of King Agbar V of Edessa being converted in the first century by Thaddeus, one of the seventy-two disciples mentioned in Luke 10:1-24, is generally regarded as legendary.

everything as citizens, and endure everything as foreigners. Every foreign country is their fatherland, and every fatherland is forcign. They marry like everyone else, and have children, but they do not expose their offspring. They share their food but not their wives. They are in the flesh, but they do not live according to the flesh. They live on earth, but their citizenship is in heaven. They obey the established laws; indeed in their private lives they transcended the laws. They love everyone, and by everyone they are persecuted. They are unknown, yet they condemned; they are put to death, yet they are brought to life. They are poor, yet they make many rich: they are in need of everything, yet they abound in everything. They are dishonoured, yet they are glorified in their dishonour; They are slandered, yet they are vindicated. They are cursed, yet they bless; they are insulted, yet they offer respect. When they do good they are punished as evil doers; when they are punished, they rejoice as though brought to life. By the Jews there are assaulted as foreigners, and by the Greeks they are persecuted, Yet those who hate them are unable to give a reason for their hostility

In a word, what the soul is to the body, Christians are to the world. The soul is dispersed through all the members of the body, and Christians throughout cities of the world. The soul dwells in the body, but it is not of the body; likewise, Christians dwell in the world but are not of the world. The soul, which is invisible, is confined to the body, which is visible; in the same way, Christians are recognised as being in the world, and yet their religion remains The flesh hates the soul and wages war against it, even though it has suffered no wrong, because it is hindered from indulging in its pleasures; so also the world hates the Christians because they set themselves against its pleasures. The soul loves the flesh that hates it and its members, and Christians love those who hate them. The soul is enclosed in the body, but it holds the body together centre: and though Christians are detained in the world as if in a prison, they in fact hold the world together. The soul, which is immortal, lives in a mortal dwelling; similarly Christians live as strangers amid perishable things, while waiting for the imperishable in heaven. The soul, when poorly treated with respect food and drink, becomes all the better; and so Christians when punished daily increase more and more. Such is the important position to which God has appointed them, and it is not right for them to decline it.[530]

Thirdly, the Christians of the early centuries do not seem to have had anything resembling what Christians in the modern Western world would recognise as a plan for church growth. This was not because the Christians of this period did not engage in evangelism or believe in church growth. They did. We can see this, for example, in the third century Syriac text known as the *Didscalia Apostolorum* which states:

> ...we by the power of the Lord God have gathered (men) from all peoples and from all tongues, and have brought them to the Church with much labour and toil and in daily peril, that we might do the will of God and *fill the house with guests* [Mt 22.10], that is His holy Catholic Church, that they might be glad and rejoicing, and be praising and glorifying God who called them to life.

> Be you then, O laymen, peaceable one with another, and strive like wise doves to fill the Church, and to convert and tame those that are wild and bring them into her midst. And (for) this is the great reward that is promised by God: if you deliver them from fire, and present them to the Church firmly established and faithful.[531]

In this quotation we find references to both evangelism and church growth. What we do not find in this text, or in any other early Christian text, is a specific plan to grow the Church, or specific instruction about how to engage in evangelism. Nevertheless, the Church grew.

[530] *The Epistle to Diognetus*, Ch. 5.4-6.10, in Lightfoot, Harmer and Holmes, pp.299-300.

[531] *Didascalia Apostolorum,* 2:56 translation by R Hugh Conolly (Oxford: Clarendon Press 1929) at https://earlychristianwritings.com/text/didascalia.html. 'Wise doves' is reference to Jesus' command to the twelve in Matthew 10:16 to be 'wise as serpents and innocent as doves.' and 'those that are wild' are non-Christians.

The reference in both the *Epistle to Diognetus* and the *Didascalia Apostolorum* to the numerical growth of the Christian Church during its early centuries reflects all the other evidence we have, which tells us that the Church grew exponentially during this period. For example, in his book *The Rise of Christianity* the American sociologist and historian Rodney Stark argues that 40 percent per decade (or 3.42 percent per year) seems the most plausible estimate of the rate at which Christianity actually grew during the first seven centuries.'[532] This rate of growth would account for there being about 6 million Christians in 300 and approximately 33 million in 350 from a starting point of 120 Christians at Pentecost (Acts 1:15).

As Kreider observes, from a modern perspective this growth seems odd:

> According to the evidence at our disposal, the expansion of the churches was not organised, the product of a mission programme; it simply happened. Further, the growth was not carefully thought through. Early Christian leaders did not engage in debates between rival mission strategies. The Christians wrote a lot; according to classicist Robin Lane Fox, 'most of the best Greek and Latin literature which remains from the later second and third centuries is Christian.' And what they wrote is surprising. The Christian wrote treatises on patience... but they did not write a single treatise on evangelism. Further to assist their growing congregations with practical concerns, the Christians wrote church orders, manuals that provided for the life and worship of congregations. The best treatment of how a second century Christian should persuade a pagan to become a believer was published in London in 1970!

> In places where we would expect to find instructions to engage in mission - for example a growing church's catechetical materials preparing people for baptism - we look in vain for references to

[532] Rodney Stark, *The Rise of Christianity* (San Francisco: Harper and Row 1997), p.12.

evangelization. The best surviving summary of catechetical topics, Cyprian's *To Quirinius* 3, contains 120 precepts for catechumens in Carthage, but not one of them admonishes the new believers to share the gospel with the gentiles. Early Christian preachers do not appeal to the 'Great Commission' in Matthew 28:19-20 to inspire their members to make disciples of all nations; they assume that the apostles (Jesus' eleven plus Paul) had done this in the church's earliest years and that it had already been fulfilled in the church's global expansion. When writers referred to the Matthew 28: 19 -20 text, it was to buttress the doctrine of the Trinity or to address the issue of baptism, not to inspire missionary activity. [533]

As Kreider goes on to say 'there were no missionary societies at that period and no parachurch mission agencies.' Apart from Pantaenus (who is said to have evangelized in India) and Gregory the wonder worker (who evangelized in Pontus in what is now northern Turkey):

'[t]he bearers of the faith are nameless. There are no iconic missionary heroes/heroines, no self-conscious successors to Paul, until the fifth century when Patrick, the evangelist of Ireland, shows what had not been present in early centuries.' [534]

'Most improbable of all,' writes Kreider:

...the churches did not use their worship services to attract new people. In the aftermath of the persecution of Nero in AD 68, churches around the empire - at varying speeds in varying places - closed their doors to outsiders. By the end of the second century, most of them had instituted what that liturgical scholars have called the *disciplina arcani,* the discipline of the secret, which barred outsiders from entering private Christian worship services and ordered believers not to talk to outsiders about what went on

---

[533] Kreider, pp.9-10. The references that Kreider makes are to Robin Lane Fox, *Pagans and Christians* (San Francisco: Harper Row, 1986), p.270 and Michael Green, *Evangelism in the Early Church* (London: Hodder and Stoughton,1970).
[534] Kreider, pp.10-11.

behind the closed doors. Fear motivated this closing - fear of people who might disrupt their gatherings or spy on them. By the third century, some churches assigned deacons to stand at the doors, monitoring the people as they arrived. They admitted catechumens to the opening part of worship, the service of the word with its readings and sermon, but not pagans; and to the service of the Eucharist that followed the admitted neither pagans nor catechumens - only the baptised members of the community and believers from other churches with letters of recommendation... Worship services were to glorify God and edify the faithful, not to evangelise outsiders. [535]

However, as previously noted, the Church nonetheless succeeded in growing exponentially in a way that enabled it to become the dominant religious force in the Roman Empire in the fourth century and to go on to shape the history of the entire world in consequence. If we ask how this growth occurred, the answer given by Kreider is as follows:

...it was primarily because the Christians and their churches lived by a habitus that attracted others. The Christians focus was not on 'saving people' or recruiting them; it was on living faithfully -in the belief that when people's lives are re-habituated in the way of Jesus others will want to join them. This happened gradually, one person at a time, largely through face-to-face encounters and not least from parents to children. As Justin's student said to the persecuting prefect in Rome; 'I received this good faith from my parents.'

Wolfgang Reinbold has developed a model for the churches growth that I find credible.

'If the Christians raise their children as Christians and the Christian man in the course of a generation also can convince only *one* of his pagan neighbours and the Christian woman can convince only one of her pagan friends lastingly of the truth of their faith, he and she

---

[535] Kreider, pp.11-12.

had done more (!) than we must presuppose in order to build to explain the growth of the church in the first three centuries.'

Not all Christians would have done precisely this. Some would have done much more: their relational gifts and contagious faith would have led a number of their neighbours and friends to find life and healing in the Christian community. Some Christians must have done less. Some children no doubt responded positively to their parents and faith communities; others didn't. And the sources indicate people who had been members of the Christian community who for some reason dropped out. But the Christians' numbers nevertheless were on an upward trajectory - not spectacularly but by patient ferment. This, the Christians believed, was God's work and not theirs. So they did not engage in frantic action to save those who are not baptised; instead they entrusted the outsiders to God. The church, patiently, also entrusted itself to God, who would bring people into 'the community of saints participating in truth' by the arduous means of catechesis and baptism. [536]

This answer is couched in polemical language which is aimed at Michael Green's study *Evangelism in the Early Church*, which Kreider sees as viewing the approach to mission taken by the Early Church through the distorting lens of twentieth century Evangelicalism. That is why he uses the term 'saving people' in quote marks and why he says the early Christians did not engage in 'recruiting' people, or in 'frantic activity.' These are all coded ways in saying the early Christians did not act like twentieth century Evangelicals.

However, if we set aside the polemical way Kreider expresses it, the basic argument he puts forward is correct. The primary focus of the Church in the early centuries *was* on fostering a new Christian way of life (a 'habitus' to use Kreider's term) both as individuals and as a community, in the belief that if they patiently lived this kind of life the

---

[536] Kreider, pp.109-110 quoting Wolfgang Reinbold, *Propaganda und Mission im altesten Christentum* (Gottingen: Vandenhoek & Ruprecht, 2000), p.22.

faith would be handed on to the next generation in their families, and those outside the Church would be led by God to enquire about Christian belief and practice. These enquirers would then become Christians through a process involving extended and detailed catechesis and eventually baptism. They would in turn become witnesses to others and so the Church would grow.

We can see how this process worked in the case of a particular individual if we put together what is said in Pontius' account of the life of Cyprian and Cyprian's own letter to Donatus. Pontius tells us that Cyprian:

> ...had a close association among us with a just man, and of praiseworthy memory, by name Caecilius, and in age as well as in honour a presbyter, who had converted him from his worldly errors to the acknowledgement of the true divinity. This man he loved with entire honour and obedient veneration, not only as the friend and comrade of his soul, but as the parent of his new life.[537]

Cyprian himself tells Donatus:

> While I was still lying in darkness and gloomy night, wavering hither and there, tossed about on the foam of this boastful age, and uncertain of my wandering steps, knowing nothing of my real life, and remote from truth and light, I used to regard it as a difficult matter, and especially as difficult in respect of my character at that time, that a man should be capable of being born again—a truth which the divine mercy had announced for my salvation—and that a man quickened to a new life in the layer of saving water should be able to put off what he had previously been; and, although retaining all his bodily structure, should be himself changed in heart and soul. 'How,' said I, 'is such a conversion possible, that there should be a sudden and rapid divestment of all which, either innate in us has hardened in the corruption of our material nature, or acquired by

---

[537] Pontius, *The Life and Passion of Cyprian 4*, in *The Ante-Nicene Fathers*, Vol.5 p.268.

us has become inveterate by long accustomed use? These things have become deeply and radically engrained within us. When does he learn thrift who has been used to liberal banquets and sumptuous feasts? And he who has been glittering in gold and purple, and has been celebrated for his costly attire, when does he reduce himself to ordinary and simple clothing? One who has felt the charm of the fasces and of civic honours shrinks from becoming a mere private and inglorious citizen. The man who is attended by crowds of clients, and dignified by the numerous association of an officious train, regards it as a punishment when he is alone. It is inevitable, as it ever has been, that the love of wine should entice, pride inflate, anger inflame, covetousness disquiet, cruelty stimulate, ambition delight, lust hasten to ruin, with allurements that will not let go their hold.'

These were my frequent thoughts. For as I myself was held in bonds by the innumerable errors of my previous life, from which I did not believe that I could by possibility be delivered, so I was disposed to acquiesce in my clinging vices; and because I despaired of better things, I used to indulge my sins as if they were actually parts of me, and indigenous to me. But after that, by the help of the water of new birth, the stain of former years had been washed away, and a light from above, serene and pure, had been infused into my reconciled heart—after that, by the agency of the Spirit breathed from heaven, a second birth had restored me to a new man—then, in a wondrous manner, doubtful things at once began to assure themselves to me, hidden things to be revealed, dark things to be enlightened, what before had seemed difficult began to suggest a means of accomplishment, what had been thought impossible, to be capable of being achieved; so that I was enabled to acknowledge that what previously, being born of the flesh, had been living in the practice of sins, was of the earth earthly, but had now begun to be of God, and was animated by the Spirit of holiness.[538]

---

[538] Cyprian, Epistle I in *The Ante Nicene Fathers*, Vol 5, p.275.

As Michael Green explains: 'Cyprian was an aristocratic orator from Carthage; rich, cultured, but beneath it all he was very much aware of his sin and wondered if there could be any chance of a fresh start for one like himself.' [539] Then he met Caecilius who told him that Christianity provided such a chance. Caecilius led him to accept the truth of the Christian message 'the true divinity' and was his sponsor, 'the friend and comrade of his soul,' when he entered the Carthaginian catechumenate. During his catechumenate he doubted whether he could ever escape the influence of his worldly past, 'the errors of my previous life' and may have backslid into his previous vices ('indulge my sins'), but Caecilius helped him to patiently stay the course towards baptism and when Cyprian was finally baptised he received a life changing experience of the power of the Holy Spirit ('a light from above, serene and pure, had been infused into my reconciled heart).' Thereafter Cyprian himself became a witness to orthodox belief and godly behaviour as a presbyter, a bishop and finally a martyr, to numerous people in his own day, and, through his writings to countless people since.

Caecilius' patient witness to, and support of, Cyprian was thus like a pebble thrown into a pond causing ripples that have spread across the world down the centuries since. Patient witness bore fruit and helped the Church to grow.[540]

---

[539] Green, p.198.

[540] In his book *Christianizing the Roman Empire A.D. 100-400* (New Haven: Yale University Press,1984) the American historian Ramsay MacMullen puts forward the alternative argument that what led to the growth of Christianity in the period before the conversion of Constantine was the reputation that Christians came to have as exorcists and miracle workers. Although there is no doubt that both miracles and exorcism were features of the life of the Early Church, MacMullen's argument is flawed on two grounds. First, there are plenty of accounts from people like Cyprian in which the miraculous is not mentioned, and the early apologists don't make miracle working a central part of their argument for Christianity, which they surely would have done if MacMullen's argument was correct. Secondly, as Larry Hurtado points out, there were plenty of other miracle workers around in the ancient world so 'why would people commit to Christian

6. The patient evangelism of the Early Church and the teaching of the New Testament.

Although we can thus see that it bore a huge amount of fruit, for many in the Western Protestant tradition who have been taught to believe that the New Testament model for mission is for every Christian to issue the unconverted with a direct call for an immediate decision for Christ, the Early Church's patient approach can instinctively seem unbiblical. However, as Graham Tomlin argues, this reading of the New Testament is mistaken. He writes:

Why doesn't the New Testament mention evangelism much? Even the most committed evangelist, reading its pages with an open mind, has to admit that its authors hardly ever urge church members to 'get out there and tell their friends about Jesus.' People like Paul, Peter, and John preach wherever they go, found churches and evangelise like mad. But when they get around to writing to the ordinary Christians in these churches later on, they never seem to do what you'd expect them to: urge church members to be active personal evangelists. There is a lot about Christian doctrine, about the person and work of Christ, the cross, and the resurrection. There's also quite a bit about the unity of the church, personal and corporate behaviour, relationships in families, households, civic society, and the rest, but disappointingly little about evangelism *per se*...[541]

He goes on to say:

The letter to the Ephesians is a case in point. It paints a picture of God's design for creation from the beginning to its end, placing the church in the centre of the frame. Yet the Greek verb *euangelizomai*, to evangelise, is not mentioned at all. As the letter has a lot to say about the church and its pivotal place in human and divine history,

faith in particular on the basis of miracle-working, when miracles were available from other sources?' (Larry Hurtado, *Why on earth did anyone become a Christian in the first three centuries?* (Milwaukee: Marquette University Press, 2016), p.110)
[541] Graham Tomlin, *The Provocative Church*, 4ed (Cincinnati: Forward Movement, 2015), Kindle edition, p.14.9

you might expect it to have quite a bit to say about evangelism but it doesn't. The nearest it gets is Ephesians 6:19 to 20 (RSV) where Paul...asks them to pray, that utterance may be given to me in opening my mouth boldly to proclaim the mystery of the gospel...that I may declare it boldly as I ought should speak.'[542]

For Tomlin, the answer to the question 'Why doesn't Ephesians (and the rest of the New Testament) mention evangelism more often?' is that according to the New Testament:

...The Church's first task is to be what it's meant to be, to display the wisdom of God to whoever looks in from the outside. This new community is called to demonstrate by the distinctiveness of its life and the harmony created among very different people, God's variegated wisdom. The task is to learn to live the Christian life before we talk about it; to walk the walk, before we talk the talk. God has chosen to work out God's will for the world not through a bunch of individuals being sent out to persuade others to believe but by creating a new community made-up of very different people, giving them the Spirit which enables them to live together in unity, to develop a new way of life, and to live this way of life publicly. Evangelism finds its place within this context. Even though it isn't highlighted as the highest priority of every Christian, evangelists are still key figures within the local church. The role of the evangelist (Paul himself is a prime example) is to articulate on behalf of the rest of the community the invitation to come under God's rule to become part of this new humanity, to join in what God is doing. That's why Paul asked them to pray for him that he will fearlessly make known the mystery of the gospel, even though it has landed him in prison. He calls the evangelists in Ephesus to do the same -there is no sense that only apostles are entrusted with this task -as he fully expected individuals in the local church to be identified as gifted in evangelism (Ephesians 4:11)...

---

[542] Tomlin, p.130.

By and large, the letter to the Ephesians doesn't tell Christians to make a priority of getting out there and evangelising. It does tell them to love each other, to learn a new way of relating in families and at work, to gain freedom from damaging obsessions, and healthy scepticism towards the idols of the age. It tells them to develop a completely new way of living. That is the priority. And when that begins to happen, the word of the evangelist or even the simple recounting of a personal journey to faith, rings true because it connects with the reality experienced among God's people. [543]

To this the Christians of the Early Church, would, I suspect, say: 'Yes, absolutely, that is what we believed, and that is what we were trying to do all those centuries ago. We are glad to see you've got the message.'

7. Back to the future: the message about Christian witness from Tomlin, Newbiggin and McAlpine

In the penultimate section of this chapter I shall explore what it means to act as God's patient people in accordance with the teaching of the New Testament and the practice of the Early Church in relation to (a) witnessing to individuals, (b) witnessing to society as a whole and (c) witnessing in a world that increasingly thinks that orthodox Christians are the 'bad guys' as we saw in chapter 4.

I shall explore these three forms of Christian witness by looking at what Graham Tomlin, Lesslie Newbigin and Stephen McAlpine have to say about them in their books *The Provocative Church*, *The Gospel in a Pluralist Society* and *Being the Bad Guys*. What is important to note is that although these three writers have different emphases, they all agree with the New Testament and the Early Church in teaching that Christian witness in the modern world has to involve the patient activity of people whose lives individually and collectively embody the truth of the Christian message. There is no short cut to effective witness.

---

[543] Tomlin, pp.157-158.

Graham Tomlin, being provocative people

In his book *The Provocative Church* that we have just looked at, Tomlin highlights the fact that in order for the good news of Jesus Christ to be communicated effectively to people in today's world it cannot be presented in a disembodied fashion. In his words:

...contemporary culture in the West (and far beyond, if the prophets of globalization are right) has become very wary of disembodied truth. Where truth is suspected of being a mere front for power games, what lies beneath the surface of truth becomes a critical issue. In other words, the connection between the truth claim, and the kind of living that emerges from it, comes under very close scrutiny. Is this truth just another bid for power and mastery over others, just like Fascism and Marxism were, the discredited ideologies to the 20th century? Evangelism that proclaims the gospel of truth yet pays little attention to the kind of community creates or the quality of life of the people it shapes, is unlikely to be listened to for very long by those who have imbibed the postmodern suspicion of disembodied truth with their mother's milk.[544]

Furthermore, declares Tomlin, Christianity itself:

...Is just as suspicious of disembodied truth. Its truth is always embodied - that's what the incarnation means: it means God's truth and reality have become embodied within a particular human life, lived like, but unlike, all the others. When Jesus came to announce the coming of the Kingdom of God, this was a truth embodied in his own personal life and it was to be embodied in the life of the communities of the Kingdom that followed. The kingship of Jesus may from the outside sound just like another claim to mastery over others. However, this only points up the necessity, especially in this cultural setting, for an understanding of evangelism that makes it dependent on and tightly linked to the enactment of the loving rule

---

[544] Tomlin, p.62.

of Christ within the Church's own life. If human life was always meant to be lived and to flourish under God's gentle and compassionate rule, then the Church, the community of the Kingdom, has to embody that truth, to incarnate it -to use Christian language - if its proclamation is to be heard. [545]

What this approach means in terms of the Church's practice is that the leadership of the Church needs to encourage Christians to do three things, to live 'public Christian lives,' to tell 'personal stories' and to issue an invitation to find out more.[546]

In order to illustrate this point Tomlin recounts the true story of man he calls 'Simon.' Simon, he writes:

> ...once noticed his neighbour looked a little crestfallen. He stopped to ask why it was told the sad story. The neighbour plans to go on vacation the next day, but his daughter had just crashed the family car and they could no longer go. Simon then offered the use of their family car, a Volvo station waggon. The neighbour thought the offer could not possibly be serious, so he declined. But when pressed further, he gradually realised that the offer was real. Slightly amazed, he took up the offer, and the next day, drove the car in the direction of the coast, waved off by Simon and his family.

> All vacation long he could not get out of his mind the generosity of his friend, for whom the car seemed something incidental to be loaned and risked, rather than something to be guarded and kept pristine, as most people did in their neighbourhood. When he returned, he couldn't help asking why Simon had done it. The answer came back: because he was a Christian he had learned that all their possessions were not really theirs at all, but God's and were to be used generously for others as well as themselves. The neighbour was intrigued and began to ask why he had become a Christian. Simon explained the story of his own journey to faith

[545] Tomlin, p.62.
[546] Tomlin, p.140.

simply. Over the next few weeks, more discussions took place, and questions arose. Simon confessed in rather an embarrassed fashion that he wasn't that good answering them all but that his church ran a course that gave people a chance to ask any question and explore Christian faith for themselves. To cut a long story short, intrigued by this liberating approach to life and possessions, the neighbour eventually become became a Christian.[547]

Tomlin comments:

It's a simple example, but makes the point. All three of the elements mentioned above were present. Simon was willing to live a public Christian life, looking for practical ways of letting God's rule extend over his use of possessions as well as cities of Sunday mornings. He was willing to tell the story of his own journey to faith when called upon to do so. He was also fortunate enough to have a church that had a regular course running for those interested in discovering more. [548]

To use the biblical and patristic terminology that we looked at in the previous sections of this chapter, Simon lived a life of patient Christian well doing. When this attracted his friend to want to know more about the Christian faith, Simon introduced his friend to his Church's catechetical programme and the patience of those who ran this programme eventually resulted in his friend accepting the faith for himself and so God's patient purposes in the world were taken forward.

As Tomlin further explains, what this story illustrates is that bringing people to faith is not simply the task of a few talented individuals. It is something that is the work of the Church as whole. As he puts it:

While many Christians will find their evangelistic ministry arising out of their living a public Christian life and the questions arising from it, others will have real gifts in the areas of explaining,

---

[547] Tomlin, pp.140-141.
[548] Tomlin, pp.141-142.

persuading, and answering difficult questions. Another key role in the leadership of evangelistic churches is identifying such people and enabling them to use those gifts in the context of an inquirers course, or some other type of discovery group. As we have seen, few churches grow without them, and a vital part of the pattern of evangelism explained here is the provision of a place where questions can be answered and the heart of Christian faith can be explained. Simon needed somewhere he could point his neighbour when the questions emerged. It was his church leader's job to ensure that the place was there, and that Simon knew why it was there.

Not everything in church is done for evangelism purposes. Running a lunch club for lonely elderly people, a visiting programme for local disabled people, or lending a car to a disconsolate neighbour - none of these are done for evangelistic effect. They are done because they express the rule of God -this is what happens when God is in charge. Yet they all have an evangelistic dimension, as they have the potential of provoking the question, and when they are done out of Christian love and care, they often will. In this sense everything a church does has an evangelistic dimension.[549]

To put it, another way, as the Early Church knew, when everyone in the Church is patiently doing the particular tasks that God has assigned to them, then the Church will grow.[550]

[549] Tomlin, pp.145-146.

[550] If we ask where times of revival such as the Great Awakening in the eighteenth century or the Welsh Revival of 1904 fit into this picture, the answer is that what the evidence tells us is that such revivals are the result of Christians patiently living holy lives and patiently and persistently praying that God will renew his Church and save the lost. (for this see R E Davies *I will pour out my Spirit*, Tunbridge Wells: Monarch 1992 and Michael Green, *When God Breaks In*, London: Hodder and Stoughton, 2014)). Furthermore, revivals, though important sources of renewal for the Church and blessing for wider Society, are occasional in nature, whereas the more usual form of church growth is long term and incremental.

Lesslie Newbigin, proclaiming Christianity as public truth

In his chapter on 'The Congregation as Hermeneutic of the Gospel' in his book *The Gospel in a Pluralist Society*, Lesslie Newbigin contends that the Church has a bigger calling than simply the conversion of individuals, vital though this is. As he sees it:

> The Church cannot accept as its role simply the winning of individuals to a kind of Christian discipleship which concerns only the private and domestic aspects of life. To be faithful to a message which concerns the Kingdom of God, his rule over all things and all peoples, the church has to claim the high ground of public truth. Every human society is governed by assumptions, normally taken for granted without question, about what is real, what is important, what is worth aiming for. There is no such thing as an ideological vacuum. Public truth, as it is taught in schools and universities, as it is assumed in the public debate about political and economic goals, is either in conformity with the truth as it is given in Jesus Christ or it is not. Where it is not, the Church is bound to challenge it. [551]

If this is the Church's calling, the question that then follows is how the Church can give plausibility to its claim 'to provide the public truth by which society can be given coherence and direction?' [552] The answer to this question, suggests Newbigin, is that:

> ...the only answer, the only hermeneutic of the gospel, is the congregation of men and women who believe it and live by it. I am of course, not denying the importance of the many activities by which we seek to change public life with the gospel - evangelistic campaigns, distributions of bibles and Christian literature, conferences, and even books such as this one. But I am saying that these are all secondary, and that they have power to accomplish their purpose only as they are rooted in and lead back to a believing community.

[551] Lesslie Newbigin, *The Gospel in a Pluralist Society* (London: SPCK, 1989), p.222.
[552] Newbigin, p.223.

Jesus...did not write a book but formed a community. This community has at its heart, the remembering and rehearsing of his words and deeds, and the sacraments given by him through which it is enabled both to engraft new members into its life and to renew this life again and again through sharing in his risen life through the body broken and the life blood poured out. It exists in him and for him. He is the centre of its life. Its character is given to it, when it is true to its nature, not by the character of its members but by his character. Insofar as it is true to its calling, it becomes the place where men and women and children find that the gospel gives them the framework of understanding, the 'lenses' through which they are able to understand and cope with the world. [553]

According to Newbigin, this community will have six characteristics.

First, it will be 'a community of praise.' [554]This means two things. It means that it will be a community: 'where people find their true freedom, their true dignity, and their true equality in reverence to the One who is worthy of all the praise we can offer.'[555] It means it will also be a community 'that acknowledges that it lives by the amazing grace of boundless kindness.' [556] While our modern society emphasizes rights and prefers to talk of justice instead of charity:

...In Christian worship we acknowledge that if we had received justice instead of charity we would be on our way to perdition. A Christian congregation is thus a body of people with gratitude to spare, a gratitude that can spill over into care for the neighbour. And is of the essence of the matter that this concern for the neighbour is the overflow of a great gift of grace and not primarily,

---

[553] Newbigin, p.227.
[554] Newbigin, p.228.
[555] Newbigin, p.228.
[556] Newbigin, p.228.

the expression of a commitment to a moral crusade. There is a big difference between these two.[557]

Secondly, 'it will be 'a community of truth.'[558] What this means is that:

A Christian congregation is a community it went through the constant remembering and rehearsing of the true story of human nature and destiny, I'm attitude of healthy scepticism can be sustained, a scepticism which enables one to take part in the life of society without being bemused and deluded by its own beliefs about itself. And, if congregation is to function effectively as a community of truth, its manner of speaking the truth must not be aligned to the techniques of modern propaganda, but must have the modesty, the sobriety and the realism which are proper to a disciple of Jesus.[559]

Thirdly, it will be:

...a community that does not live for itself but is deeply involved in the concerns of its neighbourhood. It will be the church for the specific place where it lives, not the church for those who wish to be members of it – or, rather, it will be for them insofar as they are willing to be *for* the wider community.[560]

The two errors that need to be avoided if this to be the case are (a) that 'the congregation may be so identified with the place that it ceases to be the vehicle of God's judgement and mercy to that place and becomes simply the self-image of the people of that place. Or (b) that 'it may be so concerned about the relation of its members to God that it turns its back on its neighbourhood and is perceived as irrelevant to is concerns.'[561]

---

[557] Newbigin, p.228.
[558] Newbigin, p.228.
[559] Newbigin, p.229.
[560] Newbigin, p.229.
[561] Newbigin, p.229.

Fourthly, it will be: '...a community where men and women are prepared for and sustained in the exercise of the priesthood in the world.'[562] According to the New Testament:

> The office of a priest is to stand before God on behalf of people and to stand before people on behalf of God. Jesus is himself the one High Priest who alone can fulfil and has fulfilled this role. The Church is sent into the world to continue that which he came to do, in the power of the same Spirit, reconciling people to God (John 20:19-23). [563]

The exercise of this priestly ministry by the Church, writes Newbigin:

> ...Is not within the walls of the Church but in the daily business of the world. It is only in this way that the public life of the world, its accepted habits and assumptions, can be changed by the gospel and brought under the searching light of the truth as it has been revealed in Jesus. It may indeed be the duty of the Church through its appointed representatives -bishops and synods and assemblies - to speak a word from time to time to the nation and the world. But such pronouncements carry weight only when they are validated by the way in which Christians are actually behaving and using their influence in public life.[564]

The fact that the Church has the calling to exercise a priestly ministry in this way means two further things, declares Newbigin:

    a.   The congregation has to be the place where its members are trained, supported and nourished in the exercise of their parts of the priestly ministry in the world. The preaching and teaching of the local church has to be such that it enables them

---

[562] Newbigin, p.229.
[563] Newbigin, p.230.
[564] Newbigin, p.230.

to think out the problems that face them in their secular work in the light of their Christian faith. [565]

b. ...a Christian congregation must recognize that God gives different gifts to different members of the body...Only when a congregation can rejoice in gifts which others have been given, can the whole body function as Christ's royal priesthood in the world. [566]

Fifthly, it will be a community whose members exercise 'mutual responsibility.' The root of the problems facing modern Western society is:

...an individualism which denies the fundamental reality of our human nature as given by God – namely that we grow into true humanity only in relationships of faithfulness and responsibility toward one another. The local congregation is called to be, and by the grace of God often is, such a community of mutual responsibility. When it is such, it stands in the wider community of the neighbourhood and the nation not primarily as the promoter of programmes for social change (although it will be that) but primarily as itself the foretaste of a different social order. Its members will be advocates for human liberation by being themselves liberated. [567]

Sixthly, it will be: 'a community of hope.' One of the striking features of modern Western culture is the absence of hope. By contrast: 'the gospel offers an understanding of the human situation which makes it possible to be filled with a hope that is eager and patient even in the most hopeless situations.'[568]

In summary, declares Newbigin:

---

[565] Newbigin, p.231.
[566] Newbigin, p.231.
[567] Newbigin, p.231.
[568] Newbigin, p.232.

If the gospel is to change the public life of our society, if Christians are to occupy the 'high ground' which they vacated in the noon time of 'modernity,' it will not be by forming a Christian political party, or by aggressive propaganda campaigns. Once again it has to be said that there can be no going back to the Constantinian era. It will only be by movements that begin with the local congregation in which the reality of the new creation is present, known, and experienced, and from which men and women will go into every sector of public life to claim it for Christ, to unmask the illusions which have remained hidden and to expose all areas of public life to the illumination of the gospel. But that will only happen as and when local congregations renounce an introverted concern for their own life, and recognise that they exist for the sake of those who are not members, as sign, instrument, and foretaste of God's redeeming grace for the whole of society. [569]

Stephen McAlpine, how to be the best possible bad guys

As we saw in chapter 4, according to Stephen McAlpine, Christians are widely seen as the 'bad guys' by contemporary Western society. As he goes on to write, the challenge this raises for Christians is not 'how to stop being one of the bad guys.' This is because:

...the only way to stop being a bad guy in the eyes of the world is to become what the world says is a good guy. And right now that means compromising in all kinds of ways where the world beckons one way and the Bible points another.[570]

The challenge is instead 'how to be the best bad guy you can be,'[571] or as the subtitle of his book puts it 'How to live for Jesus in a world that says you shouldn't.'

In part three of his book, McAlpine sketches out what he thinks this means in practice in relation to three topics, a strategy for the Church, a

[569] Newbigin, p.233.
[570] McAlpine, p.11.
[571] McAlpine, p.11.

strategy for Christians in the workplace, and a general strategy for how Christians should live as citizens of an alternative city within the city of this world.

On the topic of a strategy for the Church, McAlpine suggests that just as the Jews in Judaea in the time of the Persian empire were called by the prophet Haggai to complete the re-building of the temple in Jerusalem, so Christians today are called to build up the life of the Church. As he sees it, there are three parts to this calling.

First, Christians are called to 'Preference God's people' [572] What this means is that:

> We are to cultivate Christian communities in which our common characteristic is Jesus. A sure-fire apologetic for the church is its ability to create deep community across social and cultural boundaries. As Western cultures fracture into toxic tribalism it's crucial for churches to form deep, thick communities, based around more than convenience.[573]

In order to cultivate such communities:

> We need to do life together - church services, meals, times of *ad hoc* gathering in which conversations are sprinkled with grace. This is what will challenge a culture in which it is taken for granted that creating a fantastic career edifice, building a trophy cabinet of holiday and lifestyle experiences, or spending time, energy and money on self-actualising projects are paramount.

This is not about keeping Christians busy. It's about first defining ourselves as the gathered people of God and then shaping our lives around that commitment. It will mean sharing meals with people

[572] McAlpine, p.98.
[573] McAlpine, pp.98-99.

when it's easier not to. Sharing more of your finances with those who have less. Sharing more of *you* when you're tired or grumpy. [574]

Secondly, 'the church must...rediscover its core practice of proclaiming the praises of God.'[575] Specifically, this means that Christians need to focus on the person and work of Jesus. This is because:

Without Jesus we have no compelling reason to offer any vision for human flourishing beyond what the world already has. Our arguments for a Christian social and sexual ethic sound to some little more than desire to regain power. But Jesus' resurrection ushered in a new ethic. Our hope for the culture is not the image of Adam and Eve in the garden but the image of Jesus in the new creation.

That's why, both personally and in community, we should make much of praising Jesus and focusing on what he has done for us. Sure, we can spend time planning and talking about what we can do for him - but those things can only spring from our all and wonder at his grace for us. And then from letting that everyday praise make its way into our everyday conversation.[576]

Furthermore, argues McAlpine:

If we are focused on Jesus we will not become self-entitled or embittered Christians who play the victim card and get angry when society pushes against us. We will instead be filled with joy. When we don't join the cheers when our cultural enemies *lose* a battle, or when we don't shout angrily at them when they *win* a battle, it will only be because Jesus is our hope and joy -and he is our example of what it looks like to entrust yourself to the one who judges justly (1 Peter 2 v23). [577]

---

[574] McAlpine, pp.99-100.
[575] McAlpine, p.100.
[576] McAlpine, p.103.
[577] McAlpine, 104. Italics in the original.

Thirdly, Christians must 'Promote God's promises.'[578] The reason they must do this is because:

> ...there's currently an openness to the gospel message in our society, despite the hostility. Historic levels of anxiety, fear and loneliness abound. The church is a community of promised resurrection hope in a society that is terrified of death and anxious about missing out on the good stuff that advertising offers. We have something which many in the world's want but cannot find. It may not always feel as though this is true, but it is true nonetheless.[579]

As McAlpine goes on to explain:

> The church is the temple of God, headed for a glory we cannot even imagine. For the moment that description of the church may not feel true. It may not feel plausible. But because of God's future resurrection promise, it is. So we can serve a needy world in costly ways because we know the future! We can serve a world that scorns and reject us; we can be known as those who add value to our communities through resources, volunteering, social concern, financial support and professional *pro bono* work, because we look to God's promises. Churches which lovingly serve communities that are suspicious of them reveal where their hope lies. They rouse the curiosity of those who reject their message yet benefit from the outworking of their hope.[580]

What this means in practice is that:

> Whatever you do, leave your community a little bit better than the way you found it. Why? Because God has promised a new creation. We have the mandate to showcase that new creation now, in fractured but real ways, as we await its fulfilment. We can assess the brokenness of our location or end of it and investigate what

---

[578] McAlpine, p.104.
[579] McAlpine, p.104.
[580] McAlpine, pp.105-106.

pressures people in our area are likely to be under, and prayerfully respond to these things.[581]

On the topic of a strategy for Christians in the workplace, McAlpine explains that Christians in the workplace today need to follow the way in which: 'Daniel exhibited three distinct qualities that that enabled him to honour God in a hostile workplace: he was faithful, faultless and fearless.'[582] These qualities shown by Daniel provide 'a template for us as we face increasingly complex ethical situations in our own lives.'[583]

McAlpine suggests that in order for Christians to remain faithful to God in our workplaces like Daniel did two things need to happen. First, he writes, if you are a church leader then you need to:

> ...prepare your people for the week *they* will be having, not the week *you* will be having. The vast majority of their time is spent with work, study and family: places where ethical pressures arise. Have you created a preaching, discipleship, and pastoral care strategy that will support and guide them when the office, shop or kitchen table becomes a hostile battleground? Can you point them to books, courses or conferences that will help? Do you pray regularly for and with them about these pressures? A crucial task of the modern pastor is to prepare people for life in Babylon, Monday to Saturday (and increasingly Sunday!) [584]

Secondly, 'if you're out in the trenches, then you need to engage in a regular pattern of self-examination' that involves considering your private life, your prayer life, what you watch and what you read, your response to criticism, the importance of work and whether you find your justification 'in Jesus rather than in your job description, pay scale

---

[581] McAlpine, p.10.
[582] McAlpine, p.113.
[583] McAlpine, p.113.
[584] McAlpine, p.114. Italics in the original.

or career opportunities?'[585] In addition, you need to form a support group of fellow church members:

...In which together you can explore the principles that you will abide by when the pressure comes. What can you bend on without compromise? Where is the give and take? What will you hold the line on? You need to discuss and establish boundaries before the situations turn up, so that your response is reflexive, not reactive. [586]

On the issue of being faultless, McAlpine suggests that this involves not just what we won't do (the sort of conscientious objection we looked at in chapter 8) but also what we choose to do:

If, after refusing to be swayed on ethical matters, you are scorned, disciplined, demoted, or even let go from your job, it must be in spite of the way that you live, not because of it. We must cultivate exemplary, grace filled and generous lives that challenge any allegation that our beliefs lead us to be mean-spirited, hostile and dangerous. [587]

On the issue of being fearless, McAlpine declares that the key thing is to have the right view of God and other people, understanding that because God is big, we do not need to fear other people and that other people are just like us 'with all the same sorts of fears, hopes and dreams we have.' [588] If we have this right view of God and other people, we will then be people who can obey God fearlessly and answer other people lovingly when we are challenged about our faith.

In order to have this right view of God and others, declares McAlpine, we need to begin by attending a church:

[585] McAlpine, p.115.
[586] McAlpine, p.115.
[587] McAlpine, 117.
[588] McAlpine, p.118.

...in which God's bigness is front and centre, and his salvation plan through Christ for all of creation is explained and celebrated. You'll know if that's the case in your church by how people are treated, especially the broken, the annoying, the plain weird, the single, the same sex attracted. Are they projects to be involved with or family to belong to? Are these people seen as being of the same size as the wealthy impressive and good looking?[589]

The attitudes we learn in this sort of church will then:

...flow over into all of life. The gay-activist colleague and the anti - Christian fellow teacher are first and foremost made in the image of a big God. It may be that no answer you give about such matters, save fully agreeing with them, will make you anything but small in their eyes. But don't get in first. If they are to despise you it must be in spite of what the rest of your life looks like. [590]

McAlpine concludes his call to be faithful, faultless, and fearless by noting that if we have these qualities, we may:

...like Daniel...be thrown to the lions – cultural ones. You may lose your job, your influence your status. You may even lose your friends and the approval of your family, no matter how lovingly you explain yourself. Your honour and respect for your opponent may not be reciprocated.[591]

Nevertheless, even if this does happen, we can still have hope because:

...Jesus' resurrection has ushered in a new age. We have not received it fully yet, but the Spirit's down payment means that we're guaranteed that scorn, disgrace and being sidelined are not the end.

[589] McAlpine, p.121.
[590] McAlpine, p.121.
[591] McAlpine, p.122.

Not long ago, a friend of mine questioned the progressive sexual public programme being pushed at his workplace. A fairly senior public servant, he was forced to move departments in order to be able to continue working. His response has been to maintain love and respect for colleagues, all the while knowing that his vindication will one day come from Jesus. And in spite of the long-term trouble and upheaval it caused, he was filled with joy. Daniel's strategy – faithful, faultless and fearless - really does work.[592]

On the topic of living as citizens of the city of God in the midst of the city of this world, McAlpine contends that the key to Christians doing this successfully is first of all to address our own behaviour:

The key is this: are we proclaiming the gospel message, and practising the gospel ethic it demands, among ourselves first? Now is the time to get our own city in order. If refugees from the culture wars and the secular age realise that the way we deal with sin, or the way we practise forgiveness, or look after the single mother, is completely different to the city they have known all their lives -and much more likely to lead to flourishing than anything from that city – they will clamour to escape and become citizens of the new city.

Not that we need to be perfect. Acknowledging our failures is one reason why we gather as the church: we proclaim the gospel of repentance and forgiveness to each other, committing ourselves to God again and making ourselves ready to go out into the world. Then we do it again next week. Every church gathering is a mini withdrawal from the world, in order to return to the world ready for a fresh attempt to live out the gospel ethic.[593]

As McAlpine sees it:

We're at a critical juncture. We must future proof ourselves. So creating alternative education systems which are not hostile to the

[592] McAlpine, pp.122-123.
[593] McAlpine, pp.136-137.

gospel for example, is a good idea. However, engagement with the culture should continue. If we are to establish alternative institutions and workplaces that operate around the Christian ethic, we must not do so just for ourselves. There are plenty of non-Christian neighbours and professionals who will also be worn out by the secular culture and seeking an alternative.

A day may come when many public roles and private jobs are no longer open to us; But let's stay engaged while we can. While our viewpoint and actions are still legal, let's be brave enough to express and enact them. And then when we can't, or we are driven out, let's encourage and support each other, seeking creative ways to flourish – way that will give meaning and plausibility to our citizenship of a new city. [594]

In his 'Afterword' McAlpine concludes his book by saying that rather than giving into despair we should:

...accept that this time and this place in history, we might we just might have to put up with being the bad guys. And that can drive you back into the community of God's people and to all the richness that dwells there, thanks to the unity gifted to it by the Holy Spirit. You can refuse to allow the atomising nature of modern individualism to get its grip on you and pull you away from God's people. And you can go forward together to engage with the world bravely and courageously and with love and concern: to continue to be all that Jesus has called us to be even when all the world sees is a black hat coming in his direction, and humbly but resolutely to hold out a different story, and a better way and a happier ending.[595]

8. Patiently passing on the faith to the next generation

When thinking about evangelism and church growth there be a tendency to focus on the conversion of those outside the Christian community. It is vital that this happen, but it is equally vital that

[594] McAlpine, pp.137-18.
[595] McAlpine, p.140.

Christians bring up their children to believe and practice the Christian faith.

As we have already seen when looking at the evidence from the early centuries of the Church, part of the reason that the Church grew was because the early Christians passed on the faith to the children of the Christian community. As Stark argues, the early Christians seem to have had a higher rate of fertility than their pagan neighbours, due in part to their rejection of abortion and infanticide.[596] In addition, Christians also adopted babies that non-Christians had left to die of exposure. This meant that there were a large number of children in the Church and the Church baptised them[597] and patiently brought them up in the Christian faith, thus creating a new generation of Christian believers.

We can see evidence for this process at work in New Testament times in 2 Timothy 1:5 where Paul tells Timothy: 'I am reminded of your sincere faith, a faith that dwelt first in your grandmother Lois and your mother Eunice and now, I am sure, dwells in you.' In the words of John Kelly: 'Paul's point is that, just as his own religious life had powerful family roots, so Timothy's was grounded in that of his mother and grandmother.' [598]

Another example comes from the record of the interrogation of Justin Martyr and his students by the Roman prefect Rusticus in the mid second century. Although Justin himself had been converted to Christianity from paganism, to quote Kreider:

> ...several of the students responded by expressing their indebtedness to their parents. 'I listened gladly to the teaching of Justin' said Evelpistus, 'but I also received my faith from my parents [in Cappadocia].' Another student, Paeon, similarly said that he

---

[596] Stark pp.122-128
[597] For the evidence for the baptism of infants from New Testament times onwards see Joachim Jeremias, *Infant baptism in the first four centuries* (London: SCM, 1960).
[598] John Kelly, *The Pastoral Epistles* (London: A&C Black, 1986), p.157.

received his faith from his parents. And a third, Hierax, simply said, 'I have long been a Christian and ever shall be.' To be sure their Christian faith could be deepened and refined, which was Justin's work, but it was rooted in the lives of their families and local churches whose task it was to 'discipline their children in the reverential fear of God.' [599]

It is important to note the last point made in this quotation, which is that it not the responsibility of the parents alone, but of the parents and the church together to teach children to accept and grow in the Christian faith. As Mark Griffiths notes, this recognition of a dual responsibility in this matter is a Christian continuation of the teaching of the Old Testament in Deuteronomy 6:5-7 and 11:18-19 in which it is laid down that it is the responsibility of both the *bayit* or family and the *mishpachah* or wider community to teach the faith to the next generation.[600] Down the centuries the Christian Church has continued to believe in this dual responsibility, which is why in the Church of England's *Book of Common Prayer*, for example, it is seen as the responsibility of parents, godparents and the Church's ministers to see that children are 'brought up in the fear and nurture of the Lord, and to the praise of his holy Name.' [601] and as we saw in chapter 7 this call to engage in the catechesis of children and young people still exists today.

It is now sometimes argued that it is inappropriate, and indeed abusive, to seek to raise children to accept the Christian faith since this is a form of indoctrination that fails to respect their right to personal autonomy in belief and behaviour. The Christian response to this argument is that no form of child rearing is ideologically neutral. All children will in fact be brought up to accept some givens in terms of belief and behaviour. Furthermore, since accepting and patiently living out the Christian faith is the only means by which human beings can fully flourish in the life

[599] Kreider, p.103 citing *Acts of Justin*, 4, Recension B, in Herbert Musrillo (ed), *The Acts of the Christian Martyrs* (Oxford: Clarendon Press, 1972), pp.50-51 and Polycarp, *To the Philippians* 4 and *Didache* 4.9.
[600] Mark Griffiths, in *Faith at Home* (Cambridge: Grove Books, 2024) pp.6-8.
[601] *The Book of Common Prayer*, 'The Form of Solemnization of Matrimony.'

and the next it is in fact not only permissible, but a positive responsibility, to seek to patiently and non-coercively persuade children to embrace Christianity for themselves. [602]

A final point to note is that in our society at the moment this responsibility will need to include teaching children that to be a Christian is to be a dissident. In chapter 7 we saw that Yuri Sipko's family taught him that to be a Baptist Christian meant refusing to become part of the Communist Young Pioneers movement. In similar fashion Christians need to teach their children today that to be a Christian means to say 'No' to numerous ideas and forms of behaviour that they will encounter at school, among their friends, on television or online and to be prepared to patiently go on saying 'No' to them even when it is very difficult to do so.

---

[602] It is also worth noting that worth noting that there is legal recognition of the right of parents to raise their children according to their own faith in any number of documents, for example the UN Convention on the Rights of the Child, the European Convention on Human Rights (Protocol 1, Article 2) or Article 8 when taken in conjunction with Article 9 (the younger the child, the more intimately their Article 9 rights will be tied to those of their parents), and Article 5 of the UN Declaration on the Elimination on All Forms of Intolerance and of Discrimination Based on Religion.

Chapter 10
In conclusion

In this book I have done five things.

First, in chapters 1-3 I have explained how the Christian belief in freedom of religion, based on the teaching of the Bible about God's freedom and the freedom he has given to his human creatures, led to the principle of freedom of religion becoming enshrined in international and national law in the years following the Second World War.

Secondly, in chapter 4 I have also explained that in spite of freedom of religion having formal legal protection it is under attack across the world today, with Christians being the world's most persecuted religious community.

Thirdly, in chapters 4-5 I have noted that attacks on Christian freedom are growing in the Western World, and that this is linked to a process of historical development in Western society since the seventeenth century that has resulted in Christians now being increasingly widely seen as the 'bad guys.'

Fourthly, in chapters 6 and 7 I have argued that this pattern of historical development has to be seen in theological terms as being a result of the Devil distorting the positive effects of the influence of Christianity in Western society and that in spite of the growing hostility to orthodox Christianity that has been the result of this Christians still possess the God given freedom to live in the ways that he wants them to live.

Fifthly, in chapters 8 and 9 I have argued that living in the way that God wants them to live involves Christians living lives marked by a conscientious refusal to act in ways that contravenes God's will for his human creatures as summarised in the Ten Commandments. I have also argued that in addition Christians need to be vocal in calling for freedom of religion and active in working with non-Christians for the common good. Finally, I have argued that Christians today need to copy the example of the Christians of the early centuries of the Church by responding to the patience of God by living lives of patient Christian holiness which will commend the Christian faith to those who are currently unbelievers and so cause the Church to grow, drawing on the works of Graham Tomlin, Lesslie Newbigin and Stephen McAlpine to illustrate what such patient holiness should look like in practice today.

What is important to note in conclusion is that I am not arguing that if we follow the pattern of Christian activity seen in the Early Church, and updated by writers such as Tomlin, Newbigin and McAlpine we will see sudden and massive Church growth leading to the end of attacks on Christian religious freedom in Western society.

God being sovereign, that might happen. However, in his wise patience God may have decided that this is not the right thing to happen and that he wishes the Church in the West to continue to endure hostility and widespread Institutional decline for a period known only to him. The fact is that we do we do not know in specific detail what God's immediate plans are for the Western Church anymore that we know the date of Jesus' coming in glory to judge the living and the dead (Matthew 24:36).

If the argument of this book has been right and Christians need to learn to be patient people, then part of what this means is learning to live with ignorance about God's specific plans for the future and learning to live patiently with whatever circumstances he has decided to send our way.

It may be that Justin Brierley is right to suggest that: 'Matthew Arnold's long withdrawing Sea of Faith is beginning to reach its farthest limit and that we may yet see the tide of faith coming rushing back in in our lifetime' and that: 'we are seeing the first fruits of the returning tide in the lives and stories of a number of public intellectuals who are finding themselves surprised by the continuing resonance of the Christian story.' [603] On the other hand, such intellectual converts may remain exceptional, and the prevailing social imaginary may remain secular and indifferent or even hostile to Christianity. Only time will tell.

The key point to grasp, however, is that, whatever happens, the commission given by Jesus to his Church will remain the same: 'Go therefore and make disciples of all nations, baptizing them in the name of the Father, the Son and the Holy Spirit, teaching them to observe all that I have commanded you' (Matthew 28:19-20). The Church's permanent calling is to create not simply nominal converts or adherents, but disciples, men and women from all nations who have been grafted into the life of the Triune God through baptism and who have been taught to observe the commandments of Jesus (which in context means the teaching of the Old Testament Scriptures as interpreted and applied by Jesus and witnessed to by the Gospels and the other New Testament writings).

Fulfilling this commission will involve the members of the Church, both clergy and laity, doing a number of things.

First, regardless of the approval or disapproval of the surrounding culture, the members of the Church must remain steadfast in their commitment to the teachings of the Old and New Testament Scriptures and to those teachings of the Fathers and subsequent Christian writers that bear faithful witness to these teachings. It is only those who already belong to the Church continue to be committed to these teachings that the Church will be in a position to teach the commandments of Jesus to new disciples.

Secondly, members of the Church must live lives of patient and distinctive Christian holiness that will attract those outside the Church to find out more about what Christians believe and why. Living in this

---

[603] Justin Brierley, *The Surprising Rebirth of Belief in God* (Carol Stream: Tyndale Elevate, 2024), Kindle edition p.4. The public intellectuals whom he names are Jordan Peterson, Douglas Murray and Tom Holland.

way may involve Christians patiently and lovingly refusing to do things that the law or the prevailing culture commands or expects them to do.

Thirdly, as well as running enquirers courses such as *Alpha* and *Christianity Explored* and making use of modern apologetic works that are the equivalent of the work of the apologists of the Early Church, members of the Church must be diligent in patiently explaining in detail to their children and young people, and to adults who are new to the faith, what the Christian faith teaches and what it requires in terms of godly behaviour. Good examples of the topics that such catechesis needs to cover can be found in the list of catechetical topics found in Cyprian's letter to Quirinius (Appendix 1), the Large and Small Catechisms of Martin Luther and in the ACNA catechism *To be a Christian*.

Fourthly, this catechetical activity must be supplemented by preaching that week by week expounds the teaching of the Old and New Testament Scriptures and shows how it applies to the day to day lives of Christian believers in the particular circumstances which the Church faces today.

Fifthly, those members of the Church who have pastoral authority must make use of it in both disciplining those who have disobeyed the commandments of Christ and in restoring to fellowship those who have repented of their disobedience. In the words of Dietrich Bonhoeffer:

If the Church refuses to face the stern reality of sin, it will gain no credence when it talks of forgiveness. Such a Church sins against its sacred trust and walks unworthily of the gospel. It is an unholy Church squandering the precious treasure of the lord's forgiveness. Nor is it enough simply to deplore in general terms that the sinfulness of man infects even his good works. It is necessary to point out concrete sins, and to punish and condemn them. This is the proper use of the *power of the keys* (Matt.16.19: 18,18: John 20.23) which the Lord bequeathed to his church. Even the Reformers laid great emphasis on this power. It is essential for the Church to exercise it, for the sake of holiness, for the sake of the sinner and for its own sake. If the Church is to walk worthily of the gospel, part of its duty will be to maintain ecclesiastical discipline. Sanctification means driving out the world from the Church, as well as separating the Church from the world.

But the purpose of such discipline is not to establish a community of the perfect, but a community consisting of men who really live under the forgiving mercy of God. Discipline in a congregation is a servant of the precious grace of God. If a member of the Church falls into sin, he must be admonished and punished, lest be forfeit his own salvation and the gospel be discredited. [604]

Sixthly, members of the Church should be persistently and patiently praying for God to send seasons of revival such as the Great Awakening in the eighteenth century, or the Welsh revival of 1904, since historically such seasons have led to the creation of numerous new disciples and have had a beneficial effect on society as a whole.

Finally, the members of the Church need always to bear in mind that the Church is ultimately Christ's Church. He has promised to build it and he will do so. Christians may not be able to understand what Christ is doing to build his Church at a particular time and in a particular place, but that is not important. What is important is that they patiently do what he has told them to do and trustingly leave the rest to him. In the words of Bonhoeffer in a sermon on Matthew 16:13-18 preached on 23 July 1933 in the face of the appalling disaster of the takeover of the German Protestant churches by the Nazi affiliated 'German Christians.'

> ...it is not we who build. He [Christ] builds the church. No human being builds the church but Christ alone. Whoever is minded to build the church is surely well on the way to destroying it; for he will build a temple to idols without wishing or knowing it. We must confess - he builds. We must proclaim - he builds. We must pray to him - he builds. We do not know his plan. We cannot see whether he is building or pulling down. It may be that the times which by human standards are times of collapse are for him the great times

---

[604] Dietrich Bonhoeffer, *The Cost of Discipleship* (London: SCM, 1959), pp.259-260.

of building. It may be that the times which from a human point of view are great times for the church are times when it is pulled down. It is a great comfort which Christ gives to his church: you confess, preach, bear witness to me, and I alone will build where it pleases me. Do not meddle in what is my province. Church, do what is given to you to do well and you have done enough. But do it well. Pay no heed to views and opinions, don't ask for judgments, don't always be calculating what will happen, don't always be on the lookout for another refuge! Let the church remain the church! But church, confess, confess, confess! Christ alone is your Lord, from his grace alone can you live as you are. Christ builds.

And the gates of hell shall not prevail against you. Death, the greatest heir of everything that has existence, here meets its end. Close by the precipice of the valley of death, the church is founded, the church which confesses Christ as its life. The church possesses eternal life just where death seeks to take hold of her; and he seeks to take hold of her precisely because she has possession of eternal life. The Confessing Church is the eternal church because Christ protects her. Her eternity is not visible in this world. Shwe remains despite the attack of the world. The waves pass right over her and sometimes she seems to be completely covered and lost. But the victory is hers because Christ her Lord is by her side and he has overcome the world of death. Do not ask whether you can see the victory; believe in the victory and it is yours[605]

[605] Dietrich Bonhoeffer, *No Rusty Swords* (Glasgow: Fontana, 1977), pp.212-213.

Appendix 1
Cyprian's *To Quirinius*

The work known as *To Quirinius* is Cyprian's response to a request from a catechist called Quirinius for help with drawing up a curriculum for catechetical instruction. Cyprian's response was to send him a list of 120 topics with a short summary of the biblical teaching relating to each topic.

I have included below the list of 120 topics covered by Cyprian with Cyprian's summary material for topics 21-23 at the end by way of example.

List of topics

1. On the benefit of good works and mercy.

2. In works and alms, even if by smallness of power less be done, that the will itself is enough.

3. That charity and brotherly love must be religiously and stedfastly practised.

4. That we must boast in nothing, since nothing is our own.

5. That humility and quietness is to be maintained in all things.

6. That all good and righteous men suffer more, but ought to endure because they are proved.

7. That we must not grieve the Holy Spirit whom we have received.

8. That anger must be overcome, lest it constrain us to sin.

9. That brethren ought to sustain one another.

10. That we must trust in God only, and in Him we must glory.

11. That he who has attained to faith, having put off the former man, ought to regard only celestial and spiritual things, and to give no heed to the world which he has already renounced.

12. That we must not swear.

13. That we are not to curse.

14. That we must never murmur, but bless God concerning all things that happen.

15. That men are tried by God for this purpose, that they may be proved.

16. Of the benefit of martyrdom.

17. That what we suffer in this world is of less account than is the reward which is promised

18. That nothing must be preferred to the love of God and of Christ.

19. That we must not obey our own will, but that of God.

20. That the foundation and strength of hope and faith is fear.

21. That we must not rashly judge of another.

22. That when we have received a wrong, we must remit and forgive it.

23. That evil is not to be returned for evil.

24. That it is impossible to attain to the Father but by Christ.

25. That unless a man have been baptized and born again, he cannot attain to the kingdom of God.

26. That it is of small account to be baptized and to receive the Eucharist, unless one profits by it both in deeds and works.

27. That even a baptized person loses the grace which he has attained, unless he keep innocency.

28. That remission cannot in the Church be granted unto him who has sinned against God.

29. That it was before predicted concerning the hatred of the Name.

30. That what any one has vowed to God, he must quickly pay.

31. That he who does not believe is judged already.

32. Of the benefit of virginity and of continency.

33. That the Father judgeth nothing, but the Son; and the Father is not honoured by him by whom the Son is not honoured.

34. That the believer ought not to live like the Gentiles.

35. That God is patient for this end, that we may repent of our sin and be reformed.

36. That a woman ought not to be adorned in a worldly manner.

37. That the believer ought not to be punished for other offences but for the name he bears only.

38. That the servant of God ought to be innocent, lest he fall into secular punishment.

39. That the example of living is given to us in Christ.

40. That we must not labour boastfully or noisily.

41. That we must not speak foolishly and offensively.

42. That faith is of advantage altogether, and that we can do as much as we believe.

43. That he who truly believes can immediately obtain.

44. That the believers who differ among themselves ought not to refer to a Gentile judge.

45. That hope is of future things, and therefore that faith concerning those things which are promised ought to be patient.

46. That a woman ought to be silent in the church.

47. That it arises from our fault and our desert that we suffer, and do not perceive God's help in everything.

48. That we must not take usury.

49. That even our enemies are to be loved.

50. That the sacrament of the faith must not be profaned.

51. That no one should be uplifted in his doing.

52. That the liberty of believing or of not believing is placed in free choice.

53. That the secrets of God cannot be seen through, and therefore that our faith ought to be simple.

54. That none is without filth and without sin.

55. That we must not please men, but God.

56. That nothing that is done is hidden from God.

57. That the believer is amended and reserved.

58. That no one should be made sad by death, since in living is labour and peril, in dying peace and the certainty of resurrection.

59. Of the idols which the Gentiles think gods.

60. That too great lust of food is not to be desired.

61. That the lust of possessing, and money, are not to be desired.

62. That marriage is not to be contracted with Gentiles.

63. That the sin of fornication is grievous.

64. What are those carnal things which beget death, and what are the spiritual things which lead to life.

65. That all sins are put away in baptism.

66. That the discipline of God is to be observed in Church precepts.

67. That it was foretold that men would despise sound discipline.

68. That we must depart from him who lives irregularly and contrary to discipline.

69. That the kingdom of God is not in the wisdom of the world, nor in eloquence, but in the faith of the cross and in virtue of conversation.

70. That we must obey parents.

71. And that fathers ought not to be bitter against their children.

72. That servants, when they believe, ought the more to be obedient to their fleshly masters.

73. Likewise that masters ought to be more gentle.

74. That every widow that is approved ought to be honoured.

75. That every person ought to have care rather of his own people, and especially of believers.

76. That one who is older must not rashly be accused.

77. That the sinner is to be publicly reproved.

78. That we must not speak with heretics.

79. That innocency asks with confidence, and obtains.

80. That the devil has no power against man unless God have allowed it.

81. That wages be quickly paid to the hireling.

82. That divination must not be used.

83. That a tuft of hair4143 is not to be worn on the head.

84. That the beard must not be plucked.

85. That we must rise when a bishop or a presbyter comes.

86. That a schism must not be made, even although he who withdraws should remain in one faith and in the same tradition.

87. That believers ought to be simple with prudence.

88. That a brother must not be deceived.

89. That the end of the world comes suddenly.

90. That a wife must not depart from her husband; or if she departs, she must remain unmarried.

91. That every one is tempted so much as he is able to bear.

92. That not everything is to be done which is lawful.

93. That it was foretold that heresies would arise.

94. That the Eucharist is to be received with fear and honour.

95. That we are to live with the good, but to avoid the evil.

96. That we must labour with deeds, not with words.

97. That we must hasten to faith and to attainment.4144

98. That the catechumen ought to sin no more.

99. That judgment will be in accordance with the terms, before the law, of equity; after Moses, of the law.

100. That the grace of God ought to be gratuitous.

101. That the Holy Spirit has often appeared in fire.

102. That all good men ought willingly to hear rebuke.

103. That we must abstain from much speaking.

104. That we must not lie.

105. That they are frequently to be corrected who do wrong in domestic service.

106. That when a wrong is received, patience is to be maintained, and that vengeance is to be left to God.

107. That we must not use detraction.

108. That we must not lay snares against our neighbour.

109. That the sick are to be visited.

110. That tale-bearers are accursed.

111. That the sacrifices of evil men are not acceptable.

112. That those are more severely judged who in this world have more power.

113. That widows and orphans ought to be protected.

114. That while one is in the flesh, he ought to make confession.

115. That flattery is pernicious.

116. That God is more loved by him who has had many sins forgiven in baptism.

117. That there is a strong conflict to be waged against the devil, and that therefore we ought to stand bravely, that we may be able to conquer.

118. Of Antichrist, that he will come as a man.

119. That the yoke of the law was heavy, which is cast off by us; and that the Lord's yoke is light, which is taken up by us.

120. That we are to be urgent in prayers.[606]

Topics 21-23
21. That we must not rashly judge of another.

In the Gospel according to Luke: 'Judge not, that ye be not judged: condemn not, that ye be not condemned.' [Luke 6:37] Of this same subject to the Romans: 'Who art thou that judgest another man's servant? to his own master he standeth or falleth. But he shall stand; for God is able to make him stand. [Romans 14:4] And again: 'Wherefore thou art without excuse, O every man that judgest: for in that in which thou judgest another, thou condemnest thyself; for thou doest the same things which thou judgest. But dost thou hope, who judgest those who do evil, and doest the same, that thou thyself shalt escape the judgment of God?' [Romans 2:2-3] Also in the first Epistle of Paul to the Corinthians: 'And let him that thinketh he standeth take heed lest he fall.' [1 Corinthians 10:12] And again: 'If any man thinketh that he knoweth anything, he knoweth not yet in what manner he ought to know.' [1 Corinthians 8:2]

[606] This list of topics can be found in 'The Treatises of Cyprian' in *The Ante-Nicene Fathers*, Vol.5, pp.528-530.

22. That when we have received a wrong, we must remit and forgive it.

In the Gospel, in the daily prayer: 'Forgive us our debts, even as we forgive our debtors.' [Matthew 6:12] Also according to Matthew 'And when ye stand for prayer, forgive, if ye have ought against anyone; that also your Father who is in heaven may forgive you your sins. But if ye do not forgive, neither will your Father which is in heaven forgive you your sins.' [Matthew 11:25-26] Also in the same place: 'In what measure ye mete, in that shall it be measured to you again.' [Mark 4:24]

23. That evil is not to be returned for evil.

In the Epistle of Paul to the Romans: 'Rendering to no man evil for evil.' [Romans 12:17] Also in the same place: 'Not to be overcome of evil, but overcome evil with good.' [Romans 12:21] Of this same thing in the Apocalypse: 'And He said unto me, 'Seal not the words of the prophecy of this book; because now the time is at hand. And let those who persist in hurting, hurt: and let him who is filthy, be filthy still: but let the righteous do still more righteousness: and in like manner, let him that is holy do still more holiness. Behold, I come quickly; and my reward is with me, to render to every man according to his deeds." [Revelation 22:10-12]. [607]

[607] These extracts are from 'The Treatises of Cyprian,' pp.541-542.

Bibliography

Primary Sources

Rex Adhar, 'The Vulnerability of Religious Liberty in Liberal States,' *Religion and Human Rights* 4 (2009).

ADF International, 'Prosecutor files appeal against Finnish MP's major free speech victory' at: https://adfinternational.org/prosecutor-files-appeal-against-finnish-mps-major-free-speech-victory/.

ADF International, 'BREAKING: Finnish parliamentarian found NOT GUILTY of "hate speech" for Bible Tweet and other expressions' at: https://adfinternational.org/breaking-finnish-parliamentarian-found-not-guilty-of-hate-speech-for-bible-tweet-and-other-expressions/.

Aid to the Church in Need, *Religious Freedom Report 2023* at https://acninternational.org/religiousfreedomreport/reports/global/2023.

Alcuin, Letter 113, in Timothy Shah and Allen Hertzke (eds), *Christianity and Freedom – Volume I: Historical Perspectives* (New York: CUP, 2016).

The Anglican Church in North America, *To be a Christian* at: https://anglicanchurch.net/wp-content/uploads/2020/06/To-Be-a-Christian.pdf.

Thomas Aquinas, *Summa Theologica* (Claremont: Coyote Canyon Press, 2010).

Augustine, *The City of God,* (Harmondsworth: Penguin, 1981).

Augustine, *The Confessions* (Oxford: OUP, 2008).

Augustine, 'Letter 173,' in *The Nicene and Post Nicene Fathers*, Vol.1 (Edinburgh and Grand Rapids: T&T Clark/Eerdmans, 1994), pp.544-547.

Augustine, *On Grace and Free Will,* ch.4 in *The Nicene and Post Nicene Fathers*, 1st Series, Vol. V (Edinburgh and Grand Rapids (T&T Clark/Eerdmans, 1997), pp.457-477.

Augustine, *On Lying*, in *The Nicene and Post Nicene Fathers*, First series, Vol. III (Edinburgh and Grand Rapids: T&T Clark/Eerdmans, 1998),

The Barmen Declaration, in John Leith (ed), Creeds of the Churches, rev. ed. (Oxford: Basil Blackwell, 1973).

Karl Barth, *Church Dogmatics II.1* (London and New York: T&T Clark, 2004).

Karl Barth, *Church Dogmatics* III.1 (London and New York: T&T Clark, 2004).

Karl Barth, *A Letter to Great Britain from Switzerland* (London: Sheldon Press, 1941).

The Basic Law for the Federal Public of Germany, at https://www.gesetze-im-internet.de/englisch_gg/englisch_gg.html #p0030

Richard Bauckham, *God and the Crisis of Freedom* (Louisville and London: John Knox Press, 2002).

Bede, *History of the English Church and People,* (Harmondsworth: Penguin, 1977).

Rosaria Butterfield, *The secret thoughts of an unlikely convert* (Pittsburgh: Crown and Covenant, 2014).

Rosaria Butterfield, 'Why I no longer use Transgender Pronouns—and Why You shouldn't, either,' *Reformation 21,* 3 April 23 at: https://www.reformation21.org/blog/why-i-no-longer-use-transgender-pronouns-and-why-you-shouldnt-either.

Niggel Biggar, *Aiming to Kill: The Ethics of Suicide and Euthanasia* (London: DLT: 2004).

Jonathan Bennet (ed.), John Locke, *Toleration,* at: http://www.earlymoderntexts.com/assets/pdfs/locke1689b.pd.

Boethius, 'A Treatise Against Eutyches and Nestorius', in H F Stewart *The Theological Tractates* (London: Heinemann, 1918)

Boethius, *The Consolation of Philosophy*, (London: Elliot Stock, 1897).

Dietrich Bonhoeffer, *The Cost of Discipleship* (London: SCM, 1959).

Dietrich Bonoeffer, *No Rusty Swords* (Glasgow: Fontana, 1977).

The Book of Common Prayer, (Cambridge: Cambridge University Press, N.D.),

Joe Boot, 'On the brink: the criminalisation of Christianity in Canada,' *Christian Concern*, 10 October 2020 at https://christianconcern.com/resource/on-the-brink-the-criminalisation-of-christianity-in-canada/.

Julian of Norwich, *Revelations of Divine Love* (Grand Rapids: Christian Classics Ethereal library).

Justin Brierley, *The Surprising Rebirth of Belief in God* (Carol Stream: Tyndale Elevate, 2024).

Harold Browne, *An Exposition of the Thirty Nine Articles* (London: John W Parker, 1847).

Leonard Busher, *Religion's peace: A plea for liberty of conscience* in Edward Underhill (ed), *Tracts on Liberty of Conscience and Persecution, 1614-1661* (London: J Haddon, 1846).

John Calvin, *Institutes of the Christian Religion*, (Grand Rapids; Eerdmans, 1975).

Canadian Charter of Rights and Freedoms, at: https://www.canada.ca/content/dam/pch/documents/services/download-order-charter-bill/canadian-charter-rights-freedoms-eng.pdf.

Canadian Ministry of National Defence, *Minister of National Defence Advisory Panel on Systemic Racism and Discrimination – Final Report – January 2022*, Part III section 6, Redefining Chaplaincy at https://www.canada.ca/en/department-national-defence/corporate/reports-publications/mnd-advisory-panel-systemic-racism-discrimination-final-report-jan-2022.html.

CARDUS, 29 April 2022, 'Memo: Redefining Chaplaincy,' at: https://www.cardus.ca/research/faith-communities/policy-memo/memo-redefining-chaplaincy/.

Care, 'Abortion the leading cause of death in 2023, at: https://care.org.uk/news/2024/01/abortion-the-leading-cause-of-death-in-2023.

Don Carson, *Divine Sovereignty and Human Responsibility* (London: Marshall, Morgan and Scott, 1981).

Stephen Carter, 'Liberalism's Religion problem', *First Things*, March 2002, at https://www.firstthings.com/article/2002/03/liberalisms-religion-problem.

Sebastian Castellio, *Concerning heretics, whether they are to be persecuted and how they are to be treated – A collection of the opinions of learned men both ancient and modern,* (New York: Columbia University Press, 1935).

The Catechism of the Catholic Church (London: Geoffrey Chapman, 1994).

Catholic News Agency, 8 September 2024, 'Queensland passes law requiring priests to break confessional seal,' at: https://www.catholicnewsagency.com/news/45756/queensland-passes-law-requiring-priests-to-break-confessional-seal.

Christian Concern, 'Bernard Randall,' at: https://christianconcern.com/cccases/rev-dr-bernard-randall/.

Christian Institute, 3 February 2022, 'EXCLUSIVE: Australian pastor explains draconian Victorian conversion therapy ban' at https://www.christian.org.uk/news/exclusive-australian-pastor-explains-draconian-victorian-conversion-therapy-ban/.

Christian Post, April 2024, 'French gender equality minister wants priest prosecuted for saying homosexuality is sinful 'weakness,' at: https://www.christianpost.com/news/france-may-prosecute-priest-who-called-homosexuality-a-weakness.html.

Christian Today, 13 January 2024, 'Finnish state prosecutor to appeal Christian politician's 'not guilty' verdict, 'at:

https://www.christiantoday.com/article/finnish.state.prosecutor.to.appeal.christian.politicians.not.guilty.verdict/141260.html.

Clement of Alexandria, *Exhortation to Endurance*, text at: https://catholiclibrary.org/library/view?docId=Synchronized-EN/anf.ClementofAlexandria.ExhortationNewlyBaptized.en.html&chunk.id=00000001.

1 Clement 13:1-3 in J B Lightfoot, J R Harmer and Michael Holmes, The Apostolic Fathers (Leicester Apollos, 1989), pp.65-78.

Darrell Cole, *When God says war is right* (Colorado Springs: Waterbrook Press, 2002).

Joseph Collins and Rudolph Bandas, *The Catechetical Instructions of St Thomas Aquinas* (Baltimore, 1939) at: https://www.documentacatholicaomnia.eu/03d/1225-1274,_Thomas_Aquinas,_Catechismus,_EN.pdf

The Commonwealth of Australia, Constitution Act, at: https://www.legislation.gov.au/C2004Q00685/latest/text.

The Constitution of Finland, 11 at https://finlex.fi/en/laki/kaannokset/1999/en19990731.pdf.

The Constitution of the Hashemite Kingdom of Jordan, Articles at: https://www.refworld.org/pdfid/3ae6b53310.pdf.

Constitution of the Islamic Republic of Pakistan, at 1333523681_951.pdf (na.gov.pk)

Constitution of Kenya, at https://kmpdc.go.ke/resources/Constitution_of_Kenya_2010.pdf.

Constitution of the Republic of Ecuador, at: https://pdba.georgetown.edu/Constitutions/Ecuador/english08.html.

Constitution of the Republic of Fiji, at: https://www.laws.gov.fj/ResourceFile/Get/?fileName=2013%20Constitution%20of%20Fiji%20(English).pdf.

Constitution of the Republic of Singapore, at: https://sso.agc.gov.sg/Act/CONS1963.

The Constitution of the Russian Federation, at: http://www.constitution.ru/en/10003000-03.htm.

Constitution of Rwanda, Chapter IV, at
https://www.constituteproject.org/constitution/Rwanda_2015?lang=e
n.

*Conversion Therapy Prohibition (Sexual Orientation and Gender Identity)
Bill* [HL] at https://bills.parliament.uk/bills/3512.

Court of Justice of the European Union, *Council Directive 2000/78/EC of
27 November 2000* at:
https://curia.europa.eu/juris/document/document.jsf?text=&docid=27
3313&pageIndex=0&doclang=EN&mode=lst&dir=&occ=first&part=1&c
id=3078169.

Cyprian of Carthage, Epistle I in *The Ante Nicene Fathers*, in in *The Ante-
Nicene Fathers*, Vol. V (Edinburgh and Grand Rapids: T&T
Clark/Eerdmans, 1995), pp.275 280.

Cyprian of Carthage, *On the Good of Patience* in *The Ante-Nicene Fathers*,
Vol. V, pp.484-491.

Cyprian of Carthage, in *The Treatises of Cyprian,* Treatise XII in *The
Ante-Nicene Fathers*, Vol.V, pp. 507-557.

John of Damascus, *Exposition of the Orthodox Faith*, in *The Nicene and
Post-Nicene Fathers*, second series, Vol. IX (Edinburgh and Grand
Rapids: T&T Clark, Eerdmans, 1997), pp.1-101.

Richard Dawkins, *The Blind Watchmaker* (London: Penguin, 2006).

Declaration of the Establishment of the State of Israel at
https://www.jewishvirtuallibrary.org/the-declaration-of-the-
establishment-of-the-state-of-israel.

*Declaration on the Elimination of All Forms of Intolerance and
Discrimination Based on Religion or Belief,* at:
https://www.ohchr.org/en/instruments-
mechanisms/instruments/declaration-elimination-all-forms-
intolerance-and-discrimination

Alexis de Tocqueville, *Democracy in America* (Chicago: Chicago
University Press, 2000).

Arielle Del Turco, 'Hostility Against Churches Is on the Rise in the United States - Analyzing Incidents from 2018-2022,' *Family Research Council,* December 2022, No, 1522 LO, p. 2-3 at: https://downloads.frc.org/EF/EF22L24.pdf.

Arielle Del Turco, 'Hostility Against Churches Supplemental Report – First Quarter 2023', *Family Research Council*, April 2023 | No. IF23D01, pp.2-3, at https://downloads.frc.org/EF/EF23D04.pdf.

Arielle Del Turco, 'Hostility Against Churches Is on the Rise in the United States - Analyzing Incidents from 2018-2023,' *Family Research Council* Issue Analysis February 2024 | No. IS24B01at: https://downloads.frc.org/EF/EF24B78.pdf.

The Didache in Lightfoot, Harmer and Holmes, pp. 145-158.

Didascalia Apostolorum, translation by R Hugh Conolly (Oxford: Clarendon Press 1929) at https://earlychristianwritings.com/text/didascalia.html.

The Doctrine Commission of the Church of England, *The Mystery of Salvation* (London: CHP, 1995).

Sean Doherty, *The Only Way is Ethics – Part 2: Life and Death* (Milton Keynes: Authentic Media: 2016).

Rod Dreher, 'Finland Persecutes Christian Lawmaker,' *The American Conservative*, 29 April 2021, at: https://www.theamericanconservative.com/finland-persecutes-christian-lawmaker-paivi-rasanen/.

Will Durant, 'Freedom of Worship' at https://www.saturdayeveningpost.com/2017/12/will-durants-freedom-worship/Will Durant Freedom of Worship.

Epistle Concerning the Martyrdom of Polycarp,' in *The Ante-Nicene Fathers*, Vol.1 (Edinburgh and Grand Rapids: T & T Clark/Eerdmans, 1996).

Epistle of Barnabas in Maxwell Staniforth, *Early Christian Writings* (Harmondsworth: Penguin, 1978).

Equality Act 2010 at
https://www.legislation.gov.uk/ukpga/2010/15/contents

Joel Forster, 'Risk of 'state intervention in Christian doctrine if recommendations of UN expert on LGBT issues are followed, warns WEA,' *Evangelical Focus*, 23 June 2023, at: https://evangelicalfocus.com/world/22512/un-risks-state-intervention-in-christian-doctrine-if-recommendations-of-un-independent-expert-on-lgbt-issues-are-followed.

'Free Church criticise 'anti-Christian' attacks on Kate Forbes, *The Herald*, 22 February 2023, at: https://www.heraldscotland.com/politics/23338967.free-church-criticise-anti-christian-attacks-kate-forbes/.

Georg Froelich, *Whether Secular Government has the right to wield the sword in matters of faith*, in German History in Documents and images, 'Radicals vs. Protestants – An Attack on Religious Claims to Temporal Authority (1530),' p.1, at: https://germanhistorydocs.ghidc.org/sub_document.cfm?document_id=4316.

Stefano Gennarini, 'Religious freedom ends where LGBT rights begin.' *C-Fam*, June 21, 2023 at; https://c-fam.org/friday_fax/un-attempts-to-impose-lgbt-orthodoxy-on-all-religions/?inf_contact_key=4e8d673 07858c899074b9c8bcdfeae0dd18a532c4142cb79caf2b269de1401fa.

Government of Queensland, *Queensland Health, Conscientious Objection*, at: https://www.health.qld.gov.au/clinical-practice/guidelines-procedures/voluntary-assisted-dying/information for-healthcare-workers/conscientious-objection.

Government of Victoria, *Change or Suppression (Conversion) Practices Prohibition Act 2021*, at: https://content.legislation.vic.gov.au/sites/default/files/2021-02/21-003aa%20authorised.pdf.

Jonathan Grant, *Divine Sex* (Grand Rapids: Brazos Press, 2015).

Vaclav Havel, *The Power of the Powerless* (London: Vintage Classics, 2018).

Walt Heyer, *A Transgender's Faith* (Walt Heyer 2015).

The Heidelberg Catechism, in Mark Noll, *Confessions and Catechisms of the Reformation* (Vancouver: Regent College Publishing, 2004), pp. 133-164.

The First Book of Homilies, 'A Sermon against whoredom and uncleanness,' text in Ian Robinson, *The Homilies* (Bishopstone: The Brynmill Press, 2006), pp. 88-99.

Human Rights Watch, 'Reproductive Rights and Abortion' at: https://www.hrw.org/topic/womens-rights/reproductive-rights-and-abortion.

Ignatius, *To the Romans,* in Lightfoot, Harmer and Holmes, p.106.

International Covenant on Civil and Political Rights, at https://www.ohchr.org/en/instruments-mechanisms/instruments/international-covenant-civil-and-political-rights.

Bl. Franz Jägerstätter (1907-1943) Layman and martyr' at: https://www.vatican.va/news_services/liturgy/saints/ns_lit_doc_2007 1026_jagerstatter_en.html.

David James, *Lifesite*, 27 May 2023, 'The Australian gov't is forcefully taking over a Catholic hospital because it is pro-life,' at: https://www.lifesitenews.com/opinion/the-australian-govt-is-forcefully-taking-over-a-catholic-hospital-because-it-is-pro-life/.

Julie James, 'Rugby Suicide: The Unedited Emails of His Mother,' *The Daily Telegraph*, 18 October 2008.

Jonathan Jeffes, *Abortion, Breaking the Silence* (Chichester: Lean Press, 2013).

Justin Martyr, *The First Apology*, 16, in *The Ante-Nicene Fathers*, vol. I (Edinburgh and Grand Rapids, T&T Clark/Eerdmans, 1996), pp.159-187.

Tim Keller, *Counterfeit Gods*, (London: Hodder and Stoughton, 1979).

Thomas Ken, *The Practice of Divine Love* (London: 1685) at http://anglicanhistory.org/ken/divine_poor.html.

Roger Kiska, 'Assessing the Coronavirus Act 2020: what you need to know,' *Christian Concern*, 17 April2020 at: https://christianconcern.com/resource/assessing-the-coronavirus-act-2020-what-you-need-to-know/.

Roger Kiska, 'Is a conversion therapy ban compatible with human rights?' at: file:///C:/Users/mbarr/Downloads/CC-Resource-Briefings-Conversion-Therapy-Ban-Opinion-Roger-Kiska-220407.pdf.

Jason Koppel, *The Christian Institute, Private Member's Bill to prohibit Conversion Therapy, Advice*, at

https://www.christian.org.uk/wp-content/uploads/Burt-CT-Bill-Coppel-Legal-Opinion.pdf.

E H Kossman and A F Mellink (eds), *Texts concerning the Revolt of the Netherlands* (Cambridge: CUP, 1974).

Alan Kreider, *The Patient Ferment of the Early Church* (Grand Rapids, Baker Academic, 2016).

Lactantius, *Of the manner in which the persecutors died*, in the Ante-Nicene Fathers Vol. VII (Edinburgh and Grand Rapids: T&T Clark/Eerdmans, 1994), pp.301-322.

Lactantius, *The Divine Institutes,* in the Ante-Nicene Fathers Vol.VII, pp.9-223.

Lactantius, *The Epitome of the Divine Institutes,* in the Ante-Nicene Fathers Vol.VII, pp.224-255.

The Lausanne Movement, *The Cape Town Commitment*, 2010, at https://lausanne.org/wp-content/uploads/2021/10/The-Cape-Town-Commitment-%E2%80%93-Pages-20-09-2021.pdf.

Ryszard Legutko, *The Demon in Democracy* (New York and London, Encounter Books, 2018.

C S Lewis, *Prayer: Letters to Malcom* (Glasgow: Fountain Books, 1977).

C S Lewis, *Mere Christianity* (Glasgow: Fount, 1984).

C S Lewis, *The Great Divorce* (Glasgow: Fontana, 1972).

C S Lewis, *The Screwtape Letters* (London: Fount, 1998),

Martin Luther, *On the Bondage of the Will.* Pt I, in Gordon Rupp and Philip Watson (eds), *Luther and Erasmus: Free Will and Salvation* (Philadelphia: Westminster Press, 1969).

Martin Luther, *Large Catechism*, at: https://www.lutheranlibrary.org/pdf/194-jacobs-luther-large-catechism.pdf.

Duncan MacLaren, *Mission Implausible – Restoring Credibility to the Church* (Milton Keynes: Paternoster Press, 2004).

James Madison, *Memorial and Remonstrance*, 1785, text at https://founders.archives.gov/documents/Madison/01-08-02-0163.

Victor Madgrigal-Borloz, *Freedom of religion or belief, and freedom from violence and discrimination based on sexual orientation and gender identity* at: https://view.officeapps.live.com/op/view.aspx?src=https%3A%2F%2F www.ohchr.org%2Fsites%2Fdefault%2Ffiles%2Fdocuments%2Fhrbod ies%2Fhrcouncil%2Fsessions-regular%2Fsession53%2Fadvance-versions%2FA_HRC_53_37_AUV.docx&wdOrigin=BROWSELINK.

Paul Marshall. 'Patterns of Anti-Christian Persecution' in Allen Hertzke and Timothy Shah (eds), *Christianity and Freedom – Volume II, Contemporary Perspectives* (New York: CUP, 2016).

Stephen McAlpine, *Being the Bad Guys* (Epsom: Good Book Company, 2021),

Observatory on Intolerance and Discrimination Against Christians, *OIDAC Europe Annual Report 2021*, at: https://www.intoleranceagainstchristians.eu/fileadmin/user_upload/p ublications/files/Annual_Report_2022_-_ONLINE_Web_View_Final.pdf.

Observatory on Intolerance and Discrimination Against Christians, *OIDAC Europe 2022/2023 Annual Report*, at: https://www.intoleranceagainstchristians.eu/fileadmin/user_upload/p ublications/files/Annual_Report_2023_-_ONLINE_Version.pdf.

John Nickalls (ed), *Journal of George Fox,* (London: Religious Society of Friends, 1975).

Julian of Norwich, *Revelations of Divine Love* (Grand Rapids: Christian Classics Ethereal library).

Oliver O'Donovan, *Begotten or Made?* (Oxford: OUP, 1984).

Oliver O'Donovan, *The just war revisited* (Cambridge: CUP, 2003).

Oliver O'Donovan, *On the Thirty Nine Articles* (Exeter: Paternoster Press, 1986).

Oliver O'Donovan, *Resurrection and Moral Order*, 2nd edition (Leicester and Grand Rapids: Apollos/Eerdmans, 1994.

John Owen, 'A Discourse of Toleration,' in *The Sermons of John Owen*, at: https://ccel.org/ccel/owen/sermons/sermons.ii.iii.vi.html.

John Owen, *Truth and Innocence Vindicated* (Louisville: GLH Publishing, 2020).

J I Packer, *Knowing God* (London: Hodder and Stoughton 1973).

William Penn, *A Collection of the Works of William Penn* (London: J. Sowle, 1726).

Daniel Philpott, 'Why Christians Deserve Attention' Georgetown University, Berkley Center, 2 September 2014 at: https://berkleycenter.georgetown.edu/essays/why-christians-deserve-attention.

Caritas Pirckheimer, *A Journal of the Reformation Years, 1524-1528* (Cambridge: Boydell and Brewer, 2006).

Pliny the Younger, *Epistle X* in Henry Bettenson (ed), *Documents of the Christian Church* (Oxford: OUP, 1979).

Pontius, *The Life and Passion of Cyprian* in *The Ante-Nicene Fathers*, Vol. V, pp. 267-274.

Pope Callistus II, *Sicut Iudaeis*, in Edward Synan, *The Popes and the Jews in the Middle Ages* (Lightning Source Inc.2008)

Pope Gelasius I, letter to Emperor Anastasius, Fordham University, 'Gelasius I on Spiritual and Temporal Power, 494' at https://sourcebooks.fordham.edu/source/gelasius1.asp.

Pope Gregory the Great Epistle 1, in Shah and Hertzke, Vol. 1.

Pope Gregory the Great, *Epistles*, Book XIII.XII, in *The Nicene and Post Nicene Fathers*, Vol. XIII (Edinburgh and Grand Rapids: T&T Clark/Eerdmans, 1997).

Glynn Harrison, *A Better Story* (London: Inter-Varsity Press, 2016).

Gregor Puppinck, *Brief presentation on Conscientious Objection*, European Centre for Law and Justice, 2016, at http://media.aclj.org/pdf/Brief-presentation-on-conscientious-objection---ECHR-Seminar.pdf.

Matthew Roberts, *Pride, Identity and the Worship of Self* (Fearn: Christian Focus, 2023.

Norman Rockwell, 'Four Freedoms' at: https://rockwellfourfreedoms.org/about-the-exhibit/rockwells-four-freedoms/.

F D Roosevelt, State of the Union address, 6 January 1941 at: https://www.presidency.ucsb.edu/documents/annual-message-congress-the-state-the-union.

Jean-Jacque Rousseau, *Confessions* (Oxford: OUP, 2008).

'Michelangelo Signorile, Bridal Wave,' *Out*, December 1993/January 1994.

The Shepherd of Hermas, in Lightfoot, Harmer and Holmes, pp.219-221.

Menno Simons, *The Complete Works of Menno Simons* (Elkhart: John F Funk, 1871).

Lauren Smith, 'The Persecution of Felix Ngole,' *Spiked*, 6 April 2024 at: https://www.spiked-online.com/2024/04/06/the-persecution-of-felix-ngole/.

Sozemen, *Church History*, in *The Nicene and Post Nicene Fathers*, 2nd series (Edinburgh and Grand Rapids: T&T Clark, 1997).

Jeremy Taylor, *Discourse of the Liberty of Prophesying* (London: Joseph Rickerby, 1836).

William Temple, *Christus Veritas* (London: Macmillan, 1949)

Tertullian, *Against Marcion*, in *The Ante-Nicene Fathers*, Vol. III (Edinburgh and Grand Rapids: T&T Clark/Eerdmans, 1997), pp.243-275.

Tertullian, *Apology*, in *The Ante-Nicene Fathers*, Vol. III, pp. 17-60.

Tertullian, *Of Patience*, in *The Ante-Nicene Fathers*, Vol. III, p..707-418.

Helmut Thielicke, *Man in God's World* (Cambridge: Lutterworth Press, 2016),

Carl Trueman, *The Rise and Triumph of the Modern Self* (Wheaton: Crossway, 2020).

Carl Trueman, 'Can Christians Attend Gay Weddings?' *First Things*, 25.1.24 at: https://www.firstthings.com/web-exclusives/2024/01/can-christians-attend-gay-weddings.

Philip Turner, "ECUSA's God and the idols of Liberal Protestantism,' in Ephraim Radner and Philip Turner, *The Fate of Communion* (Grand Rapids: Eerdmans 2006).

The Universal Declaration of Human Rights, Preamble, at https://www.un.org/en/about-us/universal-declaration-of-human-rights.

United Kingdom Government, *Abortion Act 1967*, at: https://www.legislation.gov.uk/ukpga/1967/87/contents.

United Nations Charter, at: https://www.un.org/en/about-us/un-charter/full-text.

United States Commission on International Religious Freedom, 'Russia's religious freedom violations in Ukraine,' July 2023 at: https://www.uscirf.gov/sites/default/files/20207/2023%20Russias%20Religious%20Freedom%20 Violations%20in%20Ukraine%20Issue%20Update_07.05.2023.pdf.

Vatican II, 'Declaration on Religious Freedom,' in Walter Abbott (ed) *The Documents of Vatican II* (London: Geoffrey Chapman, 1967).

Kallistos Ware, *The Orthodox Way* (London and Oxford: Mowbrays, 1979).

George Washington, *Washington's Final Address to the People of the United States*, at: https://www.senate.gov/artandhistory/history/resources/pdf/Washi ngtons_Farewell_Address.pdf.

Christopher Watkin, *Biblical Critical Theory* (Grand Rapids: Zondervan Academic, 2022).

Carolyn Weber, *Surprised by Oxford* (Nashville: Thomas Nelson, 2011).

John Webster, *Confessing God* (London and New York: T&T Clark, 2005).

The Westminster Confession, in Leith, pp. 192-230.

Roger Williams, *The Bloody Tenent of Persecution* (London: J Haddon, 1848).

The Witherspoon Institute Task Force on International Religious Freedom, *Religious Freedom: Why Now? – Defending an Embattled Human Right* (Princeton: Witherspoon Institute, 2012).

World Council of Churches, *Declaration on Religious Liberty*, 1948 at: https://original.religlaw.org/content/religlaw/documents/wccdecrelig lib1948.htm.

Chris Wright, *Here are your Gods!* (London: Inter-Varsity Press, 2020),

R Carlton Wynne, 'Could Jesus Have Sinned? -The Temptations and Triumph of Christ,' *Desiring God*, 2 September 2019 at https://www.desiringgod.org/articles/could-jesus-have-sinned.

Secondary sources
Scott David Allen, *Why social Justice is not Biblical Justice* (Grand Rapids: Credo House, 2020).

R E Davies *I will pour out my Spirit* (Tunbridge Wells: Monarch 1992).

Thomas Altizer, *The Gospel of Christian Atheism* (Philadelphia: Westminster Press, 1966).

'Apologists' in F L Cross (ed) *The Oxford Dictionary of the Christian Church* (London: OUP, 1963).

Kenneth Bailey, *Jesus Through Middle Eastern Eyes* (London: SPCK, 2008).

Roland Bainton, *Here I Stand* (Tring: Lion, 1978).

William Barclay, *The Gospel of John* Voi.1 (Edinburgh: St Andrew Press, 1982).

William Barclay, *The Gospel of John, Volume 2* (Edinburgh: St Andrew Press, 1963).

Willam Barclay, *The Gospel of Luke* (Edinburgh: St Andrew Press, 1981).

William Barclay, *Gospel of Matthew*, Volume 2 (Edinburgh: St Andrew Press, 1963).

Bruce Barron, *Heaven on earth? the social & political agendas of dominion theology* (Grand Rapids: Zondervan, 1992).

Richard Bauckham, *The Theology of the Book of Revelation* (Cambridge: CUP, 1993).

Philip Booth, 'Pope Francis condemns usury, but what is it?' *Transatlantic Blog*, 12 February 2018 at https://www.acton.org/publications/transatlantic/2018/02/12/pope-francis-condemns-usury-what-It.

David Bosch, *Believing in the Future: Towards a Missiology of Missiology of Western Culture* (Harrisburg: Trinity Press International, 1995).

Callum Brown, *The Death of Christian Britain* (London, Routledge, 2000).

Steve Bruce, *God is Dead: Secularization in the West* (Oxford: Blackwell, 2002).

Tara Burton, *Strange Rites: New Religions for a Godless World* (New York: Public Affairs, 2020).

George Caird, *Saint Luke* (Harmondsworth: Penguin, 1963).

John Calvin, *The Complete Biblical Commentary Collection of John Calvin* (kindle edition).

Don Carson (ed), *From Sabbath to Lord's Day: A Biblical, Historical and Theological Investigation* (Eugene: Wipf and Stock, 1999).

Owen Chadwick, *The Secularization of the European Mind in the Nineteenth Century* (Cambridge: CUP, 1974).

Ben Chang, *Christ and the Culture Wars* (Fearn: Christian Focus, 2023).

Andrew Chapman, *Human Rights, A Very Short Introduction* (Oxford: OUP, 2007).

Edmund Clowney, *The Message of 1 Peter* (Leicester: Inter-Varsity Press, 1988).

Charles Colson, *The Charles Colson Collection* (Carol Stream: Tyndale House Publishers 2005).

Winfried Corduan, *In the beginning God – A fresh look at the case for original monotheism* (Nashville: B&H Academic, 2013).

Charles Cranfield, *I and II Peter and Jude* (London: SCM, 1960).

Charles Cranfield, *Romans, Vol.1* (Edinburgh: T&T Clark, 1987).

Joy Davidman, *Smoke on the Mountain* (London: Hodder and Stoughton, 1959).

Martin Davie, *The Athanasian Creed* (London: Latimer Trust, 2019).

Derek Davis, 'The Evolution of Religious Freedom as a Universal Human Right: Examining the Role of the 1981 United Nations Declaration on the Elimination of All Forms of Intolerance and of Discrimination Based on Religion or Belief,' *BYU Law Review*, Volume 2002, Issue 2, Article 2, at: https://digitalcommons.law.byu.edu/cgi/viewcontent.cgi?article =2109&context=lawreview.

David Dickson, *Matthew* (Edinburgh: Banner of Truth, 1981).

Elizabeth De Palma Digeser, 'Lactantius on Religious Liberty and His Influence on Constantine' in Shah and Hertzke, Vol.I.

J D Douglas (ed), *The New Bible Dictionary* (Leicester: Inter-Varsity Press, 1962)

Rod Dreher, *Live not by Lies* (New York: Sentinel, 2020).

Abigail Favele, *The Genesis of Gender (*San Francisco: Ignatius Press, 2022),

Edward Feser, *All One in Christ-A Catholic Critique of Racism and Critical Race Theory* (San Franciso: Ignatius Press, 2022.

C Ryan Fields, 'A Generous Reading of John Locke: Reevaluating His Philosophical Legacy in Light of His Christian Confession' *Themelios*, Vol 45. 3 at https://www.thegospelcoalition.org/themelios/article/a-generous-reading-of-john-locke-reevaluating-his-philosophical-legacy-in-light-of-his-christian-confession/.

John Finnis, *Aquinas* (Oxford: OUP, 1998).

Nazila Ghanea, *Landscape of freedom of religion and belief* (New York: United Nation's Human Rights' Council, 2023), at: https://documents-dd ny.un.org/doc/UNDOC/GEN/G23/006/31/PDF/G2300631.pdf? OpenElement.

A D Gilbert, *The Making of Post-Christian-Britain: A History of the Secularization of Modern Society* (London: Longman, 1980).

Mary Ann Glendon, *The Forum and the Tower* (New York: OUP, 2011).

Charles Gore, *The Epistle to the Ephesians* (London: John Murray 1909).

Michael Green, *When God Breaks In* (London: Hodder and Stoughton, 2014)).

Mark Griffiths, in *Faith at Home* (Cambridge: Grove Books, 2024).

Os Guinness, *The Gravedigger File* (London: Hodder & Stoughton, 1987).

Colin Gunton, *A Brief Theology of Revelation* (Edinburgh: T&T Clark, 1995).

Norman Hampson, *The Enlightenment* (London: Penguin, 1990).

Stanley Hauerwas and William Willimon, *The Truth about God – The Ten Commandments in Christian Life* (Nashville: Abingdon Press, 1999).

J W L Hoad, 'Patience,' in J D Douglas et.al *The New Bible Dictionary* (Leicester: Inter-Varsity Press, 1980), pp. 938-939.

Tom Holland, *Dominion – The Making of the Western Mind* (London: Little, Brown, 2019).

James Hunter, 'What is Modernity?' in P Sampson, V Samuel and C Sugden (eds), *Faith and Modernity* (Oxford: Regnum/Lynx, 1996).

Larry Hurtado, *Destroyer of the Gods* (Waco: Baylor University Press, 2016).

(Larry Hurtado, *Why on earth did anyone become a Christian in the first three centuries?* (Milwaukee: Marquette University Press, 2016

J P Hyatt, *Exodus* (Grand Rapids and London: Eerdmans/ Marshall Morgan & Scott, 1980).

Joachim Jeremias, *Infant baptism in the first four centuries* (London: SCM, 1960).

The Josias at. https://thejosias.com/.

J N D Kelly, *Early Christian Creeds* 3ed (Harlow: Longman, 1972).

Derek Kidner, *Love to the Loveless* (Leicester: Inter-Varsity Press, 1981).

Peter Leithart, *A House for My Name – A Survey of the Old Testament* (Moscow: Canon Press, 2000).

Peter Leithart, *The Ten Commandments* (Bellingham: Lexham Press, 2020),

Ian Levy, 'Liberty of Conscience and Freedom of Religion in the Medieval Canonists,' in Shah and Hertzke, Vol.I.

Alastair MacIntyre, *After Virtue* (London: Duckworth, 1983).

Ramsay MacMullen, *Christianizing the Roman Empire A.D. 100-400* (New Haven: Yale University Press,1984)

J W Marshall, 'Decalogue' in T Desmond Alexander and David Baker (eds), *Dictionary of the Old Testament: Pentateuch* (Downers Grove and Leicester, Inter-Varsity Press, 2003).

Scott McKnight, *The Real Mary* (London: SPCK, 2007).

Alec Motyer, *The Message of James* (Leicester: Inter-Varsity Press, 1985).

Andrew Murphy, *Conscience and Community: Revisiting Toleration and Religious Dissent in Early Modern England and America* (University Park: Pennsylvania State University Press, 2001).

Michael Novak, *On Two Wings – Humble Faith and Common Sense at the American*

Founding (New York and London, Encounter Books, 2002).

John Nurser, *For All Peoples and All Nations – Christian Churches and Human Rights* (Geneva: WCC Publications, 2005).

Ian Paul, *Revelation* (London and Downers Grove: Inter-Varsity Press, 2018).

J I Packer, *Keeping the 10 Commandments* (Wheaton: Crossway, 2007),

Daniel Philpott, 'Christianity: A Straggler on the Road to Liberty?' in Shah and Hertzke, Vol. I.

Adina Portaru and Robert Clarke, *Freedom of Conscience: Protecting our Moral Compass* (Vienna: ADF International, 2020).

David Prior, *The Message of 1 Corinthians* (Leicester: Inter-Varsity Press, 1985).

Gregor Puppinck, *Conscientious Objection and Human Rights: A Systematic Analysis* (Leiden: Brill, 2015).

Gerhard von Rad, *Genesis* (London: SCM, 1972).

Thomas Renz, 'Do we ignore the biblical teaching on usury?' *Psephizo*, 25 January 2024 at https://www.psephizo.com/biblical-studies/do-we-ignore-the-biblical-teaching-on-usury/

Philip Rieff, *The Triumph of the Therapeutic* (Chicago: Chicago University Press, 1966).

J C Ryle, *Expository Thoughts on St. Matthew* (London: William Hunt, 1883).

David Scaer, *James the Apostle of Faith* (Eugene: Wipf and Stock, 2004).

Wilhelm Schmidt, *Der Urspung der Gottesidee*, Vol. VI (Munster: Aschendorff,1935).

Thomas Scott, *Commentary on the whole Bible*, Vol. III (London: Jordan and Maxwell, 1803).

Glen Scrivener, *The Air We Breathe* (Epsom, The Good Book Company, 2022).

Timothy Shah, Matthew Franck and Thomas Farr (eds), *Religious Freedom: Why Now? Defending an Embattled Human Right* (Princeton: Witherspoon Institute, 2012).

Jean Edward Smith, *FDR* (New York: Random House, 2008).

'Special Rapporteur on Freedom of Religion or Belief,' at: https://www.ohchr.org/en/special-procedures/sr-religion-or-belief.

Rodney Stark, *The Rise of Christianity* (San Francisco: Harper and Row 1997),

Rodney Stark, *The Victory of Reason* (New York: Random House, 2006).

John Stott, *Issues Facing Christians Today* (Basingstoke: Marshall, Morgan and Scott, 1984).

John Stott, *The Message of Galatians* (Leicester: Inter-Varsity Press, 1988).

Charles Taylor, *A Secular Age* (Cambridge Mass and London: The Belknap Press of Harvard University Press, 2007).

MD Toft and M Christian Green, 'Progress on FoRB? An analysis of European and North American government and parliamentary initiatives, *The Review of Faith and International Affairs*, vol 16, 2018,

Thomas Torrance, *The Apocalypse Today* (London: James Clarke, 1960).

Jeremy Waldron, *God, Locke and Equality: Christian Foundations of Locke's Political Thought* (Cambridge University Press, 2002).

Thomas Watson, *The Ten Commandments* (London: Banner of Truth, 1962),

B F Westcott, *The Epistles of John* (London: Macmillan 1883).

William Wigram, *An Introduction to the History of the Assyrian Church*, London: SPCK 1910).

Wikipedia, '2021 Canadian church burnings,' at: https://en.wikipedia.org/wiki/2021_Canadian_church_burnings.

Robert Wilken, *Liberty in the Things of God* (New Haven and London: Yale University Press, 2019).

Bryan Wilson, 'Secularization: The Inherited Model' in Phillip Hammond (ed), *The*

Sacred in a Secular Age (Berkeley: University of California Press, 1985).

Tom Wright, *Romans Part 1: Chapters 1-8* (London and Louisville: SPCK/Westminster John Knox Press, 2004).

Perez Zagorin, *How the idea of religious toleration came to the West* (Princeton: Princeton University Press, 2003).

Subject index

Page numbers with 'n' refer to a footnote. For example, 51n45 means footnote 51 on page 45. FoR refers to 'freedom of religion' in this index.

Scripture and ancient sources index

www.ingramcontent.com/pod-product-compliance
Ingram Content Group UK Ltd.
Pitfield, Milton Keynes, MK11 3LW, UK
UKHW022312040225
4448UKWH00009B/370

9 781838 182854